P9-CJN-469

SECOND SERVE

THE RENÉE RICHARDS STORY

SECOND

SERVE

Renée Richards
with John Ames

STEIN AND DAY/*Publishers*/New York

With the exception of the author, her father, and well-known personalities and institutions, the names and descriptions of living individuals and of establishments have been changed.

First published in 1983
Copyright © 1983 by Renée Richards
All rights reserved
Designed by Louis A. Ditizio
Printed in the United States of America
Stein and Day/*Publishers*
Scarborough House
Briarcliff Manor, N.Y. 10510

Library of Congress Cataloging in Publication Data

Richards, Renée.
  Second serve.

  1. Richards, Renée.   2. Transsexuals—United States—
Biography.   3. Ophthalmologists—United States—Biography.
4. Tennis players—United States—Biography.   I. Ames,
John.   II. Title.
RC560.C4R5   1983   305.3 [B]   82-48510
ISBN 0-8128-2897-6

To M.H.V. and N.B.R.

Special thanks to the Brain Trust:

Allan Botter
Stuart Byron
Robert S. Cohen
Michael Rosen
David Werchen

Contents

When a trout rising to a fly gets hooked on a line and finds himself unable to swim about freely, he begins with a fight which results in struggles and splashes and sometimes an escape. Often, of course, the situation is too tough for him.

In the same way the human being struggles with his environment and with the hooks that catch him. Sometimes he masters his difficulties; sometimes they are too much for him. His struggles are all that the world sees and it naturally misunderstands them. It is hard for a free fish to understand what is happening to a hooked one.

—Karl A. Menninger

1

In the Beginning

My mother was a headstrong woman. On the day of my birth she suffered a massive hemorrhage. Her reaction to this was to get into a 1934 coupe and, bleeding profusely, drive the rutted roads from Queens all the way into Manhattan. Apparently it didn't occur to her to have someone else drive the car or even try to reach a closer hospital. The important thing was that she give birth in the right place and with the right person in attendance.

The right place was the Infirmary for Women and Children in New York and the right person was Dr. Helen McLoughlin, the most important woman obstetrician in the world. Had she gone to another hospital the physician would have been unknown and quite probably a man. She might have made do with an unknown but not with a man. All her life she had been in conflict with the world of men. Time and again she had been faulted for wanting to be what only men were encouraged to be. In spite of this, she had always been first: first in her high school class, first at Bryn Mawr, first at the Women's Medical College in Pennsylvania, and finally, the first woman resident at the Neurological Institute at the Columbia Presbyterian Medical Center in New York. Still, too much of her energy had been devoted to making headway in a world run by men. She had been forced to attend women's schools and to fight to enter the field of neurology, a specialty dominated by men. She had always won before, and she was not knuckling under now just because blood was pouring out of her. This baby would be born without the aid of men.

Dr. David Raskind, my father, knew nothing of this jolting and dangerous ride. He spent most of the time at his office near the factories of Long Island City where his chief clientele were the victims of industrial accidents. He and my mother had agreed that the summer heat would be more bearable for her near the beach at Neponsit in Queens, but it was only convenient for him to visit on weekends. She had agreeably gone into labor on a Saturday—August 18, 1934—but he still wasn't there. In her opinion, he never was. She accepted this as part of his masculine nature, but that did not stop her from wishing he were different. It was a frustration that she bore lightly since she knew that she could easily survive without him. Of her own strength she had no doubt. It had been tested too often.

Strangely enough, she hoped to give birth to a male child. Perhaps she felt that *she* could make a worthwhile man if given the chance. My mother's desire for a male child had been thwarted five years earlier by the birth of my sister, whom she perversely named Michael Bishop, after her own father. This did nothing to alter the fact that the child was a girl.

When she arrived at the hospital, she was admitted under the name S. Muriel Bishop, M.D. This identity had been too dearly won to abandon when she married. Her husband would be "Dr. Raskind." One Raskind was enough.

Dr. Bishop was examined by Dr. McLoughlin and informed that she had placenta previa. The afterbirth had come down below the baby's head and was wedged against the pelvis, bleeding like a great sponge being pressed with force. There were two possible remedies. The first was a maceration maneuver. This is a violent process wherein the baby's head is crushed and the uterine contents are pulled out through the vaginal canal. The child is killed for the sake of the mother's safety. The second possibility was a Caesarean section. Unfortunately, much blood had been shed during the long ride to the hospital. My mother was weak; a section could kill her. Then again, my head was in the birth canal making extraction difficult and, so, doubly dangerous.

Dr. McLoughlin emphasized in great detail the risks involved in a section. Though she left the decision to my mother, her recommendation was clear. I should die.

But, as I said, my mother was a headstrong woman. Against

the advice of one of the world's premier obstetricians, she gave birth by Caesarean section. It was the morning of August 19, 1934. I was named Richard Henry Raskind after King Richard the Lion Hearted, though it was my mother who had shown the courage. Perhaps I've been running to catch up ever since.

2

Seeds of Confusion

Recalling the events of my childhood is a little embarrassing. Like most adults I feel remote from these occurrences of so many years ago when my body and personality were unformed. Added to that are the anguishes of identity that filled the intervening years of my life and the eventual transformation of my physical makeup and my sexual psychology. When I look back on my childhood, it is like remembering what happened to a little boy I knew very well, perhaps a nephew. It is hard to accept that the male child I was developed into the woman I am now.

Another reason why the remembrances are unsettling is that they seem so contrived. If I sat down to write a case history of an imaginary transsexual, I could not come up with a more provocative set of circumstances than that of my childhood. The peculiar thing about this is that the cause of transsexualism may someday be proven to be biochemical. If this happens, I can only conclude that fate has a sense of humor because my early life is strewn with unsubtle touches that beg to be seen as reasons for my sexual confusion. If they aren't the true cause they ought to be.

My mother brought me home to a house full of women. In addition to her, there were my sister, Michael; my mother's spinster sister, Molly; and Grandma Bishop my mother's mother. These female relatives were augmented by a housekeeper, Jenny Threet, and my nurse, Hattee. My father was also an official resident, but he was at the office during the day and spent many

5

evenings away from the house. As a child, I never really understood why he had so many of these after-work activities. It was a little hurtful that he chose to be absent so much. It was only later that I realized the reason for his busy schedule. It was no doubt a defense mechanism, his way of escaping the smothering control of his wife, a woman who utterly dominated the household and with whom he never won an argument.

To an outsider he must have seemed to be giving a good account of himself. He was a large man, handsome and somewhat gruff. I'm sure he was seen as an intimidating figure, what some might call "a bear of a man." He would argue bravely and loudly with my mother, but only to a certain point. He was like a great oak that shrugs off the wind and seems unbreakable but suddenly snaps through some hidden weakness. His later life was an unbroken string of "could haves" and "should haves." In his student days he had been brilliant. In spite of being the immigrant son of a Jewish tailor from Russia, he had earned a scholarship to Yale. His careers as an undergraduate, as a medical student, and as an intern were distinguished. Later, when he had the opportunity to do specialized training in orthopedic surgery, he rejected it and stayed with his private practice in order to finance my mother's psychiatric training. This was a generous gesture, but one that continually frustrated him. Though he did do some teaching and was associated with a good hospital, he never acquired the laurels that he could have earned if he had worked at his academic career. Father regretted this for the rest of his life, often saddening his friends by brooding aloud about what might have been: "I could have, I should have."

How could my father seem so strong, yet prove himself time and again so passive? I remember watching him play a tennis match at the local club. The "Sunrise Tennis Club" consisted of a row of dirt courts, bordering the railroad tracks. A shed with an aluminum roof served as office, dressing room, and lounge. In spite of this seediness it represented the pretensions of our neighborhood: Sunnyside, New York. The members were struggling young professional men, largely frustrated and fiercely competitive. On these dumpy courts the struggles of their daily work lives were re-enacted in the straightforward geometry of the tennis matches. The desire to win at any cost permeated the atmosphere of the club.

My father and another, fitter man faced each other in the course of a tournament being played on a swelteringly hot day. They were even at two sets apiece. The tie-breaking fifth set was bitterly fought and left both men exhausted. My father lost. I recall watching them sit in the shade of the shed, their upper bodies bathed in perspiration. The winner said that he had been so tired in the fifth set that he had doubted whether he could continue. My father answered him by saying, "If I had only known that, I might have pushed myself to win."

Even as a child I questioned this. If he could have won, why hadn't he? Of all the people in our household, I loved my father best, but this love was tempered with suspicion. He could only be trusted so far, and then his strength was gone. At that point I was on my own.

Because my father seldom seemed to be home, my mother's personality dominated our apartment at 41–44 44th Street off Foster Avenue, or as pronounced by some Sunnyside kids, "Faudy-one faudy faw, faudy fought street, offa Fosta Av'new." She had had the wall between two smaller apartments removed, making one unit big enough for her to have an office right in our home. It was a vivid reminder of her true identity.

She practiced private medicine only as a part-time vocation. Her real job was as a resident at Columbia Presbyterian Medical Center's Neurological Institute. More specifically, her job was to be a *woman* resident. Being a student doctor was like play for her. It was being a woman that was work. All her chiefs at the institute were men, and every day she struggled with their pompous condescension.

I knew little, at that time, of how she spent her days. My impressions were formed by what came before and after she went to school. I usually woke early, padded to my parents' room, and crawled into their bed. I wedged myself between my father and mother, cuddling against her warm, soft body. I was fascinated by the smoothness of her skin and the texture of her long black hair. It reached to her waist and, when loose, spread out like a cape. Tendrils of it seemed to be everywhere, and often I would hold a lock of it as I lay against her. The Arpege fragrance from the night before always lingered about her body.

My mother awakened slowly. She was comfortable with me in

her bed and took her time, stretching a little and coming to full consciousness in a languorous way. Once she was awake, however, she wasted little time in beginning a transformation that always struck me as incredible. I sat, rapt with attention, and, frequently wearing her slippers, watched as she washed and dressed her hair. There was a gentle self-indulgence in the way she did this task. She treated herself well, seemed to take real pleasure in handling herself. I've seen many women abuse their hair, scrubbing it indifferently and ripping combs almost viciously through the snarls. My mother prized her hair, gloried in it, treated it fondly.

When she had finished with her hair she started the second phase of her morning ritual. Over her recently powdered and scented body, she put on her underthings. A lacy brassiere tightly contained her large breasts. A panty girdle compressed her hips. Smooth stockings covered her shapely legs. A slip, heavy with lace, was the final softness.

Over this feminine underlayer went a shell of a different sort. First she rolled her abundant hair tightly over a "rat," a sausage-shaped piece of felt, then tied it in a severe bun at the back of her neck. Her next step was to pat a pale powder over her face and throat, covering up the healthy glow of her skin. She wore no lipstick. Her face was complete when she put on a pair of horn-rimmed glasses. Next came a white blouse, tailored and severe. Over this went a suit. In the winter it was usually wool, preferably gray, perhaps with a pinstripe; in warmer weather it was a lighter fabric. The skirt came to midcalf. The jacket had large lapels, pointed and wide. The shoulders were squared with padding. Her shoes were flat and heavy-soled. A sensible hat crowned the outfit and matched her substantial leather bag. At this point she was no longer Mommy, she was Dr. Bishop.

Then the fun was over. The newly emerged professional turned her attention to *my* wardrobe. Since Michael was old enough to dress herself, I got individual attention. This resulted in a fight every day of the year. Both Michael and I were forced to wear long white cotton stockings. These were vestiges of an earlier generation and had long ago been discarded by almost everyone else. Every day I protested against this indignity, and every day I was overruled. Dr. Bishop's reasoning was simple: white stockings were correct. I couldn't see anything correct about looking different from everyone else in the world with the exception of the Buster Brown shoe boy. Nonetheless, I wore stockings in the fall, winter, spring, and summer. Over the stockings went a pair of longish short pants. These were, to my mortification, fastened to a starched white blouse by means of buttons sewn onto the blouse at waist height. I don't know which irked me more, the buttons or the stockings, but it didn't matter—neither was negotiable. For a woman who had broken so much new ground she certainly contrived to keep her children living in the past. At breakfast I ate hot cereal—ate it and hated it. Dr. Bishop so decreed.

When she left the house after breakfast, I was both relieved and sad. I hated her power and her senseless dictates. They meant daily failure and humiliation; yet I knew somewhere beneath that severe crust was the yielding softness of my mother. Upon her return in the evening the mannish suit was cast off. For dinner she usually chose an evening dress, perhaps something with sequins. Nearly always it was low-cut and showed off much of her bosom. She supervised the preparation of dinner, and the entire family sat down in a rather Victorian way, my father in his velvet smoking jacket across the table from my mother, to consume a seven-course meal. Occasionally my mother interrupted the boring adult talk to order me or my sister to eat properly: "You left the best part" or "Eat the fat too." This event took two hours every evening, and, when it was finally over, my sister and I were liberated to play until bedtime.

I really found my mother only in the mornings during those warm times before she was fully awake. In her bed was the softness and motherly acceptance that was absent in the dictatorial Dr. Bishop. Then, each day I would watch her slip away from me.

My mother's dual nature was probably the result of a peculiar childhood. Grandpa Bishop was a drunk, a wastrel, and a womanizer for the first half of his life and a reclusive mystic for the second half. After a religious experience of some kind, he retreated into his room over the family business, a candy store, and studied the Talmud. His new life-style was ascetic and celibate. This seemed to make little difference to his unsmiling wife who continued to run the store. He died before I was born, but I saw pictures of him. He looked like Rasputin. I gather he was a maniac.

According to my mother, before Grandpa Bishop got religion, he had been "fun loving." I found out later that this was her euphemism for "screwed every woman in town." The town was Bryn Mawr, and Grandpa had made the rounds both above and below his station. Like most scoundrels, he demanded that his daughters be absolutely virtuous. His tactic with my mother, Sadie Muriel, was to turn her into the son he never had. She received the intense attention usually lavished on the oldest sons in Jewish families. They are given the educational advantages; they are loaded down with the responsibility for bringing respect and pride to the family; and they are the recipients of the badgering and the guilt that pass for support in such stereotypical households. Sadie received these dubious rewards, yet she remained a girl.

The other two women in the house, Grandma Bishop and Molly, mother's sister, were nothing like Sadie. I remember these women as dour and unimaginative. It was natural therefore that, after her father went into seclusion, mother became the head of the household as any good son would have.

Thus it was her responsibility to decide what to do about the lump on her father's back. It felt as if it were attached to one of the ribs. She took him to the Women's Medical College of Pennsylvania where she was a student. She had the best surgeon examine him. She assisted in the operation to remove the growth. She watched him die on the table. The tumor was vascular. When it was cut, it bled; and the bleeding couldn't be stopped.

I can only guess at the horror of this scene because Dr. Bishop always spoke of it in a flat, monotonous tone of voice. She was helpless and so was the "best surgeon" in spite of the curt professionalism of the operating room. When such a dam is opened, everyone fumbles. They fumble expertly, to be sure, but the blood flows nonetheless. It gets all over everything.

My mother stood there and saw this as the fruit of her efforts. This wild and uncontrollable man had put himself in her hands, and, when he failed, she failed. His death was a deep reproach, and I don't think she ever trusted a man again. She certainly never forgave herself. This may have been the point at which she decided not to make any more mistakes, to do the right thing ever after.

Dr. Bishop apparently also decided to try to make her father live again. She started this project before I was born, naming my sister "Michael," after Grandpa Bishop.

For the five years before my birth, Mike, as she came to be known, had been the sole focus of Dr. Bishop's attention. Since all the doctor knew of child raising came out of her experiences with her father, she made the same mistakes he had made. While Michael's femaleness was grudgingly accepted in practical matters, the emotional climate of the family reflected disappointment and encouraged her to be masculine. She grew up as a flagrant tomboy.

Mike was obsessed with proving her competence. For her, interactions with other children, especially boys, were contests, opportunities to prove she was as good as they. Unlike my mother, who had been myopic and unathletic, my sister was physically talented as well as highly motivated. She mounted a significant challenge to every boy she met.

My mother indulged this approach and even promoted it, though she recognized that protocol demanded some concessions to Mike's femininity. On social occasions, Mike would often have to wear girl's clothes. The logic of this, as with so many of Dr. Bishop's pronouncements, escaped the child. Having been given strong emotional support for acting like a boy, Mike didn't fancy taking a backward step into dresses, even on rare occasions. Whenever Dr. Bishop refused to hear of such nonsense, it struck Mike as an utter betrayal, and invariably she flew into a rage. These rages were prolonged and very loud. They included violent physical activity—running, door slamming, and the like. It was common for Mike to lock herself in the bathroom and continue screaming protests for as much as an hour. This did no good, for when she opened the bathroom door the situation had not changed.

There was seldom any physical punishment although my mother would sometimes smack us if driven too far. This was usually preceded by the statement, "I am going to haul off and crack you." Generally, though, our rebelliousness was handled through my mother's ironclad tenacity. Sooner or later we would give in, if only after screaming ourselves hoarse and being screamed at in return. If there was any detail that characterized our household, it was the noise level. My mother and father argued, my mother and sister argued, and my mother and I argued. My mother always won.

When I was born, Mike wasn't impressed. The normal distaste that a firstborn child feels for the second was increased by the fact that Mike had been hustling to be a boy for five years and I came into it with no effort at all. This natural animosity was further irritated when I was moved into Mike's room. This made my encroachment physical as well as psychological, but it also gave her many opportunities to get even.

Mike was torn between her instinct to protect her hard won but perverse position as the family son and the clearly stated dictum that she love her little brother as any proper sister should. She practiced a mixture of brutality and affection. Most of this seemed to center around my head. I think she was offended by the shape of it or, more probably, that the shape of it could be seen because of my short haircut. She, in spite of her boyish dress, had to wear long hair. She showed her dissatisfaction by delivering blows to the back of my head. This did not always happen, as you might expect, during the course of play. These unexplained attacks could come out of nowhere. I might be preceding her down the hall, on a perfectly ordinary expedition to the kitchen, when suddenly she would dish out an openhanded smack to the back of my head. It hurt all right, but the arbitrariness of it was the most disturbing thing. She was on a truly random program. There was no way to predict when I might get the next blow, no sensible way to protect myself. As a result I learned to be constantly on guard.

Another approach she took to acting out her fantasies was make-believe smothering. As we roughhoused together, she sometimes picked up a pillow and, holding me down, pressed it forcefully over my face. For the person on the bottom, there is really no such thing as make-believe suffocation. This would go on until I thrashed about so wildly that I either freed myself or Mike, out of fear, let me up. I would lie gasping while she showed great concern and lavished affection on me. These moments of near strangulation brought on some of the warmest moments between us.

Mike could be very warm; she showed me more affection during my childhood than my father and mother put together. Still it was often affection with psychic strings attached. She was never nicer to me than when dressing me as a girl. Although the feminine clothes in her closet disgusted Mike, she took absolute delight in putting these same clothes on me. Starting when I was about two years old, Mike would periodically dress me in her panties and slip. She would then praise me for being so pretty. Strangely enough, my mother was present at several of these sessions and was as charmed as my sister by the sight of me so transformed. I was, in fact, a pretty child, and I was so delighted by the unusual positivity, that I'm sure I was quite lovable. My mother, ordinarily so stern, treated me as if I was a delicate fairy child, a changeling who couldn't be blamed for the shortcomings of my other self. Whatever fears and hates my masculinity stirred in them were apparently neutralized by this simple action.

However, my strongest memories of my sister are of her brutalizing and nearly killing me. As for my mother, with the exceptions of our mornings in bed together and these episodes of crossdressing, I think of her as a calculating force of nature: no more feeling than an avalanche.

My sister sometimes played another game with me when we were naked together—or at least when *I* was naked. She would take my penis and push it up inside my body, make it disappear. Then she would say, "See you're not a little boy, you're a little girl." She'd let it go, and it would come back out, sometimes much bigger than before. We both thought this remarkable; so my sister would push it in again and again and again.

I think it was from such beginnings that my sense of isolation came. Every significant person in the house was a paradox. My father was so big and gruff and strong, yet so prone to crumble under pressure. My mother was so soft and yielding in her womanly guise, so cold and intellectual as a professional, yet so ready to enter into a screaming argument at home. My sister was so obviously a girl, yet trying so hard to be a boy. The rest of the family members were simply overpowered by this insanity. They moved about the house as if it were perfectly normal, and I looked on wondering why I couldn't adjust. Perhaps if it had been completely insane I would have fared better, but my mother seemed always able to cover the craziness with a patina of rationality. After all, she did become an eminent psychiatrist. This started in 1937 when she discarded her plans to become a neurosurgeon after a disagreement with her chief of service. She diagnosed the cause of a patient's headaches as migraine. The chief diagnosed it as a tumor and ordered useless exploratory surgery. Once again she had been thwarted by an arrogant male, and she walked out to take up psychiatry. She decided I would become the brain surgeon. I was three years old at the time. To her, this sort of thing made sense, and she made the rest of the family believe it.

The dynamics of our family are probably best expressed through an episode that occurred when I was four. It was Halloween evening, and I had been invited to a costume party at the home of another boy who lived a few blocks away. My mother and sister decided that I should go as a normal little girl. I had been doing this in their presence and enjoying it for some time, but the idea of anybody else seeing it, especially my father, sent chills through me. I explained, quietly at first, that if I had to go as a little girl, I'd rather not go at all. Here again I met my mother's unyielding hardness. Perhaps she thought such a costume would be more subtle than the usual caricatures. She had seen me in girl's clothes many times and knew I could carry it off. Perhaps she thought it would reflect well on Dr. Bishop if she sent her son in such a clever costume. Whatever her reasons, she and my sister teamed against me, and, as I sensed the inevitability always associated with my mother's will, I became terrified. The depth of this terror was increased by the guilty knowledge that I had been enjoying this play more than I should. With the support of my mother and sister it had seemed natural, even good, but the possibility of demonstrating it to the world threw it into its true light. It was perverse, abnormal, disgusting.

I appealed to my father for help, and he argued in my favor. It did no good. He buckled as usual and sat quietly watching while they held me down on the floor, thrashing, and dressed me in my sister's underpants, slip, and lace petticoat. Over these went a flower-print dress with the sash tied in a bow behind the back. Naturally, I wore long white stockings. There were patent-leather Mary Jane shoes, a blue wide-brim hat, a blue coat with brass navy buttons, and a little blue purse on a brass chain. Each of these items was forced onto me in spite of my continuous and exhausting struggle. Each one represented another step toward degradation. By the time the coat was buttoned up to my chin and the purse thrust into my hand, I was trembling with fatigue and apprehension, utterly numb.

When my sister led me into the party, I must have looked a lot like *Alice in Wonderland*, a perfectly groomed little girl surrounded by animals, knights, and cartoon characters. In fact, the parents of the child who gave the party wondered why the little girl with my sister wasn't in costume. They didn't conceal their surprise very well when they found out it was me. After a few horrible minutes the tumult died down, and I was able to blend in a little though I still felt strangely naked, as if by looking at my costume people could see into my mind.

I managed to get through the evening and even forgot myself somewhat. Meanwhile my mother, in a characteristic lapse of judgment, had arranged for my Uncle Al to pick me up from the party. This young man, about twenty at the time, was the best male role model in my circle. He was a fine athlete and would soon become a pilot in the Army Air Corps. Probably my mother thought I'd be glad to see him after the turmoil of the early evening, but when I saw him at the door a new wave of humiliation swept over me. Uncle Al looked nonplussed. "I didn't know you were a little girl," he said kiddingly.

"I am not," I yelled. "I'm only dressed like one."

I don't mean to give the impression that scenes as pointed as the Halloween incident were the norm. Certainly yelling and screaming were the norm, but the cross-dressing was at all other times a secret shared by my mother, my sister, and myself. Most of the time both my sister and mother expected, even demanded, that I act like a little man.

My mother, especially, cared deeply about what people thought about us. Though strong, and willing to blaze new trails, she had very real limits. She was obsessed with success, and, in order to pursue success, you must have some regard for society. My mother wanted to be a forceful human being, and she sought to obtain leverage in all spheres. She did not disapprove of housewives. On the contrary, she felt she could be a housewife and a psychiatrist as well. It was the achievement of purpose and the successful playing out of the role that attracted my mother, not its contents or the personal rewards associated with it. She wanted to be a mother but she had no real feel for it. Her actions were dictated primarily by a very conventional and sometimes archaic set of standards. She felt that if these were adhered to, things would turn out all right.

Once she had intellectualized these standards, no amount of

emotional response could change her mind, and even rational arguments were of no use. She was like a fundamentalist Bible thumper who maintains that if you interpret the word of God, then its authority is undermined. Life would have been far too complicated if she had allowed herself to be swayed. An example of this was the painful weekly enemas she insisted on administering to me. I was not irregular as a child, and I certainly cried bitterly and protested loudly but without effect. To be sure, there was a school of thought in those days that held regular enemas to be beneficial, but really! My humiliation alone might have touched a softer heart, without regard to the weekly emotional disaster to myself and anyone within earshot. My mother, however, was unmoved.

This seems an unpromising character study for a psychiatrist, especially one who handled many children's cases, but the fact is that she probably helped many people. Certainly her practice flourished. This may have been because she thought of her patients' problems as intellectual games. They were analyzed completely within her head, and the solutions were developed there also. When a patient reported improvement, she received it like a cannoneer receives the report of a direct hit on a target miles away. If all is done properly, you blow something up. Under those circumstances it's easy to remain aloof from the carnage about you.

Dr. Bishop's home life was another matter. She was relatively emotionless in her dealings with the family (unless quelling an uprising), but her standards were not Freudian; that was for work. Rather, she adhered to a muddled set of dictates learned largely from her father, a very mixed-up man.

So it was that she expected me to be a model boy, perhaps not even to *be* but to appear to be. As long as the appearance of normality was maintained, my mother was satisfied. Such shallow thinking also allowed her to participate in the sessions when I was dressed in my sister's clothes. I looked cute. Nobody but us knew about it; so what harm could it do? Whatever satisfactions she derived from my emasculation remained in her unconscious.

My understanding was far different. I was told to be a boy. In fact, Dr. Bishop decreed it. But, when I was a girl, Mommy loved me.

Mike also played it two ways. She gained prestige when she

reinforced my masculine behavior. Her tomboy personality was, officially, only just tolerated. Emotionally, it was reinforced. If it was turned to the sanctioned task of teaching me to be a little boy, then it served an accepted purpose and so gained some official respectability. And, even though it did jeopardize her position as the family's surrogate boy-child, it also provided her with an opportunity to assert her mastery over me.

While my father was off attending his many meetings, Mike taught me to ride a two-wheeled bike, to play baseball and football, and to swim. She was fearless in the face of physical danger, as are those who desperately want to prove themselves; I learned this trait from her though it nearly killed me. Once, when I was six, she encouraged me to swim more than a mile across a mountain lake. I collapsed on the opposite shore.

3

Solo Venture

When I was five my family moved to Forest Hills. It would be natural to assume that my interest in tennis began there because of the great tournament associated with the community, but this is not so. My tennis roots go back to that rundown court in Sunnyside where I used to spend hours shagging balls for my father on weekends. Though I didn't start playing seriously until I was ten, I think those hours, during which I was alone with my father and felt I was providing a real service to him, were the basis for my eventual fascination with the game. Even when I began to concentrate on tennis I never played at Forest Hills. I played at the Sunnyside club.

What Forest Hills provided were open spaces and more children to play with. Thanks to Mike I was already ahead of most of the kids my age. I became a good pitcher and batter in baseball and a good quarterback or end in football. I could swim long distances and was better underwater than most of my peers. I was competent in all sports, and, though I remained a little small for my age, my superior agility kept me equal. I was a bit too pretty to be considered a rugged little boy, but no one considered me a sissy. For one thing, I had inherited my father's voice. My speaking voice was low and masculine even when I was a child. I also had aped many of his mannerisms, and, though henpecked in reality, he appeared to be a very forceful man. Occasionally some insensitive adult would say something like, "My, you're so pretty, you should have been a little girl," but many boys have to put up with this. The difference between me and them was that they were simply irritated by it; I was terrified. Still, I pitched for the Kew-Forest Bluejays and never gave a hint of my guilty secret, though this secret was beginning to take on a more clearly defined form.

Our family had moved into a section of town called The Association of Old Forest Hills. It was posh and zoned on a strictly residential basis to preserve its character. Our house was a turn-of-the-century mansion with fifteen rooms. It was a tribute to the earning power of my parents that we were able to afford this fortress, and it eased the domestic tensions somewhat because we could get farther away from one another. You could still hear the screaming, but it was muffled.

Here, for the first time, I had some privacy. My new room, the smallest in the house, provided some refuge from my sister's sneak attacks. I was also released from an almost nightly show she used to put on for me in the old apartment. This consisted of using the light from a street lamp outside to make scary shadows on the wall over my bed: "And now, here comes a great big bear to eat you up!" The frequency of the penis game fell off, too.

I noticed grumpily that my sister's new room was twice as big as mine. I took this as a symbol of where the affections of my parents were actually centered. They cared for her, I reasoned, about twice as much as they did for me. Of course, the needs of a five-year-old are very different and demand much less space than those of a ten-year-old. She remained a tomboy through adolescence, yet she was provided with as large a wardrobe as any girl child in our neighborhood. The fact that she chose to wear only flannel shirts and blue jeans was beside the point. It was to this closet full of unused clothes that I found myself drawn.

Things really hadn't changed so much in the new house. I still made the daily trek to my mother's bed, and daily I watched her dress. As I got older, however, I began to appreciate how unusual this was. Every morning I experienced my mother's naked body as she softly went through her cycle. The slight sag of her breasts, the shape and color of her nipples, the soft muff of dark fur between her legs, these were as familiar to me as any of her flannel suits. I sensed that this was not the case with most of my friends, and so I never mentioned it. I think my mother continued this pattern so long, until I was nearly an adolescent, because she too realized that these moments were the only warm, emotional communication between us. It was not sexual, at least not openly so; rather it was sensual and direct.

When we were not screaming at one another, my mother and I had excellent communication. I was intelligent and quite early picked up her clinical mode of speech. Factual material passed easily between us. Our conversations sparkled with precision. Instructions were clearly expressed and clearly understood. She helped me with my studies. I had been placed in a special class for bright students, and she helped keep me there. She really *did* help. We worked well together, but we never felt anything much, except in the mornings, and nothing was ever really said about the mornings.

In the afternoons, alone in my room when school was over, I began to have funny sensations. In our old house I was under attack much of the time. When the delicious acceptance associated with being dressed in my sister's clothes was given to me, it was without forewarning—just like one of my sister's slaps. It might as well have been a slap for all the control I had over it. In the new house I had a room into which I could retreat. She couldn't hit me if she wasn't in the room. For the first time I was a little bit free, and it began to occur to me, perhaps even unconsciously, that if I could stop the bad stuff I might also be able to make the good stuff happen.

The best thing that had ever happened to me was being dressed in my sister's clothes. It was hardly even an idea at first. Maybe it was just that being in that room alone allowed me to relax, and relaxation reminded me of those times. At any rate, the idea to dress up by myself and for myself came to mind. I know my first reaction must have been, "No, Mike has to be here for that." Still, the notion persisted, and the very fact that doing it alone might be wrong added to its attraction and, at the same time, to its horror. Since the Halloween party I'd been pretty sure it was wrong.

My first solo venture at the age of six would have been a pathetic yet ludicrous sight for a secret observer. It was early afternoon, and my sister was out playing baseball. The other women had congregated downstairs at the south end of the house. I had been lying on my bed as the urge to do this thing grew stronger and stronger. I tried to do some of my homework. I tried to look at pictures. I tried to play with a toy truck. Finally, I got up, went to the door, cracked it open slightly, and listened: faint screaming from the far end of the house. I stepped out into the hall. I had become an interloper in my own household. The screaming stopped. I couldn't decide whether that was a good sign or a bad sign. My sister's room was upstairs on the same floor as mine. Really, it was only a few steps. I decided to risk it. Moving slowly so as not to make telltale footfalls on the ceiling below, I slithered down the hall.

The latch made a little clicking sound as I opened the door to my sister's room. I froze. This was a good measure of my nervousness since *I* could barely hear the click, let alone the people downstairs. As I stepped inside my sister's room, I began to tremble. My breathing came in short little gasps. I was afraid these might be heard, too. I walked to my sister's dresser and opened a drawer. Inside were a dozen pairs of panties. I grasped one and held it for a moment. This was as far as I had planned to go. One pair of panties would not be missed. I could take them back to my room and hide them away for occasional use. This would have been the safe way, but, at the last minute, I was seized with a stronger impulse. I pulled open other drawers and took out a blouse, a slip, some stockings. I went to the closet and pulled down a dress. As I moved around the room my pace began to pick up. I found shoes, a hat. Festooned with these articles, I bolted out of the room and down the hall. In the distance they were screaming again. In the relative safety of the bathroom where the door could be locked I threw off my own clothes and then stood naked, trying to quiet myself. I checked the hall again. The idea that someone might sneak up on me and burst in kept flaring in my mind.

What such a person would have found was a rather dowdy little boy. My frenzied selection of clothing had resulted in a droopy outfit since my sister's current clothes were too big for me. I knew that somewhere in her closet were items that would fit much better, including some very nice things that she had outgrown; but these would have to wait for another time. Yet, at that moment, I had no idea whether there would be another time or not. The whole process, up to the point when I was actually in the clothes, had been so nerve-wracking that I kept vowing to myself that I would never, never do it again. When I actually had the clothes on, though, I calmed down. An overriding anxiety still existed, but that had to do with the threat of discovery. The feeling of wrongness, on the other hand, was much diminished. In that regard I felt surprisingly at ease. The feeling was very much the same as it had been with my sister and mother present. It had the taste of serenity about it, of rest. I hardly gave myself time to enjoy this sensation. I really don't remember exactly what I did, but I did it fast. Once back into my own clothes, I tiptoed briskly back down to my sister's room and carefully replaced everything I had taken. I even put the panties back though I knew they probably wouldn't be missed, or, if missed, not traced to me. I just didn't want to take any chances.

The whole episode probably took no more than ten minutes, but, when I arrived back in my room I felt as if I had jogged to Manhattan and back. I was exhausted. That feeling of self-revilement, which had diminished so markedly when I put on the clothes, now returned to plague me. The sneakiness of the whole process turned my stomach. Even a six-year-old, or perhaps especially a six-year-old, knows that sneakiness is wrong. When that sneakiness is directed toward the goal of putting on your sister's underpants, then you know that both heaven and earth must be against you.

I lay there with the enormity of this perversion bearing down on me. Up to the moment when I stepped into the hall on the way to my sister's room, I had not been responsible; my sister and mother had done it to me. Yes, I had enjoyed it, felt guilty about it, but I hadn't been responsible. But now I was a sneak, and I felt more alone than I ever had. The world was no longer just a place where I felt uncomfortable; it had become an adversary. In the background I could hear muffled shouting. My sister had come home from the ball game.

4

Soft Enemy

Strangely enough though no one but I knew of my secret desire to cross-dress, many of the arguments in our house concerned clothing. My sister continued as a tomboy right through puberty. She wore jeans, buckled low around her hips, and flannel shirts worn outside so as to hide her waist. She was quite pretty, but she was overweight. I suspect she may have done this on purpose to eliminate any hint of delicacy in her appearance. Even if it was done unconsciously, I'm sure that overeating was at least a symptom of her problem. The battles over her wardrobe continued unabated and, if anything, increased in intensity. These fights might also include disputes over the question of what activities were appropriate for a young lady, a subject more violently contested in the 1940s than today.

My battles with my mother over clothing took a different turn; I was anxious to wear clothes appropriate to a young boy of my age. My mother's insistence on dressing me in styles about twenty years behind the times was galling. I felt conspicuous in those dated, stiff, and excessively formal clothes. Since I was struggling against a desire to dress in a truly radical style, my variations from the norm in public caused me considerable anxiety. I didn't want to arouse any suspicions.

As usual, my mother's logic in this matter was obscure. Once my father and I went to a store in Manhattan and picked out a leather flight jacket with a small upturned fur collar. It was tight-fitting, came to the waist, and was exactly what every young boy would have chosen considering the military atmosphere of the time. According to my mother this jacket was unacceptable because it was too short. It did not cover my whole body. I explained that it was hard to ride a bicycle wearing a full-length coat. The hem could get caught in the spokes. I could get hurt. My father sided vigorously with me. Of course, the jacket went back.

Naturally, there were plenty of other arguments. My mother's office was still in our home, so she was on hand a good deal of the time. By the time I was ten our battles had become titanic. Strangely, she encouraged me to be strong with others. If another boy tried to take my bat and ball, I was to fight him. But when she told me to eat the repulsive broccoli, I was supposed to bow my head respectfully and start chewing. Somehow, I couldn't reconcile these two. Maybe if I had been allowed to win a few times I might not have become so hard to handle. As it was, I never saw anyone win an argument with Dr. Bishop, least of all me. When I was younger, my sister's battles with my mother were the main event around our home, but, as time wore on, I began to require equal time. My mother and sister didn't fight any less; I just screamed a lot more, and the general strife increased by a third. I got so hostile and loud that my mother took to giving me an occasional cuff on the head. This offense to my dignity usually prompted me to go into a complete withdrawal, characterized by passive resistance, although, on some occasions, I ran away and stayed with friends for several days.

During these prepubescent years I also conceived the notion that my family considered me the inferior child. It could be that, seeing Mike's obvious problems in adjustment, they took to praising her accomplishments inordinately so that she would feel more valued. Since she was something of a social misfit, the praise lavished on her was directed toward what were deemed the "more important" areas: her scientific aptitude and her general intellectual capabilities. Her overt hostility toward me had ended when I was about seven. We carried on a relatively normal relationship, though ironically she thought of me as being the spoiled little brother while I was convinced that the family regarded her as superior to me.

In fact, we were both indulged in many ways. We were given any toy within reason as long as my mother approved. The intellectually respectable amusements were available to us at any time. We heard a lot of concerts and visited many museums. Summer camp was a regular part of our lives. We were encouraged to take lessons in anything we pleased. I took piano lessons, violin lessons, oil painting lessons, and, eventually, tennis lessons. The longest periods of time that my mother spent in my company were when she read the classics to me; those sessions could go on for hours. The premium was on structured activity, and, as you might imagine, this left little time for the spontaneous, the emotional.

Meanwhile, my forays into my sister's wardrobe were happening with greater frequency. Sometimes I would go into the bathroom where the door could be locked, but I really preferred my room where I was among personal objects and could move around. It would be natural to think that this cross-dressing must have been associated with some sexual activity. In fact it was not. I would sometimes get an erection as I pulled on some silky underthing, but this was pretty much a response to the soft touch of the fabric. It was not associated with the transformation to a girl. The same thing might happen as I dried myself with a soft towel after a bath. Then again, there was a prohibition against masturbation which, though not explicitly stated, was understood clearly by every American child of the 1940s. It is peculiar indeed that I could control the desire to masturbate but not the desire to dress in my sister's clothes. I did have wet dreams; so the mechanism was in perfectly good shape.

Those years also correspond to what psychologists call a "latency period" in children. This lasts from about age six to thirteen and supposedly is a time when sexual matters are repressed and concentration is focused on the development of nonsexual skills. Maybe this had something to do with my lack of sexual activity.

Whatever the cause, the fact is that my actions during cross-dressing were really uninspired. Aside from being dressed like a girl, I wanted everything to be absolutely normal. I liked it best when I did some common thing like reading a book. The most sexual act I did at these times was to regard myself in the mirror. I would stare, longingly I suppose, into the face of the little girl opposite me. Somehow, in the mirror my femininity was more real. Like Narcissus, I was fascinated by that unattainable image, and, like him, I pined. But most of the time I just did the normal stuff and wished that my being a girl was normal, too. My

27

dedication to normalcy was so steadfast that I usually kept my mind pretty well centered on the present moment. I didn't ordinarily sit around and fantasize though I did have some fantasies that gave me pleasure.

One of them related to a story that my mother had read to me. It concerned a circus troupe. A little girl who performed on the trapeze was injured, and her place had to be taken by a boy. He selflessly donned the girl's costume and performed her act. Everybody thought he did a good job. I used to imagine that I was that little boy, thrust by forces beyond my control into the role of a little girl, but with the approval of my family.

Another fantasy cast me as the ice-skating partner of one of my school chums. He and I performed a pairs routine. I wore a little skating skirt, and we really impressed the crowd. Afterward there was great applause.

An artsier fantasy was the one where I was Chopin as a child. I had a book about him that contained a picture in which he was wearing a long nightgown. His beautiful curls cascaded down his back. I didn't play the piano or move around much in the fantasy. I just imagined what it would feel like to have those curls and to wear a long flowing nightgown.

If there were more fantasies, I don't remember them. As I said, I kept it as simple as possible. The whole point was that by transforming myself I could transform my situation, make it bearable. I could fantasize as easily in my own clothes as I could in my sister's. What the dressing offered was a real, material change, not a dream. When I dressed in my sister's clothes I felt relaxed. In spite of a pervading anxiety about being discovered, these moments provided a few peaceful sensations in the middle of an ocean of stridence. The fact that I felt relaxed, while at the same time suffering spasms of fear that someone might walk in on me, is a comment either on the depth of my compulsion or on the incredible level of tension in the Raskind house. Probably both.

Sometimes these sessions would last only a few minutes and sometimes as long as a few hours. I was flexible and would grab my pleasure when I could. At this point in my life the desire to be like a girl did not fully dominate me. If I was playing in a baseball game, I did not think wistfully of putting on a dress. In school I did my school work; I wasn't haunted by my other life. I didn't even do it every time I was alone in the house, but I did it most of those times and many times when others were there. Sometimes it would be brought about seemingly by nothing, but often I would try to do it after an especially big argument with my mother or sister. If I was threatened with some failure that I thought might support the family's sense of me as inferior, that often brought on a session. These could be utterly silly things like not leading my sandlot football team to victory. Certainly I magnified my family's expectations far beyond their actual scale, but my conception was based in reality. Dick Raskind was expected to compete and to be successful.

I had worked out the mechanics of cross-dressing pretty thoroughly. For safety's sake I got the clothes from my sister's room each time I dressed. Only on rare occasions did I keep any of her clothes in my room between sessions. Getting them again each time took a few minutes extra, but, in the long run, I was less likely to be undone by the chance discovery of an incriminating article of clothing. Another reason why this approach worked well is that I didn't like to wear the same outfit all the time. To the average person a statement like this sounds silly. What possible difference could it make? Somehow, it was important for me to see myself in all possible guises, as if by assuming many different aspects I could make myself into a real little girl. I was not drawn only to the really feminine attire, although it was the most attractive since it represented the greatest break with my normal masculinity. I also enjoyed casual wear like slacks and sweaters. I even tried on some of her jeans and flannel shirts though these were the least satisfactory of all.

For some time this activity satisfied me. However laughable it may seem, these stolen moments of doing dull things in dresses were the highlights of my life. Probably every kid in the world gets into his sister's or mother's clothes at one time or another. They usually do it as a joke or maybe to satisfy their curiosity. The difference between me and them was that I was hooked. Like a dope addict who must have ever increasing fixes, I felt the need to escalate my activities. I wanted to be seen. I knew that this was insane, but I kept feeling the urge to go outside and meet people. There are two reasons why this appealed to me. First, I associated the best times of my life with being away from the house. Probably the best example of this was summer camp. I started at the age of six and continued until I was too old to go. I spent seven summers at Camp Deer Lake and, unlike some kids who cried at first because they were away from home, I was overjoyed from start to finish. I even enjoyed my parents' visit at the midpoint of the two-month season. I would have liked to live at camp all year round and see my family once a month. Since this arrangement was not possible, I spent as much time as I could at school and on the playing fields. It should not be hard, then, to understand why I wanted to go outside dressed as a girl. I was already experiencing a satisfying relaxation under those circumstances; it seemed that it might be even better if I could get away from the atmosphere of the house.

The second reason was that I wanted verification from other people. Looking at myself in the mirror gave me some satisfaction. The rustle of the clothes as I moved about was comforting, but I still didn't feel completely real. The only way for me to create a more believable identity for myself was to be seen and accepted as a girl by other people. Since I couldn't show myself to my family, strangers would have to do.

The female personality that had slowly been asserting itself was becoming more clearly defined. By the time I felt the urge to go outside, I had named this feminine side of myself "Renée." It was so different from the image I showed to the world that I had to differentiate it somehow. I wholeheartedly wished that these nerve-wracking impulses would go away. Naming the source of them helped the Richard side of my personality feel less guilt. I would say to myself "Renée is coming back," and Dick could remain intact even if subservient. For Dick, the chilling thing was that Renée was getting stronger, and she was lonely. She wanted to go outside. She wanted to meet people.

This split was similar to the rare cases of multiple personalities that have become familiar in psychiatric literature. The confusing thing about my case was that the personalities were of different sexes. In some ways these personalities overlapped. I did not have special books for Renée to read. She read and enjoyed Dick's books; she did his homework. When she daydreamed, the characters often came from his life. Dick never lost consciousness and then came out of it dressed in girls' clothes. The two personalities were always aware of one another. The only clear line of demarcation was that one was male and one was female.

When I was alone, these two states would vie for ascendance. Like the desire for sweets during an austere diet, the craving for the other identity would come over me. Sometimes I short-circuited it by rushing out of the house, but most of the time I gave in. Dick would recede, and Renée would come forward.

Leaving the house cross-dressed was a tricky as well as dangerous business. The best time was in the late afternoon during winter. It was dark or nearly so but still early enough so that the rest of the family would be involved in their daily affairs. My father would still be at his office in Long Island City, and my mother would be sequestered with a patient in her office, which she referred to as her "foxhole." My sister would usually be at a friend's house. I would steal down to her room, outfit myself, and slip out into the dark. These trips might last an hour or, at the most, four hours. Leaving for less than an hour wasn't worth the anxiety. Staying out for more than four hours was pushing good fortune too hard.

I don't believe I was ever recognized on the street. No one would have identified the athletic young boy in the figure of the willowy Renée. At least I fancied that was so. The fashions of the day included a variety of hats and kerchiefs and I used these to hide the length of my hair. I had inherited my mother's flawless complexion, so I really didn't need makeup. My features were well-molded, and my carriage neither excessively masculine nor feminine. No one ever suspected me or even threw me a questioning glance. These expeditions all blur into one another because nothing exceptional ever happened.

I kept on the move. It wouldn't have been smart to stay in one place too long. I was well disguised, but I couldn't allow myself to be scrutinized. My interactions were with shopkeepers, clerks, and other pedestrians. They were all transitory, but Renée fed on them because they represented a casual and ready acceptance of her femaleness. Men held doors open for me, young boys and sometimes older men looked me over appreciatively. I used the ladies' bathrooms; I window-shopped in women's stores. Everywhere I went I was accepted as a girl.

While I did this I was not concentrating fanatically on my situation. I was not saying to myself every moment, "They think I'm a girl! They think I'm a girl!" Actually, I slipped easily into the role and forgot for long periods of time that there was anything strange about it. If I went to a movie for example, I paid attention to the film, got involved in the plot, rooted for the good people to win. It was not necessary to focus constant attention on my success as a girl in order for the experience to be fulfilling. I was like a patient whose breath has been constricted. After his recovery, just not having to pay attention to the breathing process fills him with pleasure. So, Renée breathed during these outings and kept herself alive.

Getting back into the house was the most dangerous maneuver of all. Luckily our house had four separate entrances. I would steal up to the house and peer in the windows to establish the positions of the people inside. After I had done that, I chose the door farthest from where they were concentrated. The neighbors might easily have spotted me skulking around the outside of the house. Maybe they did.

I was caught by my family only twice, but never entering or leaving the house. When I was eleven my Great Aunt Bess made a surprise visit to our house. Both she and I got a bigger surprise than anticipated when I walked out of my room dressed in my sister's clothes. We both froze. There was a long moment while we stood facing one another. Finally she said, "My, you certainly look like your sister." I was too numb to speak. I retreated to my room, closing the door after me. Once inside I lay down on the bed and shivered uncontrollably. I don't know if my aunt told anyone or not. I rather think she didn't. She probably thought it was a harmless lark, a one-of-a-kind thing that she had stumbled onto by chance.

Another time my sister walked in on me while I was in the bathroom. I had forgotten to lock the door. I don't remember what excuse I gave for being in her clothes. I only remember that it was silly and delivered in an utterly panic-stricken voice. My sister never mentioned it again. I was twelve at the time.

It seemed that no one was willing to recognize Renée in spite of the evidence. The increasing risks that I took were probably an unconscious bid for recognition—for some support—but it was not forthcoming. Either I was too compulsively competent at these intrigues or my family turned their backs, preferring not to confront such a potentially explosive situation. I do have the feeling that there were suspicions. Once, when I was fifteen I overheard my sister ask my mother, "What do you do with men who want to be women?" My mother answered, "You send them to Scandinavia."

5

All-American Boy

When I was ten years old I won my first tennis championship. It was the Sunrise Club championship for boys. I still have the brass cup that I received. This championship symbolized a lot for me. It was important because I had seen my father falter so many times there. I had accompanied him, chased balls for him, and eventually taken up the game under his instruction. It was almost as if my victory helped to vindicate some of the weaknesses that I perceived in him.

Another thing was that this championship symbolized that I was the best at something. All during my childhood I felt unfavorably compared to my sister. Academically we were roughly equivalent, but our strong points were in different fields. I was strongest in literature and other humanities. She was strongest in math and science. In our household there was a tacit understanding that the important fields of learning were scientific. How could it be otherwise when both parents were doctors? Thus, however much I excelled, the triumphs did not equal those of my sister because I was excelling in a lesser arena. This extended to athletics as well. I was always expected to do well, but the emotional support was always less than that given to my sister. Nonetheless, I was feverishly competitive, always attempting to rise as high as I could though I knew it would never be high enough.

My concentration on and attachment to tennis were a reflection of this ranking. I was an equally good baseball pitcher and was once looked over by major league scouts when I pitched for my high school team. But baseball is a team sport, and when you win the success is split nine ways whereas in tennis the focus is on the individual alone. I felt it would be harder for my family to ignore such individual glory. They would have to admit that I could carry my own weight. Interestingly, my sister, an excellent player, gave up tennis when I began to excel.

Although my hunger for success dictated my choice of tennis, I think my despair of ever really achieving as much as was expected interfered with my game. Often I would defeat the best player somewhere in the course of a tournament and then lose to an inferior one in the title match. When this happened I loathed myself.

Still, life on the tennis courts was ever so much less complicated than life at home. Tennis is one of the cleanest and most straightforward of games. The play is elegantly simple, yet challenging. It is physical without being brutal. With the exception of an occasional fuzzy line call, the mechanics of the game are completely in the open, and the results are clear-cut. How different from the confused dynamics of the Raskind household where things appeared one way but were actually another. I treasured my times on the court as periods of clarity in the midst of an often terrifying muddle of conflicting signals and impulses.

I found my first girlfriend while playing tennis. She was the girls' champion at the same time that I was boys'. Louise was a sturdy little girl, very much a tomboy. I liked that. We played tennis happily together. Most of our interactions were vigorous play. We kissed a bit but not with passion or even more than passing interest, really. It was a benign relationship, marred only by a secret envy that I sometimes felt. She was a real girl and could express it openly. Sometimes, lying in my bed at night I would whisper into the darkness, "Why can't I be a little girl like Louise, and like Mike?"

There was never any real physical intimacy between Louise and me. My only experiences of intimacy had been with my sister when she manipulated my penis. Mike and I were thereafter rather standoffish and then when I was about twelve we came together again. It probably happened on one of the rare occasions when we slept in the same bed in order to make room for overnight guests, but I don't remember exactly how it started. I do have the distinct impression that it was initiated by her. I was far too intimidated by Mike to ever have made an advance. Perhaps my hands brushed against her when we were in bed together or she saw me looking interestedly at her and was a little excited by it. My specific memory of our first time together begins with her taking my hand and placing it on her bare breast. This moment carried with it a lot of the same warm excitement as when I watched my mother dress in the morning, only here I was not just a spectator but a participant. This sense of involvement was probably the most attractive thing about this episode which was more exploratory than sexual. It was unusual for me to feel that I was making some impact on Mike who normally dominated me. When I felt her respond a little it was a source of deep satisfaction.

There were more interludes like this; I explored all of my sister's sexual parts. She provided me with a very thorough knowledge of female anatomy. It was always at her discretion, however, and I was not made to feel that it could happen at my insistence. In addition, she seemed uninterested in exploring me. She may have gotten enough of that years earlier.

One more peculiar note was that I never got an erection when I was with my sister. As I've said, I never masturbated, and it may have been that lack of an active sexual life that inhibited me with my sister though I got erections at other times. It may also have been the Renée side of my personality expressing hostility to my sister and her woman's body.

Between the ages of twelve and fifteen Renée began to assert herself more and more frequently. At this time, when I was establishing myself as an excellent tennis player and developing interests in women, it seems strange that Renée strengthened too. My classmates at the Horace Mann School, to which I had transferred at the age of twelve, were beginning to perceive me as a self-assured, perhaps even cocky, guy. I excelled at academics, sports, and being one of the boys. At the same time I had a very late puberty. I didn't get the secondary sex signs until I was sixteen years old. This made it much easier for Renée to exist. I was still small for my age, slender, smooth-skinned, and damned attractive in a dress. If I had had to shave and if my features had gotten heavier, Renée might not have had such an easy time of it.

As it was, she flourished. At the same time that Dick began to theorize about his future, so did Renée. Dick had very concrete ideas. He took for granted that he would be a success in whatever profession he chose. He might even be an actor. He knew that he would marry a beautiful and sensitive woman by the time he was twenty-three. She would not be a professional woman like his mother. His children would have the complete attention of their mother; the Richard Raskinds would do a damn-sight better job of bringing up the kids than *his* parents had. Renée, on the other hand, looked forward to growing into womanhood, marrying happily, and starting a family. Of course, all of this was just daydreaming—neither Renée nor Dick took it seriously. But it still occupied some of Renée's time, and the wish to be a woman found its way into my nightly prayers. In one area Renée was ahead of Dick. She was beginning to feel some erotic tinglings when she dreamed about skating in the arms of a man.

The male component of my personality finally caught up at age fifteen. I was attracted to a girl who attended my summer camp. The girls' side was located across the lake, and I met Beverly on a combined outing. We continued seeing each other after camp was finished, and one evening we found ourselves alone at my house. At her suggestion we decided to stay home rather than go to a movie. We ended up naked on my bed, happily feeling each other up. This time there was no problem with an erection. Bev kept her hands busy stroking my penis, and I used my fingers between her legs. We brought each other to climax in a flurry of rubbing and probing. It was a very successful evening. For the first time in my life I had ejaculated in the presence of another human being. Prior to this my only experience with orgasm had been in my sleep. This was a great leap in the right direction. For the first time I had a feel for male sexuality. It put a little swagger into my step. I looked forward to the next session, but the following day I received a phone call from a distraught Beverly. She was overcome with remorse over the incident. Somehow she blamed me although if there was any seducing done she had done it. Still, all the guilt was effectively transferred to my shoulders. There were sobs and accusations followed by a reproachful farewell. We never saw one another again.

I'm sure that this was a scene that has been played with slight variations millions of times, especially in the forties and fifties. Fortunately most of the boys who received these calls were not walking a tightrope between genders. This call badly undercut my confidence. Renée took advantage and stepped up her schedule of appearances. She had pretty easy sailing until I turned sixteen and began a growth spurt that left me a six-feet one-inch tall, fully developed man.

Those years of adolescence prior to my puberty were a parade of contradictory impulses and actions. The two different genders struggling for pre-eminence created some wild juxtapositions. For example, at the age of thirteen, though not encouraged by my parents, I insisted on a Bar Mitzvah, where I proclaimed, "Today I am a man." Though sincerely meant this resolve lasted only a short time. Soon I was going out again as Renée.

I cannot describe the loneliness and terror that I experienced. I wished that I could trade this aberration for any other kind of sickness. If I had had a heart condition at least I would have had some company, and that would have made it more bearable. As it was, I felt that I was the focus for some singular nastiness, the carrier of a germ specific to me and only me. I had fought against it very hard, and Dick seemed to have won many battles. At age twelve he had prevailed in the matter of his boy's wardrobe. After that, he was unidentifiable as far as his clothes were concerned. He was the Eastern States tennis champion in his junior and senior years in high school. He was president of the school orchestra and editor of an award-winning yearbook. Though not fully awakened, his heterosexuality was beginning to emerge. When he stood on the field and discussed a career in baseball with a scout from the New York Yankees, he seemed to have arrived at the climax of an all-American boyhood.

Yet Renée, like a siren, beckoned him into the softer realms, into the gentle rustle of fabric, into the disturbing harmony of aloneness, into the smooth but impossible night.

6

Richard's Buddies

The hours I spent as Renée were a very small part of my active life, but they cast a continuing shadow over all the relationships I formed. There was no time as a child or as a teenager when I could say that anyone really knew me. They knew Dick, but I kept the female component of my personality deeply buried. The idea that it might get out haunted me. Had I been able to talk to someone, it would have decreased my isolation, but I never met anyone to whom I gave even passing consideration to telling my secret. No matter how kind or understanding people seemed, even my good friends, I couldn't imagine that they would forgive me.

Yet, however deep I buried the existence of Renée, her presence made itself known in subtle ways. For example, my friends were mostly handsome boys. This was partly because I was handsome as well and there is always a tendency for likes to be attracted to each other. In spite of this, I think that my association with handsome males had some relationship to Renée's unspoken preferences. Another feature of my taste in friends was that without exception they were all tall young men. Since I was somewhat smaller than average, they tended to tower over me. I felt a strange kind of security with these males. Though we were competitive in many respects, I gladly bowed to them in the matter of physical strength. I had no desire at all to be as strong as they were. I enjoyed that distinction between us.

I met many of my friends through my activities in tennis. Once

I began to compete seriously, I spent approximately four hours per day on the courts, either in competition or in practice or in just hanging around. It as an ideal way to keep out of the house. Tennis was an approved activity, and the dedication I showed was considered creditable by my mother and father. If I stayed a little too long at the club, well, it was forgivable. Meanwhile, I was able to escape the oppressive presence of my mother who held court all day in her foxhole and then emerged in the evening to run the family.

The tennis courts provided me with the best friend I had during my junior high and high school days. His name was Barry Wiseman. We were on the same tennis team at Horace Mann and later at Yale. Our athletic interests were the catalyst for our relationship, but the element that took it beyond that realm was our mutual love of literature and the dramatic arts. Barry was an intelligent boy whose emotional nature was near the surface. I don't mean that he was subject to uncontrolled emotional outbursts. Rather, he could be moved in ways unusual for a boy athlete. Most jocks save their emotionalism for the heat of the game. Off the field they may be rather controlled and often unable to express their feelings. Part of what draws them to sport is that it allows them emotional release. Barry was a good enough tennis player to be an assistant to the club professional during the summer vacations his family spent at their seaside house in New Jersey, but despite his devotion to the game he didn't suffer from the kind of self-conscious jockism that often subverts the more refined aspects of personality. He and I would actually sit and read poetry to each other. Our favorites were Shelley and Keats though we also read Tennyson; Barry later became a professor of Victorian literature at a midwestern college. At that time we were not interested so much in the meaning of the poetry as we were in the sound of it, the excitement of the rhyme and exotic expression.

This is not to say that we spent all our time with books. We attended lots of ball games at Yankee Stadium where we saw many of the great players of that period, such as Joe Dimaggio, Hank Bauer, Phil Rizutto, and Yogi Berra. We spent a lot of time at the movies as well. We liked war movies best. My favorite was an obscure one called *Purple Heart*. Along with everyone else I liked *From Here to Eternity*. My favorite stars were vigorous action types: Burt Lancaster, Kirk Douglas, Alan Ladd, Richard Widmark. Both Dick and Renée took their role models largely from movies. Renée's favorite female stars were feminine women like Linda Darnell, Hedy Lamar, and Greer Garson, and she loved costume epics.

Barry and I also did some double-dating when we were in high school. This usually consisted of a movie and a soda afterward. Sometimes we parked in a secluded spot and made out with the girls, but it was only light petting. Our dates were always with nice girls, and they didn't let us get away with much even though we tried. At bottom we were nice boys ourselves and believed in the sanctity of the American Girl. Had they acquiesced to our rather mild demands they would have been consigned to the category of loose women. We didn't really feel that the back seat of an automobile was the right place for serious involvement, but it was fun trying to get somewhere, especially when you were confident that the girl wasn't going to let you. In this regard Barry and I were typical teenagers of the time.

Whenever I would become so incensed with my mother or father that I couldn't stand it anymore, I would run away to Barry's home. It was a large apartment located in Manhattan. His parents were understanding. Mr. Wiseman, Barry's father, liked me especially well because he was a tennis nut himself. I would stay over there for as much as a week at a time stewing over the last blowup with my family. I loved the atmosphere at Barry's. They hardly ever yelled at one another. Days would go by without a single screaming tantrum on anyone's part, parent or child. At first I had trouble taking this in. I thought that I was in the middle of a tremendous calm before an equally tremendous storm, but the cataclysm never came.

Whatever rancor was shown at the Wiseman home would hardly have comprised a passing remark at the Raskinds.

My parents were probably equally glad to have me out of the house and may have complimented themselves on being modern when they agreed to allow me an extended stay at Barry's. Such a cooling-off period, they probably felt, was good for everyone concerned. Besides, Barry often stayed at our house for days at a time himself. I was surprised that he liked to do this, considering the strife in our household, but I guess our home in the suburbs was a welcome change of pace from an apartment in the city. We actually had a yard with grass, and there were playgrounds and tennis courts within easy distance. Staying at our place must have seemed like a vacation. After all, nobody ever actually yelled at *him;* so he could be an uninvolved witness to our feuds—interested but untouched.

On these visits Barry and I would sleep in the same bed. For most of our relationship my sister was away at college, and we'd use the double bed in her room. Naturally this arrangement bred horseplay and led to the most erotic contact I had with any male during my adolescence. I don't think Barry was consciously aware of it, and I'm not sure that I fully realized what was going on. We were two repressed innocents, and it is only in retrospect that the circumstances look suspicious.

It was my habit to sleep nude. I had done this from about the time I was twelve, the age at which I finally established my right to dress like the other boys my age. The battle over the white stockings and other old-fashioned trappings was won when I simply became too big for my mother to manhandle in the morning. This seemed to break her resolve, and soon I was as up-to-date as the next kid. As a part of my victory I refused to wear pajamas. I considered them restrictive and pointless. Barry didn't feel this way and always dutifully wore his pajamas when we slept in the same bed. We made a peculiar pair. One a large muscular character in striped pj's and the other a small, finely boned child with a silky complexion, utterly naked. I'm sure Renée must have been stirring somewhere deep inside me. The situation was too close to her fantasy of being in a cozy bed with her husband for her to be unaware of what was going on. Yet, I never assumed Renée's perspective while Barry and I were together. Consciously I felt no more than boyish camaraderie. Like all boys we were full of energy and were forever challenging each other. As we lay in bed we tried to determine who could remember the most world series winners, the most lines of poetry, the most radio or television jingles. Often our contesting was raucous, and my parents would come into the room and tell us solemnly that we'd have to be a little more quiet. Usually they would add that the bed was not a trampoline. Part of our routine of roughhouse included wrestling. We did this over and over again in spite of the fact that I had no chance of of winning. Barry was just too much bigger than I although I was very agile and could often escape his grasp. That did me little good since Barry would invariably recapture and subdue me once again. He was so strong that he could grab my ankle and just sort of reel me in no matter how I twisted about and tried to extricate myself. If he felt like it, he could, by bringing his hands, arms, feet, and legs into play, arrange himself so that he could hold me absolutely immobile. Thus enmeshed I would struggle futilely.

Eventually I would have to surrender to his compelling strength. There was something about this situation that pleased me. The restricting feel of his limbs about me was overpowering but comforting. I could expend all my energy, all my cunning, all my strength, but it made no difference. I was caught, yet I felt important. Barry's effort was all directed toward me, just to hold me still. Don't get me wrong, I struggled like hell because that was crucial to my feeling. I had to know that his dominance was real. I would push and pull and arch myself, but when I had tried everything, when I was in the middle of my greatest effort and I fully realized that I could do nothing more, I would collapse utterly. My body would go limp, and my breath would come fast. It was very sensual to surrender like that, and the strangest thing about it was that the decision to do so was not conscious. It just seemed to happen as a natural extension of the situation—as a result of Barry's strength as opposed to my weakness.

Barry would usually think that this was a ploy, and sometimes I passed it off as one. He'd loosen his hold, and I'd slip out of his grasp. Other times he'd tighten so as to withstand what he thought sure would be renewed struggling from me. When I didn't respond he'd say, "Dick, are you all right?" I'd answer, "Sure," but from far away. Then I'd shake it off, and we'd get back to our normal play. The circumstances that caused this reaction came up only on rare occasions; so these funny sensations seldom occurred. I remember enjoying them greatly as well as being nude in Barry's company. There was never any obvious sexual excitement connected with our interactions, but this was characteristic of all Dick's activities. When he was in masculine situations, even ones that might appeal to Renée (like being in the shower room with a bunch of naked guys), she always stayed out of them—except in subtle ways.

After I went away to college, I drifted out of close touch with Barry, though we both played on the Yale tennis team. Once we graduated, we hardly ever saw one another. However, there are three other friends from my teenage years who remain in my life to this day; they are Josh, Len, and Joel.

Josh Frick was Horace Mann's resident outsider. Once he kept the entire student body at bay by heaving ice balls at them. The school was located on a hill, which everyone had to climb in order to get to the doors. One winter day Josh arrived at school early. He accumulated a huge pile of icy clods and positioned himself at the top of the hill. When the rest of us came straggling up, we were met with a hail of ice. I don't mean snowballs, I mean heavy chunks of frozen snow. Josh was another of my big friends, and even at that time he was well on the way to his adult height of six feet five. He tossed those ice blocks in high arcs down the hill, sending groups of students scurrying in all directions. When the ice hit it made a kind of explosion as it broke into pieces. It was like being under a mortar attack. Josh was fast, accurate, and couldn't be outflanked. Two groups would start up the hill on opposite sides of the street, but Josh, with his command of the high ground, could shell both groups fast enough to keep them thoroughly intimidated. It might have been different if we weren't wearing our Horace Mann uniforms, that is, slacks, blazer, dress shirt, and tie. We couldn't afford to get them messed up; so we took the discretionary course: we waited.

Eventually some of the teachers noticed the uncharacteristic calm inside the school building and came outside to investigate. They found Josh patrolling back and forth at the top of the hill and the rest of the student body standing out of range at the bottom. Occasionally Josh would pause to heave a warning shot in order to discourage any new tactical maneuvers on our part. From our vantage point all we could see clearly was Josh raging to and fro, but we all heard the sharp cry, "Josh!" He stopped, turned around, then walked slowly but with head high into the school building. A teacher came forward and waved us on up. Neither the teachers nor the students were at all surprised by Josh's behavior. It was just the most recent in a long sequence of such stunts. "Why," you might ask yourself, "did he do this?" I won't try to psychoanalyze Josh. Suffice it to say that the world at large seemed to be consistently offensive to him. He was always attempting to get back at it. I think he felt that if he didn't get even, somehow his position in the scheme of things would be irreversibly eroded. The Horace Mann student body had apparently done something as a group that was an affront to Josh. As a consequence we found ourselves under attack. As simple as this ethic was, it kept him busy a lot of the time. Take the affair of the candy-store owner.

This was a vendetta in which Josh enlisted my participation and that of another boy named Alan. It was never clear to me just what this man had done to get on Josh's bad side. He may have shortchanged him or given him the wrong kind of candy. In such cases Josh didn't complain, he just counterattacked. In the formulation of this plan, Josh had used his considerable knowledge of chemistry and his knack for organization—he was a genius, though his grades did not always reflect the fact. Intrinsic to his purpose was butyric acid. This vile stuff occurs naturally in fermentation but, when isolated, smells like vomit. If you spill it on something, that thing will hold the odor for weeks. A normal human being will begin to gag if he comes as close as twenty feet to a puddle of butyric acid.

We walked into the store as if to make a normal purchase. Alan went up to the counter and pretended to mull over the selection. I kept a watch at the door for other customers. When the store was clear of customers, Alan made his decision and produced his money. Josh had positioned himself at the exact center of the store but behind a counter so that he couldn't be seen from the cash register. While the owner was busy making change, Josh kneeled down, produced a beaker of butyric acid from underneath his coat, and poured it quietly onto the floor. Alan finished up, and we all hurried out before the smell spread to the owner's nose. Safely down the block we watched the door of the store until the owner came coughing and wheezing into the street. We were all greatly amused. It was days before anyone could go in the store, and, despite vigorous cleaning, it was weeks before the awful smell was completely gone. Josh felt that the punishment fit the crime. After all, the man was in the *food* business.

My friendship with Josh was confusing to most of my other friends at Horace Mann. He seemed an unlikely companion for me, but we hit it off well. I met him when I gave a talk on photography in one of his classes. He was a photographer himself and even had a darkroom of his own. This was the catalyst for our friendship. We would develop pictures together and talk photography. He was a science whiz and eventually became a brilliant doctor himself. Although we shared this interest in science and medicine, it was really the antisocial side of Josh's personality that attracted me. I identified with his alienation. The kids at school considered him an overpowering though admittedly brainy, wise guy. Though I was popular, I could understand his apartness. He was a public example of what I was privately. Of course, he was not (like Renée) entirely without friends, but he was definitely out of the mainstream.

Josh did me a big service during one of the times that Renée was making herself felt in one of those subtle ways. He and I went to the same summer camp, and one summer at about the time when most boys are going through the change from juvenile to teenager, Josh gave me some valuable advice. The onset of puberty had caused most of the boys to start being concerned with manly behavior. The cuteness of childhood was being shed for the more aggressive and in some ways less refined adolescent mannerisms. Since my puberty was so late, I didn't have this helpful hormonal boost. At the same time Renée's strong femininity was being felt even in my male persona. It was less noticeable when I was a child, but in the adolescent period I was in danger of standing out. I don't mean that I was swishing about; my sins consisted of giggling a little too much or maybe getting a little too girlishly excited in the presence of my fellow campers. Let's say that something unusual had been announced, perhaps an overnight outdoor expedition. Everyone would be humming over this, but my level of activity would be a cut above the ordinary. I might be rushing around comparing notes, talking a mile a minute, making up stories about what might happen when we were on the trip, and generally displaying an unseemly gushiness. To some this behavior might have seemed coquettish. It did to Josh, and he took me aside one day. "Look, Rastus [this was his pet name for me], you're acting kind of funny."

"Oh?" I said innocently, even though I had a pretty good idea of what he was talking about. One strange thing about repression is that whenever someone confronts you with the thing you've repressed, you always know in some way what they're talking about. You either get mad and deny it, or you pretend you don't know what they're getting at.

"All this giggling and stuff looks bad, kind of sissyish."

"Oh."

"You need to quiet down and stop acting like, well, like a girl. I don't want to hurt your feelings, but that's how you're coming across."

"Oh."

This was one of Josh's more tactful moments. Ordinarily he didn't mince words so much. As a result of this conversation, I began to pay closer attention to my personality. I began to pattern myself after Josh. If anything he was obnoxiously male. Since I was so far from that plateau, there was no danger of my ever becoming too much like him. Still, having Josh around as an inspiration for macho behavior aided me. Josh helped me stay in sync even though my own puberty was years away.

Len Rosen and Joel Larkin were the two other friends that I made during my teens who have remained close to me ever since. For several years the three of us formed a very tight unit. All of us played tennis, and we became acquainted on the courts. When I first met them I was a far less skilled player than they were. They used to call me "Weenie" because I was much smaller and because I was so easy for them to beat at tennis. Before a match they would be in the club pool for a leisurely swim while I was fiercely warming up. For a long time the result was always the same; I lost regardless of which of them I played. Slowly, I drew even, and they began to have to work harder and harder to win. Eventually, I became the best player of the three, perhaps not so much because I had more natural ability as because they set such a high mark for me to reach. Then again, my parents demanded by their attitude that I become number one, and I accepted that challenge in the vain hope that winning might gain me some approval. It did, but I never received enough approval to satisfy my craving.

Once I drew even in skill with Len and Joel, who were already fast friends, they invited me into their company as an equal. This was the start of an excellent chemistry between the three of us. Though I often saw them separately, we probably had the most fun when we were together.

Joel was an adventurer who enjoyed all physical challenges, especially if they included danger as a component. I would watch with admiration as he went off a fifteen-meter diving tower into a tiny swimming pool. Of the ten-meter platform, divers say, "It's thirty-three feet up and a hundred feet down." The fifteen-meter level is in another league altogether, especially for an occasional diver. From up there the pool looks like a postage stamp. That height takes a lot of building up to, but Joel, with little in the way of preliminaries, walked out on the platform and dove.

Years later it was Joel who would entice me into shantytowns and red-light districts all over the Western Hemisphere when we were playing in tournaments and exhibitions. We went into some of the most dangerous slums on earth in Mexico and the West Indies just to see how the natives lived or to see a cock fight or to pick up women. These were the kinds of neighborhoods where people were found after having had their heads chopped off with machetes. Joel didn't care. If he might be attacked, so much the better; it added spice to the outing.

Under Joel's influence I became something of a daredevil myself. The courage that I had started learning as a child from my sister was tested time and again in his company. I became a little more at ease with peril, even learned to enjoy it.

Len was a marked contrast to Joel. He was the one of whom people would say, "He's got a good head on his shoulders." By this they meant he exercised restraint and common sense. It was Len who counseled against uselessly flirting with danger. He could seldom be coerced into any of our wilder shenanigans, but when Joel and I would run afoul of the authorities or get into a jam, Len was always there with practical help. His loyalty, honesty, and reliability were unequaled.

I don't mean that Len was a stick-in-the-mud, but he *was* a man of principle, and on that score he was unassailable. Joel and I were willing to compromise our rather loose standards for the sake of some amusement. To us, half the fun was breaking the rules. Len, on the other hand, had a profound respect for them. If, for example, during a tennis match an official made an incorrect line call in Len's favor, Len would insist that the point be given to his opponent. In the same situation, especially in a close match, Joel and I would be inclined to take anything we could get. We would chalk it up to the breaks of the game. Even if you did graciously make such a gesture, you could hardly expect the same concern from your opponent when he had the chance to get an easy point. These arguments carried no weight with Len. He knew what was right. I fully believe he would have forfeited a match rather than accept a point that he had not won cleanly.

The appearances of these two sort of underscored their natures. Joel was wildly handsome with dark eyes and a lantern jaw. His countenance expressed strength in a most compelling way. He made a striking naval officer later on when he went into the service. He would have been perfect for a recruiting poster: clear-eyed, clean-cut, ready for action. Len had more serious, introspective good looks. In fact, he looked exactly like the most well-known brooding and sensitive young man of the day, Montgomery Clift. He had the same green eyes, bushy brows, and finely chiseled nose and chin. His head was large and impressive like Clift's. The primary difference between them was that Len stood six-feet five-inches tall when he had reached his full growth. However, in spite of his impressive size, he gave the impression of great compassion and evenhandedness.

I stood somewhere between these two in temperament, and my experience with the dynamics of our triumvirate taught me a lot. Joel affirmed and ministered to my tendencies as a rakehell, Len to my sense of responsibility and fair play. Len's even-tempered good sense often smoothed the waters. If Joel and I screwed up in a social situation or blew up on the tennis court, Len was always there to explain in his authoritative and believable way that we were not bad people. On the other hand Len was often seen, because of his compulsive honesty, as blunt and tactless. Here I was at my best. I was flexible and able to be charming if I could just keep from going off the deep end. I saved Len from embarrassment quite a few times.

I really believe that Len liked Joel and me partly because we were so devil-may-care. We helped him loosen up. At the same time he exercised a healthy restraint on our crazier impulses, and, even if we sometimes paid no mind to his dire warnings, those same warnings made the adventure seem all the more appetizing. It was certainly comforting to know that Len was waiting back at the starting point to bail us out if things went bad. We made a fine team.

I think that all my male friends were, in a way, substitutes for my father whom I had long before sensed was an inappropriate model. Barry provided a sensitive sounding board for my artistic side. Josh gave me an aggressive male role model and, in his extremeness, helped me traverse the long distance from childhood to assertive masculine adulthood. Joel encouraged me to be unafraid and to relish life rather than to shrink from it. Len demonstrated the way that a sensitive human being lives according to principles and accepts responsibility.

Through my friends I made a game attempt to balance off the confusion and mixed signals in my home environment. Of course, these friendships came too late to reverse the damage done during my childhood. What they provided were the models for certain personality touches that allowed me to round out at least the appearance of normal maleness. In addition, their company provided a haven of acceptance to which I could retreat when family pressures became too much to bear. They were an alternative to becoming Renée.

7

Renée Grows Stronger

My friends, my scholastic and athletic honors, and my experiences at summer camp are easy things to remember about my childhood. They seem normal. The tension-filled environment of my home, the peculiar experiences with my family, and the secret hours as Renée have not been so easily recalled. These memories arose only through anguishing sessions of analysis or after my conflicts were resolved surgically. For most of my life they were locked in my unconscious mind—repressed, denied. Though Dick and Renée were not totally separate personalities, Dick Raskind had little reason to dwell on Renée when he could possibly forget about her. He forgot a great deal of the past and kidded himself about the present. In much the same way that a seriously ill patient may rationalize his symptoms away, I tried to pretend that nothing was wrong. It was a strange sort of dual consciousness. I would struggle desperately against Renée's emergence and lose. In the relaxation of tension following her appearance, I would feel confident that I would be able to control the situation next time. Like a heroin addict I always thought I could kick the habit—starting tomorrow.

This illusion was dealt a severe blow when I was fifteen. I was browsing among the psychiatric books in my mother's study. I had done this before, and I was always intrigued by the illustrations in her medical books. These were sometimes lurid (pictures of wounds and physical anomalies) and sometimes mundane (anatomy charts, diagrams of organs) but always fascinating to me. I also was drawn to accounts of various forms of mental illness. This time I came across one called *Psychopathia Sexualis* written by Krafft-Ebing, a so-called expert on sexual aberrations. Published in the early 1900s, this book contained case histories of people described as "lunatics." Most of them had been studied while they were confined in various mental hospitals. What some of these people had were feelings that matched mine almost point for point. A knot the size of a cantaloupe formed in my stomach as I read this "expert" commentary of the early twentieth century. This man kindheartedly consigned these poor wretches into the category of the irredeemably insane. I fought back waves of nausea as I read case after case, some only a little like me and some almost exactly like me. What I felt must be very like what a terminal patient feels when his doctor tells him there is no hope. I've heard such people say wanly, "At least I know for sure." There was small comfort for me in this knowledge. True, I realized that I was not unique, but with this small dose of sugar came the bitter pronouncement that I was crazy. I had no alternative but to disagree. I was willing to admit a similarity between me and the people in the book but I reasoned that they must have other problems, which I did not. *Psychopathia Sexualis* went back onto my mother's bookshelf but that day was not the last time I looked at it; I was drawn back again and again like a criminal to the scene of his crime.

This event marked the beginning of a full-scale effort to do away with Renée. The specter of lunacy turned the struggle into a real war. For the next fifteen years I tried to kill off Renée entirely, and the very force of that effort proved how much a part of me she had become. There was no more imagining that, with a little more will power, I could triumph. I put everything I had into the effort, and repeatedly I failed. With each apparent success, Dick would exult and become more flamboyant, but when Renée would inevitably return my despondency would reach new depths. I was on this pendulum for most of my life.

The effort to do away with Renée might have met with more success if I had not discovered another point of reference when I was seventeen years old. This happened when I was playing in a tennis tournament held at the U. S. Military Academy at West Point. My roommate and I were browsing in the hotel stationery shop. I was looking over a rack of paperback books when a title suddenly stood out. Dick's eyes became Renée's eyes. The book was called *Man Into Woman*. Those words rushed out of the chaos of print on the rack like a lighthouse beacon. I glanced around, saw that I was unobserved, picked up the book, and walked straightway to the cashier. I had no real idea of what the contents might be. It could even have been a seamy novel. Still, those words held out a possibility that Renée had prayed for on many a desperate night. As I climbed the stairs back to my room, I calmed myself by remembering the disappointments associated with so many sensational headlines. "Woman Gives Birth to Frog," they would scream out, yet the reality would be some trick or some patently obvious lie. Why should this title be any different?

Upon reaching my room, I furtively retreated to the bathroom where with trembling hands I opened the book—and discovered that I had hit the jackpot. It was an account of the life of a Danish painter named Einar Wegener who was the first recorded case of transsexualism. He had been a married man who felt much as I felt. It had seemed to him that his identity was misplaced. Somehow the personality of a woman had been trapped in the body of a man. His anguish over the situation led him to a radical solution. The ovaries of a woman were transplanted into his body, resulting in hormonal changes that caused him to develop female characteristics. The accompanying surgery to change him into an anatomic and functional woman was described in detail. This operation had taken place in the thirties when much less was known about hormones or even about the basic chemistry of the body. What powerful drives operated in this man to cause him to seek this crude remedy? He had delivered himself into the hands of surgeons who were mapping utterly unknown territory, and he had paid the price. Although the book I read did not make it clear why, Einar Wegener had died within a year after this surgery. Yet, he had been a woman. This was the fact that impressed itself on the personalities of both Dick and Renée. What had seemed impossible was suddenly not so. For Dick it was a realization full of dire overtones. Renée had been, up to this time, only a persistent yet unattainable fantasy. She had thrust herself into the outskirts of reality, but that was as far as she could come. Now I could feel Renée strengthen. She had glimpsed a possible way.

At the same time Renée was receiving this glimmer of hope,

she was facing a new set of obstacles. My body had grown to a height of six feet and done so rather quickly. This growth spurt had coincided with my late puberty. I was no longer an undersized young boy and, though I was no mesomorph, I was nicely muscled from athletics. I had a beard, body hair, and fully developed genitals. These were in good working order and periodically driven to erection in the same way as those of any other teenage boy. I still did not masturbate, and the sexual tension that I endured as a result of that omission might have contributed to Renée's strength. It is ironic to think that my masculine randiness and the inability to relieve it could have helped push me into the relaxed state I associated with Renée. That change was now not so easily attainable. From puberty on, it was a monumental and energy-draining exercise.

First, I would shave my beard attentively. It was not heavy and with the addition of some makeup could be effectively eradicated. My body hair was slight although some shaving was necessary on my legs. The protocol of the times required that women shave their legs all the way from the ankle to the thigh. No matter that, on me, this area would be hidden from view; Renée demanded as much authenticity as I could muster. When I was in the guise of Renée I hated my genitals; my penis and testicles seemed ugly and abnormal. I recoiled at the cumbersome, embarrassingly external complex of fleshy parts flopping between my legs. I attacked them viciously; with my fingers I pressed the testicles up into my abdomen. Although that's where they came from originally, they didn't go back so easily. What allowed me to do it at all was my abnormally large inguinal ring. This is the opening through which the testicles descend. In most men it tightens and is then too small to allow the testicles back through. This was not the case with me, and I was able to force both of mine back into my abdominal cavity. Once I had done that the problem was to keep them up there. I accomplished this by means of a crosshatching of adhesive tape. To do away with my penis I would stretch it backward between my legs, often using more heavy adhesive tape to secure it in that position. Of course, while I was Renée I kept my legs clenched tightly together to help maintain this strained condition. I felt this added to the femininity of my presence since it gave me a knock-kneed appearance, especially when I walked. Standing and looking at myself in the mirror I felt fairly successful. The disgusting member was nowhere in sight—just an unbroken expanse of pubic hair. The strain on the skin caused by pulling my penis backward caused a crease to form under the triangle of hair. This had the appearance of a genital cleft. It looked pretty good for a make-believe woman.

This sort of abuse took its toll in pain and injury. Never really comfortable, such a setup could be endured for a short while with less pain than you might think. Beyond a few minutes though, the pressures that these delicate structures were never designed to take began to create excruciating pain. Then, too, over the years I became more and more strict in this regard, increasing the strains and inventing new ways to eliminate the hated body parts. Sometimes I would knot a piece of fishing line or strong twine around the head of my penis and use that to pull it backward between my legs. The other end would be secured to a piece of rope cinched tightly around my waist. This arrangement served two purposes: it gave me more of an hourglass figure, and it also provided much more leverage for drawing my penis back. I could pass the string between the cheeks of my ass and up under the rope. Then I would pull the string taut causing my penis to be stretched brutally around the curve of my torso. Believe me, I have great respect for the resiliency of the human penis. Over the years I put thousands of bruises, hemorrhages, and abrasions on mine; in its last days it was literally covered with scars. As for my testicles, they sustained equal damage.

I've been asked many times why I didn't simply live the life of a homosexual. This question is asked by those who do not understand that Dick was a heterosexual male and that Renée was a heterosexual female. Dick had no sexual interest in men and, when Renée fantasized, she fantasized the pleasures of sex as a woman with a vagina. This fact was at the heart of my dilemma and made a reconciliation seem impossible.

Along with my increasing understanding of my condition, and the fact that there were a few others who shared it, I became more sensitive to what factors might have caused me to suffer this confusion. As a juvenile I was hardly able to analyze in any depth the maze of conflicting signals in my home. When a human being is surrounded by something almost all of the time, he comes to accept it as normal. When as a teenager I spent a few days at the home of friends, I was genuinely amazed to find that days might go by without anyone screaming at anyone else. "How unusual," I would think to myself, hardly suspecting that their homes were the norm and mine was a hotbed of craziness.

By the age of seventeen I was beginning to catch on to the difference between my environment and theirs, to realize how far out of the mainstream life at the Raskind household really was. I was, for example, beginning to pierce through the almost reflexive reverence in which a youngster holds his parents. I became much more irritated with my father's misleading aura of strength. Knowing that he hadn't enough resolve to stand up to my mother made his often callous treatment of me all the more galling. Once when I had lost a tennis match his tactless comments included the phrase, "I am ashamed of you." Even his offhand remarks could sometimes be devastating, as when he once commented, "Your back is just like your mother's."

As for my mother, I had begun to see through the forbidding exterior of Dr. Bishop. I could see that her rigid adherence to this guise was a defense against the possibility of failure. Whatever her inadequacies as a wife and mother, she would never have to confront them. My sister's identity crisis, for example, was lost on her. She lived vicariously through my sister and so saw her as the most intelligent, the most popular, the prettiest: all the things she herself had wanted to be as a young girl. She dismissed Mike's raging conflicts as negligible. Years later when I finally confessed my own identity problems, she said, "But Dick, you were such a *normal* boy." Such was her tunnel vision.

However much my mother ignored both my sister's conflicts and mine, I had finally seen the connection between them. My sister's split had become better defined as she had grown older and left the flexible world of adolescence for the more structured role of college coed. She had acquired quite a feminine persona, which she used in her social life and in particular with her boyfriend. She even used it with me sometimes. For the most part however, the face that she presented to the family was still that of a mannish young woman insecure in her femininity. That the similarities in our conditions could have escaped me for so long seems laughable, yet I had accepted my mother's version of reality rather than forming one of my own. I too had seen her as the prettiest, the most popular, the smartest. At age seventeen the light was just beginning to break through for me. I began to understand her envy and some of her malice.

A bit dazed by this gush of previously repressed information, I welcomed the opportunity to leave home for college. My liberation from the crazy house was not without its conflicts. Mike had dutifully gone off to Bryn Mawr, following in my mother's footsteps. Now, I was expected to go to Yale, my father's alma mater. The recent stirrings of understanding about the pressures that had shaped my personality had increased my tendency to contradict the family's wishes. Mother and father and sister all prescribed Yale. I seriously thought about skipping college and joining the New York Yankees. But that radical a move was still beyond my strength. I had planned all my life to go to college, and I wanted to make the most of it. Unfortunately, one of the best schools in the country was Yale. My dilemma was that the best thing for me was what my family wanted. As disgusting as it was I felt there was no getting around it. I went to Yale.

8

Tennis and Transvestism

My father and I set off in the fall of 1951 to get me settled as a freshman at Yale. As we walked about the campus breathing the cool air and pausing occasionally while my father reminisced, I was a little ashamed of my previous reluctance to carry on in his tradition. Considering his origins he had achieved a great deal, and, in that environment of ivy-covered walls and stately architecture, I felt more identification with him than I had since those early days at the Sunrise Tennis Club. This pleasure was fleeting. Actually, the Yale of 1951 was radically different from the Yale of 1917. Those differences reminded me constantly of the differences between my father and myself. Once I asked him, "How do I get from my dormitory to the playing fields outside of town?" He answered, "You take the trolley the same way I did." The trolley tracks had been torn up in the 1930s, so I had to find a more contemporary way to make the trip. The rest of my father's advice also applied mostly to the past.

I soon established a rather dreary routine at school. I lived in a dormitory with three roommates. One bright spot was that Len, my friend from Forest Hills, was one of them. I really didn't make many other friends that first year. I felt disoriented and was keenly aware that I was one of a thousand students in a freshman class. After the attention I had received at Horace Mann it was disheartening to be on the bottom rung looking at a long climb up. There was no hectic home life to drive me out into the world. With that pressure gone I became a little lethargic and turned in a

61

passing, but generally poor, academic performance. On one occasion my mother came to New Haven for a discussion with the freshman dean. I was not living up to my predicted potential, and there was some concern that my schedule of laboratory sciences might have been too ambitious. It was typical that my mother made this trip rather than my father. She and I spent a very dry afternoon together discussing my problem. I promised I'd do better.

Another factor that no doubt contributed to my despondency during that first year was that Renée had few opportunities to emerge. With a busy academic schedule and three inquisitive roommates, there was no safe time for her to surface. On a conscious level this was a source of satisfaction. I became more optimistic about the chances of getting rid of her permanently. I was glad that my situation did not allow her to exist actively. Yet, in that secret part of me Renée crouched and awaited an opportunity. Her longing must have made its way into my awareness. Though she remained suppressed, her sadness bubbled up and colored Dick's emotional life.

Without Renée there were no women in my life. I had never been aggressive with girls, and the superficial sophistication of Ivy League dating intimidated me. I saw my classmates do it with seeming ease, and I felt very, very inferior.

Two things gave me satisfaction during my freshman year. One was tennis. Once again in the difficult hours of my life, the clean simplicity of tennis became a refuge for me. The court was an arena of effort that could not be undercut by blurred ideals or psychic ghosts. What was created there existed whole and pure, as a thing unto itself.

There were no indoor courts in New Haven in my college days; so in the winter I would come to New York on the weekends to play in one of the huge, barn-like armories on the floors of which courts had been laid. These were hardly ideal circumstances for modern-day tennis, but they were the best we had.

I won the Eastern Indoor Championship that year and had set my sights on the National Junior Championship. I had practiced hard that fall and was planning to go to the Nationals in St. Louis over Thanksgiving weekend. A few days before I expected to leave a severe pain developed in my right side. It was so bad that I had to be supported as I walked into the infirmary. My face was pale, and I was breathing spasmodically like a pregnant woman in labor. They admitted me immediately and with a diagnosis of "suspected appendicitis." I was told that I would have to stay in the hospital for observation and possible surgery. I had a fever, an elevated blood count, and pain in the right lower quadrant (doctor's talk for "right where your appendix is"). Things didn't look good.

I was incensed—stuck in a hospital room, attended by a supercilious nurse ("Time for our medication, Mr. Raskind!"), and the time before the tournament growing short. I was there for two days. On the day before the first round in St. Louis I demanded that I be allowed to leave. The doctor said no. He added that I probably had a hot appendix and refused to discharge me. My nurse tried to explain medical ethics to me. I didn't want to hear it.

I confided to my friend Len that I was going to sneak out and play in that tournament. Len said that I was crazy, I could kill myself. This was one of the many times when he gave me sound, prudent advice and one of the many times when I didn't take it. I dressed, sneaked out of the hospital, flew to St. Louis and, on the following day, played in the tournament.

At first the pain in my side was a real hindrance. It was especially bad when I stretched on my serve. Luckily I was a lot better than my opponents in the early rounds. I played gingerly, but it was good enough to win. Inexplicably, the pain disappeared by the tournament's midpoint. From then on I played with assurance and beat the defending champion in a quarter-final match. However, in the semifinal I lost. It was a close match but I lost.

I should have been pleased with myself. I had undergone a seemingly miraculous cure. My appendix was not hot after all; I had triumphed over pain. As far as the tennis was concerned I had played well, especially under the bizarre medical circumstances. Reaching the semifinals of a national tournament was in itself a considerable achievement. Yet I felt myself a failure. This was like handing my mother a report card with a "B" on it. She would certainly want to know why it wasn't an "A." I realized how thoroughly I had learned this lesson. Anything short of perfection was unacceptable.

The other activity that held my interest during that freshman year was going to Greenwich Village. In those days Greenwich

Village was a refuge for bohemians on a short budget. During my high school days, I used to dress as Renée and take the subway to the Village. There I could wander around more comfortably because half the people on the street were weirdos of some sort. The squares were busy ogling them and probably never gave me a second glance. By comparison I was pretty normal looking. After the age of sixteen when I developed my secondary sex characteristics, I used makeup to cover any shadow of a beard and to enhance my features. Although I used plenty of makeup (base, powder, rouge, eye shadow, eyeliner, mascara, and lipstick), it was used with restraint. I was always aware that I had to look as normal as possible or risk curious inquiries. I enjoyed the process of applying makeup and didn't mind practicing until I got it right. The only factors that tended to draw attention to me were my height and the size of my hands and feet. I was most at ease about my extremities in the winter when I could wear big mittens and overshoes, but during the summer I got away with sundresses and other fairly skimpy attire. As I said, in Greenwich Village nobody seemed to notice me.

There was another attraction in that area of town. In the early fifties there was only one nightclub that featured a continuing transvestite revue, the "Club 82." It was named for its location at the intersection of Eighth Street and Second Avenue. This was the low-rent district, and at that time there was nothing fashionable about it.

The Club 82 was located in a dingy building and was, in turn, dingy. It seated about one hundred and fifty people in a fairly large room with no particular decor; if it had a theme it escaped me. The customers sat at small tables large enough for four people if all of them didn't put their legs underneath at the same time. I never had this problem since I was always alone. The stage was an area measuring approximately ten feet by eight feet, and its height was no greater than a foot off the floor. There was a spotlight that was operated from the back of the room. There were also colored lights that could be switched on and off leaving the stage bathed in green, red, blue, orange, or combinations thereof. The performers entered from a curtained doorway off to one side.

The acts that appeared on the stage fell into three categories: comedians, strippers, and song stylists. The comedians often did impressions of famous women such as Martha Raye. Their routines were very close to the ones made popular by the entertainer being parodied. Sometimes the transvestite had simply plagiarized the act in its entirety. Some of the comedy acts made a point of the fact that a man was dressed as a woman. In a broad burlesque style they would lose articles of clothing or assume positions where their masculinity was obvious and supposedly humorous in comparison to their attire. One of them might lean over, causing his dress to fly up and reveal a pair of polka-dot boxer shorts.

These were the acts that pleased me the least. I felt that making fun of this somehow degraded my secret wishes even further. As I look back on it, I remember that these acts were performed with enthusiasm and surprising professionalism. It was galling that the best entertainment at the club was the least reinforcing to Renée, because, though I always dressed as Dick when I went to such places, Renée was the one looking out and longing to achieve even the questionable legitimacy of the Club 82. The sight of boxer shorts under a dress did not satisfy my secret wishes.

The strippers were more appealing. Their routines were also like burlesque but contained no element of parody. They approached their dancing with just as much energy and probably a lot more seriousness than straight strippers. Often their level of accomplishment as dancers was low but their intentions were good. Their feminine personas were so well-developed that there was really no hint of their masculinity until they got their costumes off. At the early shows they'd strip down to only their G strings. Naturally, their breasts, or lack of such, gave them away though some had managed respectable bustlines even without the surgery available today. I suppose they were born with that tendency.

At the 2:00 A.M. show they'd strip entirely naked. I didn't particularly care for this. Renée didn't like the looks of an apparent woman dancing around with a penis flapping between her legs. She spent so much time and energy destroying her own genitals that this final revelation by the strippers seemed a betrayal.

Renée preferred the song stylists. Dressed in long gowns, they tried to practice the feminine graces to perfection. Their formal dresses were often faithful copies of designer creations, and many were tasteful in a very conventional sense. Usually they would be gloved and jeweled. There was little of the extreme or the crass that characterized the comedy and the stripping. With the song stylists, the emphasis was on a complete and elegant illusion. Here were attempts at dignity and honest emotion. Most of the song stylists emulated the torchy styles of the big band singers like Peggy Lee. They stood quietly in the spotlight and allowed a simple twist of the wrist or motion of the head to carry the message of their femininity. They sang in surprisingly high soprano voices often as clear as a bell. Unfortunately, because so much was attempted the possibilities for failure were greater. In the comedy routines and the stripping there was margin for error. In the song styling there was none. If the dress didn't fit exactly, if the figure was too heavy, if the makeup was too extreme, if the voice was less than perfect, then the whole thing became a pathetic and humiliating experience for me. Luckily, I was not very discerning myself, and my wishful thinking often saved me from these moments. Still, when I recognized such a pathetic performance I took it very personally. I was afraid that someday someone might likewise see through my pose as Renée; that would be the worst humiliation. My fear was especially keen when I saw the aging drag queens, some in the revue and some in the audience, vainly struggling to retain their femininity in spite of the onslaught of time. I wondered if this was to be my fate, to turn into a harridan with a five o'clock shadow.

Each revue kept to a theme of some sort. For a while it would be Hawaiian. All the routines would be given an island look, although in some instances this only meant someone would wear a hibiscus over one ear or a stripper would wear a grass skirt. Another time it might be "A Salute to Our Women in Uniform!" The one constant in the show was a master of ceremonies in a baggy tuxedo. It was supposedly a big surprise when at the end of the entertainment he revealed that he was actually a lesbian in drag. Sometimes she'd wear a beard as a disguise.

While Renée thrived on these excursions into the world of transvestite entertainment, Dick was mortified. His appraisal of these places was that they were seamy, sleazy dumps, and he resented being dragged into them. It was Renée's idea to go in, but it was Dick's idea to sit in the darkest corner and nurse a beer. Renée would have been down front shouting out encouragement to the performers and doing some dancing of her own, but the stolid and uncooperative Dick was afraid to be seen. He would go in, he didn't seem to be able to stop that, but by god he would not make a spectacle of himself!

This uneasy truce between the two sides of my personality lasted through my late adolescence. I actually discovered the Club 82 as a junior in high school when I saw it advertised in the newspaper. There were also other show spots that advertised occasional entertainment of this sort. On some of my excursions as Renée, from Forest Hills into Manhattan, I scouted the outsides of the clubs. I could never bring myself to go in as Renée. That would have been too brazen, but I did return as Dick and went several times while I was still in high school. This pattern continued during my freshman year at Yale. I would come home on weekends, sometimes dressing as Renée and going into the city and sometimes attending a revue as Dick. Since I had roommates I couldn't keep any women's clothes in the dormitory; so, for the most part, I kept them at home in a box at the back of my closet or hidden in a drawer under several layers of men's things. There was always the danger that these might be discovered by my mother or sister when they nosed about in my room, but as I felt that I had to have these items handy I took the risk.

I also had some special clothes that I kept in a suitcase in my automobile. I had acquired these, as I had all my others, by going to tall girls stores and pretending to shop for a friend. At these boutiques I was exercising my own taste, which turned out, not surprisingly, to be much like my sister's. I bought fairly conventional college girl styles. In those days tight angora sweaters were favored, and skirts, often plaid, that fell straight down from the hips to about midcalf. Sometimes a wide belt was worn with such an outfit and a pair of uncomplicated loafers or oxfords. I had a variety of undergarments that helped me fill out these clothes in feminine style. There were several bras, some padded and some not. The unpadded ones I filled out with the traditional stuffing like rolled-up socks or facial tissues. Actually, I was fleshy around my mammaries anyway, and, with a push-up bra of some sort, I did pretty well on my own. For my hips and waist I used girdles of different styles. One of the most effective was my Merry Widow, a vicious, Scarlett O'Hara-type waist cincher. If courageously handled, this piece of armor could take four inches off my middle, leaving me with a respectable twenty-seven inch waist; however, if pushed to this extreme my breathing was impaired, and I ran the risk of going into a faint through suffocation. This was a silly chance to take, since passing out would have drawn attention to me; yet Renée demanded an hourglass figure and was usually satisfied with no less than my maximum effort. Consequently, I would wander aimlessly around Manhattan with my diaphragm impeded, my testicles driven up into my torso, and my penis stretched cruelly back between my legs, tied to the cincher with a piece of twine. Is it any wonder I used to get dizzy and have to sit down?

The suitcase full of clothes in my car was special because it contained some evening wear for use on those rare occasions when I would drive down from New Haven and take a room at a downtown hotel, usually the Biltmore or Roosevelt. This was an extremely scary procedure because of the house detectives. These men had a very proprietary interest in what went on in the hotels they patrolled. In those days it was against the law for a man to appear in public dressed as a woman unless he was part of a show or other officially sanctioned event. Such men were arrested and thrown into the tank, where they were routinely beaten and raped by their fellow jailbirds. Sometimes their throats were cut. Generally speaking the authorities didn't intervene. This still goes on, though in these more liberal times I imagine the fury of it has diminished. In those postwar days there was a passion for the normal that bred a vicious response to eccentricity. Hotel detectives had a very focused range of authority and they carefully scrutinized those who came into it. A cop on the beat had thousands of people to watch, a hotel detective only a few hundred. The good name of the hotel had to be preserved, and a coed of my type was certain to blemish the dignified ambience unless her cover was perfect.

I would literally spend hours in preparation for my exit from the hotel. As I went through each step there was the feeling of ritual, of some magic being performed. After shaving my body, I would begin the makeup. Slowly my young man's face would alter, and the mirror would begin to reflect the face of a different character—similar but redefined. After this, Renée would be stronger, more present, but the figure in the mirror would still be Dick wearing a mask. Not the same Dick who had started but an altered Dick, a less secure one, a failed version of what had existed an hour before. Next I would obliterate Dick's genitals. In the pain of this process, Renée grew stronger. This sacrifice was for her. Still, Dick remained, a rather foolish figure with whatever tape or string contraption was used that evening in full sight and his face painted like a woman's. Then would come in rapidly accelerating stages the most satisfying transformation. Panties and perhaps a panty girdle would hide the hated apparatus, leaving only a smooth, feminine contour between my legs. Renée loved that. A bra added to the effect, and when a silky slip covered my torso the result was electric. Dick was further away than ever, receding into the uneasy oblivion previously inhabited by Renée. When the undergarments were in turn covered by the dress, only one step remained: the placement of my wig. This was the crowning moment. As I lowered it lovingly onto my head, I felt my feminization was completed. With those tresses framing my face, Renée was absolutely in control. My reaction to this ritual could be compared to that of a soldier who is afraid and inadequate but takes courage from the process of suiting up for battle. As each piece of equipment clicks into place, his confidence and self-image grow stronger until, when the sequence is finished, he feels himself a potent force.

Once I was properly outfitted I would go to the door and check the hall. If there was no one there, I would skulk over to the stairs and walk up or down two flights so that I would be entering the elevator on a floor different from my own. When the doors of the elevator opened on the lobby of the hotel, it was like the curtain going up on a play. My palms were damp and my pulse rate in the nineties. I would walk across the busy space with a practiced naturalness and, arriving at the door, plunge out with relief. If it was daytime I might shop or go to a movie. If it was nighttime and I was dressed up, I would pretend to be going to or coming from a party or a date. My times as Renée were all form and no substance. She faced a blank world where her only pleasures were the goings and comings that normal people considered nuisances—the dues they paid for the moments of significance in their lives. But Renée would go nowhere and come from nowhere.

During my freshman year at Yale, Renée made an unprecedented bid for acknowledgement. It came while I (as Dick) was furtively attending a transvestite show at the Apollo Theater in

Harlem. In those days the Apollo was not an exclusively black theater, though it was predominantly so. Sometimes they would bring in unusual shows that appealed to both blacks and whites. I was there to see the most famous transvestite show of the period. It was called the Satin Slipper Revue. In general format it was similar to the shows at the Club 82, but the performances were the best. It was first-rate from curtain to curtain. The quality of the show stimulated Renée. She watched those beautiful women perform flawlessly, and she realized that they, like she, tolerated (even seemed to overcome) the hateful deformity with which they had been born. This was a chance for her to live as fully as possible, and she asserted herself as never before. After the show a mortified Dick found himself backstage asking to speak to the director of the troupe.

The Satin Slipper Revue was run by a homosexual couple known as Jimmy and Clyde. Clyde was sick with a respiratory disease. It might have been tuberculosis or even lung cancer. Whatever it was it was serious, as it eventually killed him. He stayed home most of the time, and Jimmy tended to the logistics of the performances. It was Jimmy who came out to talk to me. He was a man of about fifty, well preserved and a bit of a dude. He wore a carnation in the lapel of his sharply tailored suit. He reminded me of a taller, more robust Adolph Menjou. On his upper lip was a pencil-thin moustache. At the time I didn't know it, but in the fifties such a moustache was a discreet signal of homosexuality. I had no reason to suspect this since my father had one too.

Jimmy walked out in a flash of highly polished shoes and asked me what I wanted. I explained that I wanted to be a performer. This piece of news didn't seem to unsettle him at all. He looked me over, commenting on my height and slenderness. He had me turn around and then walk to-and-fro. Finally he said, "You've got good bearing and a great complexion. If you'll meet me tomorrow night after the show and bring some clothes, we'll see what you look like." He gave me the address of his house, and I promised to meet him there.

All this sounds pretty shady, and it was. Any sane person would have avoided such a flagrantly dangerous situation, but this was just one example of the extreme gestures that my divided personality levered me into from time to time. For Renée this was the living out of a fantasy. Had she been a pure personality she would have become an exotic dancer the minute she turned seventeen and could leave home. If Dick had been a pure personality he would have been pitching for a New York Yankee's farm club. But these two extremes lived at the opposite ends of a great middle area characterized by a very conventional and bourgeois outlook. This was the area where the personalities overlapped and which exercised control over the wilder impulses of each. Occasionally the strain of this dual existence seemed to collapse this control, and some uncharacteristically excessive move would result. Actually, I had no intention of becoming a dancer. I simply wanted to see what it would be like to be considered for the job, to be treated as if I were going to be Renée on a professional basis. After all, Dick had at least chatted with the baseball scout. Why shouldn't Renée have an equal opportunity?

The next evening I packed an overnight case with shoes, underwear, makeup, a dress, and a wig. Strangely, I had had the wig made for me shortly before under the pretext that I was a dancer who did female impersonations. It was a good one costing about seventy-five dollars, which was expensive for the early fifties. It was the same brunette color as my own hair and fell neatly to my shoulders. The dress had actually been designed for the daytime but could be worn to a cocktail party if properly accessorized. It was white silk with a print of blue and lavender flowers. There were no buttons or clasps since it was cut like a short-sleeved tunic and slipped easily over my head. The skirt fell straight down from my hips to about midcalf and was cinched at the waist. The effect was feminine but not pushy.

At about one o'clock the following morning I quietly left the house in Forest Hills and took the subway into Manhattan. Jimmy's house was located on the West Side at about Forty-Fourth Street and Tenth Avenue. It was a dangerous neighborhood. A lot of struggling theater people lived there because the rents were low, but a lot of bad people lived and worked there too. There was an active drug traffic, and robberies by desperate addicts were everyday occurrences. As I drew closer to the address, I became more and more wary. When I saw that I would have to go down an alley between two tall buildings to get to the house, I almost gave it up. Still, Renée would have her way; so I walked into the darkness and through an iron gate. I had penetrated the outer line of buildings, which enclosed the block on all four sides, and found, to my surprise, a well-tended courtyard containing several small, freestanding town houses. There were trees and shrubs, through which wound a cobblestone walkway. A gas streetlight added a warm glow to the scene. I was delighted by this orderly and attractive location after the apprehension of my walk from the subway.

Jimmy lived in one of the town houses, a tiny two-story brick structure with ivy growing on the walls. He came to the door wearing a shiny kimono and sandals. He greeted me warmly, using the name I had given him when I had introduced myself the night before, Renée. When I heard his voice, softened by a couple of drinks, pronounce that name, Renée began to elbow her way forward. This was her ball game. Jimmy suggested we get right down to the business at hand. He showed me to the stairs, and I went up to change. I did notice that his eyebrows had been freshly plucked.

The interior of the house was decorated to a fare-thee-well. Everywhere there could be brocade, there was brocade. The draperies were brocade. The upholstery on the overstuffed furniture was brocade. the throw pillows were brocade. The floor was covered with thick pile rugs. I remember that somewhere, either on the floor or casually tossed over a piece of furniture, was a wolf skin. The pictures on the wall (mostly dewy landscapes as I recall) were surrounded by heavy and very ornate metal frames. No level surface was allowed to exist without a knickknack on it. There were special shelves in the corners for more knickknacks.

When I went upstairs Jimmy gave me clear directions about which of the two bedrooms I should go into. Every so often Clyde's muffled coughing could be heard through one of the doors; I was to keep out of that one. This was a direction I needed to hear only once. Even though the hacking increased in volume as I ascended the stairs, I was too excited to be much put off by it. I hurriedly dressed as Renée. The keynote was simplicity. I wanted to transform as quickly as possible to keep pace with my mounting excitement. I put on a bra and a panty girdle and then the dress. I applied a few dabs of makeup, adjusted my wig and that was it. There was no time for the more elaborate routine of making my genitals disappear but Renée came on with a vengeance in spite of that. When I walked down the stairs to let Jimmy see me, I was like a sophomore girl invited to the senior prom: shy glances and high hopes.

Jimmy came right to me and held out his hand. I took it, and he motioned me back so that he could look at me at arm's length. he turned me around and clucked approvingly, "I knew you'd make a pretty girl," he said.

"Thank you," I replied demurely.

"Let me show you a couple of things you can do with your makeup," he said professionally. Grabbing a tin of rouge from a tabletop, he shaded my chin, my nose, and my forehead. These were three places where I had never rouged before. While he was applying the rouge I noticed that he was wearing some himself. "Stage highlighting," he explained, and led me to a mirror. I looked less like a clown than I had imagined I would. As a matter of fact, I could see how it might be effective under hot lights. The guy knew his stuff.

"Sit down, sit down," he commanded in a fatherly way. "I'll fix you a drink. Fix myself one, too."

I sank into the nest of pillows on the overstuffed couch and listened to the tinkling of the ice as he mixed the cocktails. Shortly, he sat down next to me and handed me a glass filled with yellow liquid. It tasted like oranges. I found out later that it was a screwdriver. At seventeen I had drunk my share of beer, but I had never had anything to do with mixed drinks. I was nervous and the drink was cold and tasty, so I dispensed with it as if it were orange juice. Meanwhile, Jimmy was saying things like, "You have a lot of potential but you do lack experience. I don't know if I could take a chance if I didn't have some more personal interest in you." Renée was thanking him very much and saying she certainly hoped she was worth a chance. After a few minutes she began to feel downright giddy, and the world of professional transvestism began to seem like more of a genuine possibility. Jimmy's arm had snaked around her shoulders, and he was cradling her in a most reassuring way. He painted a possible rosy future in the world of show business. He stroked her thigh and feeling no resistance moved his hand higher. He ran his fingers between her legs. A warm flush suffused Renée's person, and she opened her legs a little. Jimmy continued to stroke as he continued to whisper things. What they were no longer mattered. Renée felt as if she had found love at last. A strong man was leading her toward fulfillment. He certainly had all the moves. At one point he raised her downcast face by crooking his forefinger under her chin and gently prompting her to look into his eyes. All seemed to glow as she gazed at him and then felt his lips pressed urgently against hers. His tongue found its way gently into her mouth, and they remained so for what seemed a long time. This was the culmination of all Renée's fantasies. She had longed for some affirmation like this after so many empty hours alone and so many useless trips into the streets, hungry for even a passing word or a shoulder brushed against a stranger. Now she was in the arms of a man, and it was wonderful.

Jimmy suggested that we go upstairs. I agreed, and he led me to his room. When he removed his kimono he revealed a well-kept body, completely nude. I was still in my dress, and he came to me with another languorous kiss. I said I was a virgin. He assured me that he would show me all I needed to know. Off came the dress, and with it went some of the dewiness of Renée's perspective. The bra was next and she began to feel much less secure. In the struggle to remove the panty girdle some of the tenderness went out of Jimmy's manner, though he remained gracious. Deprived of her accouterments, Renée began to fade, and Dick, who had been sent on a vacation to parts unknown, came snapping back. He didn't like what he found. He was taking a homosexual's penis in his mouth. Renée, however, was not completely gone, and it was she who insisted that Jimmy penetrate her face-to-face as a man would a woman. Jimmy, kindly agreed to this ungainly setup. Dick lay in absolute horror as he felt his anus invaded. There was no satisfaction in it for Renée or for Dick. Jimmy pushed his way in, thrust vigorously a few times and ejaculated. He paused for a caress or two and then fell asleep. It was a stereotypical deflowering: the bloom of romance that had developed during foreplay withered quickly and left a snoring older man flanked by a bleeding youngster who lay quietly sobbing.

As I lay there in the semidarkness listening to Clyde's coughing from the next room, I felt a closer identification with him than I did with either Renée or Dick. He and I were both sick, very sick. The dimension of my perversion came flooding in on me. I could make out the chintzy details of Jimmy's bedroom. The pile rug, the mirrors, the knickknacks, photographs of the Satin Slipper Revue; it was all so incredibly tasteless, so unlike the preppy world that I had lived in for so long and so far from the proper world of a Yale freshman. And it was sick.

I got up quietly, went to the bathroom and washed myself but did not feel particularly clean afterward. Putting on Dick's clothes made me feel better. I gathered up my things, put them in my overnight case, and let myself out. During this process, Jimmy never woke or broke the rhythm of his snoring. I never saw Clyde, though I could still hear his coughing as I went through the front door.

It was nearly dawn, and I made my way to the subway in a gray light. At that hour the streets were pretty safe. Every aspect of the neighborhood looked shabbier than before. On the way to Jimmy's a few hours ago I had thought it terrible but felt aloof from it, like a stranger on a tour. Leaving, I felt as if that seediness had entered me and left my bowels burning as a reminder of the intrusion.

I reached Forest Hills while it was still early and, with practiced ease, sneaked unnoticed into the house. My room seemed a safe refuge after the morning's unsavory activities, and I slept until the late afternoon. When I woke, Jimmy's house already seemed like part of the distant past. I think I must have learned the talent for denial from my mother. By the time I was back in class the next day, I thought about the incident only when I experienced an occasional twinge of pain in my rear end.

Though I didn't relive the experience in an obsessive way, it did have a strong effect on me. I redoubled my efforts to suppress Renée. Luckily, the Satin Slipper Revue incident took place late in the school year, and I was facing a summer filled with tennis tournaments that would occupy me fully and require exhausting hours of practice. That fact, coupled with my new resolve to excise Renée, resulted in a significant reduction in her appearances, but, as always, she remained and occasionally broke through.

9

Romance

The homosexual fiasco was actually the beginning of several years during which the personality of Dick was in strong ascendance. I spent the following summer playing tournaments all over the East. I was almost constantly in the company of my two friends Len and Joel. Their strong masculinity set the tone for a sympathetic response in me. During the days we played tennis, and during the evenings we drank beer and drove our cars recklessly. I still wasn't dating much, but neither were they. Their social lives were much more active during the school year, and they seemed satisfied to spend the summer in masculine company, raising hell. Our sexual moments were primarily ones that could be shared by all, like trips to burlesque shows. Occasionally we would go on dates. These never led to any authentic sex, but they kept the thought alive. Had we known how to go about it we would have gone to whorehouses, but no one felt strong enough to enter this unknown world. In future years, Joel and I would become rather expert with prostitutes; however, that summer it was all fantasy. Perhaps on those infrequent times when we went our own ways Len and Joel had serious dates, but they were never a subject of conversation. For the most part we were three tennis bums, and we enjoyed that camaraderie. It seemed unnecessary to complicate the situation.

I returned to Yale with a refreshed outlook. The shock of my first year was over, and there was a whole new class of freshmen compared to whom I was a seasoned veteran. Some of the cockiness of my Horace Mann days reappeared. I began to assert my individuality.

Yale in the 1950s was an extremely conservative place. The nearest thing we had to a demonstration was a panty raid at a neighboring girls' school. There was also a fiery altercation surrounding the ice cream trucks that were competing over the rights to sell on the campus grounds. Somehow the larger issues escaped most of us. The average student longed to be "cool." That meant being uninvolved, above the petty concerns of men more easily emotionalized. It also meant being current in the highly insulated world of the Ivy League student. This resulted in a sameness of type that may not have been equaled since. They all wore the same outfit: narrow ties, button-down shirts, and tweed jackets with skinny lapels. Between classes the commons area would be filled with people who all looked exactly the same. Some were a little taller or shorter or thinner or fatter, but those were the only significant differences. About half smoked pipes. All sported a short, well-kept Ivy League haircut.

In the light of this uniformity, my little gesture in the direction of individualism may not seem so pathetic. I wore roomy (some might say baggy) suits and bright, hand-painted ties. To a few this constituted a snotty reproach though in actuality it was a very mild protest at the conventionality of the campus. Aside from this gesture I was indistinguishable from the hard-core Ivy Leaguers. I even joined a fraternity that was populated with campus athletes. Although not a big man on campus, I was carving a niche for myself.

My tennis career was a big help in establishing me as a worth-while citizen. I won Yale's fall round-robin tennis tournament without losing a match. That started me on my way to playing number one on the varsity squad. That year I won fifteen out of the sixteen matches in which I competed. This probably resulted in more notoriety at Yale than it might have at other colleges. Many more people at the exclusive Ivy League schools actually played the game than in the student population at other schools. Consequently, the tennis team was more newsworthy at Yale. I wasn't a campus figure in the same sense as a star football player, but I was widely known, and that added to my sense of security. It gave Dick some extra leverage against Renée.

That same fall I was given a picture book of all the girls at

Smith. At schools where the student body is all male, books like this constantly make the rounds of the campus. In looking through it I found a picture of a girl whom I recognized as being from Forest Hills. Although I had only met her in passing, she had been very popular with friends of mine who went to Forest Hills High School. It was a strong enough connection to warrant some investigation. I was looking for a girl to see socially, and such slim pretexts were common starting points for dates between Yale and Smith students. I called her, and she agreed to come to Yale on an occasion known as "Mountain Day" at Smith. This is a day when the girls at Smith journey to men's colleges for the purpose of visiting friends. The tone is rather like that of an outing or a big picnic. It was an appropriately innocent occasion for a first date between relative strangers. Neither of us were really prepared for the degree of attraction we felt for one another.

Denise Eckland was the fulfillment of many of the fantasies that I had as Dick. My masculine sex drive was low, and my threshold of excitement high. In order for me to function as an ordinary man, all factors had to be satisfied almost completely. One strong criterion was beauty, but beauty of a particular kind. When I fantasized, like normal boys I used the conventional beauties of the day as my objects, but unlike normal boys I found it almost impossible to compromise this standard, especially if I was looking for a serious relationship. All of the women with whom I fell seriously in love were beauties. I would accept no less. Denise was beautiful in the very feminine way that was most pleasing to me. Her eyes were blue green, her hair light brown, her teeth perfect. They formed the centerpiece of a beautiful smile that seemed to me more expressive of her affection than any other of her features. Her figure, though curvaceous, was well-proportioned. There was nothing about her that seemed out of balance. Her complexion was light but not pale. She had a healthy, all-American look, rosy cheeked on blustery fall days. It was delightful to see her bundled up in woolen plaids, full of energy—and to watch her well-coordinated walk as she came toward me.

I was not the only one who felt that way about Denise. Shortly after I met her, I took my friend Joel up to Smith to introduce them. Denise had arranged a date for him with one of her acquaintances. As we sat in the waiting area at their dormitory, Joel spotted a girl who interested him. I was reading a magazine, so he poked me in the ribs to get my attention. "Forget about Denise," he said, "let's try to meet that one!" I looked up and said, "Joel, that *is* Denise." He told me later that he had been attracted by her smile, but I have an idea that the rest of her had something to do with it, too.

In addition to Denise's sleek, all-American good looks, I was attracted to her personality, which was so unlike my mother's. Though she was intelligent (another of my criteria for the ideal woman), it was not an aggressive intelligence; that is, she did not use it as a weapon against men. Her intelligence was devoted to her study of the arts, an area I considered more fitting for the female temperament. I could imagine my wife-to-be as a professional in the liberal arts but not as a physician or attorney. Ironically, Dick was turning into a staunch male chauvinist. He simply could not bear to be around a woman who reminded him of his mother or sister. However intolerant it may seem, he was obsessed with not tying himself down to a woman who might turn into a domineering force. He knew that he was vulnerable.

In that regard, as my relationship with Denise developed it began to appear to the world at large that I was rather domineering myself. Denise accepted my judgment as final; she preferred it that way. I was even teased by my friends for the high-handed way I made decisions for her: "Denise will have the roast beef," or, "Denise doesn't want to go to the game." These comments would usually be made without consulting her.

Actually, much of this seemingly dictatorial behavior came out of our very thoroughgoing knowledge of one another. I didn't so much dictate her behavior as I did correctly anticipate her preferences. Such a rapport was characteristic of my relationships with the significant women in my life. With few exceptions I chose women who were quite like Renée; my ability to understand their feminine natures may have grown out of my understanding of Renée's personality.

To the outside world I may have looked like a dictator, but Denise understood that this was a defense. Underneath that swagger was a soft center, and in our private times together we shared a very gentle feeling. Our search for nooks and crannies in which to pet became the subject of a continuing joke among our friends. When anyone asked where Dick and Denise were, the answer invariably was, "In the closet making out!" We were forever sneaking away from the main group to neck. The voracious appetite we had for one another came as a complete surprise to me. I had been aroused before, but the ease with which Denise stimulated me was a source of wonder. Just looking at her might cause an erection. This was unprecedented. I gave her my school ring almost immediately.

Whenever we could, we spent days alone. On the occasions of my weekend visits to Smith, I would stay at a rooming house called the College Inn. It was a little place located on the outskirts of Northampton, Massachusetts, the home of Smith College. The inn was actually an old house and had only a few rooms for rent. It was an out-of-the-way place, and I was rather proud of having discovered it. Not many students knew about it; Denise and I really felt sequestered when we were there. It was run by an old Polish couple. The wife had only one leg and used to clump about the house on a crutch. I would lie in bed with Denise and listen to the old lady banging around downstairs; I worried that the ominous thumps would travel to the stairs, ascend them, and burst in on us—but that never happened. As a matter of fact both she and her husband knew that Denise came over and never objected when she would disappear into my room at three o'clock in the afternoon and not emerge until shortly before her dormitory curfew at one o'clock. We'd spend the days in bed making love. Our lovemaking was typical of the era. Denise had promised herself that she'd be a virgin when she married. Dick approved of this. As far as I can remember, almost everyone approved of this in the early fifties. It seems a pretty arbitrary line now, but Denise and I would go no further than what is commonly called "dry humping." This term doesn't do justice to the pleasure we gained or the romance that we felt when we were together. This act, as incomplete as it was, fulfilled us. We both experienced satisfying orgasms, and for the time being we asked for nothing more.

An unusual characteristic of my masculine side was that I could not be aroused manually. I discouraged any fondling of my penis. This attitude went along with the prohibition of the times against masturbation: not only masturbation but unnecessary touching in any form. Some of my obsessiveness in this matter may be traced to the penis game my sister had played with me many years before, although for most of my life the memory of that game was completely repressed. Somehow, I felt intruded upon if anyone touched my genitals. There was an assumption of control on the part of the toucher that turned me off. I balked at this presumptuous approach. I don't mean that I was entirely unreasonable. It was the attempt to stimulate an erection through fondling that irritated me. It was too genitally specific.

I felt similarly about oral sex. Here again, my objections probably boiled down to the fact that this action represents such an intense focus on the penis. I required a more holistic approach. In this respect my sexual orientation was more like that reported by most women: a preference for a generalized sensuality.

Denise and I were ideally matched. We gloried in the sight of each other naked. This seemed supremely intimate to us. When we lay down together and felt our skins touching along the length of our bodies, we were surrounded by an aura reminiscent of a mild electrical charge. We both had very smooth skins, and the soft friction between them produced waves of delicious sensations. With our mouths and tongues together, the feeling was as if we had melted into one another.

This idyllic romance had a dramatic effect on both my academic performance and on my tennis career. My grades began to improve impressively. As a matter of fact had I not done so poorly during my first year, I would have graduated Phi Beta Kappa. Denise attained the rare distinction of being a Phi Beta Kappa during her junior year and eventually graduated as the top scholar of her college class. Though our weekends were spent in lovemaking, we studied together as well, and our conversations tended to incorporate the material we were exposed to in class. In this way we stimulated each other's thought processes and took satisfaction, perhaps a little smugly, in doing so.

Denise's wonderfully supportive attitude helped me a great deal with my tennis. Her affection was given without strings, and her delight at my success was complete. This was in strong contrast to the mixed signals from my parents. Certainly, Denise was never ashamed of me as my father had been if I lost a match. I wanted to win in order to see the happiness that it caused in her. I tried to make her proud because I knew she would be proud without any reservations.

My hunger for Denise's company and for her approval, though

in general a good thing, once interfered comically with my tennis success. In my junior year the coach of Yale's tennis team took note of the amount of time I was spending with Denise. He decided that she was a bad influence on my game. Consequently, he forbade me to see Denise prior to the team's dual match with Williams College. He especially warned me that I was not to bring her to the match. Since I was to drive half of the team in my roomy 1954 Oldsmobile, he took pains to repeat this dictate before we left. I solemnly listened, agreed convincingly, and promptly drove to Smith College where my teammates and I spent an entertaining afternoon with Denise and her friends. The visit proved so agreeable that we forgot the time and suddenly realized that we could well be late for the match. We all clambered into the car, Denise included, and made a mad dash through the Berkshire Mountains. The roads were winding and precipitous. It was no easy matter to herd a Rocket 88 around those curves and still keep on schedule. Naturally, I had to speed.

I was making good time when I noticed a flashing red light in my rearview mirror. A state trooper had taken exception to my reckless driving. Unwilling to admit defeat, I floored the accelerator. I figured I could lose him somewhere east of the Williams College tennis courts. He turned out to be a better driver than I had anticipated. The chase ended with me spread-eagled against my car being frisked by a wary patrolman. When he had satisfied himself that I was not a fleeing felon, he ordered us to follow his patrol car back to the nearest town, Pittsfield; there I was unceremoniously tossed in the slammer. While I reflected on my rashness, the other team members made some frantic phone calls. These resulted in a return call from the Williams College athletic director. He confirmed my identity and the fact that my team did indeed have a match that afternoon. This call sprang me, and I drove, considerably chastened, to the Williams tennis courts.

When we arrived my coach was frantic. The match had been postponed, and he hadn't taken the news too well that his number one player was in jail. His anger increased to a rage when he saw Denise step out of the car along with the rest of the team. He made a lot of threats, but in the end he forgave me. I was too valuable to the squad for him to do otherwise, but I was not soon again given the responsibility for transportation.

The foregoing is just one example of the irresponsible and

rebellious behavior of which I was capable. Denise's support and the security it provided seemed to encourage it. The strength I drew from loving women throughout my life often found its outlet in this kind of macho behavior. When the drive for a feminine component in my life was filled by a real woman and not by my fantasy of Renée, the extreme personality of Dick seemed free to surface, turning me, ironically, into a supermasculine persona.

The existence of Renée was considerably altered by my relationship with Denise. In the three years during which I spent so much time in Denise's company, Renée surfaced twenty times at the most. This was a radical drop from previous years when she might appear several times in a single week. At first this gave me a lot of hope. I began to think that all I really needed to lick this thing was a good woman's love. The problem was that in my solitary moments I continued to fantasize about being Renée. However busy I kept myself, I still had to spend some time alone. At those times I'd catch myself thinking as Renée would think. These fantasies would have been perfectly normal had I been a girl. I used to imagine, for example, that I was a cheerleader in a high school. All eyes were on me, and all the people in the stands responded when I called for a cheer. Or I might imagine going out on a date with some boy I had known in New York. Interestingly, these fantasies seldom utilized the people who were in my current social circle. It was almost as if Renée, restrained in the present, was forced to cast back into a time when she was freer, in order to create a believable scenario.

As time wore on, these fantasies did not decrease as I expected. They recurred with unsettling regularity and with surprising strength. Renée refused to die. Naturally, this depressed me. I felt that my situation was ideal for excising her from my life. I was in love and sharing an idyllic romance with a beautiful woman who in turn loved me. I was recognized as the finest tennis player at Yale. My grades had become exceptional at one of the country's best colleges. If Renée could not be driven out under these circumstances, she was stronger than I had ever imagined. Her hold on me appeared unbreakable.

Denise didn't understand this darker side of my personality. Of course, I never hinted at the existence of Renée, but Denise knew that something was bothering me. I would occasionally fall into a sulk from which she had no apparent power to raise me. At one point she theorized that I had a sadistic side and that I drew back for fear of hurting her. Most upsetting was my refusal to make any firm plans for our future together. While other couples were planning to marry upon graduation, Dick and Denise existed in a kind of limbo. We discussed possibilities but never set dates or bought engagement rings. Denise knew that I was hostile to both my sister and my mother. For a while she thought that was the key. Once she said, "I wish your mother didn't like me so much, then you might feel free to marry me." I didn't contradict her theories altogether because they made good cover stories. I only objected when she suggested that there was something wrong with her. There was nothing wrong with Denise. She was just fine. My mother *did* like her. In fact, everyone liked her—even Renée!

In my junior year I began to see a psychiatrist. This came about as a result of a contact made for me by my mother when I told her about my transsexualism. I decided to reveal it to her for several reasons. First was that I had read about transsexuals in my abnormal psychology class. Rather than describing them as incurable lunatics as *Psychopathia Sexualis* had done, my text-book indicated that transsexuals were disturbed individuals who could be treated. I took heart and imagined that with the help of a therapist I might still triumph.

Another reason for confessing arose from one of Renée's infrequent appearances in physical reality. It seemed that, denied the opportunity to become real on a frequent schedule, she acted with more viciousness when she did get out. After one of my rare sessions of cross-dressing with its accompanying genital mutilation, one of my testicles enlarged to twice its normal size. Moreover there had been some hemorrhaging inside my scrotal sack causing a blackish-purple bruise in the area. My penis was also raw where it had been burned as I tore off the adhesive tape that had held it down. This was the most damage I had ever done to myself, and I had done it in a period when I fancied that I might be getting better. These wounds healed, but I was left with the gnawing feeling that Renée might go out of control and do me permanent harm. She might even become despondent and commit suicide, taking Dick with her.

I suppose I could have sought help through a clinic or a private physician, but the idea of telling my mother appealed to me because I considered her partially responsible for my situation. I wanted to see what she would say—whether she would feel guilty or not. The gradual breakthrough that had started when I was seventeen and had led me to a more realistic appreciation of the dynamics of my family, was in high gear by the time I was twenty. I was ready for a confrontation, and soliciting advice from my mother was a passively aggressive way to bring it about.

I broached the subject during a day when she was idle due to a patient's canceled appointment. I think I said, "Mother, I have something that I must talk to you about. It's been going on for some time now, and I have to bring it out in the open." She could tell that I was serious, but this was the sort of thing my mother hated to hear from family members. There was little that was psychoanalytical in her approach to dealing with family problems, and this was probably the first time any family member ever asked for such help. Her attitude didn't promote that kind of questioning. Dr. Bishop was open to the world at large but closed to her family. She would spend all day talking with patients and then after supper when most psychiatrists are simply not available except in an emergency, she would begin taking calls. It was not uncommon for her to spend all evening talking on the telephone to one patient after another. I could hear her indulgently prompting them and asking probing questions unlike any she ever put to me or my sister or my father.

When I made my statement of need, I could see she was a little confused. Finally she suggested that we go into the waiting room adjacent to her office. I guess that she considered this to be a kind of middle ground somewhere between her professional and her private sectors. The average person's response to such an ominous statement would probably have been to want to go into cozier, more familiar surroundings—to get as comfortable as possible with a loved one. Dr. Bishop was, of course, not average in this regard, but to give her credit she did move us out of the office proper.

My presentation was just as emotionless as her response. I certainly wasn't going to give my mother the opportunity to see me break down. That, I knew from past experience, would just lead to recriminations. I used the style in which we communicated best: cerebral and, on the surface at least, rational. So, the two of us adjourned civilly to the waiting room.

It was a short trip. The waiting area had been a porch when we moved into the house. Mother had arranged for the conversion when she had her office built. It was a slightly unusual room in that it was skinny. There was ample length, about twenty feet; but only about eight feet of width. The proportions were all off; under the circumstances this seemed appropriate. It was decorated in the same style as the rest of the house with one exception. Here my mother's preoccupation with knickknacks had been kept under control. These doodads were omitted out of deference to her patients. Some might have found them unnerving while to others they could have been a temptation to steal. I took a seat on the couch at one end of the room, and my mother sat in a chair at the other end. Thus there was a space of about fifteen feet separating us; this too, seemed appropriate considering the tone that we had struck.

I thought it best to start out with the academic facts as I had learned them in Abnormal Psych.: "Mother, as you know, there are certain mental disorders that are characterized by gender confusion. Somehow, the individual has feelings and impulses that are characteristic of the opposite sex." I quoted a good portion of the chapter on transsexualism with my mother nodding in agreement. Finally, having laid the groundwork I arrived at the point. "Mother, I am such an individual." She continued to nod, waiting for more information. "I've been dressing up in Mike's clothes since I was six years old." I waited for a reaction. Receiving none I plunged ahead. "Sometimes I go out in public dressed as a woman. . . . I don't seem to be able to help myself. . . . I've got a wig, too." Each time I paused I expected her to jump in with some sort of comment; yet her pursed expression never really changed. Finally she said "I realized your sister had some problems [note the past tense], what with being a tomboy and all, but, Dick, you were such a *normal* child." Then my mother added, "It was my fault. You must have identified with me rather than with your father." This statement should have been a great triumph for me. It was the only time in my life that I ever heard my mother admit to being at fault. Still, that admission was tempered by her explanation: "*You* must have identified with me." In this way the responsibility seemed shifted, at least semantically, onto both our shoulders. I wasn't aggressive enough to say, "But what about the Halloween party and the other times you dressed me as a girl?" Such an unseemly display of pique would have disturbed the academic atmosphere. There we sat, dry as dust, and my great revelation withered and became a case history.

Mother suggested that I see a psychiatrist in New Haven. She promised to look into who was available there and recommend the best. With that our interview was concluded. It took about half an hour. Thirty minutes may seem a short time to spend in explaining fifteen years of transsexualism, but my mother had heard all she wanted to hear. Amazingly enough, the subject was never mentioned from that time until she died eight years later. The nearest we came to speaking about it was when she would ask, "How are you doing with Dr. So and So?" and I would answer, "Fine." I will say this: she paid the bills for many years of analysis, and she paid promptly.

The psychiatrist whom my mother recommended was Dr. Helen Gilmore. Actually, she was just a stopgap measure. Since I was only one year from graduation, we couldn't start any serious therapy. My treatment might take years, and it did not seem wise for me to get involved with a doctor and then leave after such a short time. What Dr. Gilmore did was familiarize herself with my background and counsel me in immediate matters such as the problem of choosing a career. This was a matter of conflict to me because my parents were pushing strongly for medical school. They felt that it was the only profession worthwhile enough for a Raskind. *My* notion, that I take a few years out to develop my tennis skills, was met with horror. Of course, this increased its attractiveness. In those days there was no "open" tennis, and any career would have been as an amateur. There was not much money to be made; so this option seemed impractical for any responsible person. In spite of my occasional flurries of rebellion, I was basically practical. I had to admit that though I had considered careers in teaching, political science, and even acting, none was compelling enough to warrant throwing away the opportunity to go to medical school with my parents' financing. It was doubtful that they would support any other graduate course. Had I decided to be a tennis bum, they probably would have disowned me.

Not surprisingly Dr. Gilmore sided with my parents. She felt it would be dangerous for me to adopt what she considered the unstructured life of an athlete. She maintained that I needed the security of a well-regulated everyday existence. Medical school would certainly provide this. In addition, the pressure from my parents would be eliminated, and I would have a sense of accomplishment when I succeeded in such a demanding curriculum. Finally, I would be located in the same place for a few years running; that would facilitate the therapy that we both agreed was the key to overcoming my transsexualism.

In the face of such rationality, I could not disagree. Her gesture in the direction of compromise was that I not attend Yale's medical school. She suggested that I go to the University of Rochester. This would constitute a break with my father's tradition and at the same time put more distance between me and my family, which she agreed had an unnerving effect on me. Certainly I identified Renée most strongly with them, and it was often a family crisis that prompted her emergence. I accepted this plan gratefully and took pleasure from the fact that my parents didn't like it. In this and other matters Dr. Gilmore proved a common sense guide, and I gained a lot of benefit from our frank weekly sessions. She was the first person with whom I had been able to discuss my problem. She remained objective and helpful while I ventilated fifteen years of frustration and fear.

Denise knew that I was seeing a psychiatrist, but I never told her why. She assumed that it had something to do with my inability to commit. Still, she saw no real improvement on that score. I did become less moody but no less evasive on the subject of our future together. The situation deteriorated during my senior year, and as graduation approached we both sensed that our association was coming to an end. After three years of intense intimacy it seemed pointless to go any further if I still hadn't the courage to marry like a normal man. In 1955 there were no other options; we were terminally middle class.

In spite of this foreboding atmosphere, we became hotter for one another than ever before. Whenever possible we were groping each other in a dark corner. The prophecy that had been made earlier in *World Tennis Magazine* would not come true (the caption under our picture read, "The future Mr. and Mrs. Raskind"), but we were determined to get in as much contact as possible before the house of cards collapsed. We necked right up to graduation and then were pulled apart by the unmanageable force of my complicated personality.

The symbol of that leavetaking was a trip to Europe that I took during the summer following graduation. I went as part of the Prentice Cup tennis team; the squad consisted of a combination of the teams of Yale and Harvard. We played the combined teams of Oxford and Cambridge. The point was not simply to play tennis but also to broaden the outlooks of the graduating collegians. My chief broadening came in the form of a comparison of English prostitutes as opposed to French ones.

Of course, the official activities were meaningful, too. I was delighted to nose around in England seeing all the places I had read about in history classes and walking in the footsteps of the literary figures that I loved so much. My activities were all carefully documented in letters home and were eventually published in *World Tennis Magazine* under the title "Diary of a Prentice Cupper." The American team scored a brilliant victory over the British at Wimbledon, a site revered by all tennis players. My efforts contributed to our win, so I had nothing but success in my public activities.

In the private sector, however, I was not so lucky. My roommate for the summer was a charming and extremely macho young guy from California. Tom was also a brilliant tennis player who eventually became the captain of the Yale team in his senior year. Like my other friends he was a big strapping boy, full of lusty ideas for our off-hours. Tom promoted numerous trips into Picadilly Circus to pick up prostitutes. These girls were like Eliza Doolittle before Professor Henry Higgins started to work on her. They were hard young women (sometimes not so young) with working-class backgrounds. Their come-ons were not very genteel. "Oy mate, kaada choingeja luk?" I was not entranced, but at Tom's urging I got into a cab with one of these charmers and went to her flat. This fling got really depressing when we went inside. Her place consisted of two rooms: one for sleeping and bedding her customers, and the other for everything else. The bathroom was down the hall. The walls of the rooms were painted navy blue or, at least, had been that color some time around the turn of the century. The furniture was sturdy but had seen years of hard use. There were some cheap pictures on the wall. They were the usual landscapes available in Woolworth's. The floor was scuffed and uncovered. I think there might have been a little rug over by the bed. This woman's private life was not hinted at even though I could see everything she owned. There were no books, no magazines, no letters. There was a telly in the corner. I guessed she watched that.

We swept in, and she ushered me into the bedroom without any preliminary chat. The ride over in the cab had been largely in silence, too. Before I knew it she was undressing and urging me to do the same. I was a little slower than she was, and she sort of orbited around me as I disrobed. I would get an article of clothing part of the way off, and she would already be saying, "Oil tike thet, luv." When I'd finished, she conveyed me quickly to the bed, and we lay down on top of the spread. Needless to say, I had no erection. When she noticed this technicality she began fondling me. I was lying on my back, and she was kneeling, staring intensely at my penis and waiting for signs of activity. From my perspective I couldn't even see her face, but the orientation of her body and the tone of her muscles communicated great expectations. They were not met. Occasionally, she would turn around and look quizzically at me as if I were being purposely uncooperative. Once when she did this I sort of shrugged my shoulders. This stimulated her to lean over and begin to suck me. She must have thought that this was a sure-fire cure because when it didn't work she turned around and said testily, "Wottsa maher?" I shrugged again. She got up and began putting on her clothes. I quickly dressed, left some money, and fled. Later on, Tom and I compared notes. He had come several times with his girl. I said I had too.

I tried a few more times with the girls from Picadilly, but I couldn't make it work. These outings were just as useless as the one described above. The matter-of-factness of these girls stood squarely between me and excitement. They were so plainly businesswomen that I could be no more aroused by them than I could by a used-car salesman trying to pressure me into a quick deal. Fortunately, my stay in England included a short visit to Paris, and it was there that I had my first successful intercourse with a woman. She was a prostitute as well but of a different type.

The failures in London had seriously undermined my confidence. I was worried since I had been so successful with Denise. Although we had never had complete intercourse, I had had strong erections and strong ejaculations. My climaxes were not weak or unfulfilling in any way despite the presence of Renée. On the contrary, I enjoyed orgasm tremendously, and it offered me the same moments of transcendence as it does any normal man. There was an additional satisfaction in that it was a supremely masculine experience and made me feel more secure about that side of my personality. This was one of the things that gave me hope as I developed my relationship with Denise. My orgasms had seemed an indication that I might be able to triumph over the nagging kernel of femininity inside me. Of course, it had been a false hope but not one that I ever completely abandoned. I thought that if I could have a total sexual experience it might produce a big change. Perhaps entering a woman and actually ejaculating inside her would produce a magical effect. It would be more natural, more in line with the masculine urge; it could make a difference.

The experience with the English prostitutes, rather than reinforcing me, created new doubts. Maybe I couldn't do it in the natural way. Maybe Renée wouldn't let me. Normal men liked to be played with, liked to be sucked. None of my friends had any problems making it with prostitutes. I couldn't even tear my hair and cry out, "What's the matter with me?" I knew.

After the Prentice Cup matches were finished, I made a four-week swing through Europe. I traveled with a teammate named Hank. Toward the end of our tour we arrived in Paris. Hank was conservative and stuck pretty much to the respectable tourist spots. He preferred museums, parks, and monuments. The furthest he had deviated from this was a trip with me to see the famous prostitutes of Amsterdam. These woman recline or pose in windows. They are beautifully lighted and beautifully costumed. The window dressing often appears sumptuous. Every fantasy is catered to. Some of the women wear little girl's clothes, some nun's habits, some are completely nude in various surroundings. You might find one stretched out on an Egyptian couch, ringed by artifacts. This Cleopatra might be wearing only a smile and a headdress. Such prostitutes are very expensive; so even though I was attracted to the idea of giving them a try, I didn't. Perhaps even more daunting than their price was the relatively public nature of the whole affair. In addition to prospective customers, a lot of respectable people were around just gawking. I was afraid that such public scrutiny might disturb my already shaky equilibrium. I went back once or twice without Hank, but I still couldn't get up the nerve.

When we hit Paris I separated from Hank and made my way to the Place Pigalle. This notorious red-light section of Paris was similar in atmosphere to the present day corner of Broadway and Forty-second Street in New York City. All manner of night people cruised a street that ran around the perimeter of a poorly kept park. With the park as its hub, the street formed the rim of a wheel around which traffic moved at a snail's pace. Entry into or out of this flow of traffic was by means of a series of streets radiating from the rim of the wheel. The volume of traffic and the difficulty of breaking into the flow of cars resulted in much shouting, honking, and revving of engines. This in itself was not so unusual given French driving habits (very demonstrative), but in the garish light of the neon signs over the bars that faced the park it took on an apocalyptic quality. Drivers had their heads and upper torsos stuck out the windows of many of the cars, gesticulating or screaming obscenities. Little spaces would open up, and drivers would plunge ahead with a squeal of tires, fearful that some other car might beat them to the punch. Every now and then the crunch of metal against metal could be heard.

Around the outside of this river of cars was a river of pedestrians patrolling in front of the nightclubs. It was composed partially of hookers in spiked heels, net stockings, and skirts split to the thigh. There were a few pimps wearing an extreme style of clothing remininscent of a zoot suit. There was a sprinkling of French toughs in slacks and polo shirts or, if more affluent, in pinstriped suits with dark shirts and loud ties. Some curious adolescents hung around the doors of the clubs trying to get a look at the strip shows inside. The great majority of the crowd, though, were tourists. Many were Americans, the worst of whom actually wore Bermuda shorts and had cameras hanging around their necks. The best of them were like me, unobtrusive. I could also speak French.

At first, this scene looked less promising than London or Amsterdam. The tone was equally intimidating here, if not more so. I soon discovered, however, that inside the clubs there were dark corners where I could have a drink without drawing attention to myself. Often these night spots, called things like "Les Girls!" were surprisingly uncrowded considering the circulating mob outside. I would seat myself at a table and settle down to watch the show. It usually consisted of a few strippers who took it all off, a chanteuse, and a couple of dancers, often of the Apache variety. The music was recorded, and the showmanship of the performers was negligible. The real purpose of these clubs was to flash some skin and to sell watery drinks at exalted prices, not to serve as a showcase for serious artists. While at my table, I would be joined by one of the resident hookers. She would speak softly and in a friendly way without the grating quality of the London girls.

"Bon soir," she would say as she appeared next to me out of the darkness. She would stand close, and I'd have to turn slightly and look up to the side. Sometimes her hip would touch my shoulder.

"Bon soir," I would reply. *"Comment allez vous?"*

"Bien," she'd sit down. *"Un cocktail pour moi?"*

"Oui, Garçon!"

"Oui, monsieur?"

"Un cocktail pour madamoiselle." I would look questioningly at her. She would order champagne. All of them ordered champagne. Even I knew that it was ginger ale. I would order another drink for myself. While waiting for the drinks, she would make more conversation.

"Tu est Americain?"

"Oui."

"C'est un beau pays."

"C'est vrai."

These girls rarely taxed my college French. I suppose it was in their best interests to keep the topics superficial, but their very basic level of expression was probably the result of tact. At any rate, I felt secure and never once had to discuss Sartre. I had several such encounters in different bars and finally found a girl to my liking. She was a little more voluptuous than average and young. When she talked to me, she reached out and touched my hand from time to time. It was probably a trick, but I fell for it anyway. When she asked if I'd like to go upstairs with her, I said, *"Oui."*

Unlike the cockney hookers who lived a cab ride away, the Parisian models operated out of rooms that were either upstairs over the bar or just a few doors away. We climbed a narrow stairway up to the third floor and entered a door at the end of a long hall. Everything was dingy, dingier than the buildings I went to in London. The stairwell smelled faintly of urine. I wondered which of the doors opening off the corridor would be the one we'd enter. They all looked the same. I followed the girl, watching her move along on her high heels. She was surprisingly steady on them. As she walked she fished in a little bag that she carried and eventually produced a key. She stopped and used it to open a door. Inside was a little room with a sink sticking out of the wall and a single bed underneath the window on the opposite side. Next to the bed was a straight-back chair. The window was boarded up; I don't know where the air in the room came from. Luckily it was a cool evening. In a little curtained closet was a bidet. The toilet was elsewhere. It was probably behind one of those doors we had passed on the way to the room. The lighting was subdued. The bulb hanging from the ceiling may actually have been red, but I can't be sure. It should have been.

The girl slipped off her skirt and blouse. Underneath she was wearing a lacy half-bra, garters with net stockings and, over these, a pair of black panties. She slipped the panties off revealing a patch of thick pubic hair. Her approach to undressing was not matter-of-fact. She did it slowly, looking up from time to time to see if I was watching. I was. She turned around and made it plain that I should unhook her bra. I did, brushing my hands against her breasts as I removed it. They sagged a bit, but I found them exciting; her nipples seemed small for breasts of such size. Leaving on the garter belt and stockings, she turned her attention to my clothes. Slowly she unbuttoned my shirt, running her hands inside and around to my back when she untucked it from my pants. Then her hands came up and kind of pushed the shirt down over my arms, which hung down straight by my sides. This bared my shoulders and chest. She put her cheek against me as she pulled the shirt downward, clearing my arms. I pressed her against me, and she raised her mouth to be kissed. After I had done this she pushed me back gently, and I sat down on the edge of the bed. She removed my shoes and slipped off my socks. Then she guided me into a reclining position and unfastened my pants. She helped me shrug out of them and then sat down next to me. For a moment I thought she was going to try fondling me. She did touch me but only for a brief inspection. It was gently and respectfully done. Having satisfied herself that I was not seriously diseased, she gestured toward the lavatory. I rose, crossed to the basin, and washed myself. When I turned around she was lying on the bed. She seemed accessible, and when I eased onto the bed next to her she made no aggressive move. I passed my hand over her body. She caught the hand and pressed it briefly against her lips, then moved it to her breast. That was the most assertive thing she did. Otherwise, I set the pace of our lovemaking. I put my mouth on her breasts and gently kneaded the soft flesh between her legs. She sighed as if she was enjoying it. Her whole presence was yielding and utterly unthreatening. In spite of the shoddy room she made it seem as if we were engaged in something personal. This excited me, and her relaxed approach allowed me the leisure to nurse that excitement along. Soon I had a nice hard erection. I entered her and quickly climaxed. While I was thrusting she whispered encouragement in my ear, "Dick. Dick." It was a gratifying performance—all in a night's work for her but a very big moment for me. At last I knew the pleasure of having a woman's flesh tight about me when I ejaculated. She helped by gripping me tightly with her legs as she felt me begin to tense in the excitement of orgasm. Afterward she stroked my hair companionably.

In contrast to the English girls, this prostitute was a genuine professional. In London the attitude seemed to be that all a hooker owed a customer was some friction. The Parisian girl was more sensitive to the psychological aspects of her trade. Though she had only a bare room to work with, she managed to create an aura of romance.

I returned to Place Pigalle at least twice more before my week in Paris was over. I repeated with the same girl once and tried a new one another time. The new one had a similar approach, and I was successful with her, too. After each of these episodes I felt as if I had spent twenty dollars in an extremely worthwhile cause. Hank, however, couldn't understand it. When I proudly announced what I had been up to, his response was, "Jeeze, Dick! What'd ya do that for? You could get a disease! You don't even have anything to show for your money. You coulda gotten some nice souvenirs to take back home! That's a lotta money!" Hank preferred to pursue more concrete rewards but I felt that sixty dollars was a small price to pay for such a boost to my manhood.

10

Not the Average Medical Student

After my Parisian success I had reason to feel optimistic about the future. I would be starting both my medical career and my psychotherapy in Rochester. But, as I got closer to the beginning of the fall semester I became more and more anxious. Upon my return from Europe, I made a brief, tension-filled stop at home to pick up the personal effects that I needed to begin life in medical school. It was quickly dawning on me that I was tired of school and genuinely ambivalent about medicine. My sessions with Dr. Gilmore during my last year at Yale had increased my awareness of my parents' influence on me. The four tough years of medical school began to loom more and more as a concrete example of their wills in opposition to mine. I was determined to go through with the plan but, increasingly, was beginning to resent it.

I felt some relief upon leaving Forest Hills, but as I neared Rochester my mood darkened again. The situation I moved into was similar to the one I'd experienced during my first year at Yale. I shared a small rented house with other students, and I had very little privacy as a result. Once again I was the new kid in town, and during that first year in medical school I had no time for tennis, so even that comfort was denied me. The other students were highly motivated. Since I was ambivalent on the whole subject of medicine my participation was not whole-hearted; and I soon discovered that a lackadaisical approach is unproductive in med school. All medical students go to classes all day and study four or five hours per night. Regardless of how brilliant you are, you cannot be sluggish and still get through.

Some students pretend that they don't study. There was a little pub in Rochester called the Bungalow; it was frequented by medical students in their off hours. The pretenders would hang around the Bungalow all evening. Often they bragged about not having to study, but at midnight they went back to their rooms and studied until five in the morning. If they didn't—they flunked.

I was poorly prepared for this drudgery. At Yale I had taken only the minimum pre-med requirements. The rest of the time I had signed up for whatever pleased me, and I spent far more time in psychology classes than in science labs. One of my first term classes in med school was histology, the study of microscopic cell structure. Most of my peers had taken any and every undergraduate course where you looked through a microscope. I could adjust one, but that was about all. On the first day of class I was already two years behind. Most people, if they are familiar with cell structure at all, are used to seeing diagrams. These line drawings are misleadingly clear. Each organelle is seen in the middle of a sea of white. They all have radically different masses, textures, or shapes. What you actually see when you look through a microscope at real cells is pink chicken noodle soup. The immediate reaction is that it should be impossible for that much junk to get into such a small space. What's more, it all looks pretty much the same. Imagine that you're looking at an aerial photograph of the city dump. Now count all the orange rinds and don't count the grapefruit rinds by mistake. For the first six months I couldn't even find the rinds, never mind counting them.

It was the same story in my anatomy class. A drawing of the muscular system of the body is quite clear, but in reality all that stuff is jammed in there together going every which way. You never see a diagram that includes the circulatory system, the nervous system, the lymphatic system, the muscle system, and the gastro-intestinal system all pictured together. That would be a nightmare, and it wouldn't even include the organs, the connective tissue, the adipose, and the dozens of other materials too numerous to mention. Cutting into a cadaver is like opening Pandora's box. All kinds of stuff comes out, and not much of it resembles the drawings. Some of us doubted whether the professors could really sort it out either. Partly because of this belief and partly because I was too intimidated to be serious, I contrived a series of anatomical jokes. While the professor, a spunky Scotsman, was in another part of the dissecting room, a classmate and I would remove some structure and replace it in another part of the cadaver. I don't mean we took something obvious like the heart and substituted it for the stomach. We were subtle. For example, we took the median nerve out of the arm and laid it in a cut down the leg. Then we yelled, "Dr. McHughes, Dr. McHughes! We've got an anomalous structure here!" He strolled over, peered skeptically into the incision and then, using a pair of forceps, lifted the nerve out. Disdainfully holding it up for everyone to see, he announced in his light brogue, "Gentlemen, this is the median nerve, and it belongs in the arm. I wonder [dark glance at us] how it got into the leg." He put up with these occasional jokes because, in a way, they were instructive and maybe because he enjoyed the challenge. Still, my friends would often say, "Hey, Dick, are you going to fuck around or dissect?" I did a lot more fucking around than serious dissecting. I put in the five hours a night studying, but I did so sulkily. The time was not really well used.

Meanwhile, my analysis was proceeding under the guidance of my new therapist, Dr. Alfred Clark. Every weekday at six o'clock I would enter his office and assume a recumbent posture on his couch. Both he and his office were utterly nondescript. I never knew anything about his personal life; if I had it would have violated a basic rule of Freudian analysis. The therapist was not to be seen as a human being, not to be known personally. He was a tool to be used. It was assumed that he was utterly objective, that he had no axes to grind. If he had private feelings about a patient or a problem, they were kept out of the sessions. The therapist was simply a thinking machine who offered treatment out of a deep reservoir of knowledge and never out of his own emotional response. Accordingly, the doctor tried to make himself as inoffensive as possible. His suits were ordinary as was his haircut. His speech pattern was measured and devoid of judgmental tones. His office was nondescript. The most unusual thing in the room was the couch, designed specifically for reclining. Doctor Clark would sit at the head of it, just out of sight. The setup was exactly like the ones you see so often in magazine cartoons.

At Yale I had taken as many psychology classes as I could, and I knew how the process of analysis was supposed to work. I would talk about my problems, and Dr. Clark would gently prompt me to recall the traumatic incidents from my childhood. Of course, these were deeply repressed and would come forth only through psychic struggle. There would be denial, which the doctor would pinpoint and skillfully lead me past. Once the memories of these incidents took shape I could experience the anxiety, anger, frustration, and guilt that had been locked away with them. These feelings were responsible for my abnormal behavior. In theory, once I had confronted them the compulsive cross-dressing would cease because the first causes would have been defused.

I climbed on that couch with high hopes, but it soon became clear that the passive Dr. Clark understood little of transsexualism. Furthermore, he had no feel for the strength of my compulsion. In the first few days of analysis I explained what I had been up to during the last few years. The doctor's first response was to ask me why I didn't wear more effeminate men's clothes. Perhaps I could have a flower in my lapel; this was his idea of a compromise. I could be a womanish man. Even my friend Josh had given me better advice when he said, "Stop being a sissy." If I had followed the doctor's line of reasoning, I would have turned myself into a male version of my mother. She was a woman who wore mannish clothes. I was supposed to become a man who did the opposite. Needless to say, this suggestion didn't inspire a lot of confidence in me. Things didn't really improve much over the years that I spent with Dr. Clark. During the whole time I never had one breakthrough, and I never dredged up one repressed episode. I just talked, and Dr. Clark said "Yes . . . yes . . ."

Sometimes our sessions would start with dream interpretation. For some time I kept a journal of my dreams. I had several that were recurrent. They were all embarrassingly blatant in their overtones. One of them had me walking in a forest infested with snakes. They were everywhere. The floor of the woods was a seething turmoil of snakes. They were hanging like vines from the trees. It was hard to keep my balance because of all the snakes on the ground. I couldn't steady myself because everything I might lean up against was covered with snakes. I tiptoed around that squirming landscape always on the verge of falling. At some point in the dream, I'd lose control and pitch headlong toward a nest of snakes. Then I'd wake up gasping.

Freudian dream symbolism holds that snakes are associated

100

with sex. They are perfect male phallic objects. In this dream I was cast into a landscape of threatening penises. The doctor had refinements to add, but they weren't too impressive. I had another dream where I was traveling in high mountains, teetering along the edge of a narrow trail. In yet another I was traveling by airplane when some trouble threatened to cause a crash. These two dreams reflected my lifelong fear of falling.

The most obvious aspect of all these recurring dreams is that they threw me into a series of insecure situations. I was repeatedly in scenarios that had me searching for some solid support. This was a pretty straightforward representation of my real life.

The more I talked to Dr. Clark the more outraged I became at my parents. My frustration with the therapy fed my anger. After all, they had made it necessary. Eventually I cut off all communication with them. Surprisingly, even though their emotional support had been sparse as well as conditional, I missed it.

Denise had come up a couple of times during my first year at medical school. We were intimate but strained. After Christmas she called me and asked if I thought there was any chance at all that we would ever marry. I was so despondent over the lack of progress in my analysis that I said, "No." She dropped out of my life, and I didn't see her again until 1977 when I was playing as a woman in the U.S. Open Championships. At that time, after a few embarrassing moments, we established a warm rapport and felt an affection very similar to the one we had as college kids. Something elemental in our feelings for one another had transcended my change of sex as well as the twenty years of intervening time. Unfortunately that far-off reunion had no bearing on the desolation I felt when the last hope of reconciliation was cast away. I was left pursuing a career I didn't want, accepting the financial support of parents I couldn't stand, and fighting the urge to be a woman. In this last I was aided by an ineffectual analyst.

Meanwhile, Renée was raging to get out. In the slight privacy of my house I sometimes grabbed a fast few moments of illusion. In the bathroom, for example, I could wrap a towel turban-style around my head, push my genitals back between my legs, and then clamp my thighs together. From the front, my pubic area was feminine and the towel disguised the short hair on my head. I would look at myself in the bathroom mirror and long for a more complete transformation. Sometimes the pressure would become too much to bear, and I'd have to break out of the house and go to the Bungalow where there was loud music and a lot of activity. Even though my fantasies of being Renée made me feel like Dr. Jekyll with a troublesome Ms. Hyde banging around inside him, they provided me with my greatest release. I took no pleasure from my studies or from my therapy. Simply sitting and imagining that I was Renée entertained me when little else did. Dr. Clark's therapy made no dent at all in my compulsion. If anything it increased in intensity; only my opportunities were diminished.

Aside from fantasizing about Renée, just one other thing gave me real satisfaction. That was riding my motorcycle. I bought this machine in the fall of my freshman year at medical school as a poke at my parents. I knew they wouldn't like it. I had been asking for one ever since I'd gotten my first driver's license. They had always refused on the grounds that motorcycles were too dangerous. Since I wasn't speaking to them I didn't see any reason to respect their wishes anymore. Besides, the bike cost only two hundred dollars. It was BMW "Golden Flash." Although it was a substantial bike (500 cc's), it was by no means large or complicated. By the time I was through with it four years later, I could pretty much take it apart and put it back together again. I found dismantling that motorcycle more satisfying than dismembering a cadaver.

Along with the Golden Flash, I bought another piece of indispensable equipment: a black leather jacket that sported about sixteen zippers. Marlon Brando had recently made a big splash as a tortured rebel in a movie called *The Wild One.* He had worn such a jacket. The zippers at the wrists were supposed to tighten them down so that the wind couldn't run up your sleeves. The zippers on the pockets were supposed to keep things from falling out when the wearer was racing down the open road. The jacket had a lot of pockets and hidey-holes for stuff, but they did not account for all the zippers. I think some were included just for cosmetic purposes.

I enjoyed everything about the motorcycle. I took it for long rides at high-speed. The strong feel of the wind and the blur of passing landmarks made me feel liberated. The claustrophobic secretiveness that characterized so much of my life did not intrude when I was driving the bike.

I took up with some townies who also rode motorcycles. They

were working-class types with whom I had little in common except transportation. We rode recklessly, and I fell off a number of times. One of my associates managed to get himself killed. He roared up the entrance ramp to what he thought was an overpass on a section of the new interstate highway system then under construction. Unfortunately, all they had built so far was the entrance ramp. My friend drove right off the end and fell to his death. This should have been a warning to me, but it didn't have much effect. I drove just as fast and just as carelessly as before. From my point of view, cracking up on the bike might have solved a lot of my problems.

Fall and winter in Rochester are cold, gloomy times, and that external environment accurately reflected my internal state. I became more and more melancholy. None of the right things were working. My therapy was as placid as pudding. My studies were providing me with no satisfaction, though I was managing to pass. The plan of attack worked out with Dr. Gilmore was an apparent flop. The only things I enjoyed doing were the wrong things. I enjoyed fantasizing about Renée. I enjoyed being the Wild One.

I was saved from absolute depression by the arrival of summer vacation. Once again I would enter the clean, well-defined arena of tennis. There would be no complicated decisions to make. I would move from one tournament to the next, exercising my body and sharpening my athletic skills. Perhaps some clarity would carry over into my second year of med school.

Before the tour I was reunited with Joel and Len for a spring vacation in Miami. Once again I was under their powerful masculine influence. Our trio had been broken up when I went to Rochester; Len went to Harvard Business School, and Joel went into the navy. To our relief we found that our chemistry was still strong. I was again with my comrades, and I felt a new surge of masculine energy.

Even our arguments were good-natured. Once during the Miami vacation, Len broke off from the group and had a private date. Ordinarily this would have been perfectly all right, but he had kind of sneaked off. He didn't even tell us what he was up to. Maybe he was afraid we'd beat his time. Whatever the reason, it struck us as a bit small. Our revenge was to plan a fantastic excursion from which he would be pointedly excluded. Without mentioning it to him, we hopped on a plane for Havana, Cuba. We didn't have any distinct plans and didn't even take any luggage. The important thing was that Len would notice that we weren't around. Then he'd look for us, and we would be unlocatable. Later, we would return wearing sombreros, ready to tell about our fabulous Cuban holiday.

We arrived at Havana airport early in the afternoon and took a cab into town. In those prerevolutionary days Havana was a tourist's delight. Huge hotels catered to an international clientele, and almost all the adjacent businesses were geared for the satisfaction of travelers. Joel and I were walking along looking a bit scruffy for the neighborhood in our jeans and T-shirts when at one point we noticed a swarthy young Cuban emerge from a parked car. He walked along behind us for about a block. We didn't pay too much attention to him because he looked no more threatening than any other pedestrian. He wore a small straw hat, a flowered shirt, and white tropical-weight slacks. None of these clothes were in the best of condition, but that was normal, too. In Havana there were a lot of poor people trying to look festive for the tourists. Eventually, he closed the distance between us and said, "Buenos dias! My name ees Manuel and I weel guide for ju." We were none too impressed. He saw that we were on the verge of turning him down, and before we could speak, he added, "I can get ju anything ju want!" Both Joel and I had to agree that it was an intriguing offer. Still, after a hurried conference (off to one side as Manuel stood looking hopeful) we decided to forgo the opportunity to get anything we wanted. We thanked him but said lamely that we didn't want to walk all the way back to the car. We had covered all of three blocks during the negotiations. Upon hearing this, the resourceful Manuel said, "No hay problema!" and pointed to the street where the car, driven by his partner Oscar, had been trailing along like a hungry hound dog. Our bluff had been called. In the face of such tenacity our resistance gave way. We got in the car and had the first of countless shots of rum. For Joel and me this drink was the beginning of a massive Cuban toot.

Maybe Manuel and Oscar could really have gotten us anything, but we certainly didn't strain their powers. We asked for the commodity that they were best prepared to supply—girls. As a matter of fact, that's probably what they meant by anything.

Still, if we'd wanted drugs or sex with a pony I suppose they could have supplied those too; but we were typical, clean-cut college boys interested only in whores and liquor. Our first stop was a typical Cuban cathouse in a seedy section of town. The front of the building was pink, made out of something like stucco. Upon entering we found ourselves in a dark bar—the standard tropical joint with lots of wicker and ceiling fans. We stopped there for another couple of drinks. The two guides aimed to please and laughed uproariously at our Americano humor. After another drink, Joel and I had to admit that Cuba was one damn fine place! As for the Cubans themselves, they were beautiful! That included Oscar, Manuel, and that guy behind the bar, too!

After a merry forty-five minutes in the bar, Manuel led us through a door in the back. We emerged into a courtyard off which opened many rooms. It was nicely landscaped with healthy, well-manicured plants. The building surrounding the courtyard rose three stories. At each level was a covered walkway skirting the edge of the courtyard and offering access to the rooms. We entered a room off to the side of the courtyard. It measured about twenty feet by fifteen feet and was filled with couches and chairs. In addition to the door we had come through, there were three others leading to the interior of the house. As we entered, a dark woman who appeared to be in her fifties came through one of the other doors. She was the madam, and she greeted Manuel in a familiar way. He introduced us and then left, saying that he'd wait for us in the bar. The madam spoke a little English and asked us how we liked Havana, meanwhile clapping her hands lightly. At this signal about a dozen girls came into the room through the various doors. They were dressed in lingerie. One wore a chemise, another a silky pair of step-ins. Virtually all wore push-up bras, garter belts, and stockings. Most had thrown filmy housecoats over these scanty items. Of course, they also wore high heels. The madam apologized, saying that during the day there were fewer girls to choose from than there would be at night. Regardless of that, there appeared to be a surprising variety. There were all sizes ranging from very thin to downright chubby. Some were exotic racial combinations resulting in a broad range of skin tones. There were even some blondes, though on closer inspection these proved to be dyed, their swarthy skins giving the lie to their brassy hair. Temperaments differed as much as appearances. Some were chatting vivaciously with one another, and others seemed sullen or at least withdrawn.

The atmosphere in the room was cordial, but we weren't encouraged to agonize very long over our decision. The madam had the girls present themselves in a lineup and, when we hesitated a few minutes, she said good-naturedly, "You prefer the boys?" This brought chuckles from all the girls and appreciative laughter from us. Joel chose a small delicate girl, and I went for a larger one with a more lavish figure. Both were dark and, to our eyes, exotic. After we gave the madam ten dollars, the girls led us through one of the doors and down a hallway from which you could enter any of the rooms that fronted on the courtyard. Joel and I frolicked in adjacent rooms.

Once again, I was asked to wash before getting down to business. I found this an invariable rule in every whorehouse I ever patronized. Having Joel in the next room made the whole adventure seem less serious and less frightening than my European experiences. I was very high, not only from the liquor but from the carefree atmosphere. When we finally did have sex, there was no question about my ability to perform. I was ready—and it was delightful.

Both Joel and I were flushed with this success and demanded that Manuel and Oscar take us to another whorehouse. They directed us to a very nice frame house not far from the Malicon, a boulevard that followed the curve of the harbor. It was in what seemed to be a respectable part of town. When we went inside we were amazed to see college girls sitting around laughing and talking. We could just as well have walked into an American sorority house. Of course the girls were Cuban, but they were also young, fresh faced, and dressed as American coeds might, in summer dresses, halter tops and shorts, or some other perfectly respectable attire. They looked downright wholesome. We were much impressed by this place because it promised to fulfill a fantasy. All of those nights we had spent trying to make time with respectable girls, and getting nowhere, had bred a feverish dream that someday one would give in. Here, among these cheerful young ladies, we could experience something like that in reality. Even if the substance was lacking, at least the appearance was convincing.

The madam, or should I say housemother, came forward and welcomed us. We were invited into a sitting room and served drinks. Most of the girls spoke English. We chatted with several and finally made a choice. We were almost embarrassed to make the offer, yet the madam received it with a smile and beckoned our girls over. They came as if they were meeting blind dates for the first time. They giggled and took our arms. We might as easily have been going upstairs to make ice cream as to go to bed. Again Joel and I were in adjacent rooms, and we padded freely back and forth comparing the two girls and arguing over why one was superior to the other. Our sorority girls were also having a fine time. They were pleased to be in the company of adventurous, good-natured young men. Their sexual style was just as vigorous and healthy as their appearance. In bed they were attentive, helpful, and bright.

I found out later that these girls were often taken on dates by American college boys. They would go to a place like the Tropicana, an open air night club with a gambling casino attached. There they would mambo the night away, but instead of kissing goodnight at the door, they would go inside to make love. In Havana this could happen; in America, it almost never did.

Joel and I liked the sorority house immensely, but we couldn't stay there more than a couple of hours. The tab would have gotten out of hand; besides, we were both sexed out. *My* performance in particular was unusual. Such sexual athleticism was even more notable in the face of all the rum Joel and I had consumed. I guess Joel was a little more used to it because he remained saner over the next few hours. I, on the other hand, became more and more raucous and uncontrollable.

From the time we left the sorority house until we arrived back in Miami, the intake of rum scaled up, and my memory of events gets worse and worse. Later in the day Manuel and Oscar took us to a cockfight at a rancho in the suburbs. The audience was composed mostly of tourists, but there were a few Cubans, too. Everybody was betting and rooting loudly. I stood on my seat, inflamed by a battle between two very scrappy chickens. Joel and Manuel tried to quiet me down, but my blood was up. Eventually our foursome had to leave because of my behavior; you have to be pretty rowdy to draw attention to yourself at a cockfight.

When we had dinner there was some kind of trouble with the

restaurant management. I remember being stopped on the street by an irate waiter who accused us of not paying our check. He was right. We hadn't been able to get his attention; so we had simply walked out. It was effective. He came right after us, and we settled up on the sidewalk.

I have no memory of what happened that night. We woke up in a hotel. I guess Manuel and Oscar checked us into it. Anyway they were waiting in the lobby when we came down. After some rum for breakfast, we demanded that we be taken back to the sorority house for more fun. By the time we finished there it was getting on toward evening, so we left for the airport. On the way we stopped at yet another whorehouse, the Mambo Club, for what we called our "flying fuck," the aeronautical answer to "one for the road." We were out of money by then, but the madame cordially accepted our check.

By the time we hit the airport, I was out of control again. While Joel took care of the tickets, I climbed up on a counter and, seized with West Indian spirit, sang "Matilda" at the top of my lungs.

Matilda, Matilda, Matilda
She take me money and she run Venezuela!

Heads began to turn, but I persevered. "A little louder now! Matilda! Matilda!..." Pretty soon there was no one in the airport waiting area who wasn't staring at me. Unintimidated, I sang out in my best calypso rhythm, "Everybody now! Matilda! Matilda!..." Nobody was more shocked than I when fifty percent of the waiting passengers joined in. Slightly stunned, I stopped for a moment, but they carried on. Seized with a sense of power, I yelled out, "A leetle softah now!" The crowd obliged. On the third or fourth chorus the whole crowd was rocking. By now, I was accompanying my singing with a bit of dancing. When I sang, "A little highah now," I stretched my arms up and pranced on my tiptoes. When I said, "Very soft now," I squatted down and put my fingers about two inches above the counter top. During this maneuver I closed my eyes soulfully, and when I opened them I was looking right into the face of an airport security guard. Undaunted, I jumped up and continued singing, but he was soon joined by other officials and by Joel. Together they persuaded me to come down off the counter, a move which drew almost unanimous disapproval from my choir. Joel led me to an out-of-the-way corner of the waiting area and promised the guard that he'd keep me out of trouble. Every now and then some traveler would come by to congratulate me, and isolated pockets of singing continued to break out from time to time. Without leadership though, they were short-lived. When we boarded the plane we left a much livelier atmosphere in the airport than we had found when we arrived. As our plane taxied away we could see Manuel and Oscar standing behind the hurricane fence, waving. They had certainly been worth the fifty dollars we paid them.

On board the plane I continued singing "Matilda" but was ignored. In retaliation, I began to chuck gumdrops at the other passengers. From where I stood in the back of the plane, I could see at least fifteen bald pates, and I decided that I would bounce a gumdrop off each of these shiny targets before the plane landed. Luckily, I had bought a large bag of candy in the Havana airport. Never ceasing the singing of "Matilda," I worked earnestly toward my goal. Periodically, the stewardess would ask me to stop. If I did it was only for a short while. Then I would resume both the singing and the flinging. Meanwhile Joel was carrying on a drunken conversation with a man in the seat next to him. The man, a doctor, was appalled when Joel told him that I was a medical student. He shouted back to me, "A brilliant medical student, and you're wasting your time like this!" I bounced a gumdrop off his forehead. He turned back to Joel, "What a disappointment," he said. A gumdrop hit him in the ear. "I heard that!" I yelled.

I guess the pilot radioed for the police to meet the plane after the copilot couldn't make me quiet down. In addition, Joel had come loudly to my defense. Rather than force a tussle at ten thousand feet, they decided to let us continue to be rowdy. We really weren't being destructive, just irritating. In Miami International Airport Len was waiting. We had called during the weekend to rub it in. He had good-naturedly agreed to meet us on our return. When he spotted the police waiting at the gate, he guessed that they had something to do with Joel and me. As we got off the plane, we could see Len towering in the middle of a cluster of uniformed patrolmen. He had begun to speak in our defense even before the plane arrived. Joel and I were taken aside and given a good talking to while Len stood smugly by with an "I-told-you-so" look on his face. He had done his work well, though. They let us go.

That frenetic trip to Havana was probably the peak of my sexuality as Dick. It was neither the most satisfying nor the most sensual sex I ever had, but it was by far the most I ever packed into such a short time. This dynamic performance and the successful summer of tennis that followed it gave me a big boost for the return to school in the fall. I felt good when I started back, but I was soon deeply depressed.

My three roommates and I had moved out of the small house that we had occupied during our freshman year. The new house had an attic area that I immediately appropriated. It was a secluded nook that was not in the mainstream of activity, and I felt safer there. Renèe began to come out in the evenings. She probably would have emerged sooner or later in this out-of-the-way spot, but her forthcoming was really provoked when I found a box of women's clothes already in the attic. Apparently they had been left by a previous tenant. They were not particularly stylish or even clean, but I still couldn't keep my hands off them. As I put on one of the dresses, that familiar feeling swept over me once again. Thereafter I became Renée almost every night. I would come home, retire to my attic room, dress, and then study. The nervous and fidgeting behavior that I felt when I tried to study as Dick, left me when I studied as Renée. Ironically, though Dick's anxiety level shot up, my grades improved because of the extra time I spent studying. I didn't try to make my genitals disappear every night. Generally speaking, I'd be satisfied simply by donning a dress under which I usually wore a panty girdle. I didn't have a wig so I made do with a scarf. I couldn't use makeup since that would have taken too long to remove if someone had come to the door. No one ever came, but I didn't feel I could take the chance. Though my roommates knew I was seeing a therapist, they had no clue as to why.

Meanwhile, the second year of therapy was as docile and ineffectual as the first. Each day, the nondescript Dr. Clark prodded me gently, and I responded with a river of talk but no repressed material. Sometime during that year I relented and reestablished communication with my parents. The decision to do so

110

might have been the result of Dr. Clark's benign influence. Other than that, nothing definite came out of our sessions.

I made sporadic attempts to establish sexual contact with women. For a while I dated a girl who went to a nearby Catholic college. We would spend evenings together studying or watching television. I made advances, but she always put me off. The necking and petting that we did was mild, but it satisfied me. I was beginning to see that the companionship and identification I felt with a woman was as important to me as the sex. In this I seemed to be different from other men. I could happily lie in bed with a woman and feel completely satisfied with the intimacy of touching and simply being together in a loving atmosphere. If that was the way she liked it, then I could happily accept her limitations.

What I learned, however, was that I was poorly equipped to play the male-female games of the fifties. My girlfriend mysteriously broke up with me and started dating one of my roommates, a tall, aggressive athlete. He had been a basketball player and, though an excellent student and a basically sensitive youth, retained a lot of jockish machismo. He was very successful with women and not prone to keep quiet about it. This braggadocio was finally responsible for me hearing that he and my old girlfriend were making it on a regular basis. I assumed that he was successful where I was not because of his insistence. She had clearly been interested in me, but I had lacked the masculinity to overcome her girlish reluctance. My sense of inadequacy increased manyfold. I felt more and more that I was unsuited for life as a man.

Of course, this sounds utterly chauvinistic and it was, but I was a product of the times. As a matter of fact, I had less insight than average since my perspective was split. My feeling for appropriate masculine behavior came more from observation and impersonation than it did from any internal mechanism. A lot of times I was like a man in a foreign country trying to blend in with the population. I was so desperately worried about fitting in that I seldom stopped to think critically about the system.

Renée began to emerge even more strongly in my third year when I moved into a room in a private home. It was owned by a woman doctor who had gone to Bryn Mawr. I was out of the fraternal atmosphere of a jointly rented house, and my sense of privacy increased. Renée came forward more frequently and for longer periods of time. Under this onslaught Dick grew more despondent.

In an effort to bolster my flagging masculinity, I called a girl I had met through my basketball-playing roommate. He had told me that she was an easy mark, and I knew that his friends had been with her, too. She remembered me and invited me over. It was a midwinter night, cold and icy. She met me at the door, and after some preliminary chat we went to bed. Though she was understanding, helpful and very willing, I couldn't perform. Maybe she wasn't exotic enough or resourceful enough or close enough, or maybe I was too thoroughly depressed. Whatever the reason I failed miserably. Though she assured me that it happened to everyone at one time or another, I left mortified and defeated.

As I drove back home, I was overpowered by depression. My mind had gone numb with a generalized dread. My limbs felt heavy and I was driving in a transfixed way. The streets were icy, and the car's slippery response matched my mood in that I felt I was driving in slow motion. Everything seemed to be black or white. Suddenly two spots of brightness appeared before me. I had hardly recognized them as headlights when I heard a splattering sound and the windshield shattered into a million pieces. The horn sounded and continued to wail as I was jolted out of blackness and into a blast of light. Somehow one headlight of the other car had survived even though twisted at a peculiar angle. It was shining in my face. I opened the door and struggled out into the icy street. I slipped several times before I reached the other car. Inside was a man slumped over the steering wheel. When I opened the door of his car, he fell out onto the ground—unconscious. I leaned over and noticed the snowy ground around him was red with blood and becoming redder. Groggily, I realized that the blood was not his; it was raining down from above—it was mine. Periodically little gushes would splatter both the man and the snow. I looked down and saw my shirtfront soaked in red, yet when I felt my chest there was no wound. Confused, I put my hand to my face, which was strangely numb. When I touched my jaw it moved in a peculiar way as if it no longer was attached to me. When I touched my mouth, I found that my teeth were gone. I yanked my hand away, afraid to touch anything else. Already I could feel the shock beginning to overtake me.

The streets were deserted and the snowfall increasing. I looked around wildly and saw a light burning in a nearby house. I ran to it and found that it was the porch light on a suburban home. I pounded on the door which was eventually opened by a middle-aged woman in a housecoat. What she saw must have been frightening. My jaw had collided with the steering wheel and been smashed to pieces; a jagged chunk of it was sticking through a laceration in my neck. Blood spurted intermittently from a small artery that had been severed. The woman gulped but then conquered her fear and helped me inside. By the time we got to a couch, she too was covered with blood. Her husband, who came in while she was helping me down the hall, ran out into the street where the horn on my car was still blowing stridently. While the woman phoned for an ambulance, I managed to cut down the bleeding by exerting pressure on the artery. She came back with some clean towels and asked if there was anything she could do. Since I couldn't make my mouth work, I motioned for a pad and pencil. On a slip of paper I wrote, "Dr. Robert McCormack, University Hospital." I kept this in my pocket and gave it to the ambulance driver when he arrived.

After some emergency treatment at the nearest facility, I insisted on being transferred to the medical center at the University of Rochester. Dr. McCormack was waiting, and in the early hours of the morning he made a start on the massive repairs necessary to recreate my jaw. In a way I had been lucky. The shattering of my jaw had acted as a cushion that absorbed the force of the crash. If the point of impact had been three inches higher—between my eyes—the concussion would have killed me. If it had been three inches lower, my neck would have been crushed; this too would have been fatal. As it was, the right half of my jaw had been torn away and was floating free without connection to the rest of my skull. Eventually, this piece was reconnected with steel arch bars. As for the rest of the job, it was like putting together a jigsaw puzzle. My jaw had been almost completely destroyed. When he'd done all he could, Dr. McCormack wired my jaws closed for three months. Even after the wires were taken off I couldn't move my jaw for another four weeks. Gradually I regained normal control. For years after the accident, I

113

needed periodic attention including extensive dental work; to this day I have small insensitive areas on my jaw, places where the nerves were destroyed.

There was a dimension to this accident that continued to concern me even after the pain and inconvenience were gone. I kept wondering if I could have avoided it. I was an athlete. My reflexes were good, yet I had seen the car only a second before the collision. Was it possible that I wanted to die? I certainly had been depressed, but I had never consciously considered suicide. Still, my days were centered around an hour of psychotherapy where the mechanisms of repression and unconscious motivation were regularly discussed and applied to my actions. Why should this brush with death be treated differently? Dr. Clark, as usual, took a moderate point of view. It might have been unconsciously motivated or it might have been accidental; or it might have been a combination of the two. Though we discussed it thoroughly, no conclusion was reached.

The practical effect of the accident was that I began to feel that I couldn't really trust myself. Renée might be blindly attempting to destroy Dick without realizing that she would die too. I began to question myself at every turn, always wondering what my true motivations were, always a little confused, and always a little frightened.

I received eight thousand dollars in damages from the driver of the other car. It turned out that he was drunk. No one blamed me. Even my pediatrics professor passed me in spite of my having missed so much class time. Luckily I had an aptitude for children's medicine and did well on the written examination, so he felt the gesture was justified. I was thus exonerated by the courts, by my professors, and even by my parents who were surprisingly unaccusing about the accident. The only person who thought I might have been responsible was me.

Unaccountably, as it so often did in my life, the pendulum took a swing in the other direction after the disaster. By summer I was mended, and I spent my vacation on the old grass-court tennis circuit. I did well, beating several world-class players. One was the Mexican national champion who had also been a Wimbledon doubles champion the previous year. This success was surprising since I was playing against men who competed year-round. The best I could manage in Rochester during the winter was to sweep the snow off the hospital courts in the morning before class and hit balls with some of the other students who liked to play. One club in Rochester had an indoor court, but I couldn't play there much because school took most of the hours in a day. In spite of my handicaps, I was winning important matches. This made me wonder all the harder what I might do if I could really devote myself to the game. It also rejuvenated my self-confidence, and I returned for my senior year in a more optimistic frame of mind.

The summer's triumphs did not, however, completely eclipse my fears. I knew well that the strain of medical school might again send me into a depressive tailspin. As a precaution I rented an apartment within walking distance of school. Since the accident, I had been uncomfortable driving. As it turned out this was a needless precaution. My senior year was my most successful period at Rochester. Once again I owed the change to the influence of a woman.

In a virtual replay of the events at Yale, I met a girl who stabilized my life and lifted me out of my despondency. Lorraine was a nursing student. Like Denise, she was beautiful, bright, and sensitive. She was devoted to me, and with her support I studied as I never had before. In the clinical stages of my training, I was outstanding because of her influence. Renée was in a decline. My sex life with Lorraine was vigorous and frequent. She lived with me in the apartment and provided me with the happiest home life I had ever known. The loneliness of my first three years in Rochester was gone, yet I could feel the presence of Renée. She crouched in me waiting for her moments—the times when I was alone. Then she would come forward to press her case. As I had with Denise, I declined marriage with Lorraine. I backpedaled and refused to make the commitment. While Renée lived I could not be a husband. A marriage should involve two people, not three.

On the day of my graduation, any onlooker would have pronounced me the golden boy. I was young and handsome. I was flanked by distinguished parents, devoted friends (Len and Joel had flown up for the occasion), and a beautiful girlfriend. I was a doctor about to take up the challenge of healing, yet I could not heal myself.

11

Dick and Renée Take Turns

When I broke up with Lorraine, I left comfortable domesticity behind. The summer following my graduation in 1959 found me already a busy intern at New York City's Lenox Hill Hospital. During the year that I spent there I was unpsychoanalyzed and untroubled by Renée. Both the problem and the cure had to be suspended in the face of my work schedule. I was on duty every day of the week as well as every other night. That meant thirty-six hours of work followed by a night's sleep (rarely as much as the prescribed eight hours), which was then followed by thirty-six more hours of work. All interns followed that routine for a year. Usually at least one of us was down sick due to our lowered resistance. We fell easy prey to the infectious disorders of the hospital patients. The philosophy behind this exhausting routine was both economic and professional. The hospital wanted to get as much work out of us as it could and at the same time expose us to as much medicine as possible in a year's time. In addition, the grueling schedule had some of the spirit of a fraternity hazing. This frantic year was something all doctors shared, and it symbolized the ideal of selfless dedication to healing.

Once a man at a kibbutz in Israel explained to me why so little psychotherapy was practiced in that country. "We don't have time for it," he said. That was exactly my situation. Sexual crisis for an intern is being late for a nooner. When I worried about sex at all, it was over finding time for it, not which one I was. I spent several frantic nights squeezed together with a nurse on my cot in

117

the intern's quarters above the old Anna Orfendorfer Clinic on Park Avenue. The sex was all the more exciting for having been grabbed on the run.

This period of absolute exhaustion provided me with nothing but good memories. Never since have I dedicated myself so wholeheartedly to anything or been so rewarded. I was a good intern, and when I saw people get well under my care it was a fine feeling.

Two very important events took place during my time at Lenox Hill. The first was that I decided on my specialty. All through medical school I had evaded this question. In a strange way, it paralleled my attitude toward marriage. In neither case could I commit myself. My mother pushed for neurosurgery, the field she felt she had been denied entry to by narrow-minded colleagues. My father favored his specialty: orthopedics. Naturally, I dismissed both of these.

One day I observed a cataract operation. The eye and the complex muscles surrounding it intrigued me. They are a self-contained community of interdependent structures, complicated yet compact. I appreciated the localized quality of this area; one might be able to learn everything about it, make sense of its intricacies.

Furthermore, almost everything about the eye is visible. Problems can be diagnosed conclusively. If there is a growth or other anomaly, it is usually in sight. There is seldom a need for guesswork or exploratory surgery. If surgery is necessary, it is far less messy than other operations. Ophthalmologists hate blood. In spite of this ease of diagnosis and relatively clean technique, the operations require precision. You seldom get a second chance since the tissues of the eye don't respond well to more than one cut. Your first chance is your last, and you have to do it right. I liked the clean precision of the cataract surgeon.

I was also attracted by the mystery of the eye. Sight is perhaps the most treasured of all the human senses; it orients us and furnishes us with our primary link to the world. In addition, no other organ is so associated with the mind and personality as the eye. The eyes are considered the windows to the soul, the inlets that reach to our essence. Perhaps I was drawn to their study because of my confusion over my own true nature. For whatever reason, I was fascinated. I had the surprising sense that all my work in medicine could find focus in a study of the eye.

I began to watch as many such operations as I could and even assisted in some. My enthusiasm continued to mount, and I soon made inquiries about opportunities for studies in the basic sciences of ophthalmology. It was a little late, but luck was with me. I found an ideal situation in New York's Bellevue Hospital. Upon my acceptance the future seemed clear. The last major career decision was made.

The second important event of my internship was emotional rather than medical. Once again I was in love. I had met Gwen. Gwen seemed to be the ideal extension of my taste in women. She was beautiful, of course. Her eyes were blue green, her hair sandy-blonde, her smile radiant. Beyond her physical beauty was an intangible soft quality that struck me as purely feminine. Of all the important women in my life, she was the most retiring and the most devoted to me. In groups of people she could hardly be prompted to speak, yet when we were alone she was talkative, even kittenish. She played the piano in a fluid, natural style. I would sit for hours listening to her play Chopin or Mozart. I tried to get her to play for our friends; regardless of how much I tried to persuade her, she refused to play for anyone but me. Though I protested I was secretly pleased by this exclusivity.

I had always felt a strong psychic connection to the women in my life, but my relationship with Gwen was extraordinary in that regard. We often spoke to one another in a sort of code consisting of key words or phrases. The details were unnecessary since we understood each other's thought processes so well. Making plans was a very simple thing for both of us, almost telepathic. We would show up for a rendezvous at a certain place and at a certain time, yet neither of us could remember having discussed the particulars of the meeting. We established this connection almost immediately, and it led to an interdependence that lasted six years.

We were compatible in many ways. Gwen was not only interested in sport but active in it herself. She especially enjoyed fencing. Once, during a practice session, she dislocated her shoulder and came to Lenox Hill for surgery. When the attending physician attempted to draw a blood sample for a preoperative lab test, Gwen adamantly refused to have anyone but me touch her with a needle. The whole procedure ground to a halt as the orthopedic staff scoured the hospital for me. I stopped what I was doing and went immediately to take the sample. That incident is representative of the ways our lives were enmeshed through our obsession with one another.

Her dependence on me fired my masculinity, and we had a terrific sex life. I had no problem being aggressive with Gwen. Her yielding personality seemed to call forth more potency from me. I initiated sex often and was far less inhibited with Gwen than I had ever been before. I was still conservative in that I didn't go in for exotic positions and still didn't care for manipulation or oral intercourse, but my level of abandon increased in spite of these limitations. I became more compelling, less tentative in my lovemaking. Before Gwen I had always treated sex as a sort of continuing experiment. It was always exciting, but I never felt the degree of control that I did with Gwen. With her gentle participation, I came to think of myself as an accomplished lover. I was confident—one might even say lusty.

At the end of my year of internship, I rented a small apartment on East Eighty-Seventh Street off Park Avenue, a location that was convenient to the office of my new psychiatrist, Dr. Robert Bak. I raced home every weekday afternoon for our sessions at six o'clock. I had to be on time since any lateness was automatically interpreted as resistance. Regardless of how legitimate an excuse sounded, it was dismissed as a cover for the patient's attempt to avoid therapy. I had learned this lesson years before with Dr. Clark.

At the beginning of our analysis, which was to last three years, I was usually early. Dr. Bak's waiting room was small, with just two or three chairs. There was a picture of Freud on the wall. In that little room Freud's eyes seemed ever watchful. I couldn't help glancing up occasionally to see if he had changed his expression. He never did; he always looked as if he knew more than he should. Only rarely would there be another person in the waiting room. This was always an uncomfortable situation. Both parties avoided eye contact, just catching enough glimpses of the other person to set each wondering what the other's problem was. The room was crowded with all three of us in there: the other person, me, and Freud.

Dr. Bak himself reminded me of Freud. He was a big man, probably six-feet four and very heavy. He wore a beard and spoke with an accent that sounded appropriate. At first I thought it was Viennese, but I later found out it was Hungarian. His presentation was as forceful as Dr. Clark's had been muted. Like Dr. Clark, he would sit at the head of the couch out of sight, but when Dr. Bak occupied that space it throbbed with energy, something like having a nuclear reactor hovering just outside your peripheral vision. This impression was enhanced by the fact that he smoked a huge cigar. Periodically, billows of smoke would drift into my line of sight as if produced by a powerful mechanism working hard. Sometimes he would sit wordless through an entire session, just puffing on his cigar. I would talk about whatever came into my head. At the end of the hour he'd say, "Time's up." I would think to myself, "For this I pay fifty dollars?"

In the matter of procedure, I had little voice. Dr. Bak was considered the best psychoanalyst of his day. He was the head of the New York Psychoanalytic Society, which was like being president of all the presidents. What he said was, by virtue of the fact that he said it, the latest stuff. And he was intimidating. In addition to his physical size, he projected massive intelligence. He uttered profundities at an astonishing rate. In fact, he remains the only man to whom I have ever felt completely intellectually inferior. I don't know if this made for a more productive doctor-patient relationship or not, but when he talked I listened.

As our relationship was established, Dr. Bak outlined his theory about the cause of my sexual confusion. He felt that I had no real desire to be a woman. To the contrary, I was plagued by the exact opposite problem: that is, I was afraid of losing my penis. My transformation into a woman was a way of acting out that fear; the elaborate ritual of hiding my genitals was a symbolic castration. The more I abused myself in the process, the more meaningful and realistic was the big payoff. According to Dr. Bak, what I liked about the process was not becoming a woman but the relief I felt when I changed back to a man. Subconsciously, I was saying, "Oh, thank god, my prick is still there!" Of course, this sounds a lot like the story of the man who beat his head against the wall because it felt so good when he stopped. According to Dr. Bak, the mind works in such strange channels. I used to have a dream of a black stallion. He felt this indicated a preoccupation not with a horse but with Italians. Dark-skinned Italians apparently symbolized sexual potency to me.

Another aspect of this unconscious construct was my interest in exotic Italian motor cars. At the time, I had a Lancia and had previously owned a Maserati, but my interest in fast cars did not stop with the Italian ones. I had had Corvettes, Volvos, Mercedes. I could see his point about the sexual confusion since I seemed to vacillate between the more brutish models like the Corvette and the more refined ones like the Mercedes. Even with one of the Corvettes I was unstable. At one point I had it painted jet black and at another powder blue. Dr. Bak felt that these cars were phallic objects and reflected my desire to retain a powerful masculinity in spite of my seeming desire to be a woman.

Dr. Bak's presentation was so convincing that I accepted this interpretation of my behavior. His tracing of the problem's development was brilliant, but this understanding did not help me to a solution. Knowing that I was gratified by the change back into a man did not lessen my desire to be a woman. Actually it increased. The desire to be Renée had been growing steadily stronger for years. Even when I was preoccupied with school or with a woman and had few opportunities to transform, I still harbored the desire—and the desire grew stronger and stronger. In spite of this I was encouraged by Dr. Bak to fantasize all I wanted about being Renée. He felt that the fantasizing might provide an outlet that would lessen my desire to do it in reality, but that was not the case. Though I was strictly forbidden to cross-dress, I did it anyway.

Dr. Bak felt that my relationship with Gwen was a positive thing. He used to say, "The best part of your relationship with Gwen is your sex life. The rest of it is ambivalent and confused because of your earlier problems, but the sex is fine. The best thing you two kids do together is having intercourse."

We obliged him about five times a week. Gwen was living with her parents, but she frequently stayed overnight with me. At about eleven o'clock she would say, "I have to call Mother." Gwen would tell her mother that she was staying overnight with a girl friend. I think her parents accepted this charade because they knew we were devoted to one another and hoped that we would marry soon. They liked me. What parents wouldn't? I was from a professional family, I was a Yale man, a doctor, and a gentleman athlete. I was also polite and, to all appearances, well-adjusted. The latter was an aspect of what Dr. Bak referred to as my compartmentalized psychosis. He agreed that I was crazy, but crazy in a very specific way. Aside from causing some depression, my psychosis seldom found its way into other aspects of my life. I was like a man whose temperature inexplicably rises to a hundred and four degrees once a day but who is otherwise perfectly healthy. The isolated quality of the phenomenon makes it hard to treat, especially when it happens on a random schedule. I appeared to the world at large as a sane and reasonable young man. The first time I met Dr. Bak, he said, "Things of this sort are very sticky." He was never more right.

I had women's clothes in my apartment and wore them whenever circumstances allowed. It was inevitable that Gwen would sooner or later run across them. One day about three months after I had moved into the apartment she confronted me with these clothes, including my wig box, and demanded to know if I was seeing another woman. I said, "No. Those are for the other side of me. You know that I'm seeing a psychiatrist. Now you know why." It was a tribute to the rapport I felt with Gwen that I unhesitatingly told her the truth. Aside from my mother, she was the first nonprofessional to whom I had ever confessed. She received the news even-temperedly and really showed surprising restraint in that she didn't grill me at all. I think we both had the same attitude on the matter: we didn't want it intruding on our relationship. I didn't think it should be any of her business, and my tone didn't encourage further questioning.

This mutual silence on the issue lasted for years. When it came up, it was in indirect ways. Many times she wanted to know why we couldn't get married or at least engaged. I would say, "You know why." She made it clear that she would marry me in spite of Renée, but I couldn't make the commitment. Sometimes she'd say, "Why don't you get rid of these clothes?" I would reply that I'd like to but that I didn't seem to be able to bring myself to do it. Gwen knew that I dressed only when she wasn't with me; so as she left to go home she would always say, "You aren't going to do any stuff when I leave are you?" I would say, "No," but it reflected nothing but a good intention on my part.

Truth was that things were getting worse. I was taking more

chances than I had since I was a teenager. For example, Dick had begun to frequent the Manhattan shops that specialized in clothes for tall women. At first I used the excuse that I was buying for my girlfriend who was tall. This stood up for only a short while since I felt compelled to return to these shops more and more often. There was no reasonable excuse for me to buy so much for my girlfriend. Inevitably they began to wonder why she didn't do some of her own shopping. As I grew more familiar with the proprietors of these shops, I confided to them that these clothes were really for me. I doubt they were surprised. The revelation certainly didn't interfere with our business. Once they knew the truth I didn't have to wait until I got the clothes home in order to try them on. I could pick and choose like a normal shopper, if I came during an appropriately slow part of the business day so that I'd be pretty much alone with the salespeople.

This relationship of trust between me and these merchants marked a tremendous change in attitude. The mere thought of discovery had previously made me physically ill, and here I was confiding in shopkeepers. This as much as anything else, clearly reflected Dick's crumbling position.

As Dick, I was increasingly aggressive in my professional life, as well as on the tennis courts. I was at the top of my class in the basic science course that I took at Bellevue Hospital. When that year was finished, I became a resident at the Manhattan Eye and Ear Hospital. As usual, the support of a loving woman resulted in a high level of performance. It may also be that the discipline of my analysis with Dr. Bak was forcing me to confront the polarities inside me. As the two aspects of my personality grew more clearly defined in my conscious mind, their actions in the world were similarly affected. At work I became a dedicated and aggressive resident. I radiated the confident masculine image promoted on the popular medical television shows of the time; "Ben Casey" typified the world's idea of a young doctor, and I came pretty close to that macho yet sensitive ideal. My superiors liked me, and my patients trusted me.

I may have given the impression that, as Dick, I was a tormented and indecisive personality. Certainly this had been true in the past. In my medical school days I was sometimes dangerously depressed, but the practicalities of internship and my choice of a specialty had given real substance to my personality as a doctor. As a resident in ophthalmology, I was considered a young firebrand. I radiated confidence and competence. I plunged tirelessly ahead. During the two years of residency, I assisted in or performed myself over one hundred and fifty major operations. I witnessed countless others and, on one occasion, was drawn into the action by a peculiar twist of fate.

I was observing a cataract operation being performed by one of the senior members of the surgical staff. I was there to study his technique, which was economical and very deft. The patient was a twenty-one-year-old girl who was also suffering from diabetes. Cataracts are sometimes provoked in young people by such severe metabolic disorders. In the middle of the operation, the anesthesiologist said flatly, "I am not getting any pulse." A second later he added, "I am not getting any blood pressure either."

The old surgeon quizzically looked up from his work and asked, "What's happening? Is she dead?"

"She has had a cardiac arrest," replied the anesthesiologist. There was a pregnant pause. "I think we shall have to open her chest." The anesthesiologist was British and spoke in a very proper and controlled way. He made this announcement as if it were an invitation to tea. Then he got up and walked to a special cabinet in the operating room where the scalpel for such an emergency was stored. In those days there was no external heart massage: when a patient's heart stopped, you cut open the chest and reached in.

The anesthesiologist brought the scalpel back and held it up in front of the rest of us. Besides the old doctor and myself, the staff included a resident who was assisting in the operation. I was concerned for the patient's sake, but at the same time excited since I had never seen a live open-heart massage before. Naturally, I had received instruction in it and had gone through training to familiarize me with the technique, but here was an opportunity to actually see it done.

The anesthesiologist stood there holding the scalpel out as if we were children drawing straws. He stared at the two doctors. I had come in close and was looking interestedly over their shoulders. He repeated, "We shall have to open the chest," and then added, ". . . Dr. Raskind." The two other doctors parted like a theater curtain and he handed me the scalpel. Imagine my surprise! I blinked a couple of times like an amnesiac who has awakened to find himself at the controls of a crippled airliner. I was more surprised than intimidated; so I relaxed and let my training take over. Methodically I felt for the fourth intercostal space on the left. I cut just above the rib, avoiding the intercostal blood vessels. I split the chest wall open by pulling the ribs apart and put my hand into the cavity, gently pushing aside the covering of the lung and the lung itself. The heart is surrounded by a sac of tissue called the pericardium. I grasped this along with the heart and began to squeeze rhythmically. I was using my left hand, the tennis hand; I remember that her heart felt small and vulnerable against my strength.

Within seconds the anesthesiologist said, "I think I have a pulse. Stop for a moment." When I stopped, he confirmed, "I have a pulse." After another short period of hesitation he added, "I'm getting some blood pressure." Shortly, the heart was beating regularly. I could feel it pulse in my hand. The blood pressure climbed steadily, and I realized that the immediate crisis was over except that I was up to my wrist in the patient's chest cavity. Sweat was breaking out on my forehead. I told the supervising nurse to go get Dr. Smith. He was an Australian doctor who was actually a plastic surgeon but with some previous experience in chest surgery. Within a minute Donald Smith stood slouching in the door to the operating room with a typically Australian smirk on his face. "Jesus Christ, Dick," he drawled. "What are you doing with your hand in that bloody girl's chest?"

I answered with the evenness of a man holding a ticking bomb in his hand. "Donald, stop with the jokes. Put some gloves on. Come in here and help me sew this damn thing up." He quickly scrubbed and came in. We removed my hand, and he examined the tissues surrounding the lung and heart to make sure there had been no tears. I had done well; there was no damage and no bleeding. He sutured her chest, and the patient was sent back to her room where she made an uneventful recovery.

This was not the only time I took charge in a life-and-death situation. Early in my residency at Manhattan Eye and Ear, one of my colleagues was found slumped unconscious over a binocular microscope. Since we were all new, we had no idea of each other's medical histories. A general cry went up, and all the residents crowded around. I examined him and instructed a nurse to give me a syringe of glucose. I thought that he might be a diabetic who had gone into insulin shock. One of the other residents suggested that I draw a blood sample and let the lab determine his glucose level. I told him that if it was a case of insulin shock the man would be dead by the time we got a lab report. For about fifteen seconds, as the nurse was preparing the syringe, we argued heatedly. Finally I said, "I don't care what his glucose level is. I'll find out if he wakes up when I give him the injection." With that I found the vein and gave him a shot. A few seconds later the young doctor opened his eyes and said, "What happened?" He suffered no ill effects.

These are just two examples of Dick Raskind's aggressive and competent persona. As a professional I acted decisively and with none of the vacillation that marked my private life. When confronted with a job to be done or in straightforward social situations, I was thoroughly well-adjusted. It was only in my solo moments that I wavered.

Another area in which I excelled as a male was tennis. I played only sporadically in those days, but, even so, I played well. Naturally Gwen was always with me when I went to a tournament and, as they had before with Denise, the regulars on the circuit assumed that we were on the verge of marriage. It was a natural conclusion. We were obviously fascinated with one another; any two normal people of the period would have been picking out a china pattern by this time. Occasionally, the familiar yet romantic way we presented ourselves led some to believe that we were already married. Once Arthur Ashe, then a teenager, called Gwen "Mrs. Raskind." After all, she was around all the time, and we certainly seemed settled in our relationship. He assumed that things were as they seemed.

Unfortunately, though the show was good, Renée's personality was breaking through more violently. Her appearances were characterized by increasing violence to the hated male genitals. The techniques of causing them to disappear were the same as they had been, but the violence with which they were carried out was unprecedented. For the first time I began to think of myself (I guess I should say "my selves") as masochistic. In past years the ritual of transformation had been a means to an end. The discomfort was a by-product. Now Renée seemed to be dwelling on the pain—even enjoying it. When the penis was drawn backward between my legs it was stretched so tightly that small road-map patterns caused by broken veins would appear on the shaft. Where the twine was tied behind the head of my penis, it would cut into the flesh. As I walked the abrasion would cause extensive friction burns. When the testicles were shoved upward, it was no longer simply to get them out of the way. Renée shoved them up higher and higher, wishing that they would stay there and be in some magical way absorbed, but they weren't. When they came back down they were bruised and hurt. Often they swelled to twice normal size. The type of injury that had sent me to my mother for a confession years before was now a regular part of my life.

About one year after I began analysis, an event occurred that provided Renée with even more energy. My mother died.

If this announcement seems matter-of-fact, it's because her death was largely matter-of-fact. One day during my internship, I received a call from my mother. She said that months earlier she had been to a doctor who had diagnosed her condition as a spastic colon. She hadn't liked this much because she didn't think of herself as the type to have a spastic colon. When the symptoms continued she got a second opinion; this time the diagnosis was rectal cancer. According to her, the earliest date she could arrange for the necessary surgery was three weeks away. I was unwilling to accept this since early action is important in cancer treatment. I assured her that I thought I could do better. I put in a call to a friend who was then an intern at New York Hospital and asked him if he could pull some strings; the operation was scheduled for the following day. From the first my mother's sickness was surrounded by professional activity. It was communicated to me in technical terms, and my response was largely a technical one. Everyone in the family was a physician, and this promoted a business-as-usual atmosphere even though the subject of the crisis was a family member. As I've said before, this type of intellectual communication was what we did best. I distanced my mother's sickness in the same way any competent doctor distances the problems of his patients. It is a delicate balance between emotional concern and flat objectivism. When you tilt too far in one direction the quality of care suffers. As an intern I saw life-and-death situations every day, and my mother's was calculated in with the rest.

When the doctors opened her up, they found that the cancer had spread to the liver. They removed all the malignant material they could, but they knew that some remained. The chances were overwhelming that it would grow back again and eventually kill my mother. Still, there was the slight possibility that, deprived of the main mass those leftover cells would die off; it sometimes happens. The family had to decide whether she should be told that her case was, in all probability, terminal. We decided to say nothing, and Mother never asked. Perhaps she had a private talk with the physician, or maybe she just preferred not to know for sure. Characteristically, we didn't discuss it. All that medical science could do had been done; what more was there to say? Of course, Mother took chemotherapy and cobalt treatments and suffered the usual side effects. They made her nauseated and weak, but she went back to her practice in spite of the discomfort.

For a while she improved; the removal of a tumor always brings an immediate relief to the patient's system. Sometimes it seems almost miraculous. A sense of normality settled over the family. I finished my internship and began my study of basic science in ophthalmology. After a year or so Mother's condition had begun to deteriorate. I was often called upon to drive her to her cobalt treatments and to perform other tasks, especially as she grew weaker. My father was still at his office every day. My sister was married and living out of town, coming home only on occasion. My schedule was also demanding but more flexible than theirs. I spent an increasing amount of time with my mother as she grew weaker. I began to feel closer to her. She was stoic and courageous, but she would occasionally break down out of frustration. She had been strong all of her life, and she considered her weakness a needless indignity. I eagerly supplied what emotional support I could. I don't mean that we wept together but that we shared some understanding on an emotional level. For example, I sometimes anticipated her desire for something like a glass of water and would bring it to her without being asked. She would not only express gratitude verbally but would somehow radiate it so that I could feel a genuine emotional contact. I think that during those times I put aside all my indignation; the past was forgiven, if not nullified. I brought this up in my sessions with Dr. Bak, but he had no comment.

These emotional moments took place most often in the last six months of my mother's life, but they were never frequent. Mostly we talked about practical matters. By this time she was aware that she had only a short time to live. Among many other things, we talked about my father. He had immersed himself in the details of daily life as a protection against anxiety and grief, trying to pretend that nothing had changed. If forced into a position where he had to confront the situation, his expressed feelings were always directed into some trivial matter. When he took my mother for a treatment, he might gripe interminably about the traffic, which was no worse than usual. My mother was intimately familiar with this denial and had used it to her advantage over the years. Now that she was dying, however, she worried about how this sort of behavior would affect my father's financial affairs. She admonished me to look after him, to provide the practicality that her death would take out of his life. We also discussed the fate of her mother who had grown senile over the years; Mother did not want her sent to a home. This wish was honored by my father until Grandma's death, though she was not told when Mother passed away. Every day for ten years she would ask my father, "When will Sadie be coming home?" And every day my father would answer, "Tomorrow."

Doctor Bishop died one night in her sleep. She had been in the hospital for three months and had wasted from a robust woman to an emaciated shell.

After Mother's death, Renée became even harder to control. I theorized in one of my daily sessions that her disapproval of Renée had helped to check my transformations. Had there been a public scandal, Mother's reaction would have been of paramount concern to me; that fear was now removed. It was one more aspect of the increasing erosion of Dick's personality.

Gwen sensed this and tried to take up the slack. She stayed with me as much as possible. When she was there I didn't feel the urge to become Renée. One of her most persuasive arguments in favor of marriage was that she would always be with me and, consequently, I could never change, but I was afraid that even worse things would come out of a marriage. Renée was already outraged. If she was pressed further, I had no idea whether or not she could be controlled. If Gwen was there all the time, I could foresee myself transforming into Renée during the afternoons in some hotel or even at the hospital. Worse yet, if Renée was restricted through a marriage, she might begin to feel that there was nothing to live for. She might grow despondent and attempt to take her life. The memory of the automobile accident in Rochester came back to haunt me. I concluded that I could put little trust in my fragmented personality. The combinations were potentially volatile.

The best proof of my reluctance to marry Gwen came when she became pregnant. Why this happened is problematical; most of the time we used a diaphragm for birth control. It might have happened on one of those so-called "safe days." The birth control pill was several years away and, in those days, there was a lot of figuring that centered around menstrual cycles. We were supposedly safe anytime except the period from nine to nineteen days after menstruation. It was a relief not having to deal with a diaphragm on safe days. This was a pretty optimistic approach, and there are a lot of people in the population today who were conceived on safe days. Then again, Gwen may have "forgotten" to put the diaphragm in. I was typically male in that I left birth control up to her. My assumption was that such an important item would never be overlooked, but then I never helped her remember either. Knowing as much as I did about repression and unconscious desires, I should have been more on guard. Gwen was anxious to be married, and pregnancy is a time-worn device for bringing it about. It needn't have been a conscious plot. We forget all sorts of things that we really would rather not remember. Maybe I wanted it, too, as a further affirmation of Dick's manhood.

The main point is that we were in deep trouble. For respectable people in the early sixties there was usually only one course of action when a girl got pregnant: she and her boyfriend got married. Of course, there *were* some other alternatives. She could go away, have the baby, and give it up for adoption. This was out of the question for Gwen who was in graduate school. The second possibility was an abortion; there was no place in the United States to get one legally, so the woman either went to a seedy neighborhood where she was taken care of by an amateur with a coat hanger or to a doctor who did abortions on the sly. For those who could afford it, the best place to find a sly doctor was in Puerto Rico. The controls there were looser than on the mainland,

and abortion clinics operated without much interference. They were clean and run by certified medical personnel. In addition, Puerto Rico was a tourist spot, and clinic patrons could pretend they were going there on a vacation.

Gwen and I discussed the options and decided on Puerto Rico. Even though she would have loved to be married, she agreed without argument. She had seen the lacerations on my genitals. These made it impossible to pass my problem off as an idiosyncrasy like wearing loud ties or smoking smelly cigars. Gwen realized that a baby was out of the question. There was no way to tell what effect a child would have on Renée. She might be jealous, she might feel maternal, or she might have an unforeseen reaction. As unstable as I already was, I could not consider any course of action that might further unbalance me.

I made some inquiries among members of the medical community and found out about a responsibly run clinic in San Juan. Now that I was a resident doctor, getting time off was less of a problem than it had been when I was an intern. I arranged for some sympathetic friends to cover for me during the week I was to be gone. We timed the trip to coincide with a long holiday weekend so that Gwen would miss only a little school work. All this planning helped us keep our minds off the purpose of the trip; we had almost managed to work ourselves into a festive mood by the time we left New York.

The clinic was located in San Turce, a suburb of San Juan. The man in charge was a kindly old gynecologist who seemed a little confused by Gwen and me. We were like a married couple and obviously cared deeply for one another. He wondered aloud what our problem was; we told him nicely to mind his own business. This did not appear to offend him; he just shrugged and checked Gwen into the clinic. For me he recommended a good night's sleep, adding that I should stay away from the clinic until the abortion was over the next morning.

The doctor's advice was good, but I couldn't get to sleep. The little hotel room seemed oppressive. I replayed our arguments over the situation. There was no other choice, yet I was plagued by doubts; I guess they were not so much doubts as regrets. I didn't doubt that we were doing the right thing, but I deeply regretted the necessity. I could only imagine what Gwen was feeling, lying in a strange room, waiting.

Sometime in the early morning hours I dozed off. When I awoke it was dark; the clock showed five o'clock. I had slept through the day and into the afternoon leaving Gwen uncomforted in the hours following the operation. Guilt stricken, I bolted out into the street only to notice that there was no one around, no pedestrians, no cars. Only then did it occur to me that it was actually five in the morning. The operation had not yet taken place; I returned to my room and paced until just before noon. The doctor had said that I could come to visit Gwen at that time. I arrived promptly and found her resting in her room. Gwen was healthy and strong so that same day we checked her out of the clinic and moved into one of San Juan's luxury hotels. For the next week we pretended we were on vacation.

All this was done with little discussion. Gwen was by nature a stoic. She dealt with the abortion in the same contained way that she had received the news of my compulsion to dress as a woman. The abortion was never thrown up to me or used as a weapon. The only time I ever saw her lose that composure was when we argued over marriage. On that issue she would become hysterical. I once just barely caught up with her as she was running toward the Hudson River with the intention of drowning herself. I had my share of hysterics, and I also threatened suicide. At times death seemed better than the double life I was leading. Dick was not pleased. Renée was not pleased. Gwen was not pleased.

Though the abortion was never brought up in our arguments, it marked the beginning of a decline in my relationship with Gwen. Maybe it served notice to her that the situation was indeed hopeless. Together we had created the beginnings of a new life. It contained elements of both of us, and we both wanted to let it grow, but we could not.

Gwen started coming to the apartment less frequently, and she eventually stopped staying overnight. Our relationship dragged on sporadically for another couple of years. Then we had one final argument, no worse than many others. It was distinguished only by the fact that it was the last. After that we never spoke to one another again.

12

Masquerades

The disruption of my relationship with Gwen meant more time to myself and an increasing insecurity about my sexual identity. Renée began to emerge more frequently. My genitals were in a constant state of trauma from the repeated application of the heavy adhesive tape. Anyone who has ever removed a Band-Aid from a hairy portion of his body will identify with the pain I suffered practically every night. Imagine how much more powerful the sensation would be if wide bands of surgical tape replaced the Band-Aid and the point of application was the tender skin of the reproductive organs.

Pain was not the only issue. Renée was again insisting on bolder exercises in reality. Again she wanted to go out in the world, only now the danger was multiplied because I was a resident of Manhattan and far more likely to be recognized. I tried to minimize this possibility by never going into the world as Renée from my own apartment. If Renée was to have a night on the town, I would rent a hotel room in another neighborhood and use it as a base of operations.

The tone of these expeditions is typified by an experience that started in a beauty parlor. Since my sexual maturity my disguise as Renée had become less and less convincing. After all, I was six-feet one and weighed one hundred and eighty pounds. I had a good complexion, but I also had a fast-growing beard that required tiresomely close shaving and then the application of a pancake makeup to eliminate the traces of it. In the old days my face had been delicate, readily acceptable as feminine; now it required special attention. Truthfully, I was not very good at it. I conceived the notion that if I could just be done up in a beauty parlor by a real professional, it would make a big difference. Accordingly, I checked into a Park Avenue hotel and went to an elegant beauty shop that catered to wealthy clients. I went as a man but carried with me a suitcase full of women's things. I approached the proprietor with an elaborate story about how I was going to attend a masquerade party and had hit on the idea of going as a woman. I told him that I wanted to look as much like a real woman as possible. I showed him the clothes and wig I had supposedly bought for the occasion, and he complimented me on making appropriate choices for my height. I assured him that I had had the full cooperation of my girlfriend, who had helped pick the things out. By the time I had finished with the explanations and demonstrations, the whole shop was buzzing with excitement. Suddenly, the average workday was transformed into an adventure by this manly young guy. Other patrons in the shop began to take notice and even put off leaving when they were finished in order to see how my experiment would turn out. This publicity was exactly what I wanted. The best defense is a good offense. By placing myself in the public eye, I automatically allayed suspicions; rather than insecurity, I projected an easy-going confidence.

The proprietor put me in the hands of one of his best cosmeticians, who looked me over with a professional air. "Fabulous skin," he muttered. There followed comments about the shape of my face and in particular my jawline, which was strong. I was informed that my cheekbones were elegantly high, that my eyes needed to be "brought out." He settled the wig on my head and decided what hair style would best complement my features. In short, he did everything that I had hoped he would. Like a magician of some sort, he dipped into little containers of powder and cream. Potions were mixed. I was cleansed, masked, and then decorated according to the rituals of women throughout the ages. I even allowed a little selective plucking on my eyebrows, just enough to give them a more distinct outline. When he finished with me, I looked better than I had in years. My hair—that is, my wig—was upswept, piled high in a sophisticated arrangement. My face was impeccable; little shadows had mysteriously appeared, eliminating the hard-edged masculine qualities. My eyes had indeed been brought out. They had never looked larger or more luminescent. My eyelashes were about twice as long as they normally were. I was entranced.

When I emerged from the dressing room where I had put on my evening clothes, there was a chorus of ooh's and ah's. I was still tall and still muscular, but my impact was more feminine than it had been since I was an adolescent. For a while I was the center of attention, but eventually it became obvious that I would have to be on my way. I was reluctant to leave the cozy world of the beauty parlor. Outside there was nothing for me but the usual aimless wandering. It suddenly stood out in all its horrible emptiness. I wished fervently that there really *was* a masquerade party; I could spend the whole evening as Renée and still remain above suspicion.

While I was settling up with the proprietor, I was approached by the woman who had been in the next chair as I was being transformed. She was young and had shown an active interest in the treatment I was getting. She had even made suggestions that had not been graciously received by my cosmetologist. Ignoring my costume party story, she asked if I'd like to go and have a bite to eat with her. I sensed that she was intrigued, even excited by the presence of a man in women's clothes. She was attractive, and the approval implicit in the invitation made her even more so. I agreed and gathered up my masculine clothes. As we walked out on the street I felt a wave of confidence. The presence of a real woman gave me legitimacy. Much of my fear evaporated, and I began to feel as if we were two chums out for an evening in New York. I allowed myself to relax, and Renée came to the fore. During the meal we chattered like sorority sisters, but underneath was a confusing mixture of heterosexuality and lesbianism. Though Renée was in control, Dick's desires kept intruding. I know that my companion was confused as well; she would touch my hand and then look at me in a quizzical way as if she had gotten a slight electrical shock from the contact. This undercurrent continued throughout the evening.

When we had finished our meal, she suggested that we go to her apartment in the Bronx. She knew by then that I had no real plans for later. During dinner I had admitted that the masquerade story was untrue and that it was just an excuse to dress as a woman. She had accepted this without the blink of an eye, as if it were the most natural thing in the world for a man to spend two hours being made up in a beauty parlor.

Her apartment was unassuming. I couldn't imagine what a girl from the South Bronx had been doing at an exclusive beauty parlor on Park Avenue. Of course, I didn't ask. Maybe it was her one big extravagance. I will say that she had a nice wardrobe. For the rest of the evening I tried on her clothes. In some ways it was like a slumber party. We had a glass or two of wine which made us a little giddy; we giggled quite a bit. Every so often she'd snap her fingers and say, "Oh I have something that would *really* look good on you!" I'd happily slip into anything she suggested.

I still had my makeup on when we went to bed together. The sisterly attitude continued into our sex. There was a lot of gentle caressing and looking into one another's eyes. She was apparently turned on by my femininity. This acceptance relaxed me, and I performed well. Otherwise our sex was straight and unremarkable. When I got up the next morning and looked in the mirror, I saw that my face was a wreck. Everything was smudged and out of order. Little granules of mascara clung to my cheeks, and my beard was beginning to poke through the makeup base. I quickly scrubbed my face and dressed as a man. In the morning, as usual, my masculinity was stronger, and I felt sheepish and a little fearful about what had happened the night before. I made my good-byes to the girl; she offered to drive me home, but I didn't want her to know where I lived or to get the idea that our relationship could continue. When leaving the beauty parlor the night before I had forgotten Dick's shoes; so when I walked out of the girl's apartment building and onto the Grand Concourse dressed in a sport shirt, slacks and bare feet, I drew some stares from the residents of that Bronx neighborhood.

Dr. Bak took a dim view of Renée's excursions. After two years of analysis, he could see that I was worse off than when I had started. Our sessions were degenerating into shouting matches. Discouraged by the lack of progress, I brought up the subject of transsexual surgery. This idea had been in the back of my head since I had first heard of Christine Jorgensen in the early fifties. I hadn't considered it seriously because I had for so long held out the hope that analysis might cure me. As Dick, I had everything I could wish for. In addition to being young and handsome, I had a

138

satisfying profession and, in tennis, a rewarding avocation. Everything would be perfect if I could just lick my identity problem, but after six unsuccessful years on the couch I was ready to entertain the idea of surgery.

The still intimidating Dr. Bak would fly off the handle when I brought this up. He would stand over me like a great prophet and predict utter doom if I ever had my penis done away with. He reminded me constantly that my only purpose in cross-dressing was to achieve the satisfaction of seeing my male member still intact at the end of an episode. If it was actually cut off, I would almost surely become psychotic. The least I could expect was a debilitating depression. I would scream back, "No! That is not so! You are like all other men. You love your prick above all else, but I hate mine! I don't want it! It should never have been a part of me!" This hysterical response covered my own doubts. Dr. Bak could be right, but if he was, my last resort was denied me; and I would then face a lifetime of freakish behavior, forever vacillating between masculinity and femininity.

Realizing that he was losing control of me, Dr. Bak did two things that for him were unprecedented. First, he prescribed tranquilizers to combat my anxiety and depression. For an orthodox Freudian this was an admission of failure. These tranquilizers signaled the beginning of what is known as "directive therapy." In this style, the therapist tells a patient what steps to take rather than letting the patient fish around for his own direction. In Freudian analysis the patient should have insights and from these decide on what is best for himself. When Dr. Bak began making suggestions and prescribing chemicals, he was just trying to keep me afloat. The idea of a cure had, at least temporarily, been put aside. The second thing Dr. Bak did that was out of character was to send me to one of his colleagues for an intensive evaluation. This was like God throwing up his hands in despair and saying, "I give up, maybe the Archangel Michael can do something with you." The archangel's comments were as follows, "Well, it is obvious that you are not psychotic and you are not schizophrenic, but, Dr. Raskind, you must get over this craziness of wanting to change yourself into a woman!" So much for the archangel.

Meanwhile Renée was breaking loose practically every night, and it seemed only a matter of time before I was discovered. Dick was sinking deeper into depression as he was yanked around by the ever more powerful Renée. The subject of suicide began to come up in my sessions with Dr. Bak, and in this instance he rose to the occasion magnificently when he directed me to grow a beard.

What a fabulous charm those whiskers turned out to be! As my beard waxed full, Renée waned. Who would have imagined that such a simple thing would work so well? I came to love that beard. It was full, and the hair was of good quality, straight, not wiry. I kept it trimmed close to my jaw line so that it was neat and stayed out of my way when I was doing medical work. Best of all, when I looked in the mirror I saw no trace of femininity. I couldn't even fantasize because the beard struck me as so overwhelmingly masculine. If thoughts of Renée came to mind, I needed only to stroke my chin and her specter was banished. For the next year no article of women's apparel touched my body. I didn't even have the desire. I even considered getting back with Gwen on a regular basis, but I decided that we had already suffered too much pain together. There would always be a shadow hanging over us. Then again, in the past I had found it best to be cautious about these things. Renée had faded before and then come back stronger than ever.

In spite of my caution, I wholeheartedly enjoyed my final year of residency. Both as a doctor and as a tennis player I was more aggressive than ever. I had never been reluctant to wade into a controversial situation or to express my opinion, but that beard increased my swagger threefold. Some might have called me insufferable. As for athletics, I was ferocious. If the killer instinct had ever been lacking, it was no problem for the bearded Dick Raskind. I was like some maned beast charging around the tennis courts, showing no mercy. When I went home in the evening, even if I was alone, I was a macho guy.

During this period, I began seeing my old friend Josh Frick again. He was still a maverick and, in my shaggy state, that characteristic appealed to me more than ever. One of Josh's latest vendettas was directed at car thieves. Like all my other friends, Josh had expensive automobiles, and they were frequently stolen. Incensed, he rigged his Corvette with an alarm that sounded loudly if the car was violated. One night about three A.M. he heard the alarm. Grabbing a rifle outfitted with a Japanese sniper-scope, he flew to the window. The thief was already in retreat, but Josh took aim and squeezed one off anyway. The felon staggered but managed to gain the subway entrance and make his escape. Josh complained bitterly about the errant bullet, as if winging criminals wasn't enough. Josh Frick—my kind of guy, especially when I was bearded.

I look back on that beard as the centerpiece of an era: the time of the beard. Unfortunately, it was an era that lasted only a single year. Upon finishing my residency at Manhattan Eye and Ear Hospital, I went immediately into the navy. This had been arranged years before when I graduated from medical school. At that time, I had signed up for what was called the Berry Plan. The purpose of this plan was to defer a doctor's draft date until he had finished his specialized training. Notices started coming during my last year at Manhattan Eye and Ear. I was glad to go, but there were two areas of disagreement between myself and the navy. One was the problem of where I should be stationed. I actually went to the Department of the Navy in Washington to clear this up. The problem was that it was essential that I be stationed in New York in order to continue my analysis. I was ushered into the office of a navy commander in charge of such allocations. He showed me a list of thirty possible assignments scattered around the globe and asked me to list three choices in order of preference. I said, "New York, New York, and New York." He said, "You don't understand. You have to list three *different* choices." I told him that it would have to be the U.S. Naval Hospital in St. Albans on Long Island or nothing because I was in the middle of psychoanalysis. To my surprise, he acquiesced. I think he realized that I could probably get out of the sevice altogether if I mentioned the nature of my problem. Good doctors are prized by the armed services; so I was given my desire. He probably also appreciated the fact that I was willing to do my hitch in spite of having an excellent reason not to.

I didn't do so well with the second area of disagreement between me and the navy—my beard. I knew that some naval officers wore beards so I thought at first that I'd be okay. I was surprised to find out that beards represented a certain amount of sea duty. If you came back from a cruise with a beard, you could keep it. On this point, the area commander stood firm. Navy tradition could not be flaunted; my beard would have to go. It was with a great sense of dread that I approached the washbasin to do away with the magical beard. I could almost feel Renée stirring as I whacked away at it. Each time I sent a razorful of lather and beard spinning down the drain, the gloom settled more deeply around me. But when I finished, Renée didn't come howling forward. I thought that maybe my year with the beard had made a lasting impression.

I actually looked forward to that tour with the navy. For many years my life had been ordered by a sequence of commitments: undergraduate work, medical school, internship, year of basic ophthalmological sciences, residency, and now the navy. I was comforted by this tidy progression of events. It required only a little attention from me to move from one situation to the next. All doubt was removed from the general progression of my life so that I could spend a lot of time dealing with my main area of insecurity.

I took a roomier apartment in Manhattan and commuted daily to the Naval Hospital in St. Albans. In the evenings I would drive recklessly back for my session at six. I narrowly missed accidents on several occasions because of my haste to get back on time. Naturally, if I was late, I was scolded by Dr. Bak for doing it on purpose. It had been hard enough as a resident to make those appointments, but driving from Long Island into the city in one hour is tough, and I got quite a few tickets. I probably should have used Josh's trick for avoiding citations. He carried several containers of old blood in the back of his car. When he was stopped he'd claim that he was rushing the blood to a hospital; the cops usually waved him ahead on his mission of mercy. As cocky as I was, I couldn't bring myself to be that outrageous.

I found out quickly that the navy was perhaps more interested in me as a tennis player than as a doctor. Almost immediately, I was entered into the Third Naval District Championships. I won that and was sent posthaste to the North Atlantic Regional Championships, where I won again. Continuing, I went onward and upward, winning both the singles and doubles championship in the All-Navy tennis tournament. Suddenly, without so much as an orientation, I was the All-Navy tennis champion. They made me captain of the navy tennis team, and I led them to compete in the Interservice Championships in Illinois. I spent the whole tournament wondering who I was supposed to salute. I hardly knew how to wear my own outfit, let alone what the various insignia on other people's meant. While in uniform I kept my hand poised at my side like a gunfighter. I didn't have much trouble with the enlisted men—they saluted first. Anybody who didn't salute me before he was eight or ten feet away was trouble; I saluted first and hoped for the best. Our team made it to the semifinals, after which I was returned to Long Island where I officially began my career as a navy doctor.

There was plenty to do. The war in Southeast Asia was escalating. The casualties came pouring in, and I packed the equivalent of many years of private practice into just two years in the navy. It was a discouraging way to learn my craft. Still, I was a healer, and I liked the sensation of seeing my care produce positive results. I never questioned the legality of the war, just the stupidity of a boy's face being ripped open by a piece of shrapnel.

Like Joel before me, I made a handsome officer, and I wore my uniform proudly. Only on a few issues did my attitude differ from the navy's. One of these was military regulations. Often the eye department was not policed in the way that the inspecting officer thought proper. The navy has regulations for everything, including stuff like how shiny the floors should be. I always considered myself a doctor first and an officer second. The chiefs of the naval hospital thought it should be the other way around. I received many memos and personal comments that made it clear that we should shape up. On the other hand, the eye department turned out a large volume of good work in spite of the lack of military discipline. Just because my corpsmen did not have to hop up when I walked into the room was no reason to believe I was an ineffective leader. You can't get good work out of a clinic staff if you are not respected. As a matter of fact, my corpsmen, Bukowski and Isbell were devoted to me. They were the ones in charge of hiding my airedale puppy, Rocco, from the inspection team that came around on Friday afternoons. In turn, when they were in trouble for drunkenness or fighting, I would attend the captain's mast and speak in their defense. In spite of my offhand attitude toward the military niceties, I was promoted to lieutenant commander at the end of my first year on active duty.

In many ways I did have the attributes of a good officer. I got my staff to perform well and I showed ingenuity. At the time I was to play for the second year in the All-Navy Championships, I was temporarily the only ophthalmologist on the base. Because of this unusual gap in the hospital's manpower, I couldn't take the week's leave necessary to compete in the tournament. This problem was solved by having my doubles partner, a helicopter pilot, pick me up in front of my office at the hospital and fly me to the tournament in Newport, Rhode Island. He did this daily for the entire week of matches, returning me each evening to the hospital grounds. In spite of this frantic routine, I repeated as All-Navy tennis champion. That same year, I won the New York State Men's Championship, a title that had eluded me many times. By the time I reached the finals, my feet were bloody and raw. The calluses on the soles of my feet had cracked open and new blisters had formed. On the day of the finals, I had my father inject novocaine into the soles of my feet so that I could play. My tennis exploits finally led to a letter of commendation from the chief of naval personnel in Washington to the commanding officer of St. Albans Naval Hospital, congratulating him on "having produced a naval officer who is such an outstanding athlete and excellent representative of the U. S. Navy." I mean to say Dick Raskind was a hit in the armed services.

Night was a different story. At night I would cover my crew cut with a wig, cinch myself, and climb into a dress. Even with hours of effort, the best I could manage was a grotesque parody. I haunted the city by evening and then, like Cinderella, returned home and changed form again. As I had feared might happen, when I shaved off the beard, Renée did come back. The manly charade that I practiced during the day made her presence all the more galling. I entered another serious depression. I carried on as best I could, and managed to maintain a pretty good facade at work; but, I didn't have the energy or the inclination to hide my melancholy from my closer associates. My father, in particular, knew something was badly wrong. I don't think mother had told him about my sexual confusion, although he may have known and just chosen not to mention it. I certainly never brought it up, and to this day it has never once been a topic of conversation between us. At any rate, he didn't have to know the specifics to realize that I was morbidly preoccupied. As always, his prescription was a vacation. He had encouraged me many time over the years to get away from the strife at home by taking a trip out of town. The unusual feature of his prescription this time was that he wanted us to go together. I had three weeks leave coming to me after my first year in the navy, and he proposed a quick trip to Europe.

Ordinarily I would have turned it down without a second thought. I had no reason to believe that three weeks with my father would improve my disposition. Furthermore, he was a terrible traveling companion—the typically demanding American tourist. I think I rather surprised him when I agreed to go. My reason for doing so was that such a trip would provide the perfect cover for a plan that had been forming in my mind. During the previous year I had been furtively combing lower Manhattan's pornography shops for copies of transsexual and transvestite magazines. These cheap publications were produced in basements by people involved in the life-styles the magazines described. They were ratty little productions, usually printed on newspaper stock and rarely more than ten pages in length. They were devoted to accounts of sex-change operations, tips on where to go if you enjoyed dressing as a woman, and other similar topics of interest. I think they were a labor of love, a way for interested parties to see that there were others of their kind. Unfortunately, the seediness of the product certainly cast the subject in a bad light. Still, any such information was important to me even if it did come in a shoddy package. The magazine I remember best was called *Turnabout.* Some of the articles about transsexuals were accompanied by smudgy before-and-after photographs. Most of the transsexuals mentioned were in Europe because the operation was not legal in the United States. Though the accounts in these magazines were lurid, they furnished me with some basic information. I knew, for example, that Paris was a gathering point for many transsexuals. Often they were employed in the transvestite revues that were a show business tradition in France. This is not to say they were respectable, but, like American burlesque, they were a continuing feature of shady Parisian nightlife. The most famous of these transsexual performers was Coccinelle. I had been enthralled by her book *The Story of Coccinelle,* which I had found in the same store as the transsexual magazines. I decided that I would try to meet her; the trip to Europe with my father would provide an opportunity to do so.

Naturally, I had to engineer some way to break free of my father during the trip. What I proposed was that he and I travel to Europe separately, eventually meeting in Lucerne, Switzerland. I used his irritating approach to travel as an excuse. I said that he would drive me crazy if I had to put up with his temperament on the way over. He had heard similar complaints from others; so my comments did not surprise him. I also think he suspected that I had a secret lover whom I wanted to see in Europe. He held out high hopes that this trip would break my depression, and he willingly accepted the terms without questioning my motives. He sailed on the *Queen Mary* and I on the S. S. *Rotterdam*.

I traveled first class with eight suitcases, four full of men's clothes and four full of women's clothes. On the ship I dressed as a man. I enjoyed playing the part of a naval officer on leave. The surroundings were sumptuous and the atmosphere cosmopolitan. During the voyage I met Irene Castle, a famous dancer of the early twenties. She and her husband Vernon introduced the Castle Walk and were later the subject of a Fred Astaire and Ginger Rogers movie ingeniously titled *The Story of Vernon and Irene Castle*. The shipboard atmosphere was congenial, and I felt at home hobnobbing with international trend setters. This elegant ambience certainly made an unusual springboard for my entry into the bizarre Parisian subculture of transsexualism.

On my first night in Paris, I dressed as a man and went to a nightclub called Madame Artur. This place had been mentioned in Coccinelle's book and was of about the same caliber as the Club 82 in New York. An identical mix of gawking tourists and bohemians constituted the audience. I asked to speak to Coccinelle but was told she was at a nightclub on the Left Bank called Le Carrousel. I was disappointed, but in talking with some of the transsexual performers I picked up a valuable piece of information. I found out that many of these girls lived at the Hôtel de la Paix, near the Folies Bergère. That night I checked into the Hôtel de la Paix.

Even as I checked in I began to feel elated. Some of the women from Madame Artur were gathered in the hotel's sitting room and chatting. At last I was physically near people like me. Some of the oppressive loneliness that had afflicted me for so long lifted as I rode the little cage-like elevator up to my room. These people were not transvestites or homosexual pretenders; they were men who had realized an incredible dream and become women. I walked out onto the little balcony of my room. The street below was tidy, well-tended, picturesque. The people here were part of a community, not simply misfits slinking around in the slums. The notion that had heretofore seemed so remote began to take on a clearer outline. Renée might truly live. I went back inside and spent the rest of the evening polishing my nails.

The next day I went shopping dressed as a woman. Three thousand miles from home in civilized Paris, I felt immune from the threat of discovery. I later found out that this was blissful ignorance. The laws of Paris were just as punitive as those in New York.

I lumbered around Paris towering over the average French-woman as well as most of the men. In spite of my size, I presented a pretty benign picture, what with my camera draped around my neck. This identified me as a tourist and, though often irritating, tourists seldom made bad trouble however funny looking they were.

In the evening I went to Le Carrousel. The performers in shows at such clubs are called "les travestis." This designation comes from the same root as the English word "travesty." Originally they were heterosexual men who burlesqued the appearance and mannerisms of women. Gradually, true transvestism, the serious impersonation of women, grew out of these burlesque perform-ances. At the time I was in Paris, the most famous of "les travestis" were the transsexuals. They seemed to be the next step in the evolution of this peculiar art form. Many of the transsex-uals had been transvestite performers before their operations. This was the case with Coccinelle and another famous performer called Bambi. When I inquired again about Coccinelle I was told she was on vacation. Reluctant to go home without having talked to someone prominent, I asked to speak to Bambi and was told to wait at a table in the nightclub's main room.

In a few minutes Bambi swept in wearing a full-length lynx fur coat. Her hair was blonde and fell well below her shoulders. She had brown eyes and sharply chiseled features. She was a knock-out, and I was glad to see that she was tall, at least five-feet ten. I introduced myself and asked her to sit down. Bambi's tone was friendly but not excessively so. She gave the impression of an extremely competent and articulate person; her voice was low and seductive. She was affected, but she played her role without apology and with a clear sense of style. When I explained that I was an incipient transsexual looking for information, she didn't bat an eye in spite of my unpromising appearance. On the contrary, she was supportive. After looking me up and down she commented that my body seemed plastic enough to accept the change and provide me with an acceptable vehicle in which to live out my life as a woman. This was encouraging since she had been through the experience and her word stood for something. At last I felt that I was talking to someone who knew something. She provided me with the names of people who could provide the hormones for the long process of chemical preparation necessary before surgery could be possible. She stressed the necessity of electrolysis, the painful and extended technique whereby each hair follicle in the face is individually destroyed by a tiny electrically charged needle. Finally, she confirmed that the necessary surgery was being done regularly at a facility in Casablanca. Our conversation lasted for about twenty minutes and was packed with information. I was left with the feeling that it was all within reach, that it could be done if I wanted it badly enough. As Bambi left the room, I noticed again how gracefully she moved—and she was so tall!

After she left, I stayed on to watch her show. She took command of the stage, sang and danced competently, and finished by stripping completely nude. She was, in all observable aspects, a woman. More importantly, she seemed to be contented. In our conversation she had endorsed her own change without reservation. She had a boyfriend, an apartment, a car, and a whole social existence outside the theater—she lived a normal life. Of course, she was earning her living in the world of les travestis, but I didn't see any reason why such a woman could not be, for instance, a doctor.

The elation I felt after my talk with Bambi was short-lived. The transsexuals at my hotel were not nearly so positive. Although they tolerated my presence among them, they seemed put off by my appearance; they were all slight of build, and I was like a behemoth among them. My face was covered with pancake makeup to cover my beard, which caused a shadow no matter how closely I shaved. The rest of my makeup was equally heavy to

mitigate the mature features of a thirty-year-old man. I quickly
became known to everyone on the block where the hotel was
located. They observed the comings and goings of *"l'Americaine"*
with wry amusement. Their disbelieving looks expressed their
thoughts exactly: *"C'est impossible."* Still there was one man in
the neighborhood who kept telling me how beautiful I was and
inviting me up to his room, but I wasn't interested.

One of the rooms at the Hotel de la Paix was occupied by a girl
who was recovering from her surgery. In the evening, a group of
transsexuals usually gathered there to play an old Victrola and to
socialize. I was present during one of these sessions, and as usual I
was full of questions about the surgical process—especially how
the patient felt afterward. Did she have any regrets? It turned out
that she had none. "But," the new girl added significantly, "some
are not so lucky. There was one who was not ready, who did not
have the true feminine nature." Suddenly I became terribly
uncomfortable; my hands and feet felt three times as large as
normal. Under the pancake makeup, I blushed. "After the
surgery," the new girl continued, "he went mad!" And all the girls
around the bed threw up their hands and chorused, *"Il est devenu
fou! Il est devenu fou!"* Then I knew for sure that this was all for
my benefit. As a group they had decided that my prospects were
bleak, and (if such a thing was possible) I was casting a disrepu-
table light on the real transsexuals. Another girl said, not
unkindly, "You are a beautiful man. Take off your nail polish and
go back to the United States. Enjoy what you are."

Their story caused me to recall Dr. Bak's dark prophesies. The
young man's reaction was exactly what he had predicted for me.
In spite of the successes I could see all around me, the specter of a
horrible, irreversible castration still could not be ruled out. I
could not be sure that these slight young creatures, so at ease in
their femininity, were not a different order of humanity from me.
Certainly they seemed to think they were; they made me feel like
an ostrich trying to be a songbird.

After a week I left Paris with nothing settled. I knew that I
could have the operation, but I still wasn't sure I *should* have it. As
I rode the train from Paris to Lucerne, I experienced no problem
re-entering the character of Dick. This was surprising because
the six days in Paris were by far the most prolonged period of

time I had ever spent as Renée. The transformation had only been a matter of taking off the nail polish and makeup. Dick came back quite easily. Perhaps the girls at the hotel were right after all.

Curiously, the rest of the trip with my father was probably the chummiest time we ever spent together. We went from Lucerne to the French Riviera, where we frequented dance halls and picked up girls together. At other times, he arranged dates for me with the daughters of the women he met, and I returned the favor, fixing him up with the mothers of girls I found on my own. We sailed together on the Mediterranean, even taking a chance by sailing miles out from shore in rough water. We gambled shoulder to shoulder in the casino at Monte Carlo. My trip with my father was as masculine in tone as my days in Paris had been feminine. That was the first and last time I ever shared such an experience with my father. It seemed a poignant suggestion of how our relationship might have developed without the overpowering presence of Dr. Sadie Muriel Bishop.

At the end of our week together, I left my father and went back to Paris where I collected my four suitcases full of ladies wear. It was a quick stop, and I didn't get a chance to go out on the town as Renée. I hopped on a jet, and a few hours later I was back in the navy.

13

Renée Makes Her Move

Upon my return from Europe I really went to seed. Though I had easily transformed back into Dick after my Paris adventure, I found that I could not follow the advice of the girls and "pregirls" at the Hotel de la Paix. I tried however; I took off the nail polish and returned to the life of a naval officer, but I couldn't enjoy it. All day I would labor over the absorbing intricacies of eye surgery. What I was doing would affect the course of these men's lives. In many instances I would make the difference between a world of light and a lifetime of darkness. This important work was completely engrossing, but on the way to and from the operating room I often saw in my mind sudden images of myself slipping into a ladies gown. The juxtaposition was silly—the sublime and the ridiculous—but there it was. Renée was invading the sterility of the hospital. She wasn't interfering, mind you, but she was definitely nosing around inquisitively. Heretofore, the intense atmosphere of the medical work had pretty much kept her at bay. The manly Dr. Raskind had held court uncontested, had swaggered through the halls of healing as a pure creature, well-defined and decisive. Now there was a hint of a sashay in that swagger. To the outside world this was as yet unnoticeable, but I could feel the change. Something was bent further than it had ever been bent before.

My life after-hours was likewise changed in a radical way. In Paris, Renée had tasted something like a normal existence. She had walked the streets unafraid, had her own little room, chatted

151

with the girls, and had done these things not just for a few hours but for days! Returning to a life of skulking around and talking to strangers was unthinkable. All the elaborate scenarios that I had regularly played out suddenly showed themselves in their incredible cheapness. The comparison between my experience in Paris and the realities of Manhattan made me increasingly bitter. Renée, though she didn't throw caution out completely, began to step more arrogantly into the world.

One of the first demonstrations of this growing flamboyance took place on a routine excursion into the streets of the city. I had spent a little extra time in my makeover that evening. Renée was looking pretty good. By this I mean that perhaps only ten percent of the people I passed on the street did a double take. As I looked in the shop windows, I could almost believe that the dark reflection staring back was a tall and elegant model pausing to investigate more closely an item on display. The fashions of the time were poised between the simple designs of Chanel, made popular by Jackie Kennedy, and the Carnaby Street creations epitomized by the miniskirt. My dress was cut in the style known as Empire. These dresses were gathered under the bosom and then fell straight down from that point, perhaps flaring just a bit; often they were worn with a little bolero jacket. This was ideal for me since it de-emphasized my waistline. In addition, the jacket covered my shoulders, which have always been broad, as well as my arms, which were muscular. The season was summer, and my outfit was made of cool, light beige linen. It had a tropical look, an airy feel that I thought went a long way toward counterbalancing my unfeminine heaviness. As I strolled by Tiffany's I imagined myself similar to the tall and slender Audrey Hepburn as she appeared in the film *Breakfast at Tiffany's*. Of course, she was much thinner than I, but she was tall and had a long neck. As I gazed through the thick windows of Tiffany's at the jewels beyond, I saw my reflection spangled with the glint of diamonds. I looked positively elegant! I so seldom felt proud of my appearance that the sensation was both a pleasure and a pain. How marvelous to feel adequate and how miserable to have no warm companion with which to share myself.

I looked up and down the street. Everyone seemed to be walking in pairs or in a group. Even those who were alone walked purposefully as if on their various ways to reunions where they would be with friends. My frustration, which had grown harsher and harsher over the previous years of pretense and deception, rose in me like a half-digested meal. The first taste of it, bitter and nauseating, unleashed a torrent of feeling; my fists clenched and I saw my face contort in Tiffany's window. I thought I might scream at the top of my lungs, or fall down in a seizure, or attack a passing pedestrian. I was close to doing something very foolish. Instead, I hefted my stylishly large pocketbook, settled the strap securely on my shoulder, and strode purposefully off toward the apartment of my friend, Josh Frick.

The reason that I chose Josh's place is really unclear to me. It was probably that he was almost always home. Josh seldom went to other people's apartments; if you wanted to see him, you went to his place. In a way, this was reassuring since, though self-involved, he was dependable. I always knew where he was. On the other hand, he was, of my old and dear friends, the least likely to be understanding. Perhaps this figured into my motives. I might have been afraid to go to anyone who was too supportive of Renée. Though she was in the driver's seat on the evening in question, Dick could still shout up from the well of my unconscious and make himself heard. Indeed, as I neared Josh's apartment, Renée became less strong, and Dick began to fitfully emerge. This sputtering of my psyche continued right up to the moment I rang Josh's doorbell. However, when he opened the door he found not the desperate Renée, but the sheepish Dick Raskind decked out in a wig and a smart evening outfit. By this time I was fairly digging my toe into the rug in a fever of embarrassment. I was staring at the floor when the light from the doorway fell across me. I looked up, like Lauren Bacall in *To Have and Have Not*. Josh was standing there with a supremely inquisitive expression on his face. I could feel my hands trembling fiercely at my sides; so I closed them into fists. Josh was leaning against the door jamb running his eyes all over me. I kept looking down and then raising my gaze just far enough so that I could catch the expression on his face through my eyebrows. I must have looked like a huge child standing shamefacedly with my head hanging and my fists clenched, waiting for punishment. Finally Josh spoke.

"Is that you in there, Dick?"

"Kind of," I answered in a little voice. I chanced a look up into his face. The grinding of the gears was almost audible. Josh is a smart man, and in a few seconds the hidden and half-hidden clues of seventeen years' association were flashing into place like so many computer cards. In a trice he had achieved the massive alteration in perspective made necessary by this simple visit from me. His next statement reflected his new orientation.

"Up to your old tricks again, I see."

"I guess so."

What before had been my eccentricities, my lovable peculiarities, had in one-half minute become my "old tricks." I don't mean that Josh was vicious in his tone—far from it. Like someone who finds out that a trusted friend is a secret alcoholic, his first reaction was to measure all past activity by that standard: "So that's why you . . . And that Christmas Eve when you . . . ? Of course, your appointments with . . ." Now things made better sense; the cat was out of the bag and so might still be beaten to death by Josh Frick.

"Won't you come in, Miss Raskind."

"Josh, please."

"How ungentlemanly of me to keep a lady waiting in the hall." He placed a gallant hand in the small of my back and steered me inside. I could tell exactly what was about to happen. Josh, never one to be stymied by the subtleties of a situation, had decided that he could cure me by archly pointing out the absurdities of my condition. He was the same well-intentioned boy who had set me straight at summer camp in 1948. I'm sure he felt that since the direct approach had worked once before there was no reason why it shouldn't work again. I attempted to head off this useless exercise.

"Josh, I know what you're thinkng. I . . ."

"Actually, I was thinking what a lovely perfume you're wearing. Is that Chanel Number Five?" He touched the back of his ears briefly. In this game, Josh was a master. He was not subtle, but his instincts were unerring. Embarrassingly enough, my favorite scent was My Sin. Ignoring his question, I plunged ahead.

"You don't know how hard it was for me to come here like this."

"Yes, yes. I can imagine that walking in those heels is hell, but a girl has to pay a price for style. I, for one, appreciate the effort."

"Josh, have a heart!" The use of this archaic phrase from our youth seemed to break through his pose. For the first time, he addressed me directly.

"Well, my god Dick! You look like a fool! Am I supposed to take this seriously? I mean, I wish I had your biceps."

"The size of my biceps doesn't affect the way I feel. I feel like a woman, Josh. It's getting so I feel like a woman more than I do a man. I've been in analysis for almost nine years, and it's getting worse! What am I supposed to do?"

"You look like a fool," Josh repeated.

"Don't you think I know that? Jesus Christ, tonight I look *good!* You should see me on an off day!"

"No, thank you."

"I don't even know exactly why I came here. I knew what I'd get. It's just that I've been so damn lonely. Can you imagine what it's like to wander around dressed like this with no one to talk to, no friends, nothing? Do you know what would happen if I was caught? They'd throw me in the tank where, if I was lucky, I'd be beaten to death. If I wasn't lucky, some big ape would bugger me and then cut my nuts off!"

"Well," said Josh reasonably, "don't do it anymore."

"Where have you been, out in the kitchen? Didn't you hear me say I couldn't help myself? This isn't like cutting out cigarettes. This thing goes deep."

Josh looked thoughtful. "Do your father and sister know?"

"I don't think so. My mother knew, but I don't think she told anyone else. They might be suspicious. My sister even saw me once when we were kids, but we never talked about it. Really, I think my sister was more responsible for it than anyone else in the family, even my mother. I'm so incensed that I can hardly be civil to her. Thank god she got married and out of my hair." Josh's eyes narrowed. I didn't like the look on his face. "If you've got any idea of telling them, forget it. You'll never see me again if you do." He looked thoughtful. I figured he felt that somehow it would do me some good if my family slapped my wrists. After a moment, he stood up.

"Excuse me," he said and left the room. I thought maybe he was going to a pay phone to call my father. He walked right to the door of the apartment and went out. I fidgeted about, worrying. For the duration of my visit, I had been speaking and acting as Dick.

I'm sure I must have struck some ludicrous poses as I paced, manlike, around the apartment or sat with my legs crossed. The more I sat there alone, the more uncomfortable and out of place I felt. I thought the best thing for me to do was make a quick exit while Josh was gone. Whatever he was up to, I had the feeling that it wasn't going to reflect a compassionate understanding. I had already had all of the Frick therapy that I thought I could take for one evening. I stood up, arranged myself, and stepped to a mirror on the wall for a quick makeup check. While I was standing there pursing my lips, Josh walked in followed by two people who lived next door. I whirled around like an escaped convict suddenly caught in the beam of a searchlight.

"I'd like to introduce you to my friend Dick Raskind—doctor, naval officer, tennis champion, woman." The couple, a young accountant and his wife, were noticeably jumpy. "Hi," they said in unison, both raising their hands in small waving motions. "Of course," Josh continued professorially, "there are some problems with that latter designation. Perhaps I should say, 'budding woman, incipient woman, future woman.' At present, we have only the suggestion of things to come, the dainty feet, for example. What are they, Dick, size twelve?" I wondered what kind of radar this man had that he so accurately struck my most sensitive points. I had reassumed my chastised child position with my head down and my fists clenched. "Never mind though, I'm sure there is some kind of foot reduction surgery available." The couple from the next apartment were edging toward the door. I could see their feet slowly backing out of my line of sight. "I don't know what we're going to do about those shoulders, though," Josh continued. "I guess we'll just have to take them off and give them to some wimp who wants to look like Burt Lancaster." I heard the door close and looked up. The strangers were gone.

"That was the meanest thing you've ever done to me, Josh."

"Look, Dick," he said, "I've decided that you're not going to get any sympathy from me on this thing. It strikes me as just plain silly. You're already a terrific man, so don't mess it up. What you got tonight is exactly what you'll get again if you come around here in those stupid clothes. Now, go home and take off that dress." He held the door open for me. As I passed through, he socked me hard on the arm.

In spite of Josh's intimidating reception, I found myself going

156

back to see him. Often I dressed as a woman, and true to his word he ragged me mercilessly. If there were other people there, he invited me in without warning either them or me. "Dick, Dick, come in. Frank, Harold, I'd like you to meet my dear friend Dr. Richard Raskind, but don't get any ideas, he's a nice girl. Anyone trying to take liberties will have to answer to me!" I put up with this treatment because at least it wasn't condescending. Josh treated me as if I was a normal person who had a bad habit like biting his nails. His treatment actually made me feel less abnormal, and it gave Renée someplace to head for when she started out. Though the atmosphere in Josh's apartment was not ideal, I was tolerated. Besides, my skin was getting thicker, and I thought these encounters might do me some good. Whatever course of action I took in the future I was bound to meet resistance. At least Josh was my friend.

But after that first night, I had been devastated; rejected, betrayed by a friend, I had staggered home with my head reeling. Strangers had seen me unmasked! However, although the most horrible thing had happened, I had survived. I'd gotten up the next morning, gone to the hospital, operated on patients, and come home without incident. Being unmasked hadn't been terminal at all. I figured if I could take that humiliation and continue to live a normal life the future might not be so barren after all. That's why I became a regular at Josh's apartment.

And Josh didn't just torment me; he made other attempts to cure me. His chief device was to get me girls. In high school Josh had not been a great social success; his aggressive personality made a lot of people avoid him. Frustration at not being accepted was probably at the root of his one-man stands at the top of the hill in front of the Horace Mann School. When he reached adulthood, Josh made up for lost time. He was tireless in his pursuit of women and probably asked twenty out every day. Every evening he would go out to walk his Doberman pinscher. That dog furnished the pretense for several propositions a week. He purposely walked it in a section of town frequented by professional models. When he had to restrain his dog to keep it from eating their poodles, this gave him the opportunity to introduce himself. Using the girls he met in this way as contacts, he insinuated his way into the world of high-fashion photography. Suddenly he was everywhere. Professionals would turn around, and there would be Josh looking over their shoulders. They would wrinkle their noses, shrug, and go on with their work. No one was sure by what right he was present, but his air of assurance was undeniable, so he was tolerated.

I don't know how exactly Josh sustained this, but I imagine it was similar in tone to the technique he used when he crashed an Elizabeth Taylor-Mike Todd party being held at Madison Square Garden in the mid-fifties. He was a medical student at the time and wore his whites to the rear entrance of the Garden. He also carried his black leather doctor's bag. Josh aggressively convinced the security guard that he was the physician for the evening. He expressed this so matter-of-factly that the security guard automatically assumed that all parties had attending physicians. After all, it *was* a Mike Todd production. Once inside Josh took his tuxedo out of the black bag and joined the party. By the end of the evening he had propositioned his twenty women.

These tactics made Josh the most successful bachelor in New York, if you count having lots of women as success. There was an endless parade of beautiful girls through Josh's apartment, and he directed many of them to me. He took heart when I occasionally escorted one of these babes home. He apparently took the position that I must not be getting enough ass and that lack was causing me to dress up like a woman. He couldn't understand that there wasn't a thing in the world wrong with Dick. Renée was the problem and remained so, regardless of how many women Dick took to bed. One of these women, though, did make a superficial difference when she moved in with me for a few months.

One evening Josh caught me looking interestedly at his current steady date, Heidi. She was exquisitely beautiful—in fact, she was perfect. Her hair was long and blonde; her skin had that healthy Scandinavian glow. The eyes were crystalline blue. She had a figure that featured many curves but was in no way sloppy. You could have hunted for hours and never found any untaut skin or oversoft flesh on that body. I was looking at her as a physical phenomenon as much as a sex object. She was like an exceptionally well-executed artwork; you want it even though it clashes with the decor in your apartment. Josh noted my appraising glances, and a few days later he showed up at my place with Heidi in tow. He came no further than the door of my apartment. Solemnly he put her hand in mine and said, "Happy Birthday, Dick." Before I could respond he exited, leaving me alone with the beautiful Heidi. I felt rather honored that Josh would part with this lovely creature for my benefit. Of course, the gesture itself was degrading, but it was the best Josh could do. I don't suppose it occurred to him that Heidi had anything to do with the deal. For him she was like a fishing rod, an expensive piece of equipment that good friends could share. I looked over at Heidi. She was standing there exuding a perfect aura, but, on closer inspection, there seemed to be something missing after all. Her expression was peculiarly ambivalent, especially considering that she had just been given by one man to another man.

"What do you think of this?" I asked.

"I don't mind," she said.

Soon Heidi was living with me; she was exactly what I needed at that point in my life. She turned out to be the personification of that old saying "Beauty is only skin deep." This is not to say that Heidi was ugly underneath. What was underneath her beauty had nothing to do with good or bad or judgments of any kind. She left those up to other people. Somewhere along the line Heidi had not understood that she was capable of making, indeed was *expected* to make, decisions. When the wind blew, Heidi set sail but with never a glance at the compass. I gathered that she felt it was in the order of things that she be given to me as a birthday gift. It also never occurred to her to wonder why we never fucked. We slept together naked, we caressed each other; sometimes I idly played with her breasts, but that was as far as our sexuality went. You would think that this would have given her pause since every other man she met was wild to get into her pants. Heidi, however, was not one to make comparisons. She had a warm place to stay and someone to pay her bills. In addition to this she had her income as a call girl.

This was something I frowned upon, and when she moved in with me I made her promise not to do it anymore. Actually her clientele was limited to a small circle of people whom she casually serviced on a regular basis. Though she promised me that she'd give it up, I think she probably sneaked out to do it anyway. Heidi was just a girl who couldn't say "No." I used to sit her down and tell her, "Heidi, it is wrong for you to take a hundred dollars for servicing Jack Hightower." For one thing, though a multimillion-aire, Jack Hightower was eighty-one-years old and it took two hours for him to climax. A hundred dollars wasn't enough. Such lightheartedness was lost on Heidi. The most I could expect was that next time she might ask for more money.

Heidi was immune to philosophical arguments about the dignity of the individual. In fact, I'm not sure she knew what the word "dignity" meant. I'm not being ironic. She was a high-school dropout and didn't see much point in knowing too many words. Though she looked like a queen, when she opened her mouth to speak people were absolutely stunned. Her voice was pleasant, but her comments were often inappropriate. Once she came in unexpectedly and found me sitting in the living room dressed as a woman. This was the first time she knew of my problem. "What are you doing sitting there in that green dress?" she asked. Her intonations put the emphasis on "green" as if the situation would have been vastly different had I been wearing a blue dress instead.

It was a measure of my neuroticism in those times that I actually held out some hope that this relationship might blossom into a love affair that would save me. I even considered marrying Heidi. I took her home to dinner with my father once and watched his initial delighted expression turn during the course of the evening into one of disbelief. He directed comment after comment at her, only to be answered with a nod or shake of the head. During the whole evening she said no more than twenty words, but they were enough. As Heidi and I left the house, my father shot me a private look, arching his eyebrows imploringly: "Have I missed something?" was the question those eyebrows asked.

When I brought up to Dr. Bak the possibility of a marriage with Heidi he was flabbergasted. "A nice Jewish boy from Queens does not step under the *chupah* with a cunt-lapping lesbian whore," he yelled with finality. I had let it out in one of my earlier sessions that Heidi seemed to have a taste for women as well as men. Of course, Dr. Bak was right. Any sane person could have seen that Heidi and I were together for all the wrong reasons. As crazed as I was this eventually became clear to me, and I made the decision for both of us. Heidi packed up and blew out into the world once more.

As silly as the affair with Heidi had been, it depressed me that it was over. At least, she had been a warm body to come home to. Though our relationship was essentially sexless, it had been cozy and undemanding. While we were together I seldom dressed as

Renée. Heidi provided a mellow interlude in an otherwise desolate part of my life. After she left I began to be surer that the only
cure for my problem was surgical.

I had repeatedly seen articles about Dr. Harry Benjamin, the
man who coined the word "transsexual." He had treated Christine Jorgensen and was continuing his work with an ever more
vocal group of sexually misplaced persons. Many like me had
been through years of ineffective psychoanalysis. When I suggested that I might have a talk with Dr. Benjamin, Dr. Bak
exploded. "Quack!" he thundered. Rising up like a prophet of old,
he again repeated his warning. If I lost my penis I would lose my
sanity, at least what was left of it. Frankly, Dr. Bak had lost his
objectivity. I think he had held out special hopes for me; after all,
if I were cured I would have been a wonderful subject for a book
that would further embellish the Bak legend. The analysis, which
had degenerated to directive therapy, was now moving into what
might be called brow-beating therapy. Dr. Bak's own emotions were clearly evident in our sessions, as you may have noted
from his response to the idea of a marriage with Heidi. "Cunt-
lapping lesbian whore" is not a phrase commonly used by psychiatrists in describing their patients' girlfriends. No, Dr. Bak was
just as much at sea as I was, only he couldn't afford to admit it. I
began threatening to quit analysis; I must have made the threat
fifty times before I finally managed to do it.

Terminating an analytic relationship is rough for the same
reason that being late for a session is rough. The analyst treats it
as evidence that you are trying to avoid uncomfortable material.
If the patient says, "This is doing me no good," the analyst perversely informs him that the opposite is the case: the worse the
patient feels, the closer the analyst is to uncovering valuable
repressed data. A patient is apparently supposed to be encouraged by the fact that he never wants to see his analyst again. On
the other hand, analysts are also suspicious if you are too positive
about therapy. They reason that this is probably an attempt to
gloss over the as-yet-unrecognized core of the patient's problem;
either way you go their answer is always more therapy. Dr. Bak's
objections were increased by his realization that when I stopped
seeing him I would start seeing Dr. Benjamin, whom he regarded
as a scalpel-happy charlatan. For weeks our sessions were
devoted solely to the subject of why I should continue. There was

161

no therapy, only a bitter struggle of wills. Finally, as I sat one day in the waiting room looking at Freud, I realized that there was no fight left in me—there was no reason to fight. I went in to my session calmly. As I left the familiar little room I glanced one last time at Freud. His expression had not changed; he still looked like he knew more than he should. We had a quiet session that day. Probably Dr. Bak was encouraged. At the end of the hour I said, "Today is the last one." "Yes, yes," he answered absently. He had heard it before. I left, never to enter his office again.

Having abandoned the faint hope for Dick that analysis had kept alive, I moved quickly to contact Dr. Benjamin. Amazingly, my first appointment was set for less than a week after my first call to his office. I guessed that the transsexual business was not as brisk as certain newspaper articles had led me to believe; this impression proved to be inaccurate. When I first stepped into Dr. Benjamin's waiting room I went through a severe culture shock. I expected something like Dr. Bak's waiting room, a small space where one sat alone and waited to see the great man. After all, Dr. Benjamin also dealt with deep-seated human problems. This was not a clinic where he treated athlete's foot or lanced boils. It was devoted to fundamental changes in nature's plan.

Some held that men like Dr. Benjamin were devils incarnate, still striving to wield the power of God himself and, unable to do so, satisfying themselves by sacrilegiously altering the precious products of His divine creation. I had expected a little more pomp to be associated with the process. What I found at his little office on East Sixty-Second Street was more like a surrealistic Italian movie.

The first person I laid eyes on was a black man about six-feet six-inches tall wearing sandals and a miniskirt. He was standing in the corner by the water cooler fussing through a patent leather purse. A shoulder length blonde acrylic-fiber wig vibrated stiffly as he shook his head in frustration. His numerous bracelets tinkled in counterpoint as his hand darted around in the pocketbook. Finally, he brought out a bright yellow compact, opened it, and peered intensely into the mirror. His brows knitted together in an obvious display of concern. Out of the purse came a lipstick; he unscrewed the top, revealing a violent red color that he applied vigorously to his lips. Following this he pushed a few strands of acrylic into place and snapped the compact closed; replacing it

162

and the lipstick in the patent leather bag, he turned to face the room at large.

I had been standing half through the doorway and half outside. Caught off guard by the sight of this dark apparition I had sort of frozen, but I quickly found a seat near the door. I surveyed the room and found it full of creatures who were neither fish nor fowl. There were women who were dressed as men and men who were dressed as women. There were also some women who looked like women but only one man dressed as a man—me. A lot of them looked as if they had lost their senses. For example, what did that black giant with the fiber wig think he was up to? Six-feet six was out of the question! *I* was six-feet one and considered that just barely acceptable. Of course, on reflection, I figured that he probably felt that six-feet six was just *barely* acceptable, too. Did I detect a touch of envy in his eyes when he looked at me? Probably he was wishing that he was as short as I was. At any rate, he ought to have been ruled out on the grounds of bad taste. That miniskirt was terrible!

My attention was drawn to a rhythmic motion in the next chair; I looked to the right and saw a young man in a button-down shirt scratching his rather prominent breasts. He kept running his hands over them in an unvarying pattern. He devoted one hand to each breast. First, the right hand would circle the right breast going counterclockwise. Simultaneously, the left would be moving clockwise around the left breast. Periodically, he would reverse directions. I watched this ritual for several long moments; noticing my interest, he looked up.

"Man, these things are killing me," he said, referring to his breasts as if they were a pair of tight shoes.

"How long have you had 'em?" I asked.

"They've been growing for about five months. Pretty big, huh?"

I guess there was a note of pride in his voice. My eyes kept snapping down to where his hands were going around and around. "I don't know how much more they'll grow," he continued, "but I sure wish they'd stop itching. I'm going crazy with it." He reversed direction. "That's why I'm here, to see if they're supposed to itch. I wake up in the morning, and I've scratched myself raw!"

"Too bad," I said, tearing my eyes away. Across the room I could see the black guy staring intently at my new friend with the itchy tits. His skirt had ridden up so high that his pink panties were in public view.

I began to think that maybe Dr. Bak was right. What was a nice Jewish boy from Queens doing in this room full of half-baked creatures? Benjamin's waiting room was a far cry from the lyrical environment of the Hotel de la Paix, with its winsome and adventurous clientele. Those girls had seemed like, well, like girls. What we had here looked like a series of plans that had gone astray. Worse yet, a lot of them looked like they had been bad plans to begin with. Still, there *were* the women who looked like women. They were tidy jobs if they were really transsexuals and not just interested parties. A couple of them were even tall. I took heart when one good-looking specimen was called into the examination room. This proved that France did not have a complete monopoly on successful conversions. I later found out that all the women in the room were transsexuals—all men who became women. I thought some might be there to go the other way, but that was not the case. To this day I have not met a female-to-male transsexual.

At length I was called in and met Dr. Benjamin himself. The only figure in my life with whom I could reasonably compare him was Dr. Bak; and, at first glance, Dr. Benjamin suffered when I did so. He was a busy little gnome of a man: bald, elderly, and bespectacled. He spoke with a slight accent, the remnant of his early days in Tübingen, Germany, where he had grown up and gone to medical school. Whereas Dr. Bak had intimidated me from the start, Dr. Benjamin seemed a likable fussbudget, very much in the tradition of the Old World general practitioner. He impressed me as kindly and decent but hardly one to inspire unreserved confidence. As he listened to me reviewing my history, he tilted his head first one way and then another, sometimes nodding agreeably. Occasionally, when I would grope for words, he would supply them so casually that I didn't notice at first. Then I began to realize that this old man really did understand, so much so that he could probably have told the story without my help. The childish exploits, the futile years of psychotherapy, the driving compulsion, the skulking around—all these constituted a familiar refrain that accompanied his daily work. He listened intelligently, and he understood almost as well as I did. I began to gain respect for this little man. When we finished with my history, he suddenly took on a different tone.

"I understand the trouble you've had," he said, "but you know this operation isn't going to solve all your problems. Not only that, it will create some new ones. People may not want to have their eyes worked on by a woman who used to be a man. I don't know of a single transsexual doctor. This is a new area. There will be many hardships."

"I'm ready for that," I said confidently.

Dr. Benjamin rummaged in his desk drawer for a minute and withdrew two eight by ten photographs. Dramatically, he thrust them in front of my face. "Do you want to look like that?" he asked abruptly. The photographs showed two old men, nude to the waist. They had some breast tissue, but they also had facial hair; their skin was slack and unhealthy looking. Apparently they were failures of some sort, doomed to live their lives as freaks. They were horrible. I recoiled, and somewhat shaken looked back to Dr. Benjamin, who wore a stern yet inquisitive expression.

"I can't believe I'll wind up like them," I said.

Dr. Benjamin's face softened. He seemed to know that what I really meant was that I would do everything I could to keep that from happening to me. But even if there was a chance that I'd wind up a freak, I'd take it. This was the kind of commitment he required. Even Dr. Benjamin agreed that transsexual surgery was a last-ditch measure. Anybody who could be scared off by ugly photographs had no business on the operating table. He put the pictures away and started a physical examination. As he went through the familiar routine, he commented on my body in the light of what would be done to it. He agreed with the cosmetologist who had made me up for the imaginary masquerade party; "Good skin," he said. In general, he reinforced what Bambi had told me in Paris, that I had a plastic enough body to adapt to the transformation. The accepted term is "somatic compliance." This refers simply to whether or not an individual can be made into a socially acceptable woman. From a strictly technical point of view, any stevedore, no matter how heavily boned, hairy or huge, can be turned into a woman. The question is: How are the other patrons going to react when she walks into Sardi's? As he spoke, I kept thinking about the tall man in the miniskirt waiting in the outer room. Would he be turned down I wondered, or was he too considered somatically compliant? I quickly realized that this kind of thinking was counterproductive; I should not compare myself with others. I was going to be Renée, and she would be tall and damned elegant!

During my first meeting with Dr. Benjamin he referred me to a laboratory at New York University where I provided blood and urine samples for a huge battery of tests to assess my hormonal level and the general state of my body chemistry. I was also required by Dr. Benjamin to meet with a colleague of his, Dr. Wardell Pomeroy. He is famous for having coauthored, with Dr. Alfred Kinsey *Sexual Behavior in the Human Male.* His job was to assess the personalities of candidates for transsexual surgery and make recommendations with regard to their fitness. At the time there were no gender identity clinics such as now exist in the major American university hospitals. The field of transsexualism was in its infancy, and Dr. Pomeroy was the best resource available for psychological screening, though he, too, was learning by doing. I met with him several times and took a number of tests. Looking back, it's easy to see how his inexperience showed. He was very understanding about my compulsion but, at the same time, suspicious of my heterosexuality. According to test results, on a scale of zero to ten my heterosexuality was nine and a half. He said that he would be much more comfortable recommending the surgery if I had been active as a homosexual. Of course, he had been interviewing Dick who had always loved women. Renée had never had a legitimate shot at romance. Experience would soon demonstrate to Dr. Pomeroy that many transsexuals were like me, with little or no homosexual experience. Shaking his head ruefully as he looked over my record of nine years in analysis, he had to admit that I had given conventional treatment a very generous opportunity. Since my compulsion was not only intact but growing stronger, he agreed to authorize the first stage of the transsexual process, a course of female hormones. He suggested that since this treatment was reversible, up to a point, we could observe how I responded and make further decisions based on that. If all went well the next step would be to live for a year as a woman prior to surgery.

In all, about two weeks elapsed between my first visit to Dr. Benjamin and the day he gave me my initial shot of female hormones. On the second occasion I was ushered immediately into an examining room, and I never had to wait again. This is one of the rewards of being a physician yourself: colleagues take you ahead of everyone else. About the shot, I was quite calm. I had been very nervous during my first visit but had spent the two intervening weeks preparing myself for the first step in the transformation. I could also take comfort from the fact that it would be quite a while before anything took place that would make the entire process irreversible. Meanwhile, I could explore the sensation of growing femininity and see if it brought the expected satisfaction. I had the feeling of being a longtime traveler about to set foot on the ship that would carry me home.

Whatever high-minded images I may have had in my mind, Dr. Benjamin did not cater to them. There was no pomp in his manner; he simply had me drop my pants, whereupon he poked a needle into my butt. That was the end of the great moment. I was to take hormone pills every day and to return every two weeks for additional shots. Dr. Benjamin shook my hand and sent me home.

As part of my orientation I had been referred to a circle of transsexuals that met weekly in Brooklyn Heights for a kind of group therapy. It was run by Art Stallings, the same man who produced *Turnabout*, the transsexual magazine that I had secretively bought so many times. The idea was that these lonely people could take some comfort from congregating with others who were similarly inclined.

If ever there was a case of misery loving company, this group exemplified it. They could hardly be blamed for their melancholy dispositions; their lives had been guilt ridden and secretive. Personalities developed under those circumstances do not tend to be upbeat. Their interactions hardly constituted warm support for one another. Still, this suspicious and withdrawn group was the best the world of American transsexualism had to offer. Often, strangers would show up, sit in the shadows, and then leave— never to be seen again. Others would stay a few weeks before disappearing. The regulars of the group were in all stages of therapy and exhibited a wide range of styles, but basically they fell into two categories: those who were dressing as women too soon and those who were waiting too long. Among the latter was a person who used to show up in a business suit every week; he did this in spite of the fact that he had big tits and a woman's ass. He also smoked a pipe; imagine Bella Abzug in a gray pinstripe puffing on a Doctor Grabow. In the category of those who dressed too soon was an individual whom I got to know fairly well. Her name was Johnnie Taylor. I say "her" because, though there was nothing feminine about her presentation, Johnnie insisted upon wearing women's clothes. We talked quite a bit because our educational backgrounds were similar—she was a physicist, a fellow scientist. Johnnie was a husband and had a couple of kids but preferred the idea of being a woman. Unfortunately, she made a poor one: her teeth were bad, and her skin was heavily pitted. Worse than those factors was Johnnie's generally unfeminine effect. Her gestures, walk, carriage, and voice were all masculine. She looked less convincing than Milton Berle in drag. Even hormone therapy didn't seem to be helping; Johnnie just didn't have any feel for femininity. She sat, a glum presence in an already glum group, and said little. She opened up to me a bit, and I soon decided that she was not a true transsexual but a paranoid schizophrenic attempting to escape into the world of womanhood. If this sounds presumptuous, remember that I had been through nine years of psychoanalysis. In that amount of time you pick up a few hints. Eventually, Johnnie went to Casablanca and had surgery. When she came back she still wasn't happy. I met her by chance a year or so later; she complained bitterly that she was nothing, neither a man nor a woman. A couple of weeks later she killed herself.

You can understand why I spent only a few months in this group. If I hadn't seen the French transsexuals in Paris I might have been dissuaded by my experiences with this downbeat assembly, but I had my memories of the lighthearted atmosphere at the Hotel de la Paix. Those girls looked forward with joy; they were convinced that they would live fulfilling lives. As a matter of fact, one of them had already been engaged to a medical student, an event that had made me envious at the time but which now buoyed my spirits. The attitude of the Brooklyn Heights group was a direct reflection of the attitude of American society toward them: insecure, frightened, and confused.

My weekly visits with these people provided me with a realistic perspective on my fellow transsexuals and the problems they faced. This was valuable to me because I had a tendency to get euphoric once the hormones began to take hold. I felt no particular sensation immediately after I received my first shot, nothing except an irritating ache in my butt. Aside from the satisfaction of having started on a course of treatment that might give me some relief from my anxieties, I felt exactly the same as before. I was strangely calm and went about my daily activities in the usual way. In the mornings I would drive out to the naval hospital, and in the evenings I would come back into the city and relax or maybe see friends. The only thing missing was the visit to Dr. Bak. With no deadline to meet I could be a little more leisurely on the drive home from work. I took my pills in the morning and pretty much forgot about the process after that; this went on for approximately five days. On about the sixth day I began to feel a subtle difference in myself. What it was is difficult to explain. Imagine that you are attending a party with really good friends, people that you care for and normally feel good with. You sit down and begin to talk amiably; someone hands you a glass of fruit punch mildly spiked with vodka. As you talk you sip the drink, never giving it a second thought. Thirty minutes later you find yourself thoroughly relaxed, laughing, animated beyond the norm, and overcome with feelings of warmth toward your wonderful companions. You are feeling so good that it suddenly thrusts itself on you because it contrasts so markedly with how you ordinarily feel. You ask yourself, "What did they put in this drink?"

Essentially, that was what my experience was like. It was as if someone had slipped me a mood-elevating drug. The world seemed less antagonistic, more supportive; I had a sense of lightness as I moved through it. Dick had always been a presence of great density; many people found him aloof, superior. The burgeoning Renée found herself less inclined to isolation, more interested in the people around her. I suddenly began to feel more personally about people who had heretofore been defined primarily by my formal relations with them. So-and-so was my nurse. So-and-so was my anesthesiologist. My efforts in their behalf (and often I bent over backward) were in the line of duty. I went to the captain's mast to speak up for my corpsmen, not out of humanitarian feeling but because it was my duty; it was dictated by an abstract code of fair play. They did for me, and in return I did for them. It was all very civilized but, at the same time, distant. As

169

treatment progressed, I found myself more and more interested in personal details. In some instances my friendships began to alter. One doctor and his wife who had been longtime associates of mine noticed a peculiar shift in my orientation. For most of our relationship I had treated the wife as a tolerable but fairly uninteresting part of the duo. Her conversation centered primarily around the kids and the intricacies of homemaking. I preferred to discuss medicine and tennis strategies with her husband rather than commiserate with her over her son's inability to master a two-wheeled bike. Slowly though, I began to find myself more able to be concerned with the homey details of housewifery. If the husband left the room to go to the bathroom, on his return he might find me gone. Looked for, I could be found in the kitchen watching his wife do the dishes and savoring her chatty résumé of the day's events. I know that they discussed this between themselves. She was impressed with how much more human I had become. He thought maybe I was planning a seduction. Years later they finally understood.

Such misunderstandings were possible because I told no one about my therapy. I had to be on guard. The personality changes, though noticeable, were fairly easy for me to keep within acceptable bounds, though I did begin having what might be called uncontrollable lapses. These centered around two seemingly opposite activities: laughing and crying. I began to be frequently amused all out of proportion to the stimulus. Someone might make a remark that would elicit chuckles from everyone in the group. After they had stopped chuckling, I would continue—all the while escalating. People would wait politely for me to finish, and this would feed my amusement. The sight of them all looking at me inquisitively would strike me as hilarious. Soon the person who made the joke in the first place would be saying, "Oh, come on, Dick. It wasn't that funny!" That, too, was funny. These fits could go on for ten or fifteen minutes, their intensity rising and falling until finally they subsided as I grew exhausted. People quickly observed that the fastest way to get by these laughing episodes was to ignore them.

I also began to have crying jags. More often than not these were private, though I did break down in public sometimes. Ordinarily they would be provoked by a movie, a line of poetry, a news report, or even a casual remark that somehow carried a tragic or pathetic overtone. Imagine my surprise when I burst into tears for the first time in a motion picture theater. Dick Raskind had not cried in public since he was a child. There I was, weeping uncontrollably, smack in the middle of a group of one hundred and fifty movie fans. Heads were turning all over the auditorium. Although I tried to keep it down to a quiet sniffle, it soon scaled up into a series of breathless sobs. Finally, treating myself like an uncontrollable child in a public place, I left.

The strangest thing was that I did not feel at all regretful about these episodes; I only wished they were not an inconvenience to others. As a matter of fact, I really felt good after fifteen or twenty minutes of crying in the privacy of my apartment. I had the sensation of being purged. It was as if the control and repression of a lifetime were finally breaking down. Afterward, that lovely feeling of lightness would be doubly noticeable. I think people who witnessed these incidents thought that I must be under some severe emotional stress, and so they were generally kind and indulgent. I experienced these adjustment problems for about the first two months of my hormone therapy, then my personality leveled out and became more stable though I retained much of my newly discovered emotionality.

The physical changes were harder to explain away. It was about five weeks before I noticed any. You might think that I would be getting up each morning and racing to the mirror to check myself, but I was surprisingly blasé about the progress of my transformation. I found it hard to be clinical. I did not, for example, keep track of my measurements so that I could have a record of where I gained and lost inches. Probably the first thing I noticed was an increase in the sensitivity of my nipples. They had never been a major erogenous zone for me, and I had never given them much thought except to wish that they were more like a woman's. Suddenly they were calling themselves to my attention. My shirt would begin to chafe the newly tender tips, and I would absently reach down and pull the material out so that it no longer touched the nipple. About the fifth time I did this the truth flashed on me. I remembered the itchy young man in Dr. Benjamin's waiting room. A slight twinge of fear invaded me; was this the beginning of some unanticipated oddness that I would have to endure? On closer inspection the problem proved to be simple tenderness; and, really, that was not a problem but part of the solution. Now I would know firsthand what all the hoopla over women's nipples was really all about. In private moments I began to manipulate them experimentally. With practice, the sensation passed from slightly irritating to distinctly erotic. My experience in playing with women's breasts helped me here; I concluded that I had a good touch. The end of the nipple shaft was really a hot spot and seemed to be directly connected to my genital area. I experienced some very pleasurable, though not intense, sensations in my penis and in the area of my groin. You might call them tinglings or little pings of response; and with them came a vague sensation of the neurological connection between the two erogenous zones. I could almost feel it like a thread stretched tightly between nipple and groin. As time went on my nipples became enlarged. The boundary of the areola crept outward, and the shaft thickened to a diameter equal to the tip of my little finger. In general my breasts began to plump out. It was a great pleasure to me to feel that softness and realize that it was a very definite reflection of my growing womanhood. I had to start wearing loose clothes to disguise these new curves.

At about the same time I started noticing the tenderness in my nipples, I also began to see a change in the texture of my skin. One day I was looking in the mirror, and I thought idly, "Boy, my mother really gave me good skin. Everybody comments on it and I can see why." Then I looked more closely as I once again densely made the connection between the hormones and what I was seeing in the mirror. The grain of my skin had tightened up to an impressive degree; little flaws that had been there before were gone. Slight wrinkles and enlarged pores were a thing of the past. I ran my hand experimentally over my forehead and then my cheekbones. They were like glass. In addition, I thought I could feel a change in the tone of the muscles just beneath the skin; they seemed to be softer now. As time passed this became more pronounced, and the shape of my face changed as a result. The firm angularity of my jaw line softened, and the general shape of my face became more rounded. My already high and prominent cheekbones became more accentuated because the muscles in my cheeks smoothed out, leaving less mass to mask them. This trend extended to the rest of the muscles in my body as well. Soon I was able to wear sleeveless dresses without worrying about my muscular arms embarrassing me. The definition between bicep, deltoid, and tricep disappeared. Certain veins, forced into prominence by muscular development, receded into the contours of my arms. The muscles themselves elongated, and that gave me a smoother silhouette. My legs became less knotty as well. My behind, however, increased in size due to the fatty deposits that had begun to form there. Though most women dislike the idea of fat being linked to their asses, these deposits were a source of great satisfaction to me. They rounded me out and, along with my breasts, moved me closer to the feminine ideal.

Soon I felt a difference in my hair as I combed it. The individual shafts were smaller in diameter, resulting in a finer consistency. Luckily, I had abandoned my crew cut for a longer style; the new hair was not stiff enough to stand up properly. Other hair on my body grew finer as well as more sparse. I had never had a lot of hair on my legs anyway, but the fineness and the thinning caused by the hormones made it hardly noticeable. Most dramatic was a change in the pattern of my pubic hair. Males have a sort of inverted triangle of hair with the point running up toward the navel. Even for a man as unhairy as I had been, I had had a trail of hair shooting upward from the main thatch around my genitals. This fell out, leaving me with a neatly defined triangle, point down, very feminine in appearance.

Of course, nestled in the midst of my newly redefined bush were my male genitalia. As the treatment progressed they too began to change. For one thing, they got smaller in every way. Both the diameter and length of my penis diminished. Like all the other changes this was a gradual process. At the end of six months of treatment my penis was about two-thirds the size it had been at the start. My testicles atrophied even more dramatically. Before hormones they were about the size of robin's eggs, but they gradually shrank to the diameter of marbles. Their consistency was altered too. Rather than the tough resiliency that characterizes normal testicles, mine developed a doughy quality. They would slowly spring back to their original shape when squeezed, but they were far more malleable than they had been previously. This change was not accompanied by a lessening of sensitivity; if someone had kicked me in the balls, I would have felt the same excruciating pain as before. I also retained the sensitivity in my penis. Regardless of how small it got, I could still be excited to erection. The major change in that regard was that the erections had lost their rod-like stiffness. They were rubbery, and even at the height of excitement my penis could be bent pretty much into a right angle. I remember standing in the bedroom looking down at my penis which, as an experiment, I had bent radically over to the left. It looked so strange and unnatural that I was half amazed at how calm I was. The fact is that I had not one regret with regard to the little fellow's predicament.

Yet, the therapy was not all bad for my male parts. At least I felt less aggressive toward them. I found myself less inclined to the vicious measures I had previously used to hide my masculinity. For one thing, now that they were smaller I could tape them down with less trouble. My testicles were easily shoved up into my torso, and the smaller and more pliant penis molded itself cooperatively to the contours of my body. A few strips of adhesive tape quite easily held in check the remnants of my once average-sized organs. And I felt far less inclined to take such measures. Most of the time I was satisfied with a simple panty girdle. This garment pressed my genitals so flat that there was hardly a bulge between my legs. Renée could afford to be tolerant for the time being since she was getting her way.

Another important change that occurred during this time was in the sensation of orgasm—specifically my ejaculation. Though my erections were bendable and my testicles shrunk to a tiny size, I could still come. For awhile it was the same as ever. I had always had satisfying climaxes; when comparing notes with my friends I had verified that mine were at least as intense as the normal man's. About three months into the treatment I noticed a slight change. Like the others it came on subtly. The buildup to the orgasm remained the same, but, at the moment of climax, the discharge seemed to lack strength. I climbed toward the usual burst of sensation in my groin, and somehow that release was dribbled away. It was the difference between a dam suddenly collapsing under great pressure and that pressure being relieved by opening the gates to let the water rush out in an orderly fashion. As I became more feminized, the gates were opened ever more slowly and ever less wide. Eventually I began to experience not only an unsatisfyingly weak discharge but an actual discomfort. As the fluid exited, whatever blockage that may have existed seemed to cause an irritating sensation, as if I were pumping out not mucous material but dryer more granular stuff. Naturally, I checked the consistency and found it normal in appearance. As I rubbed it between my fingers, I could perceive no difference in texture either. Apparently the seminal fluid had not changed, but the internal mechanism was definitely deteriorating.

This climactic development was of small concern to me because I was having very little sex in those days even though I had a steady girl friend who stayed with me far into the treatment. Needless to say Patty was an understanding soul, far too understanding for her own good; maybe "optimistic" is a better word. She hoped, even as my breasts grew equal to hers, that somehow everything would turn out right. She thought maybe I'd get tired of being a woman and her love would make me a whole man again.

This kind of devotion in the face of my bizarre situation has been characteristic of many women in my life. You might think that they would have taken one look at my peculiarities, thrown up their hands, and beat a hasty retreat. The pattern was more often to take one look and throw *open* their arms to embrace me. No matter how funny looking or unsatisfying as a lover I might have been, there have always been women, mostly beautiful, mostly intelligent, who were willing to waste their time dreaming the impossible dream. At my worst, I indulged their fantasies and even kidded myself that something might come of the relationship; miracles have been known to happen. At my best, I would explain the situation rationally and paint an appropriately bleak picture. It never seemed to make any difference whether I was at my worst or my best. A lot of them were willing to hang in there against all good sense.

One of the contributing factors was that I have always liked women. Through the years I've been fascinated by them and willing to focus intense interest on them. This has always included spending time listening to them talk, watching them move, noting their taste in clothes, and so on. I think they appreciate this in a man and are drawn to it even if the basis is a sisterly rather than a masculine impulse. They probably think to themselves, "What a lovely man! He has such a good feeling for my needs. We'd be perfect if I could just dispel his silly notion of being a woman." So, they would stay around, sometimes for long periods of time, doing their best to make me see the light.

Patty even accompanied me to a symposium on transsexualism

175

presided over by Dr. Benjamin. It was the first such event he had ever held, and I was the only transsexual in attendance. The reason I was there was that I was a physician as well as a patient. The purpose of the symposium was to increase the medical community's awareness of transsexuality. Patty was there as my guest and to her surprise became the focus of attention during one of the sessions. Dr. Benjamin, coffee cup in hand, turned to her and said, "Young lady, if you expect someday to marry this person next to you," he motioned in my direction, "and if you are looking for this person to father your children, you are looking in the wrong place." Both Patty and I were flabbergasted; our mouths dropped open in unison. Never before (or after) this event had Dr. Benjamin departed so radically from his kindly and professorial approach. I think he must have watched Patty's loving glances and the familiar way she touched me and decided that she was setting herself up for a needless heartbreak. Then again he might have been a little peeved at me for permitting such intimacy under what he considered false pretenses.

Patty and I regained our composure and finished the day's activities without further embarrassment. That night she insisted that we make love. I knew that this would more than likely add insult to injury, but I wanted to oblige. I even liked the idea because I really did love Patty. It was a peculiar kind of half male, half female affection, but it was genuine. I could still be excited by her, and as I began to kiss her and caress her breasts I felt a surge of passion. My attitude was androgynous. In addition to my male impulses I felt a feminine sensation as well, possibly similar to the responses of a lesbian; however, I could never tell Patty this. The ironic thing was that she was pushing me to an orgasm that had lost its appeal. It was actually hard to bear. Like all others, Patty finally left me.

All of the effects of the treatment that I have mentioned so far were reversible, at least in theory. I had the luxury of thinking of them as an experiment that, if it went wrong in some unforeseen way, could be called off without permanent scars. Only one thing that I undertook during this period was utterly permanent—electrolysis. Female hormones do some marvelous and radical things. They make you grow breasts, they shrink your testicles, they change the outline of your body, and they'll even stop you from going bald—but they won't eliminate your beard. That is why electrolysis looms so large in a transsexual's life. Nothing proclaims manhood so publicly as a beard. You can hide your torso under a voluminous dress, your pate under a luxuriant wig but for your chin there is nothing except disgusting layers of pasty pancake makeup. No matter how expertly done it always looks suspicious. Even if you start out having shaved very closely and with your makeup looking pretty good, a beard's growth is unremitting and incredibly fast. If you go out at seven o'clock, by midnight you've got a shadow. Probably only the genitals themselves are more irritating to transsexuals than their beards. This is why so many, even though they may not take hormones for some reason, have an electrologist remove their beards. Though most people know that electrolysis exists, few know what a painful, tedious, and time-consuming process it is. I went three or four times per week for sessions lasting an hour or more. This routine continued for over three years. There are as many as one thousand hairs per square inch in the average beard; an electrologist may remove as few as twenty per minute. You figure it out.

My first electrologist was a little old lady who was also an astrologer. She was a motherly type and very nice to me. She claimed that my transsexualism was clearly indicated in my horoscope. During our sessions she would drone on like a barber with a familiar customer. I liked her and confided a lot about myself, but I didn't pay much attention to what she said while she worked. For one thing I was in pain. I would lie there, and Mrs. Grady would isolate a hair follicle and examine it to make sure of the direction in which it grew. This is important because the needle has to be inserted exactly along the shaft of the hair and at precisely the proper depth. Once this has been done a current of electricity is run through the needle, killing the hair follicle by burning it. If the needle is too shallowly positioned, the hair lives on; too deep and it burns a hole in your face. A bad electrologist can leave you with a face the texture of coarse sandpaper. Once the hair had been killed, if I was lucky it didn't grow back. Sometimes it did, and it was not always her fault. Often, because facial hair is layered, there is a dormant follicle below the active one. When the topmost root is killed the one underneath begins to produce, and you've got a brand-new hair. When this happened Mrs. Grady would have to go in a second time.

The tedium and pain of electrolysis can only be compared to that suffered in a dentist's chair, except that at the dentist you can have real painkiller. Electrologists cannot administer drugs, so you have to make your own arrangements. Many of my friends took codeine. Although I had access to stronger drugs because I was a physician, I made do with aspirin since I've always been leery of drugs except in extreme need. Besides, since I went so often, I could have become addicted.

Most people can stand the pain for only fifteen minutes or so. Not only is it excruciating but you have to lie very still while that needle pierces your flesh. If you wiggle you are liable to wind up with a little volcano on your face. To lie still while you hurt takes a lot of energy. I used to do it for an hour at a time, sometimes two hours. The worst areas were the neck and around the nostrils and ears. Mrs. Grady would have to stop periodically and wipe the tears off my cheeks. The next day I'd report to the hospital with a vivid rash on my face where she had worked. I'd tell those who inquired that I'd gotten it from shaving too close. As pleasant as Mrs. Grady was, I left her after a few months because our progress was slower than I thought appropriate. The new electrologist was not an astrologer, not motherly, and not chatty, but she was the best in the city. She worked fast and with precision. Not counting the times when I was away from New York I spent two years under her care. As a result of her efforts and my mother's gift of good skin, my face today is unblemished and smooth. Undoubtedly it's one of my best features and seldom fails to draw wistful comments from transsexuals who were not so lucky.

The first six months of my feminization coincided with my last six months in the navy. By the time I was discharged I was beginning to look a little odd in my uniform. My hips were pressing suggestively against my trousers, and my chest was suspiciously lumpy. This slightly peculiar body was crowned by a face that was much different from the Jack Armstrong good-looks of the previous year. I had had to cut back on my tennis playing in order to make time for my therapy. During the latter months especially, I was a peculiar sight in tennis outfits in which much of my body was on display. I still played a good game and, in fact, didn't notice much decrease in my general abilities though I was definitely less strong. After six months of hormone therapy I estimate that I had about four-fifths of my previous strength. Visually, my arms and legs had changed markedly, but my sense of my physical capabilities was less objective. The changes took place slowly over a long period of time, and such things as relative strength were hard to pinpoint.

I looked forward to my discharge from the navy so that I could begin living more regularly as a woman. I pictured myself in a little apartment, promoting my feminization and waiting for the time when I would have the surgery that would cap the process. Naturally, I'd have to move out of my present place and establish a new identity elsewhere in the city, but that too appealed to me. My close friends, who probably had some idea of what was going on though I hadn't told them, would carry over into my new life, but most of the trappings of Dick Raskind's existence would be laid to rest. This period of my life was one of tremendous optimism, but somewhere in the midst of my glowing fantasies must have nestled a hard kernel of doubt. Perhaps Dick, fighting for his existence and losing, played a final trump card.

No matter how it is explained, what I did sounds incredible. Of all the people in the world I could have told about my treatment, I picked my sister, Mike. Who knows what old business was boiling around in my unconscious, prompting such a self-destructive move? In fact, the whole incident is so emotionally charged that I must have repressed a great deal of it. I cannot remember the conversation. I assume it was on a visit to see her in New England, where she was on the staff of a university medical center. Maybe I thought that somehow she would be pleased since she had promoted my femininity when we were children. The fantasy we had lived together ("Now you're not a little boy anymore, you're a little girl!") was coming true in the real world. Maybe my attitude was more snide: "See what you've done to me?" I honestly don't remember. Whatever the reason I unburdened myself—and Mike did not approve. She spoke to me in rational terms though I don't recall her specific arguments. Certainly she cited my heterosexual past. She might also have thrown in a little psychoanalysis, since she was getting interested in that field. Naturally, I was immune to such persuasion after nine years on the couch. Maybe I felt more justified when I left her because I had faced these arguments and my resolve was undiminished.

When I arrived at Dr. Benjamin's office for my next shot, he was more courtly than ever. He asked me to sit down and then said, "Renée, I've decided to discontinue your treatments."

"What?"

"I know that this will come as a shock to you, but I have been reviewing your case, and I believe we should let the effects of the hormones subside, to see how you do as a man."

"Why?"

"I am concerned about your future. Personally, I don't think they will allow a transsexual to practice medicine. It has never been done before, and I think the American Medical Association or the licensing board or some other regulatory group will think you too unstable."

"I'll take that chance."

"Then there is the matter of your heterosexual background. This has always been a sore point with Dr. Pomeroy. He too feels that you should try again as a man. You may find that the experience of taking the hormones has made a difference in your male outlook. Perhaps you may carry enough femininity over into your life as a male to satisfy you."

"Being a woman will satisfy me."

"That may still come, but for now both Dr. Pomeroy and myself feel that a little vacation from therapy would be a very good thing."

"Did my sister have anything to do with this?"

"This is a decision arrived at by Dr. Pomeroy and myself. We are in agreement. How could a little vacation hurt? Don't you want to be absolutely sure?"

"Have you talked to my sister at all?"

"Well . . ." here Dr. Benjamin paused, "She did call to express her concern for you, and I think her fears are legitimate. After all, she has known you for a much longer time than I have, and she is a physician as well."

"Everybody I know is a physician. What difference does that make?"

"Well, she has had scientific training as well as close contact with you, so her opinions are doubly valuable."

"Did she threaten to raise a stink?"

"Please, Dick. Why make this so hard? It's just a safeguard, just a way of getting our bearings." His tone was so understanding and rational that I knew his mind was made up. There was really no appeal. He was the only man in America who could treat me, and he had decided, for whatever reason (I recalled Mike's titanic rages at home), not to help me any further. Still, I couldn't stand to leave without one last try.

180

"Dr. Benjamin. I love the changes I've gone through. I have no regrets. I want to continue. It would be so simple to continue. I promise you that you aren't making a mistake. Please! Please, let me go on."

"I'm sorry, Dick."

I picked up my purse and left. Months before I had started coming to the office dressed as a woman. Now, walking back through the waiting room I felt like an impostor. I no longer knew what I was. I could see Dr. Benjamin's point of view. Only a handful of transsexual operations had been done in this country. As long as they were obscure entertainers or quiet people from ordinary walks of life, the risks were few. On the other hand, eyebrows might be raised if a brilliant young doctor, perhaps suffering from mental derangement, were allowed to mutilate himself. If, moreover, that young doctor's sister, also a doctor, was to question it (as she surely would), such a case could make the national news and deal Dr. Benjamin's work a crippling blow. Certainly it was a failure of courage on his part but an understandable one.

Such an understanding did not help me deal with my sense of disorientation. I didn't even have the navy to give stability to my life since I had been discharged a couple of weeks earlier on July 5, 1965. For the first time in my life I had no orderly progression to follow. School was over, internship was over, specialization was over, the navy was over, analysis was over—and hormone therapy was over. I had nowhere to go; so I went home to Forest Hills and my room in my father's house. There I sat and did nothing. Days and then weeks went by. I rarely went farther than the backyard or occasionally to Flushing Meadow Park to walk the Airedale I had acquired as a puppy in the navy. He was now a boisterous young adult weighing about sixty pounds. Actually, Rocco was on the verge of becoming the most important creature in my life. No matter how understanding my friends and acquaintances had shown themselves to be, Rocco was the only one who had demonstrated no change in behavior when I began my metamorphosis. He liked me as a man and as a woman. He showed no surprise if he caught me in a dress, and he didn't inquire about my health when my appearance began to change under hormone treatments. It was enough for him that I had rescued him from the crate at the airport when he was just a puppy. He had been flown to New York from Cleveland where he was born into a litter with very distinguished parents. When I opened the crate I found him, about six weeks old, wearing a little green turtleneck sweater and huddling miserably against the slats in the back. I think he loved me so much because I took him out of that crate. He was a grateful dog all of his life and never gave a damn about the state of my physiology. During those weeks I spent at my father's house, Rocco seemed to be the only trustworthy friend I had.

My father, as usual, didn't speak directly to me about my state of mind. Instead he hovered around solicitously, making meals for me and occasionally suggesting a nice vacation. I was even less responsive to him than usual because I couldn't be sure he hadn't conspired with my sister in getting me kicked off the hormones. Naturally, we never discussed it, but I suspected that his solicitude might be born out of a guilty conscience. When we talked it was about superficial things.

I spent a lot of time in my room where so long ago I had furtively begun my career as a would-be woman. Now, as a strange, half-changed adult, I sat in that room too worn out to even put on a dress—without the drive to do more than read some medical journals and walk the dog. Of course, I thought about going to Europe and continuing my therapy there, but there was always the specter of surgery in Casablanca. The Brooklyn group of transsexuals had talked frequently of the mistakes that were sometimes made. One could wind up with a two-inch deep vagina, for example; or a vagina deep enough but with too flimsy a wall separating it from the rectum. Intercourse could burst such a wall, flooding the vagina with fecal matter. Such horror stories made American medical expertise seem essential even though the culture was less tolerant.

Eventually, after a month or two of sitting and staring I made my decision. Once again I turned to the structure offered by education. More than two years earlier, during my residency, I had been awarded the Head Fellowship. This is a stipend that allows a graduate of ophthalmological studies to spend a year anywhere in the United States learning from a distinguished professor. The award is considered a high honor and means that the recipient can have access to the latest techniques in his specialty from the very people who are innovating them. They were willing to pay me to step into the vanguard of my profession. As a resident, though, I had been facing two years in the navy; when I made this clear to those who administrated the fellowship, they told me to reapply when I got out. I had put it out of my mind but, almost on the day of my discharge, I got a letter inviting me to use the fellowship and informing me that no reapplication would be necessary. After considering my unsavory alternatives, I decided to become a student again and told them that I would start in September.

This choice was the beginning of my superspecialization. My area of interest was binocular vision, the study of how the two eyes work as a unit. I chose this specialty because the door seemed wide open. It is a complex field and poorly taught in most medical centers; consequently, the average ophthalmologist knows little about it. When I finished my residency I was as poorly grounded in this area (known as strabismus or ocular motility) as any of my colleagues, but I was intrigued by the vacuum—here one could be a pioneer. Another attractive thing about the field is that most problems in binocular sight occur in children. In general, I have found that children are better patients than adults. They are, if approached properly, more cheerful and less abusive than grownups; they are also loving and appreciative. I'd always had a good rapport with children; so the fact that I'd be dealing with them when I started my practice made ocular motility seem an ideal specialty.

Even though I repeated these good points over and over to myself, I couldn't build up any real enthusiasm. Too much ground had been yanked out from under me to warrant optimism and lust for life. I looked on the upcoming year as a time out during which I could regroup. Maybe a new opportunity would present itself. Meanwhile, I'd study. This aimlessness led to a rather devil-may-care attitude on my part. During that year I was quite a different personality from the conscientious naval officer who had been commended so wholeheartedly by his superiors.

14

Go West, Young Man

I flew to Los Angeles where I took possession of a Shelby Cobra. As I looked at this brute of a car I couldn't help thinking about Dr. Bak's theory concerning me and automobiles. I think it is true that the ones I've owned have formed a running commentary on my life. Perhaps it started when I was a small child and my father took me with him to look at a boy-sized car he had seen listed for sale by the parents of a rich kid who had outgrown it. That little car stands out vividly in my mind even today. It was the size of one of my pedal cars but instead of pedals had an electric motor. For a child like myself who at age three could spot a '36 Lasalle or a '29 Auburn, this little blue job was heaven on earth. The style was that of an open roadster; when I climbed in to take her for a test drive the thrill was indescribable. It was as if that little car, so much like the ones the big people drove, propelled me into another dimension. I was no longer a confused child but a *motorist!* Who could fail to respect me if I had my own car? At this moment of potential triumph, however, tragedy struck. Dad decided not to buy the car. I think he must have found out that it cost more than he had anticipated. At any rate I climbed out of it still sublimely affected, only to be hustled away with no further explanation. As we backed out of the driveway, I watched Little Blue recede into the distance and finally angle out of sight when we pulled into the street. I'll be the first to admit that no kid who doesn't get his own private motorcar can call himself deprived on that score alone, but I've always wondered why my father let me see it and drive it, hung it tantalizingly in front of me—and then yanked it away. I guess he didn't realize how much I would crave it.

When I finally got into a position to acquire cars, I satisfied this craving many times, and each time the car seemed appropriate. The Shelby was likewise appropriate. It was a special model created by the famous race driver Carroll Shelby. It was the powerhouse of its day, a special creation consisting of a 427 cubic centimeter Ford Cobra engine mounted on a small sports car chassis. This was fitted with an aluminum body built in England by the Arnold Bristol Company. It could accelerate from zero to sixty in four seconds, faster than any production model of the time. Yet, in spite of all this power the aluminum body was so delicate that you could leave a permanent thumbprint on the hood when you opened it to check the oil. It also lacked the comforts of most normal automobiles. There were no windows, only plastic curtains that could be fitted over the top edges of the doors. The doors themselves had no handles; they were opened by pulling a string inside the car. Despite these inconveniences I drove that Shelby happily and relentlessly, top down, all over the country. It was perfect for me because I too was a special creation, a combination of power and delicacy as unfinished as the Cobra. We were both created for speed with seemingly no other purpose than to go fast, but god help us if we cracked up. Our shells were too fragile to withstand much impact.

I floored the accelerator and roared north along the Pacific Coast. Rocco enjoyed the speed as much as I, leaning into the wind with his teeth bared. I camped out for several weeks in the forests of Oregon, where, for the first time in years, I felt unpressured. Except for the times Rocco was fired on by deer hunters it was one of the most peaceful periods of my life. In the morning I'd wake up to find myself staring hundreds of feet up into the towering redwoods of the Northwest. Somehow my problems seemed smaller there. In fact, my whole stay in Oregon was woodsy and basic despite the fact that I was studying a highly technical subject. I could look out from the window of my office— equipped with the finest and shiniest of instruments, the full flower of medical technology—and see Mount Hood in the distance. Everywhere there was greenery and a kind of countrified approach. I could walk to work from my nearby rooming house, accompanied by Rocco. Upon arrival I'd pat him on the head, and he'd run off to play for the rest of the day, faithfully returning at five o'clock to pick me up. He adjusted well for a dog who had been raised in Manhattan.

On the weekends, I'd sometimes accompany Dr. Swan, my mentor, to his tree farm and work on the farm's pond, which had a tendency to get overgrown and clogged if not looked after. Often I thought longingly of what it would be like to live and work permanently in this evergreen existence, but I knew I could not. I wasn't suited for a life in the garden—not as Dick anyway.

During my stay in Oregon I thought I carried off my charade pretty well, but when I left I had the feeling that my pose might have been more transparent than I had imagined. At my going away party I was presented by my associates with a flannel nightdress. Of course, they knew that I was going to Iowa for the next part of my fellowship, and the winters are icy there. But I have always wondered why they didn't give me flannel pajamas instead. During this time I was living only as Dick. Renée made no appearances at all, yet there must have been suspicions that found their outlet, either consciously or unconsciously, in the choice of that gift.

Another attitude on the part of my friends in Oregon also suggested that I was perceived in an unusual light. Two members of the hospital staff, who knew that I was going to be driving around the country, had the feeling that I was vulnerable. They suggested that I buy some protection. These friends tried to make me believe that *everyone* should be prepared, but their explanations were tinged with the concern strong men feel for women. As a result of their urging I left Oregon with a thirty-eight caliber revolver under the driver's seat.

I headed down the Oregon coast intending to drive all the way to southern California and then cut over through New Mexico and Arizona before turning north to Iowa. I hadn't gotten far down the scenic coast road when I struck a rock, which punctured the oil pan. Quickly the lubricant drained out of the engine, which froze immediately. I stopped dead in the midst of a howling gale, miles from help. Rocco and I hitched to the nearest town, a coast village called Newport, Oregon. A small garage towed the Shelby in and jacked it up. The engine was a mess and obviously needed to be rebuilt or replaced. Newport was fresh out of Cobra engines;

so I settled in for a week to help the mechanic rebuild the damaged one. I stayed at a little motel that, like everything in Newport, was located on the windswept coast where the sky seemed forever gray. The sun did not shine once during the whole week. I enjoyed the mechanical work, but at night with no place to go in that desolate town I grew lonely. For the first time in six months I felt an overpowering urge to become Renée. I purchased some clothes at a little store, and at night when the wind howled around the windows of my motel room, I became Renée. In this forbidding place she seemed appropriate, at home.

I left Newport understanding my engine far better than I had before but more confused than ever about my personality. The evenings as Renée had disturbed a melancholy but apparently stable peace. I hadn't been particularly happy since I stopped the therapy, but I had not been driven. Now I could look ahead to the old cycle: Dick by day and Renée by night. It was not an attractive prospect. I pressed the gas pedal harder and sped south in defiance of the speed laws and of my own survival instincts.

After five hours of driving, I crossed into northern California and pulled into a tiny roadside café. It was about one o'clock in the morning, and there were few other customers. The place was a typical highway eatery, dingy, with a bar and a complement of stools. Along the walls there were booths and tables. The center of the room was cleared for dancing. Outside, a storm was building, and occasionally the lights would flicker as the squall increased its intensity. I sat at the bar drinking my coffee with Rocco lying at my feet. It felt good to stretch myself after being folded up in the cockpit of the Cobra for so long. Across the room two teenage couples sat having drinks. A few minutes later the lights went out for good, and we sat in the dark until the waitress lit candles for the kids' booth and for me at the bar. Shortly, three young men about the same age as the others came in and sat at a table near them. One of the newcomers, a skinny, nervous-looking boy, began to taunt the kids in the booth. It was soon clear that this was a romantic quarrel: the taunter had lost his girl to a boy in the booth. He and his friends had apparently come in to make life miserable for the others. Insults began to fly from one group to another as both continued to order drinks. Finally, the woman-stealer stood up, and as if on signal all of the men rushed onto the dance floor and began to slug it out. The turmoil quickly moved outside. As the two boys were overpowered by the three, they retreated to the gravel parking lot outside. Frankly, I didn't give a damn if all the delinquents in northern California beat each other's brains out. I sat for a few more minutes musing about my own problems. As I was paying for the coffee I could hear the two girls screaming outside. When I walked through the door I saw why. The three late arrivals were holding the Romeo down and were meticulously beating the hell out of him. The other boy had run into the restaurant for help. The girls stood by with their hands up, screeching horribly. There was blood all over the parking lot. In the background lightning flashed, intermittently lighting the grisly proceedings. The chief tormentor was kneeling astraddle the Romeo's chest and was bashing him in the face. The other two stood by, ready to spell him if he should grow tired.

As indifferent as I was to the altercations of these teenagers, this senseless brutality offended me. Was this truly the only thing these kids could find to do? The lightning flashed again, revealing one of the attending boys as he kicked at an exposed portion of the victim's torso. I stepped to my car and removed the thirty-eight from under the seat. Holding it unobtrusively down by my leg, I walked briskly over to the scene of the beating. When I was at close range I raised it to eye level and held it out in front of me, two-handed: "You have three seconds to get off him," I said, "or I'll start with one leg and then work on the other." I didn't even have to fire a warning shot. He got up immediately and stood over by his friends, all three facing me with frightened expressions. They stood transfixed as the lightning flickered, revealing what must have been a bizarre sight. A pale, shaggy man-woman stood calmly pointing a pistol at them. I was beginning to wonder what I was going to do with them when a police siren howled, faintly at first and then louder. Within minutes a patrol car arrived, apparently called by the young man who had gone for help. The trooper looked doubtful even when I lowered my pistol and explained to him why I had been holding three of his citizens at gunpoint. Still, the victim was standing there, his face an eloquent witness in my behalf, and the waitress and bartender backed me up, too. After the explanations were made, the policeman became more interested in the Shelby than in the question of what I was doing carrying a pistol. After a brief examination of the engine and cockpit, he sent me on my way.

This wasn't the last time I called attention to myself. My appearance alone was notable. Though I had worn conservative clothes in Oregon my traveling outfit was a little more assertive. I wore tight jeans with blue work shirts and over that, in order to hide my breasts, a denim jacket. This rough-and-ready attire was in contrast to my androgynous features, especially my long hair and the unusual smoothness of my face. In Arizona I was apparently mistaken for an Indian and challenged to Indian-wrestle by one of the local good ol' boys. His idea of Indian-wrestling turned out to be what in New York we called arm wrestling. He beat me right-handed and confidently agreed when I suggested that we try our lefts. A look of angry confusion settled over his face when I easily smacked his arm to the bar; my serving arm has always been very strong. He began to search for some way to antagonize me and suggested that we introduce Rocco to a pit bulldog owned by one of his friends. While he was making the arrangements, Rocco and I went to the men's room and kept on going, through the window, out to the Cobra, and away.

I took some satisfaction on that trip in coming off as a mutinous figure, and I swaggered enough to make myself noticed. Coming out of a restaurant on the Kansas Turnpike, I found a note on my windshield that read, "Wild One, meet us at The Place in Kansas City." Without a moment's hesitation I headed the Shelby in that direction. This was ideal, an invitation that came from no one to go to a place I had never been to. What more could a displaced person ask for?

The Place turned out to be a huge, barnlike saloon similar to P. J. Clark's on Third Avenue in New York City, only bigger. The theme was Western, with the emphasis on outlaws. On one wall hung a large picture of John Dillinger. A thick wood bar ran the length of the room. All the chairs were big and heavy, made of oak. I seated myself and took a look around. It was late afternoon and the bar was sparsely populated. Those who were there seemed to be Kansas City bohemians, not too far out but weird enough to make a New Yorker comfortable. Soon I was approached by two young men, one of whom said, "Hi, Wild One, glad you could make it." They turned out to be friendly homosexuals who had been attracted partially to me and partially to the Shelby. Together, we were apparently an irresistible combination. After a few beers the talk got cozy, and I revealed that I was an actor who often did female impersonation. They were both impressed. I made sure that they understood thay *my* particular art was serious impersonation, not burlesque. As long as we were being confidential, I certainly didn't want to be misunderstood. They pressed me for details, and I fabricated a whole life, drawing on my experiences in New York for details to make it seem authentic. When I mentioned the Satin Slipper Revue their eyes lit up.

"Why, we've got a Satin Slipper nightclub right here in Kansas City!" said one excitedly. He went on to explain that it was a club that featured female impersonations. It was primarily striptease but presented straight acts like mine as well. Maybe I could do a turn while I was in town.

"Well, I don't know," I said warily "I'm on vacation." "Oh, come on," they urged. "It'll be fun—give Kansas City a taste of real professional entertainment." Finally I got to feeling that it really was my duty to spread some culture to the boonies. I agreed, and my new friends took me to meet the manager of the Satin Slipper nightclub, Ordell Lacy.

He was large and grossly overweight. During the course of the conversation he repeatedly referred to himself as a "Big Fat Fairy." I told him that I would do my act for a couple of weeks to defray the expenses of my trip but that I didn't have any of my gear with me. The Big Fat Fairy looked me over and agreed to give me a tryout the following morning. I would close the last show, the one that started after midnight. As for an outfit, I could choose from the costumes and props that were part of the club's permanent equipment.

The fact that I had never before performed as a stripteaser did not faze me, nor did the fact that I have never been a very good dancer. My idea of social dancing has always been to stand almost still with my arms around my partner, taking little bitty steps. People at college used to do impressions of me dancing—my ineptitude was that noticable. The topic of fast dancing never even came up; I just didn't do it. For all my athletic skill and grace on the tennis court, I was a klutz when it came to the dance floor.

My state of mind in those days was such that I didn't figure I owed the audience at the Satin Slipper anything but my best effort—regardless of how bad it might be. The important thing was that I live out a fantasy. Besides, I figured that I was a quick learner; and now that I had a show to do I would simply practice the next day, and by midafternoon I would be ready.

Ordell and I shook on the deal, and I checked into a downtown hotel. That evening I tweezed out by the root every single hair on my face. They had been substantially thinned out by electrolysis, but the job still took until three in the morning. I didn't have any trouble staying awake because I was in pain. Still, I had learned to live with the discomfort of the electrologist's needle; so the discomfort of tearing the hairs out wasn't essentially new, and the results were worth it. My face was as smooth as a baby's bottom and remained so for several days. The hateful beard had been eliminated. All that remained was to make myself into an exotic dancer. After a hearty breakfast the next day, I returned to my room and got down to business. Opposite the bed there was a big mirror in which I could see myself full-length. I pushed the bed to one side, creating a dance floor, and then stripped down to a bra and panties that I had left over from my lonely evenings in desolate Newport, Oregon. For music I depended on my portable radio.

One thing was immediately apparent: I was most effective when I stayed in one place. Moving was not my strong suit; when I just stood and did bumps, I looked pretty good. (My grinds were only passable.) When I tried to walk or strut in time to the music, however, I looked strangely awkward. When I tried to walk *and* bump at the same time, the result was, well, awkward would be a kind description. I gave the impression that I had been stricken with a lewd nervous disorder. My pelvis, my legs, and my torso seemed to be in the midst of a violent disagreement over what my body was up to. With practice I improved slightly; yet for anyone with much perspective the prospects would have looked irredeemably bleak. Luckily, I didn't have any perspective. I was on a high, and when I projected ahead to my debut all I could think about was the applause of my public. If I considered my awkwardness at all, I dismissed it as a minor matter that would undoubtedly correct itself under the stimulus of an actual performance. After a couple of hours' practice I had my basic moves worked out and spent the remainder of the day resting up for the show.

Go West, Young Man

When I arrived at the Satin Slipper about ten o'clock, Ordell, the Big Fat Fairy, was onstage in a circus tent of a dress, telling jokes and making fun of himself. It was a dingy little place located on a street that had apparently been zoned for strip shows and topless bars. Less elegant even than the Club 82 in Manhattan, it was a long, thin room hardly capable of holding more than a hundred customers. As always, the crowd was primarily curiosity seekers but seemed louder and more boisterous than the audiences in New York. They did seem to be enjoying Ordell, and I considered that a good sign. Actually, Ordell must have learned a long time earlier that the best way to please these crowds was through self-revilement. He did this lavishly, referring to himself repeatedly as a big fat fairy; it always got a laugh. This response was what I interpreted as a good omen. I was clearly out of touch.

Backstage there was a sort of common area where all the performers prepared. There was a makeup counter with a mirror that ran the length of it. Around the mirror was a border of naked light bulbs just like in the movies. It took me an hour and a half to do my makeup. I had remembered to put the rouge on my nose, forehead, and chin just as Jimmy had shown me so long ago when he had "auditioned" me for the original Satin Slipper Revue. As the visiting professional from out of town, I was accorded automatic respect by the locals, and my spiffy makeup job sealed their approval. For my costume I had chosen black panties and black knit stockings with a black garter belt. My bra was an eye catcher; it was one of those that have the ends cut out so the wearer's nipples show through. I could see that some of the other performers were openly ogling my breasts. For the first time in months I felt proud of them. Over the items of underwear I fastened a bunch of chiffon scarves, tucking the ends into the garter belt and the bra. Frankly, I don't see how Salome made do with only seven veils; I must have had fifteen or so artfully bedecking me. Over this banquet of flags I wrapped, sari style, a long piece of netting. To finish off the outfit I wore an incredibly huge blonde wig. With this topper and a pair of Ordell's spike heels (he was the only one with feet as big as mine), I must have stood about six-feet nine-inches tall. Everyone agreed that I was a breathtaking sight.

At last, I heard Ordell announce my act. He gave me a big buildup, dwelling on the supposed fact that I was a professional from The Coast. While he was doing the introduction I took my place on stage behind the curtains. I assumed a provocative pose, feet together, hips canted to one side, left hand elegantly raised with fingers pointing heavenward, and right arm stretching swanlike into space. The last thing I heard was Ordell's voice saying, "Let's give a big Kansas City welcome to the fabulous Reneeeeeeee!" The sound system blasted out the brassy, opening bars of "The Stripper," and the curtains parted to reveal me standing there like a gaudy monument. The one A.M. crowd went wild. This was what I had waited for; these people did not yet know how good it could get. Under those veils, I had a body like few others in the world, and I was prepared to show it all. Their whistles and cheering were a clear message: "Renée, let's see what you got!" I stepped out confidently but immediately my torso, pelvis, and legs resumed their familiar quarrel. Ordell's three-inch heels didn't help any. The catlike coordination that I had expected to surface miraculously during an actual perform-ance was not forthcoming. Moreover, the net sarong proved more difficult to strip off than I had imagined. I took my attention off the bumping to concentrate on getting the net untangled. A stunned silence fell over the crowd; they were having trouble reconciling my spastic performance with the impact I had made when the curtains opened. I managed to get the net unwrapped, dragging off five or six scarves in the process. By now the crowd had serious suspicions, and some of the less tolerant were begin-ning to make rude noises. I continued yanking off scarves in as provocative a way as I could manage, but nothing I did was good enough—or even remotely good for that matter. Rejection had robbed me of whatever presence I had possessed. Flop sweat was breaking out all over me. The audience's disgust was now unanimous. Hoots, catcalls, raspberries, and a multitude of other impolite noises came swelling out of the smoky blackness. Never have I heard an audience in such total agreement. By this time I was down to nothing but underwear and perspiration. Ordell finally turned off the stage lights and music. He was probably afraid that I would be run out of town on a rail if I actually stripped naked. A nude person is pretty vulnerable.

I gratefully made my way backstage where the respectful gazes I had previously been given had changed to good-natured smirks. No one, including Ordell, was really angry with me. Ordell said it was the liveliest he had seen a Satin Slipper

194

audience in years. He even suggested graciously that, with practice, I might get to be a competent exotic dancer. I thanked him, but I knew that the only practice I was cut out for was a medical one, and accordingly I set out for Iowa, leaving behind the exciteing world of show biz.

The Kansas City affair hadn't even dented my self-possession. Even when the audience was at its most vicious ("Look at that Adam's apple. Har! Har!"), I had remained remarkably unmoved. I had felt some momentary panic, but once off the stage the whole scene seemed more amusing than humiliating. I really had no self-image to be threatened. Before you can fear consequences you have to feel that you have something to protect, and I didn't feel that way. The real me was in an ampule somewhere back in Dr. Benjamin's office. Without that component I was a half-formed thing without much self-concept to protect.

I blew into Iowa City in the middle of a hard freeze that lasted pretty much all winter. The motel that was to be my home for the next six months was a bleak affair with a barren little courtyard and a four-lane highway just beyond that. After tossing my one suitcase full of belongings into the dresser, I dropped into the hospital to see my new professor, Dr. Burian. From him I expected to synthesize what I had learned from Dr. Knapp and Dr. Swan. Dr. Burian's interest was research into all aspects of binocular vision. He was more academic than my previous teachers; he liked to find out why things happened even if there was no immediate practical application for what he learned. If I could incorporate my practical experience from New York and Portland into Dr. Burian's theoretical framework, I would be thoroughly grounded in ocular motility.

Of course, there was clinical work to do, and to my surprise I found that I had arrived just in time to do it. Dr. Burian was absent on a lecture tour for two weeks, and even on my first visit to the hospital it seemed obvious that the residents considered me the big gun from out-of-town. Their deferential manner reminded me of the strippers at the Satin Slipper. The difference here was that I actually *was* an expert in ophthalmology. When they presented me with some of their clinical problems, I advised them confidently. In particular, I took command of the patients who had problems with their superior oblique muscles. After an extensive evaluation of one such case, I said, "Let's operate." One of the residents replied, "Dr. Burian never operates on the superior oblique. It's a complicated muscle, and he feels it's better to treat the problem by operating on another muscle." My response to this was short and to the point: "Nonsense! I'll show you how to do it." In this cavalier way I indirectly countermanded the orders of one of the world's leading ophthalmologists. During the next two weeks I supervised several such operations; I saw no reason to obey such a silly dictate. With Dr. Knapp I had assisted on dozens of operations on the superior obliques. Dr. Burian's stature and the fact that he was the boss didn't seem to me to be adequate reasons for doing precisely what he said should be done.

When he arrived back in town, he asked the residents what they had been up to with me. One of them answered as casually as possible, "Oh, we've just been operating on some superior obliques." Dr. Burian's face turned pale, then crimson. "You have been doing what?" he asked. "You know we don't operate on those muscles!" I had been standing with my arms folded at the back of the group of residents. They parted, leaving me an unobstructed view of the professor's outrage. I was unconcerned and managed to remain nonchalant throughout his lengthy tirade. I knew that I should be worried, but he was wrong and that was that.

After his initial outburst he took a look at my postoperative results and calmed down. Amazingly, he scheduled a few cases for surgery and observed my technique. He was impressed and, showing a very generous nature, never held my cockiness against me. That he didn't carry a grudge was lucky for me because I learned a lot from him and even stayed longer than my alloted time so that I could finish a research paper that we coauthored.

In addition to learning about the workings of binocular vision, I picked up other valuable information in Iowa City. I was able to see first-hand how a top-notch academic ophthalmology program is set up. I learned the basics of organization and administration since I was not only a student but a supervisor as well.

The program was very rigorous. It started at seven-thirty in the morning with a convocation of the entire staff and an examination of every eye patient in the hospital and ended at six o'clock with an academic conference perhaps featuring a research seminar by one of the residents in training. In between these two widely separated events was the usual busy routine associated with the functioning of a great medical center.

The doctoring was fun, but Iowa City didn't have much to offer me in my hours away from the hospital. A good part of the time the weather was subzero. I'd open the door to let Rocco out of the motel room for a romp, and he'd refuse to go. He was a dog of keen intelligence and had figured out that there was nothing of interest outside. There were no indoor tennis courts, so I couldn't kill time practicing. Sometimes I'd take a drive in the Cobra through the flat, frozen cornfields that made up the countryside. This was as much torture as pleasure, since the car was not made for inclement weather; the plastic curtains were a slim barrier between me and the ten-below temperature outside the car.

On one of these uncomfortable jaunts I drove past the tiny airport outside the town. There I saw some small private planes taking off and landing. Probably crazed by the cold, I decided to inquire about flying lessons. I had always wanted to learn, but my fear of high places had always deterred me. I stopped to investigate, and before twenty minutes had passed, I was high in the sky gingerly testing the controls at the pilot's urging. To my delight, being up in that little plane was not like being in a high place. At great heights, without nearby points of reference, the ground below looks little different than it does when you look down to tee off at the golf course. The experience of flying did not do a thing to cure my fear of heights (to this day I still won't go out on a balcony above the second floor), but it went a long way toward curing my midwinter blues. After eight hours of instruction, I soloed.

Though I approached flying with the same scientific attitude that I brought to medicine, I tended to be a little less careful with my own life than I was with the lives of my patients. Late one afternoon while I was concentrating all my attention on practicing turns, the sun unexpectedly went down. Suddenly it was dark, a situation that I was not qualified to handle. Up in the air over Iowa every direction looks the same at night. I had just soloed a few days before and hardly even knew how to operate the radio. While I was fooling around trying to remember how to contact the tower, I stood a very good chance of flying right into the ground. My eight hours of instruction had been spent on the really important things like taking off, landing, and turning.

Since I wasn't supposed to be up at night, details like how to turn on the lights in the cockpit had been given only perfunctory attention. I spent five minutes scanning the control console trying to figure out how to illuminate the instruments so I could tell if I was flying level or not. Eventually I got them lit in time to discover that I was on a very gradual descent into the Iowa corn. After correcting that I managed to contact the tower and explain my situation: "It's dark and I'm lost" were, I believe, the words I used. "Where are you?" they asked. "What is your present position?"

"I don't know. That's how I decided I was lost." I was having to concentrate hard to remember that I was supposed to lift my finger off the radio button when I wasn't talking. Sometimes I'd forget and hear only the last half of a remark.

". . . were you when the sun went down?"

"Over the cornfields."

". . . ich direction from the airport?"

"Uh, north."

". . . you headed now?"

"Huh?"

"Which direction are you headed now? What is your present heading?"

"North."

"Due north?"

"Pretty much."

"Well, that means that you are probably flying north away from Iowa City. Make a standard rate turn to a heading of one eighty. If you don't see the lights of town within ten minutes we'll start you on a circular pattern until you can spot the town. How much fuel do you have remaining?"

"Three-quarters full."

"Good. You should be fine. Remain in radio contact."

They didn't have to tell me to keep in touch. Pretty soon the scattered lights of Iowa Ciy were in view, and the people in the tower were able to deduce from my description where I was in relation to the airport.

This was not the only time I nearly killed myself in an airplane. Once, en route to Cincinnati, I called the nearby Indianapolis Airport and asked what time the sun set in Cincinnati. I didn't want to get caught in the dark again. The tower officials said that they couldn't speak for Cincinnati but that sunset in Indianapolis was in eight minutes. Again, I had no idea where I was in relation to the airport. As it grew dark the radar operators guided me to a small private airport that obligingly turned on its lights for me.

Another time while practicing near Iowa City, I got lost again and flew around until I was almost out of gas. Luckily another plane came by, and I followed it to the airport where I was cleared for an emergency landing. When I taxied to a stop, the fuel gauge read absolutely empty.

Not all my close shaves were due to my carelessness. Again I was over Iowa when a hailstorm sneaked up on me and pelted the plane with baseball-sized pieces of ice. After enduring about fifteen minutes of this, I finally managed to stagger back to the landing strip where I came in on a runway that was virtually a sheet of ice.

In spite of these experiences I continued to be enthusiastic about flying, although I never did get an instrument rating. I was terrible at flying blind, though I kept blundering into situations where I badly needed that skill. I even bought a plane while I was in Iowa City; I decided to do this just before I left. I had received while studying with Dr. Burian an invitation to take over the ophthalmology residency training program at Manhattan Eye and Ear Hospital. The doctor previously in charge had an exploding private practice and could not devote the necessary time to his duties at the hospital. This was a relatively common situation since "instructor to the residents" was a job often given to a gifted young doctor who had not yet established a thriving private practice. As he worked at the hospital, he made contacts, built a reputation, and slowly developed his own practice. When it was solid, he left, and a new instructor to the residents was hired. I was well-acquainted with the administrators at Manhattan Eye and Ear; in addition I had an excellent reputation among the community of ophthalmologists. Coming off a year's advanced studies as a Head Fellowship winner, I seemed to be a natural choice. Accordingly, they decided to bring their golden boy home.

As I flew up the East River with Manhattan on my left and Forest Hills on my right, I felt quite the returning hero. I was stronger than I had been a year ago when I left. Tempered by the crazy experiences that had grown out of my despondency, I felt far more in control as I guided my Piper Cherokee into Flushing

My mother, Dr. Sadie Muriel Bishop, at age 53

Age 3. I hated those outfits.

My father at age 48, posing in front of the office where he has practiced medicine for fifty years

My first two-wheeled bike. My sister taught me to ride by giving me a shove and then looking on interestedly as I sailed away, out of control.

On the Horace Mann School tennis team, 1948

Horace Mann School graduation
photograph, 1951

Horace Mann School's best dressed
baseball player, 1951

With my date at the Yale freshman prom, 1952

With two close friends in 1954.

In doubles competition against Princeton, 1955

Below: At the Bermuda Intercollegiate Championships, Dick was singles champion. The man in the suit is famous coach Herman Hickman.

The fourth doctor in the family receives his medical degree in 1959.

Below: Lieutenant Commander Richard Raskind
(U.S. Navy photograph)

Singles winner at the All-Navy Championships, 1963

(U.S. Navy photograph)

With my father before we left on the trip to Europe where I met the transsexuals of the Hotel de la Paix. Note the change in my appearance.

Above: Picking up the Shelby Cobra for my trip west in 1966

Left: A shot from a fashion layout for which I posed during my year in Europe

LONG ISLAND

leisure WEEK

LI BUSINESS REVIEW   SEPTEMBER 13, 1973

LI holds court
for tennis,
new king of sports

COVER PHOTO: Dr Richard Raskind hustles to meet
a serve in the recent Pipers 100 tournament held at
the Shelter Rock Tennis Club (Manhasset).

Featured on the cover of a Long Island newspaper supplement September 1973

Inset: With Andy in 1973

Even after transsexual surgery, I still dressed as a man when I visited my son, Andy. The stupid-looking wig perpetuates the charade.

At the La Jolla tennis tournament that was the beginning of my unmasking

Accepting the trophy as women's singles champion at the La Jolla Tennis Tournament in 1976

(World Wide photo)

Below: Before a television appearance in August 1976. On the right is Dr. Roberto Granato, who performed my operation. On the left is Dr. Charles Ihlenfeld, who has performed more than 200 sex operations. Dr. Granato told Associated Press that his patient "is a woman in every sense of the word."

(Wide World photo)

Betty Stove (bottom left) and Martina Navratilova (bottom right) team up against me (top left) and Bettyann Stuart (top right) during the U.S. Open women's doubles championship at Forest Hills in September 1977.

(World Wide photos)

At Forest Hills in 1977

(Wide World photos)

Below: At the Avon Championships in February 1979

(Photo by Christopher L. Columbus)

At the 1979 U.S. Open

After winning the over-35 division at the U.S. Open in 1979

At the 1980 U.S. Open, I joined my mixed doubles partner, Ilie Nastase, in one of his famous conversations with the umpire.

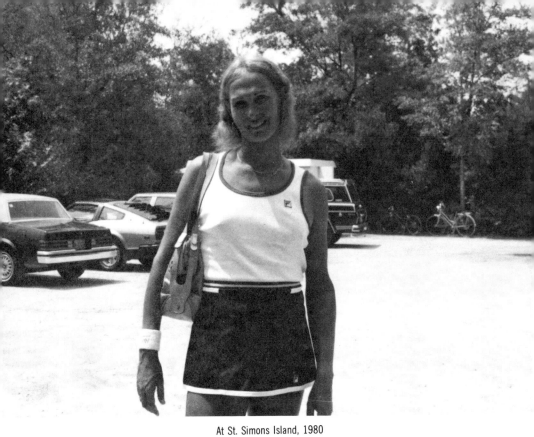

At St. Simons Island, 1980

Coaching Martina Navratilova in Stuttgart in October 1981, on her way to her summer 1982 Wimbledon title *(Photo by Angie Wim*

Outside and inside my medical office on Park Avenue
(Photos by Hank Rowland)

Below: With Tennis-ee, my most
uncritical companion, 1982
(Photo by Hank Rowland)

Airport. I knew that I was not through with Renée and could never be, but I was determined not to succumb again to the wild and self-destructive moods that had marked the past year. What I needed was a plan that would help me achieve the goal toward which I had been so happily moving a year before. With my new job would come financial security, prestige, and power. They would provide an excellent start. As if in acknowledgement of my new attitude, the powerful yet delicate Cobra did not survive the trip from Iowa to New York. I had hired a college student to drive it East, and in Pennsylvania it caught fire and burned completely.

15

Park Avenue Imposter

My first task was to make a success of my new position. The last man had allowed the residency training program to slide into a haphazard mess. Since he had to devote so much time to his private practice, there was no regularity in the instruction of the residents. They would be convened on short notice or not at all. Often they would gather for a session and wait around, only to receive a call saying that the instructor couldn't make it. This, of course, was not the way that Dr. Dick Raskind intended to run things. Though my private life had often been a disastrous shambles, I had always prided myself on being impeccably responsible as a doctor. This was not simply a choice but apparently a compulsion. At no time had I ever allowed my professional life to be disturbed by the struggles taking place in my emotional existence. If I ever suspected that medicine might suffer, I simply did not practice (as I had not practiced the preceding summer when I retired to my father's house). The medical community saw me as completely reliable. It was one of the characteristics they were looking for in an instructor of residents.

The first thing I did was to institute a routine similar to the one in Iowa City. The day started with grand rounds at seven-thirty in the morning and ended with an academic conference at five o'clock. It was a long day, and the hours between were filled with well-structured learning activities as well as plenty of practical experience. For the first few months at least I had no other outlet for my energies except my activities at the hospital. I was on top of those residents from dawn to dusk; where things had previously been slack they were now as tight as a drum. As a matter of fact, during the several years I spent in this position ninety-five percent of my time was spent supervising the residents and teaching them in the clinic. My private practice remained small and select. In Iowa City I had discovered that I could take responsibility and give clear, understandable directives. I also discovered that I enjoyed it. In New York I was able to exercise these talents in a very constructive way.

This is not to say that I didn't have to make adjustments. Almost all my life I had been a student, and the shift to authority figure was a big one. Still, another thing that I learned in Iowa City was that I knew a great deal about ocular motility, probably as much as any doctor my age. There were some towering figures in the field who stood by themselves after a lifetime of effort. I couldn't match their experience, but I certainly qualified as an expert; and in the area of the superior oblique muscles, I was especially adept.

I developed an approach to surgery on the superior oblique that was a combination of all I had learned. It was simple and direct. Previously the tendency had been to work cautiously around this muscle out of fear that its complex functions might be further impaired by surgery; however, using Dr. Swan's diagnostic techniques I could pinpoint impairments pretty accurately, and since I understood the muscle system very thoroughly I could go with confidence to the affected area and make a straightforward alteration that would restore normal function. I prided myself on obtaining the maximum effect from the least surgical interference, but I had to be bold and deft. I never attempted to solve a problem as the residents had been doing in Iowa City, by working only on an alternative set of muscles out of fear that the ones directly involved were too tricky. I was also able to make some contributions in the mechanics of surgery. I applied known techniques to muscles on which they had not previously been used. In general, I streamlined the process wherever possible.

My residents appreciated my expertise and held me in high regard, treating me with great deference though I was only a few years older than they. Theirs was an affectionate respect that did not, however, preclude some academic horseplay. One of their favorite tricks was to ask a leading question. Once baited, I would begin to rattle on in great detail about the subject. The residents would wink conspiratorially at one another and settle back while I carried the ball. My mind in the area of ophthalmology was encyclopedic, and these sessions could last a long time. If I threatened to run down, a resident would step in with an appropriately intriguing tangential inquiry, and I would be off again. This type of thing was instructive as well as amusing to the residents. They found it entertaining because my professorial gushiness was in such contrast to the quiet and efficient persona that I otherwise cultivated. At the end of one of these episodes, which usually took place during rounds, I would glance at my watch, alarmed that I had taken so much time in explanation. With a snort that said, "Here, here, we must stop all this nonsense and move on to the practicalities of medicine," I would stride purposefully to the next patient. Meanwhile, the residents would grin knowingly at one another and wait for the next opportunity to wind me up.

Though my reputation as a physician was centered around my surgical talents, I feel strongly that my greatest contributions to medicine have been as a teacher. Many doctors have taken up their practices with a substantially greater understanding of their field because they were exposed to my program. Their collective impact has been far greater than any of my individual achievements. Even today as I play in tennis tournaments around the country, I am often approached by my former students. I'm always deeply touched when they recall their days with me and mention that they learned a lot.

As my reputation flourished at Manhattan Eye and Ear Hospital, I began to be in demand to lecture at other medical centers in the city. Soon invitations began to come in from across the country. For the most part I turned these down because they would have taken me away from my duties as an instructor. Aside from an occasional appearance at a national convention and a yearly instruction course at the national meeting of the American Academy of Ophthalmology, I restricted myself to the New York scene. I became an associate clinical professor on the faculty of the Cornell Medical School and assumed the directorship of the eye muscle clinic at New York Hospital. Had I been more ambitious I could have parlayed my opportunities into an international reputation, but that might have interfered with my private life. I couldn't afford to become too widely known a celebrity because such publicity would have increased my chances of being discovered. By the end of my first year back in New York I was beginning to dress as Renée again.

In those days my life was focused in every way. I worked at my profession intensely and seldom found it necessary to leave a four- or five-block area of New York City. The hospitals at which I worked were located on Manhattan's East Side, one on East Sixty-fourth Street and the other on East Sixty-eighth. My apartment was on East Sixty-sixth, and my office, where I took care of my few private patients, was on East Sixty-fifth, off Park Avenue. Even the old wooden indoor tennis courts at the Seventh Regiment Armory were on East Sixty-sixth Street, half a block from both my office and my apartment. When I did leave the area it was usually for a trip in the Piper Cherokee to Long Island or Cape Cod or perhaps Canada for the weekend.

My apartment occupied the entire top floor of a limestone town house similar to those that serve as foreign embassies in Manhattan. My bedroom was located at the front of the building and featured molded ceilings and a fireplace. From this room, a long corridor ran to the back of the building where the living room was located. It too had molded ceilings and a fireplace. Opening off the living room was a spacious terrace, which I could enjoy if I didn't go too near the edge. Skylights admitted light into both the bedroom and living room. I put up gigantic wall mirrors that bounced the light from the terrace into the living room, down the corridor, and into the bedroom. There was a tiny but adequate kitchen and even a little dining area with its own skylight. I decorated the bedroom in light blues and the living room in dark blues and reds. It was a great place for a bachelor or a bachelorette—I was alternately both. One fine thing about that apartment was the privacy. You could only get to it by a small elevator that could hold, at most, three people. The car couldn't even be stopped at my floor without a special key. That elevator shaft served as a moat to keep the world at bay.

My apartment was like a sparkling jewel at the hub of my tight little existence. From there each day I ventured into the professional world, and to there I returned each evening. Soon it was a haven for Renée; my closets began to fill up with women's clothes as my predictable compulsion began to increase in strength. After the initial year of organization, the program at Manhattan

Eye and Ear was running smoothly, leaving me with less on my mind. As always, Renée slipped into any opening; as a result she began to organize her own life. My business trips to the city's tall-girl shops became more frequent, and soon all the owners knew that the things I picked out were for me. They were aware that I was a prominent doctor, and, like most New Yorkers, considered my peculiarities to be my own business. I was a good customer and paid promptly. That was enough for them.

During my second year back in New York, I also took a trip to Scandinavia with Josh. We spent much time in Stockholm where he busily chased one pretty Swedish girl after another with me dutifully tagging along behind. He insisted that I go with him even if I complained, for example, that I'd like to take a little time off to play some tennis. He never accepted such excuses, holding that I could play tennis anytime in New York but I couldn't pick up Swedish women there. Actually, by periodically opting out of this cruising I was trying to set the stage for a side trip; it was, of course, the real reason I had come to Scandinavia in the first place. I was determined to get to Copenhagen to talk with the renowned Dr. Christian Hamburger, one of the physicians who had taken care of Christine Jorgenson during her surgical adventures of the early fifties. I finally told Josh that I was going to visit friends in Paris. He was torn but, in the end, could not bring himself to leave Stockholm when he was having such smashing success with its blonde beauties. Gratefully, I left him to his eternal quest and caught a plane to Copenhagen.

Dr. Hamburger's hospital was called the Sang Station, which translated means Blood Station. In spite of this intimidating title I went in and introduced myself. He was an old white-haired man at the time. In spite of the familiar song that I sang, he listened cordially and answered my questions in excellent English. Much of what he said I had heard before. My body was acceptable, I was young enough, I might have a hard time earning a living, and I might not be accepted by my family and friends. Finally, the preliminaries out of the way, he gave me a prescription for estrogens. His recommendation was what I had been waiting for—an encouraging word from a responsible authority. Soon I would feel that lightness again; soon I would be on track, heading for what I knew was my destiny. The resolve that I had felt when I flew into New York eighteen months before was now yielding concrete results. Dr. Hamburger was most understanding and humane; he even prescribed the hormones in suppository form since they were less expensive that way. In addition he helped me work out a treatment schedule. That same day the hormones were again diffusing through my body—starting the soft changes that would eventually alter my life forever.

Even before Josh and I set foot again on American soil, I could feel the hormones at work. I had a bag full of medicine, courtesy of the apothecary in Copenhagen. There was enough in there to last me a long time. On this go-around no meddling sister or jittery doctor could turn off the tap. When these finally ran out, I had a friend prescribe a common birth-control drug that did the job nicely. Of course, I could have written myself a prescription, but even in these bizarre circumstances I adhered to the precept that no doctor should prescribe for himself.

Under the influence of the hormones I began to live an even more flagrant double life, man by day and woman by night. The balance was actually beginning to swing in Renée's direction since I spent most of my weekends as a woman. When my body began once again to show definite progress in its feminization, I couldn't keep Renée from going out of the apartment. My neighborhood was swarming with patients and colleagues and I knew that my discovery would almost certainly be disastrous, but I couldn't master the impulse. Not only that—I didn't sneak out or use a hotel room for cover as I had in the old days. A typical evening might find me smartly got up in fashionable fall plaid, strolling along East Sixty-fourth Street walking Rocco. Rocco was widely known in the neighborhood and, friendly fellow that he was, had many familiar people he liked to visit when he was taking his nightly constitutional. He liked to do this whether or not I was in high heels; so often our walks would become a prolonged tug of war as he innocently tried to trot over to a kindly tradesman who always had a pat for him—or a doorman who smelled interesting. When I would yank his leash to correct him, he would turn around and look at me reproachfully. This was as near as he ever came to disapproving of Renée.

I took a similar chance when I drove the distinctive red Volvo sports coupe that had replaced the ill-fated Shelby. Often Rocco's recognizable head would be ostentatiously sticking out of the

206

window on the rider's side. Certainly this dangerous behavior seems self-destructive, but as always with my actions in those days, what was destructive to one personality was life-giving to the other. That which imperiled Dick Raskind strengthened Renée, and she was clearly in control. Less and less was she willing to compromise her own needs to ensure the safety of Dick, a person of whom she did not approve—in fact, wished dead.

It was inevitable that I would sooner or later be spotted; when it happened it was impossible to deny. I had darted off the street and into the tiny vestibule of my building. Returning as usual from another successful walk with Rocco, I had every reason to be optimistic. The elevator was on its way down, and I was safe within the confines of my secure little apartment building. Suddenly the janitor confronted me. He stood approximately six feet away and eyed me doubtfully. I suppose he thought for a moment that I might be a lady friend of Dr. Raskind's doing him the favor of taking Rocco for his walk. Albert was a stereotypical macho Italian. He cut off the sleeves of his T-shirts in order to display his sizable and hairy upper arms. His hairstyle was left over from the fifties when grease reigned supreme. Though he was middle-aged and thick through the middle, he still had pretensions to seething masculinity. Momentarily his look of curiosity changed to embarrassed amazement. I felt lucky that he didn't rush over and beat me up when he figured out the situation. Instead, he mumbled a greeting and averting his eyes went on his way. I had mumbled an equally lame response and dragged Rocco into the elevator. Naturally, I was fighting panic. Who knew what this stud might feel obligated to do? What might his wife, who would undoubtedly hear the story the minute he stepped through the door that evening, advise?

For a week I heard nothing and saw nothing of Albert. Then, amazingly, he developed an acute eye inflammation. Though there were perhaps eight ophthalmologists living or working on our street, he chose to come to me. More telling even, he waited all day in pain until I finished eye surgery at the hospital. About six o'clock I came home and found him patiently sitting in the vestibule. I looked him over and prescribed for him; we both pretended that our confrontation had never happened.

My spirits took a great leap up; perhaps this man's reaction was a taste of things to come. I could hardly have picked a tougher audience; yet when the chips were down and Albert needed a good doctor, he chose to wait for me—dress or no dress. I had thought that he would cringe at my touch, but he acted normally. If he could do it, others, more liberal, would surely do the same.

Among the few friends before whom I appeared as Renée was the ever-abusive Josh. He knew about the hormones but still held out hope that he could win me back through revilement and, of course, by introducing me to women. That tactic was not working at all in those days. I was seeing only one woman, and my relationship with her was relatively sexless. Jenny was really going steady with a man she had been seeing off and on for years. Such relationships always go in and out of phase, and Jenny met me during an out-of-phase time. She eventually married the man, and they had two children. Their marriage was inevitable, and I made a nice companion for her while they went through the routine of being "just friends" for a while. The three of us became quite close, since I don't think Frank ever considered me much of a threat. Jenny was also one of the friends whom I allowed to see me dressed as Renée. She was such a good-hearted person and so strongly ruled by her emotions that all she could say on the occasion of my revelation was that it gave her a "warm feeling" to see me as a woman. She confessed that she had been meaning to tell me that men's clothes seemed inappropriate for me and that she had always felt that I was too smooth and soft to be a man. How different was this sweet response from the rejection I imagined I would get from the world. I began to think that I had been too cautious too long. Judging from the responses of Albert and Jenny, Renée would not have too hard a time: limited evidence to be sure—but heartening.

I had been continuing my electrolysis treatments; they were winding up at this time. I no longer had to go through the masculine ritual of shaving my beard. This gave me no end of satisfaction, along with the increasing size of my breasts and hips. All my suits hung on me strangely: too big in the waist, too small in the hips. The jackets fit perfectly across the shoulders, but the sleeves were peculiarly large around my arms. The lapels bulged out inexplicably, making the roominess around the waist even more noticeable. Out of the jacket collar stuck my ever more womanly head.

As the changes became more pronounced, I began to consider

seriously how I would arrange for the surgery necessary to complete the process. I was still very doubtful about the situation in Casablanca. The medical skills were my paramount concern, but I had also heard horror stories about the attitude of those in charge. One transsexual friend, a member of the Brooklyn Heights group, had told me that she had actually been detained to mop the floors when she had been unable to afford the high fee (about three thousand dollars at that time) that was payable in cash. I decided once again to investigate the possibility of surgery in the United States. In 1968 the only place that was regularly concerning itself with transsexualism was the Johns Hopkins Gender Identity Clinic. I went to Johns Hopkins every year anyway to attend the Wilmer Institute eye department meeting. That year when I went to the eye meeting I also kept an appointment with Dr. John Money, a key figure at the clinic. We talked for hours about transsexualism generally and about me in particular. He also administered several psychological tests. At the end of the process, he confided to me that the center had curtailed such surgery pending the results of follow-up studies on the ones they had already done. "What on earth," I wondered, "had all that talking and testing been about then?" I felt that my case was clear-cut; with my history there was no danger of a mistake. Dr. Money was apologetic, but he was only the examining psychologist. The surgeons were the ones who had the final say about whether surgery would be done at the Gender Identity Clinic.

The hopelessness that had afflicted me three years before when Dr. Benjamin had ceased my treatments began once again to gnaw at me. I flew to Chicago for an interview with another surgeon. Again I was subjected to hours of interviewing and testing—and again I was refused. I was beginning to feel that I was too hot to handle, that these people knew before I showed up that they wouldn't accept me but that they could not resist the temptation to gather data on my interesting case. Once they had it I was tossed aside. I could not believe that they were passing me up; if they wanted good information on the process, I was the ideal guinea pig. I had been in analysis for nine years, and I was a physician myself. If they were so hot on collecting data through follow-up interviews, I would be able to give them some beauties. Far from being a bad risk, I was the best possible risk. The potential good I could do far outweighed their lame excuses.

Ironically, these things that made me such a good candidate were the very ones that scared them the most. The fact that I was a prominent physician made my adjustment after the operation questionable. They were dead set on not robbing me of my damn career, and, like Dr. Benjamin, they trembled to think of the heat that would be generated if anything went wrong. I considered this a betrayal by my fellow physicians. I had put much labor into medicine. I had respected it, added to its knowledge, and innovated new techniques to make it more effective. Now, when I called on it to help me I found that my contributions were the testimony against me. The best advice they had to offer in Chicago was: "Go back to New York for more analysis."

I returned to Dr. Money and was turned down again. I inquired in Los Angeles and faced the same evasive routine. Desperate, I saw Dr. Money again. He could see clearly that I was on the brink of a nervous collapse. His suggestion was that I allow him to give me an injection of Provera. Read carefully here or you may miss the incredible logic of this move. Provera dampens the masculine sex drive. By doing this he hoped my compulsion to be a woman would be eliminated. He had used this treatment on some transvestites whose neurotic compulsion to dress in feminine attire was somehow fueled by their masculinity. By this time I was frantic, and even the most farfetched scheme seemed preferable to no action at all. Perhaps a miracle might happen and release me from the grip of this craziness. Dr. Money administered a long-term injection that made no dent whatsoever in my drive to be Renée. If the medical establishment was looking for the final proof was this not it? However, the failure of this treatment made no difference in their attitudes toward my case. The refusals stood.

By this time I was exhausted. The strain of my double life and the alternating hope and despair of my search for treatment had combined to sap my energies. I still managed the vigorous schedule of my medical career, but emotionally I was in deep water. More and more I felt life-destroying despair invading me. Renée no longer emerged in the evenings as a symbol of a life to come; she came out angry, frustrated, and dangerous. Clearly, I had no choice. Whatever the risks, I must go to Casablanca.

The decision to have surgery in Casablanca restored order to my life. Once again I had a well-defined, reachable goal. I calmed down and began planning my strategy. My determination was given a great boost by a psychiatrist who, ironically, had been a colleague of my mother's many years before. I had met Dr. Laidlaw more recently at the 1965 symposium on transexualism given by Dr. Benjamin. I made an appointment with him and kept it—dressed as a woman. He was good-naturedly surprised by my appearance but completely open. I told him of my frustrations and of my plans for Casablanca; to my surprise he said that he didn't think I was crazy and that I was certainly old enough to decide what I wanted to do with my life. This gentle, common-sense response did wonders for my confidence. It was especially comforting coming from a man whose familiarity with me and my family went back so far. His comments were hardly profound or openly encouraging, but they were the first in a long time that supported my right to make a decision and my competence to do so. I walked out of his office feeling freer than I had in months.

My final strategy included living as a woman for a year in Europe before going to Casablanca for the surgical change. This would give me some extended experience in facing life as a woman; it would also give me time to allow any complications to arise while I could still turn back. I didn't expect any, but I was working toward an irreversible action. As long as I felt I was progressing, I could afford patience. It was only when there was nothing to look forward to that I grew frantic. Renée would be satisfied with her life as a woman in Europe if she knew that, finally, she would be whole.

Nothing really stood between me and Europe; I had gone as far as the hormones could take me. In all respects save my genitals, I was as much a woman as I would ever be. My breasts were full-sized and normal. My hips were curvaceous. My skin was smooth, and thanks to electrolysis my beard was gone forever. In my general configuration I was like a tall, sleek woman. Only one aspect of my outward appearance displeased me, and I determined to have it fixed before I left for Europe.

One of Josh's continuing snipes at me concerned my Adam's apple. It had always been prominent. This was acceptable in a man but cause for alarm in a woman. Every time Josh mentioned it I winced because I knew he was right. It was a dead giveaway and certainly nothing I wanted to take to Europe with me. I researched the available literature on larynx and thyroid cartilage surgery and decided on a Philadelphia surgeon who might be appropriate. I drove down and kept an appointment, which I had made under an assumed name. I told him that I was a female impressionist who did exotic dancing. This silly story had been effective for the last fifteen years; so I didn't see any reason to improve on it. Telling him that I was a physician was certainly out of the question. I complained that my Adam's apple was interfering with my act and showed him my profile. "How," I asked, "can I persuade anyone I'm a woman with this big lump in my throat?" He agreed that it would be rough and after some hemming and hawing agreed to do the operation. I think he may have been intrigued by the unusualness of the procedure. I may have been the first person in the United States to have this treatment. That meant he would be the first doctor to do it; few surgeons can resist a "first" if the operation is feasible and not particularly dangerous.

Shortly, I entered the hospital and was in due course prepped for surgery. I had to keep reminding myself that I was an exotic dancer and not a doctor. Many times I was tempted to ask too knowledgeable a question or even to give directions. The operation was performed under local anesthetic. First, the skin was laid back, revealing the cartilage underneath. The doctor used an instrument like a dentist's drill with a sanding head to shave away the prominent tissue. It made the same irritating whine that I associated with having my teeth drilled. As he touched the wheel to my Adam's apple I could feel the vibration in the unanesthetized areas of my throat. I lay supine on the table watching his intent eyes concentrating on my neck; occasionally he would shift position to get a better angle on the work. In many ways, he looked very much like a body-shop repairman working on a rusty fender. He put the sander aside frequently and cocked his head thoughtfully, all the while staring critically at his progress. He proceeded carefully, but even the most careful craftsman sometimes makes a mistake. He dug too deep and broke through to the interior. A hole the diameter of a pencil opened, and through it poured bits of cartilage and other debris; I saw his eyes open wide, and at the same moment I was choked by the disintegrating larynx. I grabbed at my ragged throat and convulsively thrashed on the table, driven wild by suffocation. Hacking uncontrollably, I tried to get up but was restrained by the doctor and several burly nurse's aides who were called in. I lay there immobile, my eyes darting wildly about, convinced that I would die. The doctor produced a syringe which he plunged into my larynx to deaden my gag reflex. He worked fast, and I tried to conquer my panic and cooperate as he ran a tube down my throat to suction out the debris that had entered my trachea and bronchi. At last I could breathe normally, and everyone took a rest before the operation was concluded without further complications.

During my week's recovery in the hospital, I experienced the frustration of not getting the deferential treatment usually accorded to physicians. When I would complain about something that I knew from experience to be a legitimate matter for concern, the responses were perfunctory and sometimes curt. As far as they were concerned, I was an exotic dancer, probably gay, and hardly worth their time. This situation was compounded by the fact that my recovery was not uncomplicated; several times during that week my neck had to be drained of the bloody serous fluid that kept collecting there. These factors added up to a rather stormy confinement. I was alternately outraged by the neglect and frightened by the presence of fluid in my neck. At the end of the week, however, I was discharged after being pronounced safely on the road to recovery. One aspect of the operation stays with me to this day. The gravelly quality of my voice is the result of the damage done to my larynx during the operation. I've never been completely happy with my voice since then, but many people think that I had this done purposely to make me sound more feminine. All things considered I guess it was worth it. At least the Adam's apple is pretty much gone.

After I was released from the hospital, I took a week's vacation and then went back to work. It was not long before an amazing rumor about me began to circulate. Putting together all the peculiar factors that characterized my life at the time—my feminine appearance, my bandaged throat, my gravelly voice, and my generally haggard countenance—many people concluded that I had a serious case of cancer. It wasn't a bad theory. Female hormones are sometimes prescribed for certain types of cancer, and my throat operation certainly capped off the impression. Once started, this rumor spread like wildfire and reached such intensity that I was soon pronounced dead by some people. On two

213

different occasions, my father received a spate of sympathy cards offering consolation on the occasion of my death. Interestingly enough, no one ever bothered to ask me what the real explanation was. I suppose they were afraid to find out that it really was cancer and equally afraid to find out it wasn't; an alternative explanation would be far more bizarre than a straightforward terminal disease. I never tried to quell these rumors because they provided me with an excellent cover while I was making my preparations for Europe.

There was little more to do after I had fully recovered from the Adam's apple surgery. The programs that I was in charge of had been reorganized to my liking and were running smoothly. My personal life basically consisted of only two people; Dick and Renée. Both of them were going to Europe although only one was scheduled to return. I requested a leave of absence from the administrations of both Manhattan Eye and Ear and New York Hospital. It was compassionately granted in both instances since they naturally assumed that the leave was related to my cancer. This done, I asked a friend who was a travel agent to book passage for me on the next ship sailing from New York to Europe. He looked in his shipping guide and said, "The *Michelangelo* leaves on Tuesday."

"Fine," I said, "get me and Rocco on it." We shook hands, and as I was about to walk out the door he called after me.

"Don't you want to know where the ship is going?"

"No, it doesn't make any difference."

"Well, it's going to Genoa, in case you're interested."

"That's fine with me," I said, and left.

16

European Fantasy

During my final days in New York, I sublet my apartment, acquired the necessary papers, and said goodbye to friends. Most of my personal effects were moved to my father's house in Forest Hills. I felt a genuine pang at the thought of leaving that apartment. Though it had seen some personal struggle, for the most part it had been a safe haven, a calm place at the center of a whirl of frantic activity. No longer would I have this stable base of operations; for a time at least I would be a gypsy.

The papers required more hassling than any normal person could imagine. For most of the people in the United States, obtaining travel documents is a simple matter; but, as it had for most of my life, my peculiar personality ended up making the simple things hard. Technically, I was a man, but I would be traveling and living as a woman. Naturally, this was bound to arouse suspicion at border crossings and ports of entry. My passport had been issued in the name of Richard Raskind and contained a picture of me as a man. Therefore, I came to rely most heavily on another piece of identification, my international driver's license, that featured a picture of me as a woman and was made out in the name of R. H. Raskind. I signed it Renée Raskind. I got the international license by presenting my New York State driver's license to the appropriate agency. They provided me with the new document that had a thumbnail-sized picture of Dick stapled to it. I took the license home, removed the picture, and showed it to a photographer, asking him to duplicate the format, only this time with me as Renée. He did this easily, and I stapled the new picture on making sure to line up with the old holes; thank goodness they hadn't glued the picture on. Whenever possible, I used the international driver's license, (which had my passport number on it) rather than the passport itself. This made life much easier and almost always worked whenever I was asked for identification within any country.

At international borders, I had to show my passport and go through the rigmarole of explaining that I was a transsexual undergoing treatment. Reactions to this varied from stoic acceptance to open hostility. Under everyday circumstances though, like hotel check ins or picking up mail at the local American Express office, the driver's license worked fine. Another valuable piece of identification was my naval officer's I.D. I used this in several emergency situations, explaining that I was Mrs. Raskind. No one ever made a connection between the tough-looking lieutenant commander on the card and the woman presenting it. In the photo, I was brush cut, somber, and square jawed. As Renée, my face was so different as to be unrecognizable.

During my last few days in New York, I visited with my intimate friends and let them know what I was up to. Len and Joel were supportive but sad. I think both of them presumed that they would never see Dick Raskind again; over the previous months they had watched my violent mood swings with increasing alarm. It had become clear to them that I was approaching the breaking point. Though their impulse was to advise against the change, they knew that any postponement would be dangerous. As my anxieties grew so did my potential to harm myself. Had either of them thought of an alternative course of action, I'm sure he would have suggested it, but both realized that I had exhausted all the other options. Josh, on the other hand, had a rooting interest in what I did. Seeing that I was determined to go through with the operation, he had strongly advised that I live for a year as a woman. Of course, this was not a new idea. Dr. Benjamin, Dr. Pomeroy, and others had suggested the same thing, but it was largely at Josh's insistence that I overcame my impulse to fly immediately to Casablanca after my disappointing experiences with American medical men. I did not follow Josh's suggestions to the letter since the best idea he could come up with was that I practice medicine as a woman some place in the states. I believe

216

his specific recommendation was Oklahoma City. Now, I'm sure there are many wonderful things about Oklahoma City, but somehow it didn't have the romantic flavor I was looking for. This was probably what the ever practical Josh had in mind. If Renée could survive in Oklahoma City, then she might have a chance in the rest of the world. She would have had her mettle seriously tested. On the other hand, I saw no reason why I should struggle among the oil derricks when I could vacation in Europe. Besides, Europe was a lot closer to Casablanca, and that's where I was going to end up. Even in our last few meetings Josh continued to press for the harsh realities of Oklahoma as opposed to some fantasy trip through the Old World.

In a way, he was right. I was definitely on a fantasy trip. I looked forward to the sea voyage as if I were a character in an F. Scott Fitzgerald novel. I had always been attracted to his elegant, upper-crust heroines, so often troubled, so often situated in posh, exotic surroundings. On the day of the *Michelangelo*'s sailing, I got my six suitcases together and crammed them into the little elevator that ran to the door of my apartment. These suitcases were full of women's apparel. Somewhere pushed to the back was a change of men's clothes. But other than that one safety measure I was uncompromising. I had no desire to be a man anymore. As the elevator descended, I watched the entrance to my cozy apartment slowly rise out of view. A feeling of nostalgia swept over me but quickly dissipated when I ran into my landlady in the vestibule. The day of my departure was the first time she had ever seen me as a woman. It seemed an ironic beginning to Renée's yearlong coming-out party. My landlady was even more shaken than Albert the superintendent had been; she did not even venture a hello but simply pretended not to have seen me. I was grateful since I had no real desire to start life as Renée with an explanation to someone from Dick's past.

As the stewards settled me in my cabin, they told me that the *Michelangelo*'s departure had been delayed until the evening. After inspecting the area of the kennel where Rocco was supposed to stay, I left the ship and spent the rest of the afternoon doing some last-minute visiting. When I returned to the ship I was greeted by the chief steward as "Dotoressa Raskind." This puzzled me because I had not identified myself as a doctor. The steward also deferentially gave me a package that had been left for me by a visitor; it turned out to be a gift of Swiss chocolates. I never learned the identity of my caller, but I've always suspected that it was my father. It would have been like him to ask for "Doctor Raskind" instead of using the name Renée. In addition, the staff members on the ship seemed to have doubled their attentiveness to me. All first-class passengers get good service, but I could hardly make a move for the rest of the voyage without being offered assistance of one sort or another. I think Dad spread some money around to insure that proper care would be taken of me. When the ship sailed that evening, I felt that in a way I took my father's approval with me. It was a typically indirect interaction but warming nonetheless. Naturally, we never discussed it.

The *Michelangelo* lived up to my romantic expectations. The decks were wide and full of picturesque chairs where I could sit with a blanket tucked tightly around my body and reread *Tender is the Night*, which I'd gotten out of the ship's library. If I felt more active, there was a large swimming pool and even a gymnasium. Off the stern of the ship I could shoot skeet, an activity that had a definitely aristocratic air about it and so added to my feeling of having stepped into a novel. We all dressed for dinner, the men in tuxedos and the women in evening gowns. Formal attire seemed the only appropriate dress for a dining room so spacious and elegant. Far larger than many fine New York restaurants, the *Michelangelo*'s dining area was lavishly appointed and fairly sparkled with the refraction of light off the crystal and polished silver. When the steward asked if I would like to sit alone or at a table with others, I chose to eat by myself; I was not yet confident enough to talk at close quarters with random strangers. Besides, I liked the image of a solitary and mysterious woman, perhaps hiding a secret sorrow.

I paid special attention to my preparations for my first public dinner. My hair was not yet long enough to suit my female persona; so I wore a shoulder-length brunette wig. I wasn't wholly satisfied with this because a hairpiece however good, always signals dissimulation, and I was extremely sensitive on this point even though I realized that many women wore wigs and that, alone, it did not amount to a giveaway.

As the result of years of attempting to hide my maleness under thick makeup I still had the tendency to use too much, such as a person with bad skin might use. I was also too liberal with eyeliner and mascara. Although not grotesque, the effect was slightly excessive and was noticed by at least one of the people on the cruise with whom I eventually became friendly. At the time, however, I felt relatively confident and was genuinely pleased with the clothes I had bought for the trip. These included two fancy gowns: one was a shimmering sheath covered with rhinestones and slit modestly up both sides to about calf level; the other was an elegant black velvet number, very bare around the shoulders and bosom with only spaghetti straps as a nod in the direction of modesty. It was the latter dress that I chose to wear for my first appearance in the grand dining room. It suited my pretensions to quiet elegance. At the same time, the darkness of it minimized my size as much as possible. Painfully sensitive about my height, I chose low-heeled shoes; since the other women were wearing high heels, my tallness was less apparent though still noticeable.

In speaking to members of the dining-room staff I tried to make my voice feminine. It had long ago recovered as well as it was ever going to from the effects of the Adam's apple surgery. At best it could be compared to Lauren Bacall's voice, at worst to Gene Kelly's. I had resigned myself to the rough-edged quality; what I practiced aboard ship was introducing variations of tone into it. I had noticed that men, myself included, tended to klunk along inside a very narrow range whereas women's voices fluctuated more readily between highs and lows. I tried to acquire this extra dimension without going overboard and sounding like a campy transvestite. There is also a difference in the way that women pronounce their s's, with slightly more sibilance than a man; I worked a bit on that too. The *Michelangelo* was my transitional vehicle. Whatever moves I made toward my feminine destiny were extremely tentative on that crossing. I was not confident enough to be bold.

One thing did happen that improved my confidence considerably. On my first appearance in the dining room I caught the eye of a retired Italian military officer. He was a distinguished-looking man in his sixties. About my height, he seemed a bit taller because, although he was stocky, he stood with the erect bearing of a *commendatore*. His hair was gray and thinning, but I found his maturity attractive. He conveyed a sense of strength, which I still find very attractive in older men. The commendatore approached me after dinner in the salon where I was having a drink. He spoke only a little English and a little French; Of course, I spoke English and enough French to get by. The nearest thing to Italian that I was familiar with was Latin, which I tried tentatively but with no success. Our level of discourse remained very basic from the moment he presented himself.

"Buena sera!" He stood there in his tuxedo with his heels pressed together and his hand extended. He bent slightly at the waist.

"Good evening," I replied, putting out my own hand to touch him in greeting. To my surprise he grasped my fingers firmly, bent, and kissed my knuckles. Renée suddenly felt very warm and nice. Hand kissing! This was more like it!

"May I sit?" He accompanied this question with a gesture indicating an empty chair at my table. I nodded slightly, and he settled heavily into the place opposite me. "I saw you eat," he said by way of explanation, pantomiming, at the same time, someone looking across a large room at someone else. "Was it good?" In order to make up for the juvenile level of our conversation he was smiling a little more than was warranted. I didn't mind because in spite of his age he had excellent teeth as well as a strong jaw and eyes that appraised me with obvious interest. This was the first time I had ever been openly, unreservedly ogled by a man. I quite liked it.

"The food on the ship is delicious," I said in response to his question. "I have to be careful not to eat too much."

"Ahh," he blustered doubtfully, "you are so . . ." he searched for the correct word. Finally he gave up. Looking down at his thickened waist he said in a rueful way, "I must watch! You are . . . bellisima."

This man was not hard to take at all. In spite of his limited vocabulary he knew how to make a girl feel appreciated. The more he appreciated me the more I felt like a girl. He became my companion for the evenings; together we would walk the decks, gamble at the horse-race game or sit and have drinks in the company of the few other passengers with whom I'd become acquainted. Sometimes we danced, and I found to my surprise that, though Dick was a poor dancer, Renée was rather good at it when she had a man whose lead she could follow. With the commendatore's hand firmly in the small of my back, I glided with unprecedented smoothness across the floor. We pirouetted, dipped, and generally made a success of it. At other times, the commendatore used Dick's old techniques of simply standing quite still and taking small steps. I felt good in his arms and discovered, to my surprise, that an older man can be quite strong. I guess I expected a man in his sixties to be doddering, but the commendatore was vigorous and sometimes overpowering. This was most noticeable when he became ardent. Normally, he didn't have much of a chance to get physical because I restricted most of our association to public places; but in the privacy of the deck elevator, I would suddenly find myself under romantic attack. It was in this situation that I felt his strength most. Though I tried to control his arms and hands, he was simply too strong. He swept my hands aside with surprising ease and suddenly, he would be groping my breasts. I didn't mind some of this—as a matter of fact, I liked it. The danger was that the commendatore would become too ambitious and try to move into more intimate areas. If I gave him my breasts without a fight, he would surely become optimistic about getting a hand between my legs. I regularly wore a panty girdle that gave me a smooth line, but I was understandably reluctant to have anyone feel me. Try as I might I couldn't keep him from scoring a few fleeting feels down below the waist. However, he didn't seem to notice anything alarming, and usually by the time he had progressed to that stage, the elevator door would be starting to open.

Before the commendatore left the ship I even spent some time in his stateroom in the early hours of the morning. I felt I could handle him and was anxious to experience his excitement, to be the object of his desire. I had told him that I was recently divorced and was recovering from a traumatic relationship with my husband. I added that I had not yet learned to trust men again. He took my struggles against his advances to be a symptom of my bruised sensibilities and was understanding. A less kind man might have pronounced me a cock teaser and forced himself on me. Instead, the commendatore played a tactical game of advance and retreat. These maneuvers were punctuated by time-outs during which we would enjoy snifters of brandy. I must confess that I enjoyed feeling his lips pressed against mine and inhaling his breath, tangy with the brandy's bouquet. I think that a hand slipped into the bodice of my gown to cup my breast was as much satisfaction as he ever got, but he seemed relatively content. I was genuinely sad to see him leave the boat in Naples and, even more surprising, I was seized with a slight fit of jealousy when I saw him greet his wife and children on the dock. I stood by the railing of the ship mildly stunned by what I was feeling. Certainly I had no designs on this fatherly foreigner, yet I could not deny my pique when I saw him embrace his stocky wife and equally stocky teenage daughter. Part of my feeling was brought about by the fact that he had never mentioned his family, though that certainly would not have kept me from wrestling with him. I think that this was the first time that Renée had ever had the chance to feel possessive about anyone, and she seized it. After all, he was really her first man, and there had been intimacy of a sort. Besides, it was romantic to stand there amid the festivities of docking and watch my amour disappear into the crowd, never to be heard from again. By the next day I had recovered nicely.

The commendatore had provided me with a light introduction to a woman's role in the game of the sexes. My confidence had risen tremendously as a result of his pursuit. As the *Michelangelo* steamed through the quiet Mediterranean waters, I felt myself sinking more and more into the persona of Renée. It was not a role anymore. I felt myself to be a woman, and except for the much atrophied genitals between my legs I really was one. The distance I had covered and the prospect of a radically different European culture were helping me to dissociate myself from the old life as Dick. Renée had flourished for her longest period in Paris years ago. What I moved toward as I sat watching the ship's wake spread out into the Mediterranean was like a homecoming, a return to reality rather than an escape. I thought again about Josh's plan, which would have had me in Oklahoma City practicing ophthalmology amongst the oil derricks. Where would I have found a courtly Italian commendatore in Oklahoma? Clearly I had made the right decision.

However, my feminine presentation was not accepted without reservation by everyone. I could see curiosity and confusion in some people's faces when they talked to me. Those with a critical eye and a suspicious nature spotted me. By and large, I stayed away from them, but even some of the people that had befriended me apparently had their suspicions. One was a middle-aged woman named Anita who had kindly cared for Rocco when I was struck with seasickness during the rough first few days of the trip. I had taken Rocco out of the kennel as soon as we had cleared New York Harbor but while I was sick I couldn't keep him in my stateroom or look after him. Anita had taken over in a very comradely way saying that she liked Rocco and enjoyed the opportunity to be with him. We socialized for the rest of the trip. After the third or fourth day out I got the distinct feeling that she was on to me. Anita never said anything directly; but, when she left the ship in Gibraltar she kissed me and said, "Renée, I hope you find what you want in life." It was such a simple sentiment and so sweetly offered that I wanted to cry. In a way, Anita's acceptance of me in spite of what she knew was as important to my morale as the commendatore's unsuspecting desire.

When the time came for me to leave the ship in Genoa, I had my first brush with passport officials. They came on board and checked the passengers' papers in one of the large parlor rooms. My tension built slowly as the official in charge examined document after document. The fact that I might be questioned in public put me in a sweat. At last the man arrived before me; he wore a dark uniform with shiny buttons and flashed an equally shiny smile at me as he took my passport. Flipping it open crisply, he stared for a moment, raised his gaze to my face, and then looked down at the passport again. A quizzical look replaced his official smile. He was opening his mouth to speak when the chief steward of the ship stepped forward and whispered in his ear. The passport officer snapped his eyes over to me, smiled, and said, "These are in order. Let me see the papers on the dog." He spent the next few minutes examining Rocco's papers far more carefully than he had mine. I have no idea what the chief steward said to him; it may have been something my father had said, assuming that he was the one who left the chocolates for me back in New York. On the other hand, the steward might have simply discerned my situation and taken it upon himself to explain. Whatever the case he immediately became a good friend of mine and fell heir to a hefty tip.

In Genoa, I boarded a train which would take me to Modena by way of Bologna. I was scheduled to pick up a Maserati at their factory in Modena. I had ordered the car before leaving New York and happily looked forward to the freedom of movement it would give me. Once I had it I would again feel that sense of completeness that an appropriate automobile afforded me. Meanwhile, I was aboard a picturesque train rushing through the Italian countryside. In its way, the train was just as romantic as the *Michelangelo* had been. I occupied a small compartment with room enough for perhaps six people if everyone sat close together. As it was, I had it to myself for quite some time. I sat watching the well-groomed fields and groves through which the little train chugged, occasionally making a distinctive European "toot toot." I began to get the feeling that I could well be a fictional heroine lost in her thoughts aboard, say, the Orient Express. I shifted languorously in my seat and placed my cheek against the window glass. I could see the reflected outline of my woman's face overlaid on the streaking countryside. Suddenly my eye caught a new movement in the glass; it was the compartment door being slid open. I turned and standing there in the doorway was a tall, dark, and handsome man. Things certainly were falling into place. A scriptwriter could not have concocted a scenario more to my liking, and a casting director couldn't have picked a better player. He remained motionless for a moment and then entered the compartment, closing the door after him. Seating himself opposite me, he fussed momentarily with a briefcase and then, sighing heavily, placed it tidily next to his hip. While he was doing this I discreetly sized him up. He reminded me strongly of George Plimpton. The thing I remember best about him is the sense of warmth that he projected; from the beginning I pegged him as a nice guy. For his part, he showed an active interest in me. He spoke excellent English and upon learning that I was an unmarried doctor expressed a heartfelt concern over the loneliness that surely must afflict me.

"It is so wrong for a woman like you to live only for the work," he said solicitously.

"It's not so bad," I replied, making sure not to sound too positive.

"Ha! But what about the romance? One does not live fully without it!"

"Well," I said demurely, "I have not lived entirely without romance. I was married, but we divorced."

"How could he let you go? Was he mad?"

"He left me for another woman."

"Surely he was out of his mind." At this point he moved consolingly across the compartment to sit beside me. "You are too much the woman for a man to look elsewhere." He was such a good natured fellow that I almost believed him. Carried away with the potential of the situation, I think he really felt himself to be my savior. He took my hand reflectively and said, "This hand was meant to be caressed." He bent his head and kissed the tips of my fingers. Here was a matter considerably different from the hand kissing of the commendatore. This man was young, vigorous, and no older than I was. I felt a pleasurable ping of excitement. "These lips," he continued, "should be kissed." And he did so.

I was having such a good time that I gave little thought to what might happen next. Though passive I was more than willing to be on the receiving end of those warm caresses. He never pinched me or hurt me in any way, and when I had to stop him from moving below my waist he agreeably turned his attention back to my breasts. Our passion was interrupted a couple of times by passengers coming and going in the compartment. Federico would respectfully leave me alone and amiably include the newcomer in conversation. He was equally fluent in both English and French, and we spoke as much in one as the other. Perhaps the intruders sensed that there was something going on between Federico and me because no one stayed for more than fifteen minutes. Alone again we would heatedly return to our pleasure. After about an hour and a half of this kissing and fondling, the train approached Bologna. That was Federico's destination; when he got off the train, I, my six suitcases, and Rocco got off with him.

I felt that I owed myself at least one night with this good-natured con artist. I was sure that he'd show me a good time. Besides, how often do these romantic encounters happen on European trains? How often would I be propositioned by an utterly benign George Plimpton look-alike? It seemed too good to pass up.

Federico checked us into a modest hotel. During dinner I brought up the subject of my recent divorce. Again he expressed his disbelief over how any man so fortunate to have me would look at another woman. Needless to say, this was the kind of thing I wanted to hear, but I had another reason for broaching the subject. The most important part of the fabrication was yet to come. "After the divorce," I said quietly, "I was lonely."

"This is natural," he replied, taking my hand understandingly. He was kissing the tips of my fingers again.

"I took a lover," I went on, casting my eyes down at my plate. "He turned out to be the wrong man for me." Federico grasped my hand more tightly and made sympathetic sounds. "He was a nice man, but we were not . . . *simpatico*." Federico gave me a great smile which clearly indicated that in a short while I would find out the real meaning of the word *simpatico*. "We parted in a friendly way, but there was a complication." Raised eyebrows. "I found out that I was pregnant." More sympathetic sounds. "Naturally, I couldn't have the child." Reassuring nods of agreement from Federico. "An abortion was the only answer." Even more profound nodding. "Actually, this trip is part of my convalescence." Federico's eyes narrowed a bit, and the pressure on my hand lessened.

"You are not yet recovered?" he asked plaintively.

"No." I shook my head to emphasize the point. "I can't be truly intimate with a man."

"Why did you not tell me?"

"It's not easy to discuss. I knew that you'd be disappointed."

"But you agreed to stay with me! Certainly, if I was very gentle . . ."

"No," I said again. "It would be dangerous."

"Ah, yes. Well, we must not endanger your health." He looked so crestfallen that I reached across and patted his shoulder with my free hand. "Don't worry, we'll find a way to have fun together." With that his good humor began to revive, and we spent a pleasant hour eating and drinking.

Once back in the hotel room we prepared for bed. Federico liked to sleep nude. I, on the other hand, slipped beneath the covers dressed in a yellow nightgown under which was the indispensable panty girdle. Federico was on me in a flash, and we spent the next two hours in an agreeable tussle. He wasn't too happy about the panty girdle, but after a couple of wistful tugs he left it pretty much alone. I think he held out the hope that I had overstated the case earlier, perhaps out of shyness or fear. The uncompromising panty girdle put that notion to rest once and for all. Resilient fellow that he was Federico was soon busying himself with my breasts to which I allowed him unrestricted access. He seemed delighted with them and his expert attention gave me much satisfaction. Federico and I happily climbed all over one another until finally he climaxed and we fell asleep in each other's arms. I remember feeling very tender toward him as I lay there drifting off to sleep.

The next morning we woke, dressed companionably, and had breakfast. Federico gallantly saw me to the train and gave me a juicy good-bye kiss. As the train pulled out I looked back and saw him waving vigorously. I thought to myself once again, "What a nice man!" Renée was lucky to have found him and to have had such a success so early in her new life.

The Maserati I picked up in Modena was a reconditioned model. Previously owned, the car had been lovingly rebuilt by the craftsmen who had originally made it. The guarantee was the same as if it had been new. My automobile seemed a perfect reflection of my personal state. I too was reconditioned or at least on the way to being so. As I toured the Maserati plant I marveled at the attention to quality. In one room were ten men painting a car; in the next, ten more were working on the chassis of another. They were intent in their work, as dedicated as surgeons. I hoped that my reconditioning in Casablanca would be performed with as much tender care and that at the end of the process the workers would be as unabashedly proud of the product. As the foreman handed me the keys to my silver-blue Mistral coupe, he fairly glowed with satisfaction. He even treated me to lunch at a charming restaurant, during which we discussed the intricacies of the wonderful machine—this in addition to the hour of explanation that I had received at the factory. His deference was the second gratifying thing about claiming the Maserati.

I had used my navy I.D. card, and the plant executives automatically assumed that I was Mrs. Raskind, the wife of an important military officer. Italian men are extremely gallant with any woman they consider a lady of "class." I was squired around the facility with considerable pomp and felt rather regal sweeping along with two or three attentive retainers, all anxious to answer my questions and to compliment my obvious appreciation of fine craftsmanship. There was hand kissing just before I climbed into the cockpit of my car and many solicitous remarks warning me to keep this powerful machine under control. "You must accustom yourself to the personality of the automobile," said one executive as he opened the door on the passenger's side so that Rocco could take his place. "Then you will find that she serves you well, but you must get to know her."

I got to know her flashing along the Autostrada at a hundred and forty miles per hour. In Europe there are no speed limits. The fastest machine has the right of way—and there was nothing faster than my Maserati. The inside lane is the high velocity one, and a flash of the lights in the rearview mirror of a slower car brings an immediate response; deferentially, it swings into the right lane leaving the way clear. I hardly lifted my foot off the accelerator from Modena to Milan. I felt protected in the elegant *cabini* of my Mistral. It was quite a change of pace from the only other time I had driven so fast. That was through the deserts of Arizona and New Mexico with the wind whistling under the plastic screens of the makeshift Shelby Cobra. The 427 engine had filled the air with a wild, throbbing roar. On the Autostrada all was quiet, comfortable, refined, complete. I was like one of Milton's spirits in *Paradise Lost*: "For spirits when they like can either sex assume or both." In the back of my mind hung an image of Casablanca; exotic and white, shimmering in the African sun. There I would surrender my dual nature and my days as a hermaphroditic spirit would be finished. At last I would know the pleasure enjoyed by ordinary mortals—to be one entity.

In Milan I reluctantly consigned the Maserati to a garage for safekeeping. During my short visit there would be no need to drive it around town in traffic. I spent most of my first two days in Milan at La Galleria, an attraction within easy walking distance of my hotel. It was a huge shopping district enclosed in a soaring glass arcade; one of those ornate, wrought-iron structures dating from the nineteenth century. Inside were typically Italian shops. It was as if a piece of Italian culture had been put under glass. Rocco and I wandered among these shops; on my second day we stopped in a little pâtisserie for some chocolate. While I was debating my choice I was approached by a man and a woman who used Rocco as a pretext to start a conversation. The conversation quickly shifted to me and my business in Milan. Carlo D'Angelo, short, bald, and stocky, was an architect and, as I gathered, was very successful. His wife, Dantine, was Scandinavian. She was almost as tall as me but very curvaceous, the Anita Ekberg type. We chatted for over an hour as we drank coffee and snacked on pastry. At length we parted company with vague promises that we'd get together again before I left the city.

The next morning a bouquet of roses from Carlo and Dantine was delivered to my hotel room. Here was proof of the warmth for which Italians were famous. Later that day Dantine called and asked if I would like to go to the opera at La Scala. The prospect of an evening at the opera fit right into Renée's fantasies. Dantine said that Carlo had a business meeting and couldn't attend, so it would be just us girls, which suited me fine. I was far more interested in Dantine than in Carlo, whom I found good-natured but loud and excitable. Dantine and I made an eye-catching pair.

That evening I wore my rhinestone evening dress. In those days I was not in training as a professional athlete and so looked slender and, ironically, more feminine than in the years following my operation. Dantine, also tall, complemented me nicely. She was blonde; I was brunette. She was fair; I was deeply tanned. She was curvaceous; I was slender. The only better companion might have been a handsome and sophisticated man. Still, such a man would have meant problems, and with Dantine there was only relaxed, sisterly fun—with no complications. Both of us enjoyed the lecherous glances that were cast our way as we walked down the aisle to take our seats before the curtain went up on *Boris Godunov*. (Actually, I found the lecherous glances to be the highlight of the evening as anyone who has ever sat through *Boris Godunov* will understand.)

Carlo met us for a late supper after the opera. He was full of compliments and playfully pinched both our behinds. While we ate he talked of his work and asked if I'd like to see their home. He hadn't designed the building but had supervised the refurbishing of the interior; since he seemed anxious to show it off, I accepted. Truthfully, I was beginning to feel like a character in a Fellini movie. This gesticulating upper-class architect was very much like the sort of Italians who populated his films. Carlo talked fast but not very well in English. Often he would turn to Dantine, who spoke fluently, for the correct word. She would quietly supply it, and he would charge ahead until the next stumbling block arose. As he spoke he tended to lean closer and closer, like those people trying to get Guido's attention in Fellini's *8½*.

This impression was further enhanced when we arrived at their home. It was a town house, compact and modern, yet charming. There were three floors, four if you count the basement where the indoor pool was located. The ground floor contained a small kitchen, a dining room and a salon furnished in an eclectic combination of ultramodern and antique furniture. It was tasteful in a Fellini sort of way. The second and third floors were devoted to bedrooms and to Carlo's den. These rooms were reached by means of an elevator that was located in the center of the building. The bedrooms were done in the same style as the salon but were cozier. The beds were antiques, so high that a little step stool had to be used to get into one.

The tour was concluded on the top floor, and we all rode the elevator back down to the salon where Dantine fixed us drinks and we chatted for awhile. Carlo seemed surprised that I understood his professional conversation and was able to comment appropriately on what he said. "Renée, you are so intelligent," he observed, pronouncing "intelligent" with a hard g. Actually, he was difficult to understand, not because of his intellectualism but because of his broken English. For that reason the conversation was a bit labored, and he soon suggested that we dance. He walked to an impressive-looking stereo system, flicked a switch and the exuberant strains of "Quando" filled the room. He swept me into a clear space and began a kind of cha-cha, complete with dips. I was relieved when the next song turned out to be a ballad and Carlo relaxed into a slow two-step dance. However, I soon noticed that Carlo had more than dancing on his mind. The hand that at first had rested respectfully in the small of my back crept downward to my ass. He began to massage my right cheek, slowly at first and then with increased fervor. Gingerly he worked his hand down to the point where the cheek curved under. My rhinestone gown was so tight that he couldn't make much progress, but it was not for lack of trying. I glanced anxiously around to catch Dantine's reaction, but she was no longer in the room. Carlo was beginning to make little growling sounds.

The ballad ended, and I suggested that we sit the next one out. Dantine re-entered the salon, and Carlo danced a turn with her. I noticed that he was not nearly as bold with his wife as he was with me. During our next dance she disappeared again, and Carlo paid some attention to my breasts. Although I was a little surprised by this behavior and Carlo was not really attractive to me, I was grateful for any masculine attention. I was actually flattered that he'd be interested in me when his own wife was so beautiful. I chalked it up to the Italian temperament and took what pleasure I could, though I was made nervous by the prospect that Dantine might catch us. That didn't happen, but soon I asked to be taken back to my hotel. On the way Dantine said, "Renée, why don't you come and stay with us for a while."

"Well, that's very nice, but I couldn't impose."

"Nonsense. We have a beautiful house to share, and both Carlo and I are quite fond of you. We'd like to enjoy your company for a few more days, and it would be unfair to ask you to stay at your expensive hotel."

"It sounds nice but . . ."

"Come, come, be my sister for a few days."

Carlo added his assurances, and before I knew it I was scheduled to be their house guest. The prospect wasn't hard to take: these people were wealthy, well-connected, and cosmopolitan. I was utterly alone and by no means on an open-ended budget. If Carlo liked me a bit more than he should, well, could I be blamed? Besides, a certain amount of goosing seemed to be the accepted form of behavior in Italy. Carlo's groping was the private extension of what had happened to me a dozen times in public. Strangers yelled, whistled, and poked at me every day. In crowds, I had felt strange men's hands on my ass so often that I had almost stopped paying attention. In the light of this national preoccupation Carlo seemed pretty normal. I accepted their invitation.

For the first couple of days, my stay was uneventful. We woke at midmorning and had a cup of strong coffee and a croissant in the little kitchen. Carlo was usually dressed by that time and left afterward for work. After he had roared away Dantine and I would dress and spend the day shopping or sight-seeing. In the evening Carlo would take us out to dinner, and then we'd return to the house for more drinking, dancing, and feeling up. On my second night as their guest Dantine no longer left the room while Carlo made free with his hands. I looked at her questioningly; she looked back mildly and, almost as if this were a cue, Carlo stepped up his advances. He locked his arms more tightly around me and thrust his pelvis against mine. One hand began to gather the material of my skirt so that the hem rose slowly in the back. A decision was called for and, in sexual matters, Renée likes to be led. She has always been responsive to a forceful presentation. I was already giddy from the drinks and the dancing. If Dantine had no objections—I looked at her again, and she was still smiling blandly—I would simply relax and go along for the ride.

Carlo seemed to sense this decision. Almost immediately, he led me to the elevator and put it in motion. While we rose, he continued to fondle me and then started to unzip my clothes. We stepped off into the master bedroom and the elevator descended, leaving us alone. As he went about disrobing me I could hear the elevator coming up again. When it stopped, Dantine stepped out already unzipping the back of her dress. By this time Carlo was himself naked and sporting a perky erection. His body was covered with curly hair; though he was short he looked kind of cute. Dantine had shrugged out of her clothes and was looking on as Carlo tugged at my panty girdle. This was a crucial moment. I felt utterly secure about my breasts and really didn't even mind being felt between my legs. I had inserted a piece of foam rubber in the girdle and this gave me quite a natural feel. My genitals were so small and soft that they molded themselves unobtrusively to my body. Naturally, though, the panty girdle had to stay on. I glanced enviously at Dantine's pubis, covered with a thick mat of blondish hair. Her hips were generously curved and her breasts, though heavy, were firm and sagged only slightly. "Actually," I thought, "mine are better than hers." This bit of feminine competitive spirit flashed only briefly in my mind since Carlo was pulling at the girdle again.

"Please," I said, "I can't take it off. I've had an abortion." This halted Carlo although I saw suspicion in his eyes.

"Ah, Renée," he said and put his mouth on my breast, all the while letting his fingers play around the waistband of the girdle. He was apparently used to driving women wild with this attention because he launched a couple of sneak attacks on the girdle when he figured I was distracted. But I was more than a match for him since my participation in this scene was almost totally cerebral. It was as if I were the camera on a motion-picture set—Fellini's camera. Certainly what I was seeing was interesting, but Carlo was not about to catch me off guard. He had worked me around until I was leaning against one of the high beds. Dantine had already climbed up on it and was viewing the action from a height about level with my rib cage. Unable to make any headway with the girdle Carlo shifted his attention to

Dantine. I think he figured that the best way to win me over was through a demonstration of the good things in store for me if only I would relent. The way he went about it was rather comical; he arranged Dantine with her pelvis at the edge of the bed; her legs were doubled up so that her heels contacted her hips, knees in the air. Carlo then pulled up the step stool and stood on it. This raised his groin to the height of the bed, allowing him to stand there with her knees in his armpits like a pair of crutches. So positioned, he made passionate love to her. I moved the camera around to get various perspectives on the action, but it was Fellini however I looked at it. Occasionally Carlo would glance over at me to see if I was getting the idea. I would smile back noncommittally. Both partners climaxed noisily and Carlo fell forward on her. We lounged around on the bed for another hour or so, and then I retired to my room.

This sequence of events was repeated a couple more times with diminishing interest on my part. At the end of the fourth day I began to feel a bit like a captive. Both Carlo and Dantine had been hinting broadly that I should accompany them on a trip to Africa. They intended to hunt some obscure man-eating fish. The deck beside the pool in the basement was piled high with scuba equipment that they planned to use on the expedition. I politely declined their invitation, but they were hard to convince. Each time I attempted to move on, Carlo and Dantine refused to let me go. They were adamant in a friendly way, but adamant nonetheless. At the end of a week I had to brush aside their good-natured insistence and make a break for it. Reluctantly, they helped me pack my things in the Maserati. To the last suitcase they were still browbeating me. I drove away with a sigh of relief. In the rearview mirror I could see Carlo and Dantine waving wistfully. I think they had held out fond hopes of getting into that panty girdle; instead they would have to settle for a man-eating fish.

Speeding north toward France I reflected on the trip so far. It seemed fair to call it a success. My personality as Renée was well in hand. I hardly had to think when I answered questions about my past. I was a professional woman. My marriage had disintegrated (possibly because of the demands of my career as an ophthalmologist, though I never discussed it—too painful). Further, I was using my vacation in Europe to recover from an

233

abortion. I had repeated these fabrications so often that I almost believed them myself. Socially, I had moved easily through the international mix in the *Michelangelo*'s first-class section. Of course, I had been spotted by a few people, but that was early in the trip. During the last couple of weeks I had received plenty of reinforcement. Nobody seemed very suspicious. I figured that my presentation was improving. Certainly Carlo and Dantine had been taken in. Their friends whom I had met casually on a couple of occasions had likewise been fooled.

On the sexual front I had been more successful than I had any right to expect, considering the limitations of my anatomy. My gratification had been mostly cerebral, to be sure, but the potential for a fulfilling sex life was obviously there. Strangely, the only time I really experienced any erotic sensation between my legs was at night when I dreamed. On a couple of occasions I awoke in the middle of what in a normal man would have been a wet dream, but I had neither an ejaculation nor an orgasm. The sensation was more as if my gonads were vibrating. It was a very warm and delightful feeling, but it never peaked in anything like a climax. The vibration would continue for about ten seconds, tapering off slowly. An interesting point is that I was a female in these dreams. Though I sometimes assumed the male role in other types of dreams, the ones associated with this sexual sensation always featured me as a woman. Even so, my male sex organs responded as best they could.

If anything had been suspicious about my experiences up to that point it was that they had been so unnaturally eventful. As Dick, I had been in the middle of many bizarre situations, but there had also been long periods of more or less normal day-to-day life. So far, Renée had been in one unusual encounter after another. Granted, she was on a trip to Europe, and she was open to all sorts of encounters; yet these peculiar episodes had presented themselves—they hadn't been sought out. Renée seemed to draw them like a magnet; I wondered if she would be capable of a normal life.

That question was answered in Paris. For a month I lived a comparatively uneventful existence. By uneventful, I mean that nobody seduced me on a train or offered to take me to Africa. The nearest I came to a sensational episode was when I was spotted in a beauty parlor by a well-known fashion photographer. He was impressed with my appearance and asked if I'd like to pose for some pictures. I agreed without hesitation. This tribute from a beauty expert was too flattering to pass up. He even took some shots of me in filmy lingerie though the one he eventually used was an outdoor shot featuring a full-length fur coat. My relationship with the photographer was friendly but strictly platonic.

With the exception of those photographic sessions, my life in Paris was refreshingly normal. On a brief stop in Chamonix, France, I had met a Parisian doctor who had given me the name of a colleague to look up when I arrived in the city. He felt that we'd have a lot in common since she was a female, an ophthalmologist, and an avid sportswoman. Incidentally, she had also been an operative in the French underground during World War Two. Making Yvette's acquaintance gave me entrance into a fascinating circle of people associated with the French medical community. I became friends with two other women ophthalmologists. One of these, Nicole, was the Parisian version of what I had been in New York: an expert on ocular motility in children. She became a great friend and along with the others provided a social fabric into which Renée could fit herself. With them I experienced acceptance and warmth within an everyday context.

Typically, my day in Paris would begin with a breakfast in the dining area of the modest hotel where I stayed. It was run by a family with whom I became friendly. Their son struck up quite a love affair with Rocco; so after his morning walk I never had to worry about him. The boy was happy to care for him during the day. These walks with Rocco were a significant part of my routine and might last as much as three hours if the weather was nice and the shopping good. Often it would be the lunch hour by the time we had returned from one of these outings. Usually, I had lunch with Yvette or Nicole or one of my other new friends. It amused them to show me the restaurants and cafés that were an everyday part of their lives. In the early afternoon, I frequently visited Nicole at her place of work, l'Hopital des Enfantes Malades. Here I was accorded all the courtesies of a visiting physician and even sat in on clinic sessions. Many times Nicole would confer with me and encourage me to examine the patient. Though I had no official say-so these afternoons gave me a feel for what it would be like to practice medicine as a woman. Judging by the experiences I had at the hospital and the obvious success of my French colleagues, I didn't see any real obstacle for Renée.

As a matter of fact, it was Yvette's prominence in her field that eventually led to her finding out my secret. Because of her high standing she had been chosen to make the "Report to the French Society," a yearly report made by an eminent specialist to the French Society of Ophthalmology. The report is a synthesis of the worldwide literature available on a particular subject. Yvette had chosen as her subject the diseases of blindness in children. Although being chosen to make this report is considered a great honor, it entails an overwhelming amount of research, which must be done in addition to the doctor's daily work load. Yvette would finish work in the late afternoon and then spend the evening reviewing the international literature on blindness in children. She enlisted me to help her review the articles written in English. Though she was fluent in it, my help in culling out the pertinent literature speeded her task. At one point I reviewed an article from an American medical journal. It was by a Dr. Richard Raskind. Following our discussion of the article's contents she asked me if I was related to the man who had written the article. I could have said that it was my cousin or brother or uncle, but I sensed no danger from her. She had befriended me, and I took little pleasure in lies for their own sake. "Yvette," I said, "that article was written by me." Her reaction was mild. "I'm not surprised," she replied. "I've been a little suspicious about your situation." I told her pretty much the whole story; she listened to it like a true sophisticate, leaning back in her chair, nodding sympathetically, and occasionally shaking her head in disbelief. Her attitude toward me didn't change a bit. We continued to be friendly, and if she ever told any of the others they never bothered to mention it. I don't think it went any further. My life in Paris moved along at the same tempo as it had before. In addition to my medical activities I took trips into the countryside, sometimes alone and sometimes with a friend. At last, Renée was acting like an ordinary traveler. It was a welcome change of pace; however, Paris in the winter has cold and damp weather. In spite of its companionable atmosphere, I began to long for warmer zones. Again I thought of the shimmering heat of Africa. Certainly

Renée had proved herself. It was time to move on to Spain; Barcelona would be my last stop, the staging area for my transit to Casablanca. I headed south.

As if my leaving Paris had been a cue, strange things began to happen to me again almost immediately. On the autoroute, my windshield iced over, and I had to pull onto the shoulder of the road. A truck promptly stopped a few hundred feet ahead of me, and the driver hopped out. Both the man and his truck were familiar because he had been honking and waving at me all afternoon as we crept along the slippery highway. Sometimes we passed in rest stations and at other times on the highway when one of us would decide to take a chance and increase the pace a bit, passing the other in the process. As he approached my car I could see that he had a scraping tool in his hand. Without saying a word he set to work and quickly cleared the windshield; that done he walked purposefully to the rider's side, opened the door, and hopped in. He was unusual for a truck driver in that he was thin and wiry, not broad abeam. He had a nice face, square jawed, not unlike Jean-Paul Belmondo's. I started to thank him, getting only as far as *"Merci bie. . . ,"* before he jumped at me. Luckily, there was a console between the seats or he would have been in my lap. I don't want to give the impression that this man was a rapist. Rather, he was like a music-hall version of an amorous Frenchman. There was no malice in him; he just had a very basic idea about male-female relations. For my part, I wasn't struggling too awfully hard. After all, he had done me a favor and deserved something for his trouble. It was fine with me if he wanted to steal a kiss rather than accept five dollars, but I had to draw the line when he tried to parlay the kiss into an affair to remember.

"Monsieur! S'il . . . vous . . . plait!" I took both of his hands and forced them into his own lap. When I turned him loose he grabbed my breasts again.

"Monsieur! S'il . . . vous . . . plait!" I redeposited his hands in his lap and held them there for about thirty seconds. *"C'est fini,"* I added. He shrugged his shoulders and with one last longing look left the car. I figured he had already gotten more than he'd hoped for. It's not every day that a truck driver gets to make out with a classy dame in a Maserati. I imagine he's still telling the story.

In Spain, near Gerona, the Maserati began to act up. It coughed, backfired, and then broke down completely. The local mechanics were all intensely interested in the car but more as a phenomenon than as a thing to be repaired. They would raise the hood and respectfully look impressed; for them, this exotic engine was an incomprehensible marvel.

"Que es la problema?" I would ask hopefully.

"No sé, Señorita." The only satisfaction in this answer was being called "Senorita." Eventually, I had to abandon the car in Gerona. Shortly before it failed I had picked up a couple of American hitchhikers; now we were all stuck. At another time in my life I might have felt miserable and lost, but I accepted this as another episode in Renée's European adventures. Me, the two hitchhikers, Rocco, and my six suitcases thumbed our way into Barcelona. Renée was a model of efficiency in the face of tribulation. I found a hostel for the hitchhikers and an elegant hotel for myself. The next morning I informed the local Maserati dealer that my fully guaranteed, reconditioned Mistral was immobile at a filling station in Gerona. Then I took off for a vacation in Majorca while they fixed the car. The trip to Majorca stretched into an idyllic few weeks of sunbathing, tennis, and hiking. I returned to Barcelona relaxed, confident, and ready for Casablanca.

I had only a few loose ends to tie up before I took that final step. The key thing was to arrange for the shipment of the Maserati back to the States. It took me just a couple of days to take care of everything. On my last night in town I went to a small café for my evening meal.

All during my trip through Europe I had been noticed because of my height, but the problem was even more acute in Spain. Most of the men were at least five inches shorter than I, and women virtually never came in my size. However, I had become overconfident because of my successful trip to Majorca. My tennis partners there were a very chauvinistic bunch. They were amazed at my skills and enjoyed playing with me, but, when I missed a ball, they were quick to blame it on my being a woman. I didn't mind these jibes because they affirmed my womanliness. At that time, even the putdowns were welcome reinforcements. I was undoubtedly foolish to be misled by the opinions of these men. They were mostly expatriate Americans and Europeans with an international outlook—people who could easily accept the validity of a tall woman.

The café that I chose for dinner on that last night was not full of cosmopolites. It was full of very short, very touchy, very macho Spanish men. After the initial ripple of attention that followed my entrance, most of the patrons went back to their dinners; however, there was one group of about five men at the bar who continued to notice me. They were clustered around one guy, indistinguishable from the others, except that they all seemed to be paying attention to him. He would say something in Spanish, and they would laugh. At first, I didn't get the connection between them and me. I ordered my wine, noticing with a bit of irritation the loudness at the bar, but I thought little of it until I got that unmistakable feeling of being watched. I turned and saw that they were all pointedly staring at me. While I looked back, the ringleader uttered a sneering Spanish phrase, in the middle of which glowed the English words "fucking American queer." I quickly turned around and stared down into my wine. The abuse from the bar continued; now and then the air would ring with the words "fucking American queer." The sensible thing would have been for me to get up and leave, yet I felt trapped. I kept thinking that the ringleader must be on the verge of running down. Sometimes he'd go back to his drink for as much as a couple of minutes. I'd think the worst was over, and then another stream of vitriol would be unleashed. After ten minutes I was well past the point at which I could have made a graceful exit. Besides, I was getting angry; after all, I had never been an American queer. This absurd technicality seemed to grow in importance as I sat there comprehending nothing of his remarks except that one hated phrase.

Finally, I could stand it no longer. I began to glare at him; this tactic excited him to greater efforts. He slipped off the bar stool and accompanied his remarks with some body English. The Raskind stubbornness rose in me. When I stood up his friends slipped further to each side, leaving him exposed. He hitched up his pants and repeated his favorite phrase. I covered the fifteen feet between us in about four strides and stood in front of him trying to stare him down.

"Fucking American queer!" he hissed.

"Shut up!"

"Fucking American queer!"

"I said shut up!"

"Fucking," he poked his finger into my chest, "American," another poke, "Queer." Then he poked me one last time for emphasis. He had been aiming his pokes at my breastbone but got the last one off center and sank his finger into one of my breasts. He didn't even have time to look surprised before I gave him a slap across the face. It wasn't very hard, just a gesture really; but he reacted immediately by punching me in the nose. The swiftness of his action caught me completely off guard; before I knew it I was suffering the degrading pain familiar to anyone who has had his nose flattened. That pain, piled on the previous insults, galvanized me. I snapped a straight right to the point of his chin; the sneering face whipped backward, and his hands dropped to his sides. This left his belly enticingly open and I buried my left fist in it. The air whooshed out of him, and his head came forward in just the proper position for a right hook. I brought one around from right field, and he crashed backward into a wall, winding up in a heap at the baseboard. I stood there over his inert body with my fists still clenched, waiting for him to get up—but he didn't. I looked at the nervous Spanish faces around me, and I saw that I didn't have a shred of support. I was in trouble. This realization had no sooner come over me than two policemen arrived. They were patrolmen who had been summoned by the café owner. They didn't like what they saw: a huge foreign woman standing threateningly over a stone-cold local. Each took an arm, and they hustled me outside and into their tiny patrol car. As we pulled away, two more patrol cars and an ambulance arrived on the scene. I craned my neck around and saw that they were carrying a stretcher into the café. For the first time I began to wonder if the heckler might be seriously injured. It seemed impossible, yet the blows had been undeniably solid. I remembered as a boy having knocked out a playmate during a tussle; it had frightened me. I felt that same icy lump in my stomach as we rode to the station house.

Once there, the two patrolmen presented me to the local police chief. The worst cliché you might think of would not do justice to this small-time official. He was fat, he was pockmarked, his teeth were bad, his eyes were beady, and his breath was rank. When he talked his jowls flapped. His tongue darted like a fat pink snake as he blitzed me with a stream of unintelligible Spanish. The more I couldn't understand, the more he glowered and the faster he seemed to talk. I tried French as well as English, but he understood neither. Even if he had understood I doubt whether he would have been sympathetic. We finally boiled it down to two phrases. He kept shouting, "*Tu es hombre! Tu es hombre!*" and I replied, "American consulate! American consulate!" Eventually he dismissed me, and I was taken to the cell where I was to spend the night.

It was a room measuring about eight feet by eight feet with a ceiling so low that I couldn't stand up to my full height. In the middle of the ceiling was a single, naked light bulb enclosed by wire mesh. It was turned on and off from a switch outside the cell. The walls were gray stone; there was no window save for a small opening in the door. A narrow wooden bench ran the length of one wall. Next to it was a bucket, that I assumed was my toilet. The cement floor inclined downward from the four walls, converging on a drain in the center of the room.

I sat down on the bench and tried to pull myself together. My hands were already beginning to swell, and my nose was throbbing from my antagonist's punch, which had also split my upper lip. For some reason, my back ached, too; I thought maybe I had dislocated something when I threw my combination. Tears began to well up in my eyes as I glanced around the room at the light bulb, the stone walls, and the heavy door with its little window. Soon I was weeping uncontrollably, wringing my hands. I was not so much afraid as I was miserable and maudlin.

I kept weepingly remembering how my mother had insisted on my taking boxing lessons. This was one of her ironic crusades to round me out as a proper little man even while her dominating personality was crushing the life out of my masculinity. I went at least once a week to be instructed by a college student. He taught me where to hold my hands for defense and how to turn my fist over for more power in my punches. He and I sparred, in a manner of speaking. He must have been twenty and I was only ten, but we did the best we could. I liked that part least; I was afraid I'd really hurt him. I even had a speed bag in the basement of our house in Forest Hills. I enjoyed punching that bag more than any other part of the lessons; it took real skill to keep it going.

Strangely, one of the major triumphs of my youth was associated with boxing, though it had nothing to do with me hitting someone. My father, taking into consideration my boxing lessons, decided that it would be profitable for me to attend a live boxing match. He proposed to take me to a boxing program being offered at the old outdoor Queensborough Arena. It was a small fight club where the standard of skill was not generally high but which provided a springboard for up-and-coming athletes and steady work for a pool of local pugs. The audience was composed of bloodthirsty fans along with some tough guys out to pick up a few pointers. There were seldom any women in the crowd. For these reasons my parents decided that it was not an appropriate environment for my sister who had expressed a strong desire to go. When she found out that I was going and she wasn't, Mike flew into a titanic rage. Though my mother was inclined to relent in the face of her raving, which was accompanied by the smashing of household items, father stood firm.

This incident was virtually the only time I can remember him putting his foot down and sticking with his decision. He and I went to the fights alone. We sat right down front and saw the brutality at close quarters. Mouthpieces were sometimes blasted out of men's mouths by the force of their opponents' punches. Noses and eyes gushed blood. Participants staggered about the ring almost senseless. All this was accompanied by the frenzied screaming of the fans. The atmosphere was undeniably exciting, but the gore took away whatever ideas I may have had about the glamour of boxing. Even meeting Rocky Graziano, who was at the arena to look over young prospects, didn't fire my enthusiasm. The best thing about that night was the fact that I was sitting alone next to my father and Mike was at home. In that sense I had been a winner.

As I stared blearily at the gray stone wall opposite me, I wondered how Mike would size up my present situation. She would undoubtedly use a phrase that she had picked up from her friends in the psychology department. She had used it like a club many times. "Oh," she would say flippantly, "Dick's just acting out." She articulated this phrase as if it clarified all things and rendered further discussion inconsequential. The anxieties, the self-mutilation, the lies, the machinations, the hormones—all these amounted to a simple case of acting out.

I looked down toward my feet where I saw my bucket/toilet.

Kicking it across the room raised my spirits a little. I dried my nose on my sleeve and began to pull myself together. This sniveling was doing no good; so I decided to go on the offensive.

I stood up, hunched over to the door, and began to bang on it. For a long time the only response was a face that would appear in the little window in the door, scrutinize me for a moment, and then disappear. Nothing I said made any impact, but I kept banging anyway. Eventually, the repulsive police chief went home leaving two night men in charge. One of these spoke French and amiably agreed to call the American consulate and to have food sent over from my hotel. I began to feel that I had re-established some control over my life even though I was still stuck in the cell. About an hour later he returned; to my surprise, he invited me out into the office area adjoining my cell. There we opened the package from the hotel and spread out the white linen napkins to make a tablecloth; on that we placed the containers of chicken, rice, and vegetables. There was also a bottle of dark red wine that I immediately uncorked, filling glasses for each of us. The hotel had included some cigarettes, which I also distributed. This transformation from dungeon dweller to picnicker took about three minutes. The sudden change, along with the wine and cigarettes, made me high. My rescuers seemed like lovely and generous young men; they evidently bore me no malice. What's more, I don't think they suspected my true condition. I felt quite giddy and a veritable party atmosphere ensued. When the worried consulate official arrived, he was openly amazed and said so.

"My God, Miss Raskind, I thought you might be beaten up or raped. It wouldn't be unusual."

"Well it hasn't always been this good. Have you seen that cell back there?" He nodded sympathetically. "I can't even stand up straight in it."

"I know."

"They've got a bucket for a toilet."

"I know. Unfortunately, there's nothing much I can do for you this evening. I don't even know what you'll be charged with. They probably suspect you of antigovernment activities."

"Antigovernment activities?"

"Oh, they suspect everyone of being antigovernment. That probably won't stick, but I don't know how badly the man from the café is hurt. A lot will depend on that."

He did his best to buck me up, but he was a realistic man and didn't raise my hopes unreasonably. After supper, I was led back to the cave, where I arranged myself as best I could on the bench. I woke them up twice to let me out so that I could use the toilet in the front room; I drew the line at that bucket.

Early in the morning I heard the key clanking anciently in the medieval lock on the door. I felt like the Count of Monte Cristo as I walked out of the building and into the sunlight, blinking and marveling at the brightness. I had been rushed out of the local station house so as not to keep the paddy wagon waiting. It sat chugging at the curb, an antique vehicle with thin rubber wheels. They opened double doors at the back and waved me inside. I sat down on one of the benches, they closed the door, and off we bounced. I was alone for a while, but shortly the van began to fill up with reprobates of both sexes. My station house may have been the first stop because the rest of the ride took about four hours and covered every section of the town. The vehicle in which we rode must have been built before they invented auto-suspension systems, and as we bumped along the cobblestone streets, my lower back began to ache. Nobody paid much attention to me. I think they pegged me as a prostitute. Finally, the squalid mass of which I had become a part was herded into the modern central police headquarters. I was placed in a cage-like cell with a high ceiling; at least I could stand up straight. I cooled my heels there for the rest of the day and through the night. Periodically, I would be given a starchy meal. Other than that I was incommunicado. Naturally, I thought a lot about the man I had beaten up. I hoped he was as wiry and resilient as he looked. I had to fight back a sickish dread when I considered the possibility of spending years locked up in Spain.

In the morning, a guard escorted me down a series of long corridors that led eventually to the office of the inspector general of police. I was relieved to see the representative from the American consulate who had visited me two nights before. He told me that he was going to plead my case momentarily and had the additional good news that the man from the café had recovered with little more than a sore jaw. Everything else, including the antigovernment charges, was up in the air. Shortly, we went in and confronted the inspector general; he and the consulate representative carried on a long conversation in Spanish that I gathered concerned my "mission" in Barcelona. Apparently, he thought that the only men who dressed as women were spies. The representative tried hard to translate "transsexual" into Spanish. Finally, we were both asked to wait while the inspector general discussed the case with some colleagues. For an interminable period I sat with the consulate representative in an outer office, listening to Spanish voices filtering through the door. Some were angry, some were conciliatory. At length, an aide informed the representative that I was free but that I should get out of Spain—to which I readily agreed.

The helpful representative offered me a ride back to my hotel, but I declined. I felt like walking, and the hotel was only a few blocks away. I wanted to enjoy the feeling of being free. We parted, and I strolled off toward a warm bath. Unfortunately, my misfortunes were not over. In all the apprehension of the previous days I had not been paying very close attention to my body; but now, as I walked along I noticed that I couldn't use my right foot normally. I had a steppage gait that compelled me to put the ball of my foot down first and then my heel instead of the other way around. There was also an ache in my back; I remembered the ache I had noticed in my cell at the station house as well as in the police van. I had probably pinched a nerve, and this had caused the foot problem. I limped to my hotel, dirty, humiliated, and hurt. When I opened the door to my room I found all of my belongings strewn around; I couldn't see even one patch of floor. The contents of all six suitcases were covering it. Apparently the police had not simply taken me at my word; they had made a good run at finding my secret documents. This intrusion seemed the final indignity; I broke down and wept uncontrollably. The next morning I left for Casablanca.

I limped off the plane in Africa, hired a car at the airport, and had myself driven eastward along the Mediterranean Coast. I knew that I would have to spend some time recuperating from the ordeal in Spain before I could face surgery. I needed to be in top physical shape, and, perhaps even more important, I had to have a positive attitude. Neither my body nor my mind was in decent shape after two days in Barcelona jails. I told the driver that I wanted to go someplace quiet, outside the city. He took me to a little town called Mohamedia about twenty-five kilometers down the coast from Casablanca. I checked into a small hotel with a beautiful view of the sea. For three weeks I spent the days lying on my back by the pool. I reclined on a hard mat, that in turn lay directly on the flat concrete patio. Plenty of rest on a firm surface is the standard first step in treating what I thought was my problem—a popped disc, causing a sciatic nerve compression, that was deadening my foot. I hoped that I could avoid the second step, which would be to go into traction. Every day I had the African equivalent of a chiropractor come in to massage my back and my legs. To my relief, the foot began to come around. Moreover, lying in the baking African sun seemed to have burned away the depression with which I had arrived. I had lain there much of the time in something like a trance. My mind did not cast itself backward or forward but just held its own from moment to moment, full mostly of heat and brightness. When I looked into the mirror at the end of three weeks I saw a woman darkly tanned, healthy. When I walked it was with a firm step. I was ready.

Back in Casablanca, I checked into a hotel near the clinic. That same day, I arranged for Rocco's care and took a cab to the address that I had come to know by heart years before. At that time, perhaps fifty transsexual operations had been performed, and nearly all of them had been in the Casablanca clinic. All over the world furtive people held a fantasy image of this place in their divided minds. Actually, the building in front of me was unremarkable: two stories, plaster, white. In Hoboken, New Jersey, it might have been exotic; but in Casablanca it was strictly run-of-the-mill, maybe even a bit below. I felt in my purse for the roll of one hundred dollar bills. There were forty of them. This was not a Johns Hopkins where I would be interviewed for hours and then forced to spend more hours filling out questionnaires. There would be no waiting period while my fitness was evaluated. If I handed them the money, I would be on the operating table the next day.

I stood at the curb willing myself forward, but somehow my feet wouldn't respond. Before me were the steps up which Bambi had traveled, as well as the other Parisian travestis. Here was the reality about which I had been dreaming, yet it still had the quality of a dream. It stood shimmering in the heat, wavering like a mirage. Perspiration began to dampen the sleeves of my dress; slowly a thought began to penetrate. This whole trip had been a fantasy: on the boat it was F. Scott Fitzgerald; in Italy it was

Fellini. Even my most normal experiences had taken place in Paris, the city of romance. What had this trip told me about Renée? That she could have fun on holiday in Europe? That she could get herself thrown into jail in Spain? That she looked good in a Maserati? Perhaps Josh was right; perhaps a fairer test would have been to spend a year in Oklahoma City. I took a step forward and felt a knot tighten in my abdomen. Suppose Dr. Bak was right? Suppose my silly charades were to no purpose other than the glorification of my cock—an elaborate ritual that allowed it finally to rise again like the Phoenix? And, if I had it cut off, might I not go mad like the French boy described by the travestis? Issues that I had considered settled years ago assailed me again as I stared at the clinic shining in the sun. For fifteen minutes or more I continued to stand, waiting for these ghosts to be gone; yet they persisted, became stronger. Finally, I turned away and walked the distance back to my hotel.

I told myself that such second thoughts were only natural. Who would skip carefree up those steps? Any sensitive and intelligent person would be concerned. In spite of these reassurances, I became disoriented. I felt that, somehow, I was no longer worthy to be a woman, though I certainly was not a man. I was something horrible—something in between—something like a monster. My points of reference were gone and with them my equilibrium. In a veritable daze I collected my things and hired a car and driver.

"Get me out of Casablanca," I said.

"Where shall we go, miss?"

"Anywhere . . . someplace nice."

He took me to Marrakech. It is an oasis surrounded by red desert. In the distance I could see the snow-covered Atlas Mountains. They looked cool, but they were far away. I treated myself to a luxurious hotel, the Maumonia, but I didn't take any pleasure from the sumptuous surroundings. I was still in a daze. The simple act of dressing became a trying set of decisions. At the end of the process I looked like the creation of a quarrelsome committee. I wore a powder-blue man's blazer over a black turtle neck sweater. Naturally, if the coat was open my breasts showed. In addition, I sported a pair of wheat-colored unisex trousers. On my feet were nondescript loafers. Though my face was obviously that of a woman, I could not bring myself to put on makeup anymore. I did, however, continue to wear my loop earrings. I was indifferent to the impact I made around the hotel, but I must have cut an

intriguing figure. I certainly caught the attention of some homosexual men who were vacationing together. They diverted me,
but it was tiresome to be treated as if I were a gay man. Of course,
I wouldn't have denied it. I wouldn't have denied any allegation at
that point. Quite frankly, I had no idea what I was. Up until that
moment of truth in front of the clinic, I would have said confidently that I was a woman trapped in a man's body; but I had
stood paralyzed, not fifty feet from the remedy and had been
unable to cross the remaining space. The only identity that I could
clearly claim was that of a failure.

After a couple of days the gay men left. Without their company
I fell to brooding, and my depression deepened. I began to spend
large segments of the day sitting in the hotel garden staring at the
desert. Again and again I ran over the rational objections to the
operation. I began to wish that I had never listened to the stories
of bad surgery which had often been the subject of conversation
among that woeful band of transexual misfits in Brooklyn
Heights. I despised Dr. Bak for his cleverness in working out the
dry yet brilliant analysis of my compulsion. Still, I knew that
these were only the convenient pegs upon which I hung fears that
were probably deeper and more meaningful than simple uncer-
tainty. Somewhere inside me, the previously failing masculinity
was rising up again and making a bid for life.

In the late afternoons or early evenings a man began appearing
regularly in the garden. He was not a hotel guest but apparently
came specifically to be near me. At first he sat far away or
strolled nonchalantly by, pretending not to notice me. Then he
became more pointed in his attention: he began to stare. I did not
find this offensive; at that time, I would have responded to any
expression of interest. He was a North African, swarthy but not
exotic, with a pockmarked face. His clothes amounted to nondescript sports attire. I had a hard time reading his expressions. He
seemed to make faces at inappropriate times, smiling when
nothing was funny or looking serious when I had said something
perfectly ordinary. He spoke to me in French, but the accent was
unfamiliar and we had trouble communicating. From the moment he asked if he could sit down, though, his romantic intentions were clear. He leaned toward me suggestively; sometimes I
could even feel his breath. Our conversation centered around me;
he wanted to know who I was, what I was. As I revealed a little his

eyes began to glint with increased interest. The looks became more intense. He complimented me lavishly, dwelling on what an exotic creature I was.

This was an unusual turn of events. My gay friends had kidded me about my breasts and curvy hips: *"Tu est gros!"* Their jokes were good-natured, but they emphasized my half-formed condition and so depressed me. This man seemed to find me attractive for the same reasons that I despised myself. It was a refreshing change. He invited me to his villa, and I accepted, though his only attractive feature was that he was attracted to me.

His house was located in a questionable section of town. The area was sparsely populated, mostly desert and rocks with an occasional hovel. By the time we reached his place night had fallen, and I had lost track of the route we had taken. The building in front of which we stopped was nice enough. It was an upper-middle-class home and seemed to be a part of a cluster of such dwellings, though I couldn't see any of the other houses. I just had a sense that they were there.

During the ride I had grown more and more apprehensive about this adventure. The feeling increased as it grew darker. Still, I had naively cruised through Europe for the last few months and had had only one bad experience; and that had been through a loss of self-control. All my other experiences had been positive; I was in desperate need of another one after my failure of courage in Casablanca.

Inside the house, the ceilings were low, and the furniture was low as well. I believe the living room was sunken. There was an oriental rug on the floor; in one corner was a rolltop desk. Two long couches faced one another over a long heavy wooden coffee table. He lit an oil lamp, making it the only illumination in the room. From an ornate cabinet against one wall, he withdrew a small ebony box containing a pipe and a little copper vial of hashish. He shaved a chunk of it into thin pieces and placed them in the bowl of the pipe. Setting it down on the coffee table, he disappeared into another room but soon returned with two cups of tea. All the while he was talking in his difficult French, little of which I could catch. I had the impression that his remarks were complimentary; his delivery was certainly lyrical. The tone of his voice ranged from lighthearted to hoarsely suggestive. While he was in the other room I stretched myself out on one of the couches, thinking naively that he would have to sit on the other one if I took up all the room on mine. Ignoring this tactic, he pointedly sat down next to my hip.

Now things were more uncomfortable than before because he towered over me, with the pipe to his lips, puffing out clouds of potent smoke. He offered it to me, but I declined. He thrust it at me insistently. Finally, I pretended to take a couple of drags but didn't get much smoke in my lungs. He seemed satisfied at this and put the pipe aside.

I expected him to make an advance, but instead he took up his tea and slurped it noisily. I tried to drink mine and found it overpoweringly sweet. Next, he made it clear that he wanted to show me the rest of the house. All the while we had been on the couch he had been getting more and more familiar. He touched my shoulder, my cheek, the curve of my hip. These contacts were not held long, but they communicated much. On the other hand, I had been getting less and less interested.

There was something menacing about this man. Of course, that would have dawned on any sane person back at the Maumonia Hotel. At any rate, the peculiar quality of this man was beginning to make itself clearer. His whole manner was characterized by a sense of stealth. His approach at the hotel had been circuitous, indirect. The drive to his home had seemed needlessly complicated. His preference for the dim light of an oil lamp now seemed suspicious. Lastly were these little touches—nothing really, but in their way, everything.

I welcomed his suggestion that we look at the house. I longed to get up from that couch. On my feet I felt more in command of the situation. He took my hand and led me into another room. It was the bedroom. He switched on an overhead light; there was not really much to see. It was neat, the bed was made. On the night table was a picture of the man in his younger days. I turned back to him and saw that he had closed the door, had his shirt off. He rushed over, and threw his arms around me, pinning my arms to my sides. I stood there helplessly as he lavished kisses on my face, attempting several times to thrust his tongue into my mouth. He was strong, and he had me in a very awkward position. I made some protests, but he disregarded them, continuing to slather my face with kisses and repeatedly saying my name, "Renée! Renée! Renée!" His manner was insistent, unsubtle, as if by simple repetition of my name I might be won over. It was quite a change of pace from his previous stealth.

This shift scared me more than any of the other things. It suggested instability; it hinted that he might be more dangerous than a simple man on the make. There was an urgency in his voice that I associated with bad acting, but he was obviously serious. He threw me back on the bed, releasing my arms and jamming his hands underneath my sweater. When he let go of my arms I flailed them upward to make sure they couldn't be pinned to my sides again. In doing this, I thrust my hand under the pillows on the bed and found something hard and heavy there. Reflexively, I grasped it with the idea that I might hit him on the head with it. The man by then had my sweater up and was pulling at my bra, but when he saw my hand beneath the pillow, he grabbed that arm viciously and holding it immobile, removed the object from my hand. It was a revolver.

"This is in case someone breaks in on me," he said. I didn't reply. "Life can be dangerous." He laid the pistol on the nightstand. This put the situation in an entirely different light. I was dealing with a man who hid a gun under his pillow, who had placed that gun suggestively within reach. "Renée," he spoke again, looking at me hard, "fais mon plaisir." It was a simple request; yet I didn't know what his pleasure was. He stood up next to the bed and took off his pants. Now that the action had slowed, I noticed for the first time that he suffered from some sort of skin disorder. Spotted all over his torso and legs were warty sores about the size of quarters. I tried to keep a straight face, but inwardly I recoiled. Until I saw those sores I had seriously thought that I might be able to service this man in some way. After all, I was hardly a prude. He didn't appeal to me and the circumstances didn't appeal to me, but it had hardly seemed worthwhile to provoke him, not with a pistol by the bed.

And what were my options? I could fight him though he was clearly stronger than I. This was a man of substantial size, not some bantam rooster in a Spanish café. I might possibly run out into the dark. Assuming that he didn't shoot me or catch me and drag me back, I would be lost at night in a Marrakech slum. These considerations made sex seem the easiest and least dangerous course of action, but when I saw those sores my half-formed resolve failed. Finally, I proved myself the master of action through inaction. When he came to me on the bed I was about as responsive as a sack of potatoes. I didn't fight, but I didn't help either. He managed to worry most of my clothes off me, but that effort took at least twenty minutes. At every chance I turned my body subtly so as to make his access as difficult as possible; he undressed me all right, but he worked hard. I felt the perspiration on him when he pressed himself against me. I kept myself in a kind of fetal position, always contriving to present him with the least-satisfying approach. I was in luck because he didn't seem interested in anal intercourse, so curling up in a ball was an effective way to thwart his desires. He alternated between gruff demands and wheedling but what he said was always the same whether in the form of a command or whining request, "*Renée, fais mon plaisir!*" Occasionally, he would stop talking and just hunch suggestively against me. When he did so I could feel the lesions on his skin.

After an hour of this tiring struggle, I began to feel his strength fade, I tried a new tactic: "I'm expected at the hotel. They'll miss me. I have to go back." This resulted in a new frenzy of trying to open me up, but his energy level by this time was low and he couldn't maintain it for long. "*Fais mon plaisir,*" he repeated tiredly. "I have to go," I whined in response. This went on for another hour; my constant reminder about the hotel was my best bet. All important Westerners stay at the Maumonia Hotel. I had seen one of the Rothschilds in the gardens a day or so before. The man knew this, knew that he couldn't go too far without repercussions. If he had been seen leaving with me, he would be under suspicion. Eventually, he gave in, but all the way back in the car he kept entreating me, "*Fais mon plaisir. Fais mon plaisir.*"

Back in my room at the hotel I scrubbed myself raw. The memory of those sores haunted me. Who knew what they were? Possibly they were the manifestations of an African disease, tootsie gamoochee fever or something. The next day I headed back to Casablanca; my night of fear had convinced me that there was no future in this halfway stuff. It had to be all or nothing at all. I checked into the same hotel in Casablanca. Once again I made provisions for Rocco, and once again I made the taxi trip to the clinic—and once again I stood paralyzed on the steps. This time there was no rationalizing. I simply could not move; I stood there in the blazing sun for thirty minutes and then left. Forty-eight hours later I was back in New York.

17

Family Man

When I arrived in Manhattan I was depressed. At the airport my father asked if I had had a good trip. I said, "Fine." He didn't inquire any further. Nobody did. Josh, Joel, and Len were happy to have me back with my fragile masculinity intact. I was hardly the rakehell they knew in college, but at least I had my cock. They were pleased that I was still, technically at least, a man. As for my less intimate friends, they said nothing more than: "Nice to have you back." I wished like hell that it really was nice to be back, but it wasn't. The plans that I had been pursuing for the past two years had fallen through on the steps of the clinic in Casablanca, and that left me really dangling. The only course of action open to me was to become a man again, to make a panicky retreat from femininity. Considering my previous futile efforts in this direction, it was hard to have much faith in this scheme; but I attacked it with a vigor born of desperation. I had to make it work.

In May of 1968, I reassumed my positions at Manhattan Eye and Ear, at New York Hospital and on the teaching staff of Cornell Medical School. I also acquired the position as civilian consultant to the St. Albans Naval Hospital, where I had served out my military obligation. In addition, I leased a larger private office than I had occupied before I left and set to work vigorously building up my private practice. Soon I was working at least sixty hours a week, not counting the time I spent on articles for medical journals. I took refuge in this whirl of activity, which as before centered around my peaceful apartment, into which I had moved as soon as the sublease ran out. What free time I had was devoted to tennis and backgammon with my circle of male friends. Occasionally, I attended parties, and at one of these I met a woman who became my regular companion. A stewardess for TWA who had come originally from Denmark, she was the standard-issue girlfriend for a young Park Avenue doctor. We all went with models or stewardesses. Livvie was very calm in the peculiar style of most Scandinavians; our relationship was extremely peaceful. She expected little and applied no pressure whatsoever. My low-key masculinity was enough for her.

Naturally, I had stopped my hormone treatments in conjunction with my new campaign to be a man. By the time I met Livvie my genitals were functional again; so we were able to have pretty normal sexual relations. One peculiar thing about our sex centered around the fact that Livvie was the only woman who ever stimulated me to an erection by manipulating my penis. This form of sex play had never been exciting to me, but when the calm and undemanding Livvie fondled me some previously untapped current of sexuality was broached. In prior relationships I had always seen this as an ultimatum that said, in effect: "Get it up!" Somehow Livvie did not inspire this reaction; she was in all ways unthreatening. Shortly after we met I asked her to live with me. She calmly accepted.

Though I had stopped the hormone treatments, my body did not spring back to a noticeably more masculine state. I had the use of my genitals, but my skin remained fine, my muscles smooth and elongated, and my breasts sizeable. By now the rumors of cancer in Dr. Raskind had been pretty much dissipated, replaced by a more accurate complex of suspicions. I discovered years later that my condition had been a topic of widespread speculation; most of it centered around the probability that I was a transsexual though opinion differed with regard to my true condition. Most thought that I was still male, though I was frequently mistaken for a woman. Most often this happened on the tennis courts where it was difficult to conceal my breasts. Generally, I played in a warm-up jacket or a baggy sweatshirt, but sometimes it was simply too hot for those bulky items. On a few occasions my partners were asked, "Who was that tall woman you were hitting with?" My friends would relate this to me in a nervous, joking way. These reports were as near as any of my uninformed associates ever came to confronting me with my peculiarity. I usually passed it off with a comment like, "Oh, did they think I was attractive?" I was pleased to find out that usually they did.

It would be natural to think that I would have suffered a lot of abuse in the form of rude or snide remarks, but I didn't. This was partially because I moved in relatively sophisticated circles, but even on the street or in other public places I was left pretty much alone. Dick was a lofty character even when he was womanish. Though the comments may have been thick behind his back, he was seldom troubled to his face.

One glaring exception occurred on a trip that Livvie and I took one Sunday to Bear Mountain State Park, about thirty miles north of New York City. Toward the end of the afternoon Livvie and I visited the public rest rooms; these consisted of a large shack divided into two sections with the women's entrance at one end and the men's at the other. Inside were primitive but serviceable plumbing arrangements that I used gratefully. When I came out I nearly ran into a sturdy state trooper straddling the path to the toilet.

"Excuse me," he said politely, "may I see some identification?"

"What?" I replied, flabbergasted.

"I would like to see some identification."

"Is something wrong?"

"Nothing. Just show me your identification." He was growing more stern.

I produced a wallet full of cards and licenses, all substantiating my identity as a very solid and very male citizen. While he was going through them Livvie came around the corner looking for me. "Dick, what's the matter?" She stopped next to me and put her arm through mine. "I don't know," I replied innocently, "this officer is questioning me." At Livvie's appearance, the trooper had become noticeably agitated. When he heard the word "questioning," he embarrassedly handed back my papers and said, "No problem, sir. Sorry to have bothered you." He touched his hand to his hat brim and briskly walked away. He had apparently spotted me going into the men's room and thought I was up to no good. I can only speculate on what illicit purposes he might have ascribed to me. Why would a woman dress up as a man and sneak into the outhouse at a state park? At any rate, the incident is an example of how confusing my image was in those days.

State troopers and tennis players were not the only ones who were confused. The most confused party was me. In spite of my furious efforts to once again seize my manhood, within months I was feeling that familiar urge to dress and act as a woman. Along with that urge came the old despair; the masculine world of Dick Raskind, even when supplemented by the presence of a loving woman, was not enough. I began buying women's clothes again. When Livvie was out of town on a flight, I would dress up and venture into the streets. By this time I was so despondent that I didn't give a damn who saw me. I no longer dashed furtively in and out of my apartment building. I never took the precaution of going to a hotel and leaving from there. I no longer bothered to yank Rocco away from his sociable encounters with the regulars on the street though I still didn't initiate conversation. Again I began showing up dressed as a woman at Josh's apartment. Moreover, I sometimes visited Joel or Len. This was a new wrinkle, and I took some perverse satisfaction at the shocked reactions I drew from their friends. Gradually, the women's clothes began to crowd out the men's clothes in my closets; Livvie must have noticed this, but she didn't comment—and she never saw me cross-dressed. The finale to this binge was the acquisition of a full-length mink coat for which I paid two thousand dollars wholesale. This certainly demonstrated in a tangible way my commitment to the feminine side of my personality.

Seven or eight months after my return from Casablanca, I went back on the hormones again. Livvie noted this but as usual kept silent. Josh, on the other hand, did not hold back. He resumed his abrasive therapy but did not restrict it to me. At his apartment one evening I overheard him talking to Livvie in another room.

"Kid, I've got some news for you." Josh's voice was filtered through a closed door but was loud enough for me to hear plainly. Livvie must have responded though I could not, as yet, hear her. Josh continued. "You aren't doing it for Dick." I moved closer to the door.

"What do you mean?" Livvie was saying.

"I mean Dick is back in his Halloween costumes again. It's

worse now than it ever was. He's showing up at Joel's and Len's places scaring the hell out of their friends. I saw him one night last week parading down Fifth Avenue with Rocco, for God's sake!"

"I know he has this problem," Livvie said sweetly, "but I hope he'll get over it."

"Do you know he's taking the drugs again?"

"I guess so."

"You guess so? The man you're living with is turning himself into a woman right under your nose, and you're not sure about it? Don't you feel a little responsible?"

"Me?"

"If you were strong enough, he wouldn't be mincing around like a Powers model. He needs somebody who can take charge and get his mind off this shit. You're too soft! For Dick's good, I think you should move on and give somebody else a shot." There was a long silence. "I have nothing against you. I'm thinking of Dick. If you love him, you'll agree."

After this, I heard some movement and so returned to my original position. Josh came through the door a second or two later. He chatted with me for five minutes before Livvie finally entered the room quietly; she sat stiffly for the rest of the evening, seldom saying anything. On the way home she repeated what Josh had said. I told her not to pay any attention to him, but it was obvious that she was deeply hurt. Nor was that the last conversation of this nature that Josh was to have with her. I told him to stop this nonsense, but there was no controlling him; there never had been. In one way he was right. I *was* getting worse and worse, but it wasn't Livvie's fault.

By late fall of 1969 I was ready to try for surgery again. I didn't want to go back to Casablanca, but I thought there might be a chance that, after two years, I could get the surgery in a proper American hospital. With that in mind I began making inquiries. I was still bitter about my experience with the Johns Hopkins people; so I ruled them out from the start. The best bet seemed to be a Chicago center that was then performing the operation. One Friday I came home, took off my business suit, and changed into a dress in preparation for my trip to the Windy City. It was cold and I put on my mink, which I hoped would make an impression,

257

signal in some way my seriousness. Joel drove me to the airport. In spite of his shyness about such things even Joel agreed that I looked good.

On Saturday and Sunday I was interviewed by an administrator, a social worker, a psychologist, and a psychiatrist; in short, everyone but a surgeon. I took several hours of tests, all of which I had seen before—at least three times. I should have brought photo copies of my previous answers and saved everyone a lot of time. These shenanigans cost me five hundred dollars, and in the end I was undone by one lapse of judgment. When the psychiatrist asked me if I had ever undergone psychoanalysis, I told him about Dr. Bak. I could see he was impressed, and I had meant him to be. I thought he'd reason as follows: "If the eminent Dr. Bak couldn't make any headway with this guy, he must really be incurable." Apparently he didn't reason at all; he just called Dr. Bak and asked him what to do. Later, when I contacted the Chicago people I received the advice to go back into psychotherapy. Their feeling seemed to be that ten years of analysis was not enough.

I was given this news during the Christmas holidays, and I went into a depressive tailspin. Time was running out; at that time I was thirty-five-years old. It wouldn't be long before I would be too old for the surgery. On the other hand, I couldn't keep taking hormones and expect that there would be no permanent effect. I thought back to the horrifying pictures that Dr. Benjamin had shown me years ago when I had first consulted him; were these old men with breasts my spiritual cousins?

The trappings of Christmas that surrounded me only intensified my despondency; they represented a lot of stuff that had little to do with me. I was not merry, and I did not feel much goodwill toward men. I didn't bother with a tree or any of that stuff in my apartment, but everywhere else I went, Joyeux Noël was oppressively present. On Christmas Eve I went over to Josh's. I figured that his sarcasm might bite through the sweetness of the season. He had a date that night, but I had joined him many times under those circumstances. As a matter of fact, my threesomes with Josh were often designed by him with the idea of introducing me to a likely female. Then again, given Josh's penchant for women, these three-sided evenings were often the only chance to socialize with him.

I sat in the living room of Josh's twenty-sixth floor apartment staring at a panoramic Manhattan skyline. He had gone to pick up his date, and I was putting the time to good use—brooding. Shortly, I heard a rustle in the foyer and looked up. I had seen at least a hundred different girls come through that door in my time, all of them beautiful. I even saw Julie Newmar, the actress, enter one evening. I remember her especially because she was so tall, yet so strikingly feminine and beautiful. Practically every evening at Josh's would be an occasion for the unveiling of a new beauty; so when I looked up I was expecting female pulchritude in some form. What I did not expect was the buzz that swept through me when I made eye contact with the woman who entered the room; she was simply the most beautiful girl I had ever seen. Josh was shepherding her into the apartment with much flapping of his overcoat and prolonged hanging up of winter items on the rack near the door. Without looking he called out, "Dick, say hello to Meriam. Meriam, say hello to Dick." Meriam in the meantime was walking as straight as an arrow toward me, her eyes locked with mine. She was about five-feet seven with delicate features, a classic Cupid's mouth, and a tiny yet perfect nose. Her eyes were bluish gray but tended to change hue as they picked up and reflected the colors around her. These features were set in a complexion that was literally like porcelain, exquisite! Her hair was auburn and hung softly to just below her shoulders. She settled herself like a cloud on the couch next to me. I was amazed at how close she sat; yet it seemed right. She reached out and lightly touched my face.

"Your cheekbones are so high," she said. "Are you part Indian?"

"No," I answered, continuing to stare at her, transfixed, "they're part of my Russian heritage." The banality of these opening remarks covered a multitude of unspoken messages. This trivial conversation continued to the absolute exclusion of Josh who sat in a chair monitoring us, turning his head to and fro as if watching a tennis match. First she'd ask a question, and then I'd answer it. Then I'd ask a question, and she'd answer it. I imagine Josh was appalled at the intense attention we paid to this superficial chitchat. Underneath however, chemical sequences were popping like chains of firecrackers. Josh stood this embarrassing intensity for as long as he could and then suggested that we all go out and get something to eat. He had to make the suggestion about three times before we heard him. Finally he said, "Hey! I hate to disturb this seminar but what about some food?" Meriam and I turned and looked at him like groundhogs suddenly dragged into the bright sun. "Uh, okay," I said. She and I walked out of the apartment with Josh trailing along behind like an unwanted little brother. In the restaurant, Meriam and I continued in the same vein.

"I play tennis. Do you?"

"No, but I'd like to learn."

"Suppose I teach you?"

"That would be wonderful."

"It's not that hard."

"I bet you're a good teacher."

Josh weathered this in a stoic fashion, only occasionally interrupting with a brutally sarcastic remark to which neither Meriam nor I paid any attention. At length she went to the powder room. I then turned to Josh and said eloquently, "You son of a bitch."

"Why do you say that?" he asked, though he knew full well. For years he had paraded women in front of me, hoping to entice me back into the world of men. He finally had found one that clicked, and it was too late.

"You son of a bitch," I repeated.

"Never say die, Dick. C'mon, you can do it!"

Meriam returned to the table, and the party broke up. Josh went home alone, and I went home with Meriam. Everybody seemed tacitly to accept this arrangement. When we arrived at her apartment I kissed her goodnight, and we made a date for the next day, Christmas. The idea was to get together and walk our dogs in the freezing cold of Central Park. Clearly we were out of our minds, but it seemed romantic at the time.

I arrived the next day with a Christmas gift for her. It was an exotic Christmas plant featuring an unusual salmon-colored flower. I presented her with this token and was touched that she had a gift for me as well. We unwrapped our presents and found ourselves sitting there, each holding the same damned plant with the same salmon-colored flower. This spooky synchronism put the preliminary seal on a match that fate had apparently ordained. Four days later we were in Bermuda together, sunning ourselves and getting acquainted. Though I felt she was my soul mate, there was a lot of bookkeeping to be done. I wanted to know everything about her. She was young, only twenty-two, and we really didn't have many common experiences, but the fabulous electricity between us was undeniable. As I lay beside her on the beach, I noticed with amazement that I had an erection in spite of the fact that I had been back on hormones for over a year. It was stimulated by her proximity alone. Though I was still rooming with Livvie, we had not had intercourse for some time, and I seldom felt any stirrings in my genitals.

We returned from Bermuda with stars in our eyes. In June we were married.

The attitude of my friends was typified by Joel's early reaction to Meriam's effect on me. When Joel drove me to the airport for my useless trip to Chicago, I was dolled up like a woman and sporting my full-length mink coat. Two weeks later he watched me stroll into Orsini's dressed in a tweed jacket with leather patches on the elbows and smoking a pipe. Meriam was on my arm, and I was lavishing her with adoration. As I passed by Joel's table, I glanced at his face. Disbelief, amazement, hilarity, and irony were all struggling for domination. Of course, he never said anything to me directly, no one ever did. Most of my other friends and acquaintances were just as stunned. The turn-about was dramatic; they came from all over the country to marvel at the wedding. This extravagant affair, followed by a European honeymoon, set the tone for my life with Meriam. From the start we lived beyond our means.

Meriam insisted first of all that we move to a new apartment; I agreed. The new apartment was larger and only a half a block from the old one. Naturally, we immediately redecorated it; this was the first of many redecorations. Meriam, young and with little to do during the day, kept the Raskind household in a constant state of evolution. We became intimately acquainted with paperhangers, plasterers, and painters. Added to this were our vacations to St. Moritz for skiing, to the Caribbean for sunning, or to any of a dozen other expensive spots where whim might take us. Our food bill alone could have accounted for the salary of an average man. Although she was an excellent cook Meriam didn't prepare meals often, and I didn't particularly want her to. We preferred eating at La Côte Basque or some other elegant restaurant. Our Jaguar sedan was just one of hundreds of expensive objects that we acquired. The closets were full of fashionable attire. Names like Gucci and Halston graced the labels on our glad rags. We spared ourselves nothing.

Luckily, my private practice was flourishing, but no matter how it grew the income never kept pace with our mounting bills. In some mysterious way, the combination of Dick and Meriam created a whirlpool that sucked money into oblivion at a rate far exceeding what either of us was capable of alone. The only way we kept within shouting distance of our expenditures was through the increasing volume of private patients. This increase was due greatly to Meriam's urging; she was proud of me and encouraged me to enlarge my reputation and to accept challenges. One challenge that I accepted was to take over the entire practice of a fellow ophthalmologist who had suffered a debilitating stroke. This move effectively doubled my workload, but it doubled my income too. Still, the debts stayed ahead, even though I was on the go six days a week from seven in the morning until six in the evening. This pace helped me establish a tremendous reputation as a private practitioner.

My clinical work continued at its former pace, and, stimulated by Meriam's expectations, I began to broaden my reputation. Whereas before I had kept my speaking engagements pretty much on a local level, I now began to lecture at national meetings and stepped up my schedule of regional appearances. I became a professional's professional. When a child in a doctor's family needed ophthalmological care I got the call. This is perhaps the highest compliment the medical community can bestow. Building on my already solid base I reached a position of eminence in just a couple of years.

Though I was at the top of my profession, my private life was not such a success. The primary strain was not our debts. I think, rather, the debts were a symptom of the more basic problem. After my incredible surge of potency toward the beginning of our relationship, I regressed. In spite of the fact that I was off the hormones for good, my sexual potency as well as my drive remained low. I occasionally made love to Meriam but it was not done vigorously. Naturally, Meriam was disappointed. I had seemed so ardent at the start that this drab follow-up was like a slap in the face. Without telling her, I consulted an endocrinologist who was one of my colleagues on the teaching staff at Cornell.

He presented a pessimistic picture. After all my years of taking female hormones, it was doubtful that I'd ever regain my full potency. My testicles were permanently atrophied, and my sperm count was low. I told him that I'd settle for any improvement. He started me on a course of pituitary hormones to stimulate the function of my testicles, and in addition he prescribed testosterone, the basic male hormone. After several months of this treatment, I was no better. My potency was as low as it had ever been, and my breasts were still the same size. The latter had become a continuing source of embarrassment. Not only was their presence difficult to explain to acquaintances, but they were an obvious and continuing reminder of the problems in our physical relationship.

This failure spurred me to even greater efforts in the professional world. I was obviously attempting to compensate for my unmanly private life. My efforts to establish a potent professional persona began to affect my personality. Ironically, though I was incapable of performing adequately as a lover, I became ever more macho in my external behavior. My increasing success as a doctor fed this arrogant streak. Meriam was confused. Like many women before her she had been attracted to Dick's softness. It caused a sympathetic vibration in her. He seemed to understand something about women. On the other hand, she wanted her man to be all man, and that certainly included professional success, which she urged me toward without apology. Yet, when I developed the less sensitive shell that I needed to accomplish this job, she felt a loss.

Of course there was a middle ground, and I might have found it if my body had been in acceptable working order. As it was, though, all the masculine energy that should have found expression in vigorous sex had to be displayed in some other form. I became more callous and more arrogant. The tension between us continued to build; as it did so, the feeling was drained from both of us.

In spite of our problems we did not simply abandon ship. We tried very hard, and both of us profited from our difficult times. Certainly Meriam was tempered by them and came through as a stronger and more mature human being. Her explorations of her own strength often helped me draw upon mine. One example of this occurred when I was playing in a national championship at

Forest Hills. It was the quarterfinals and my opponent was an excellent player. Both the temperature and the humidity were hovering around the hundred mark. After two hours under the broiling sun, we were even with one set to play. I sat in my chair exhausted; the sound of my panting could probably be heard by everyone within a radius of fifty yards. I didn't feel I would be able to answer the call for the last set. Meriam could see that I was at the end of my rope. She stepped forward and spoke to me: "Dick, you know that this game is all mental, and if you want to you can get off that chair and win the third set . . . that is, if you want it bad enough." I looked up at her with appreciation. She had spoken decisively and with strength, equal to equal. What's more she had chosen exactly what I needed to hear at that moment. This was far from the flat, albeit enthusiastic, cheering that I had received when we were first married. "You're right," I replied. "It *is* all mental." I got up and won the match.

This incident is a trivial one, but it demonstrates that Meriam's growing assertiveness was finding applications in our everyday life. As a matter of fact, we were both trying very hard but laboring under extremely difficult circumstances. Meriam's situation was unenviable; she was married to a macho guy but suffered all the disadvantages of that predicament without any of the supposed advantages. However insensitive such men are made out to be, they're at least supposed to be sexy. I was macho but sexually unmotivated as well as looking feminine. I took a step toward eliminating that handicap when I had breast reduction surgery.

Considering the problem I had previously experienced in trying to get someone to cut off my penis, I expected a little more waffling from the doctor. Instead, he immediately agreed that I had a big problem and scheduled me for surgery; there were the usual medical tests and such, but the whole presurgical process was very quickly completed. At least this time I could go in as a doctor and be given due respect. Moreover, I chose a personal friend who was also one of the finest plastic surgeons in New York. I didn't want a repeat of the Adam's apple episode.

As I checked into the hospital I was keenly aware of the ironies involved. I had been so pleased and proud years ago when I first saw my breasts filling out; I had marked their growth with smug satisfaction. My thoughts had raced ahead to a time when the bottom half of my torso would match the femininity that those new breasts brought to my upper half. Now I was entering a hospital where they would be whacked off to make more of a man.

That night the surgeon came into my room and drew on my breasts with an indelible pencil. First he drew a line on the areola of the nipple, then he proceeded to make some little triangular designs on the outer curves of my breasts. The operative procedure would be to make a cut in the tissue of the areola; this tissue is unusual because it does not scar. The incision in the areola would be used as an entry to the interior of the breast. The glandular tissue within would be cut loose and withdrawn through the opening. When the breast had been sufficiently hollowed out, the areolar incision would be closed and tucks taken in the sides of the breasts in order to eliminate the slack in the skin. My friend the doctor was very cheerful as he worked—no more concerned than a geometrician working on a theoretical problem. The fact that tomorrow a knife would be tracing those lines in blood seemed to concern him not at all.

I know nothing about my time in the operating room. The procedure is done under general anesthesia, so I was totally unaware of what was going on. When I woke up my chest was bandaged. Even with the bulky pads and adhesive tape, I thought it looked strangely flat. The doctor came in later in the day and said that everything had gone fine; I would be a normal man in about a month. I left the hospital the next day and in a month my chest looked average, but I was far from being a normal man.

My newly created silhouette eased some of the social discomfort. There was no longer any need for bulky cover-ups on the tennis courts; I could even go barechested at the beach without raising a single eyebrow. I suppose these changes did us some good, but there was little decrease in our private stress.

For one thing, I had to grapple with my personal reaction to the surgery. Sure, I was trying to be a man and had agreed in principle that the breasts should go, but I suffered a real depression once they were gone. The feeling that I was an amputee was hard to shake. This caused me even further soul-searching as I wondered if such a reaction were normal—or if it indicated that I still held a deep-seated hope that someday I could be a woman. On this issue, there was no one whom I could approach for an opinion.

I was probably the only person in the world who had ever had breast reduction under such bizarre circumstances. These ruminations had the effect of pushing me even harder to play the hombre. I threw myself into work and tennis.

My life has been full of ironies. Some are so pointed that they almost seem the work of a malevolent fate determined to make me either a clown or a figure of tragedy. In my time I've been one or both a hundred times over. Seldom have these ironies been good for me; a lot of them make interesting stories in retrospect, but at the time all they meant was pain and sadness. Only one stands out as good beyond question, a thing that eventually gave me the greatest joy of my life: the irony of Meriam's pregnancy.

In spite of our infrequent lovemaking and in spite of my meager sperm count, I found myself on the road to becoming a father. At first, the situation seemed no more serious than a couple of missed periods; Meriam's first thought had been that she might be sick. A check with the doctor confirmed that a baby was on the way. One of my supposedly below-par sperms had demonstrated the old Raskind pluck and gotten the job done. Under the circumstances there was nothing to do but settle down and await the blessed event.

I could not deny myself the satisfied feeling that came over me when I thought about the baby. I had set out to become a man. I had built a career. I had married. Now would come the tangible evidence of my success: an offspring to carry my genes into the future. He or she would be an extension of me and yet a whole new soul. I felt such prideful sensations with an intensity that was probably greater than the average man's. My peculiarities made these feelings all the more precious to me.

From a physical point of view Meriam's pregnancy was uneventful; just after midnight one winter morning, Andy was born.

I felt closer to Meriam than I had in many months. It occurred to me that this triumph might really make a difference to us. I asked her if there was anything that I could do for her; she sent me to the cafeteria for some ice cream.

After eating the ice cream, she fell asleep. I held the baby several times during his first few hours of life. His face seemed a perfect composite of my face and Meriam's. I felt a strong bond between us, a sensation similar to the electricity that I had experienced two years before upon seeing Meriam walk through the door to Josh's living room. Something had clicked, and that click was echoed in the pleasing face of our child. No matter that the original energy between Meriam and me was much diminished; it had found new life in this baby boy.

I went out into the hall and, in spite of the fact that it was two o'clock in the morning, began to call everyone who I thought might be interested. In sequence, the sleepy voices of my father, of Josh, of Len, of Joel, and of many others came on the line and received the news: Dick Raskind has a son. At eight the next morning I even called Dr. Bak whom I hadn't seen in years. He said, "I am very happy for you." This was my last contact with him; he died shortly thereafter.

After six days in the hospital, we brought Andrew Bishop Raskind home. Our household consisted of Meriam, me, Andy, and his nurse, Maria. She was from Colombia and did not speak English well, but she projected tremendous warmth. "Mia," as Andy came to call her, provided a wonderful continuity of experience for him in the troubled times that loomed ahead. At all times she was there with her love and understanding—a companion upon whom he could rely absolutely.

Meriam and I grew close again for a brief period after Andy's birth, but the forces that had been pushing us apart reasserted themselves, and soon we were back to our distant relationship. We could both recognize the worth in each other but only in an intellectual sense. What had started out as an emotional bonding had become no more than a polite tolerance. As near to our old selves as we came was with Andy; luckily for us all, he was a magic token that brought out the best in Meriam and me when we were in his presence. I don't think he ever heard us argue. Around him we could be genuinely warm to one another, yet in our own bed we were cold. Meriam would lie reading a book and occasionally sharing with me some insight. I would lie with my head at the opposite end of the bed reading ophthalmology journals until I fell asleep. Often we'd pass the entire night in this topsy-turvy configuration.

I spent a lot of time with Andy and especially enjoyed feeding him. At lunchtime Mia would often bring him to my office. We'd eat together, and I would let him play with my eye instruments; in general, he'd make a lovely nuisance of himself. When he got a little older, I even started teaching him the names of the parts of the eye, using a big model that I kept in the office. He loved to take it apart, though it was a little harder to get him to put it together again. In the afternoons, home from work, I'd place Andy in the little child's seat on my bicycle, and we'd ride in Central Park until night fell. After his dinner and bath I'd read to him or make up stories to tell until he fell asleep. Strangely, in all my life I never felt more like a man than when I was fathering my child.

By contrast, I was defensive and cold with Meriam, who I'd come to feel had no appreciation for my predicament. She used to say, "Dick, it would be better if you'd get angry and yell at me! I can't stand this stonyfaced silence!" But I wouldn't talk: this lack of communication was probably the key factor in our eventual breakup. She had no other men, and I had no other women. Renée was out of the picture from the start and less likely than ever to come up once I had the breast-reduction operation. I even had some plastic surgery to close my pierced ears. Meriam tried, too, but we were by then completely at odds, and I thought that talking would just make it worse.

In 1973, I tried out for the United States Maccabiah team. The Maccabiah Games, held in Israel every four years, bring together Jewish athletes from all over the world. I had always wanted to participate but never felt that I could spare the time when I was a young player. I was always in medical school, internship, or something else. By 1973, my career was well-established, and my marriage was shaky. Even though I was in my late thirties, I decided at last to try for the team but lost to one of the fine younger players who was eventually chosen. It was a disappointing loss but a couple of days after the tryouts I was called by Nat Holman, the head of the Israeli Olympic Committee. Since I was an older man as well as a strong player, they thought it would be a good idea if I coached and captained the team. I accepted on the spot. The committee felt it was getting a bargain: an authority figure and an extra player, all in one. Of course, in 1973, sports were not the only issue in an all Jewish athletic competition. Only one year before, in Munich, eleven Jewish athletes had been killed by terrorists. It was thought that the Maccabiah Games might be a prime target for more such violence. In accepting the job as coach, I also accepted the challenge of keeping the five boys and five girls on the team safe from harm. I took this responsibility seriously and on one occasion had cause to take action. On the day of the team's departure for the games we took a chartered bus from our hotel to Kennedy Airport. During the ride we spotted a stranger on the sidewalk; he was carrying a Maccabiah Games flight bag. These had been issued to team members only. Thinking that he might be a terrorist attempting to infiltrate the team, one of the other coaches and I ordered the bus stopped. We got off and approached him; when he saw us walking in his direction he broke into a run. We took this as evidence that he was up to no good and chased him for several blocks before he melted into the Manhattan crowd.

My persona during that trip was commanding and throughly masculine. I even had a short fling with an Israeli woman during the stay. Our team won the silver medal and returned to the States safely.

By the time Andy was 18 months old, Meriam and I were at the separate vacation stage. Mia, Andy, and I spent time in the French Alps where I was participating in a doctors' tennis convention. Afterward, we toured through France, spending some especially lovely days on the beautiful coast near Bordeaux.

Andy and I loved to ride the winding mountain roads on a motorcycle. We wore identical blue warm-up suits and often attracted attention because we looked so cute together. Andy would clutch me tightly, and we would speed along, occasionally dropping down to a coast road to watch how the sun glittered on the waves as we flashed by. We felt very much joined on that powerful machine, isolated from all others, yet thrust at great velocity into contact with the natural elements around us. Though very young I know Andy felt the same sense of union. When we'd stop, his face would be radiant and he'd say, "I love you, Daddy." I'd reply, "I love you too, Son," and we'd embrace.

Andy was an equal, even when he was a little boy. On our trip to Europe we shared a depth of understanding that I continue to think was unique because it was expressed in both the emotional and the intellectual spheres. "I feel close to you, Daddy," he'd say. "It's different than at home," I'd answer. "That's because we're alone and far away." He'd nod sagely, and I think he actually did grasp it.

Andy and I returned from Europe with a relationship that was closer than ever, but my situation with Meriam was worse. I became increasingly uncivil. Often I would go through the whole day without speaking to her; I even kept my eyes averted. It was a very punishing routine and finally she said, "I can't stand it anymore. If you can't even look at me, why don't you get out?" I stared at her for the first time in days and said, "I shall."

For a while I slept at my office or on the couches of friends. My week consisted of seven different beds on seven different nights. At last I accepted the finality of our separation and took an apartment on East Seventy-first Street, close enough for me to see Andy every day. I increased my tennis playing and felt a renewed sense of accomplishment. Since I was past thirty-five, I was competing in the junior veterans class. Being amongst the youngsters in that category, I was winning rather consistently. The tennis helped fill in the gaps that used to be occupied by a time-consuming, if strained, home life. Andy and Mia came to many of the tournaments, so the tennis was doubly enjoyable. I reached the finals of the National Championships that year, finally losing to my friend and later staunch supporter, Gene Scott. My reputation as a top player remained secure and helped me to retain a sense of identity in the first days of my separation from Meriam.

18

Renée Richards/Richard Reborn

Shortly after my abrupt leavetaking, Meriam met a man with whom she developed a continuing relationship; eventually, they married. I continued as a heterosexual man and dated a tall woman artist for several months; she loved tennis and came to all my matches. I continued to win, spurred on by her support. My private practice was flourishing. I maintained my close relationship with Andy. The whole situation had a familiar ring to it; once again, I was in an enviable position. I was still young; I was divorced and freewheeling. I had a beautiful girl friend, a delightful child, and yet . . .

Renée was beginning to tug at me again. It was probably because I was alone in my apartment for long periods of time. During my marriage I had seldom been alone. I think that Renée had, as in those days long ago in college and many times since, shrunk from emerging when I lived with someone. Dick was strong when he had the continuing presence and support of another; but when I was alone for long periods of time I could always feel Renée's strength. Then again, there was the breakup of my marriage and the specter of my advancing years. If Renée was going to make a serious bid for existence, it would have to be soon. As she had after other periods of suppression, she came back stronger than ever. I fought it. I even went to a psychiatrist though I had vowed never to do so again; his insulting suggestion was that I go out and get laid. Instead, I began to think about suicide. It would be easy; as a doctor I had access to all sorts of painless yet lethal substances. The force of my feeling for Andy was the most compelling reason why I didn't kill myself. The sense of betrayal that he would have felt made suicide an impossibility.

The only alternative was to allow Renée to emerge. It was not even an alternative; it was a necessity. She was coming out whether I liked it or not. In the evenings I began to dress again in women's clothes. Shortly after this development, I went again to see Dr. Benjamin. When I greeted Virginia, his secretary, she said, "You know, Dr. Benjamin has retired. His young associate, Dr. Allenfield, has taken over the practice." It was a poignant commentary on how long I had struggled with the step that now seemed inevitable. Dr. Allenfield was sympathetic. "Dr. Raskind," he said, "I think the medical profession has let you down. There is more than enough evidence that you are a genuine transsexual, and I'll give you my backing all the way." He started me on estrogens, and once again I felt that peculiar sense of well-being settle on me. The physical changes came faster this time. My recently flattened breasts began to plump out again. Because of the reduction surgery, however, they only reached about half their former size. The feminine adipose in my thighs and hips also came quickly. It was as if my body had been waiting patiently for the opportunity to be womanly again and then, given the chance, rushed toward it with unprecedented speed. Within three months I was fully feminine.

I gave up seeing my girl friend and began to ready myself for the surgery that now seemed imminent. Every evening I would dress as Renée. I no longer cared about being seen; my only concerns were for Andy and my professional life. I continued practicing as a man during the day though I looked more and more weird in men's clothes. Physicians who referred patients to me had to warn them with statements something like: "Dr. Raskind is an unusual-looking individual but he's the best in his field. Don't be alarmed by his appearance; he's a respected physician." Friends also came forward. "Dick," one said, after a tennis match, "I want you to know that your good friends are aware of the changes that you are going through." "How long have you known?" I asked. "For a very long time," he stared at me for a moment. "And it doesn't make a damn bit of difference to us." The support of my colleagues and of my friends helped me to set my mind as much at ease as was possible under the circumstances.

During this period my father celebrated his seventy-fifth birthday. Responding to strong urging from the immediate family, my sister, Mike, traveled from her home in the north to Long Island for the occasion. I sat visiting with her after the party, and she asked me abruptly, "Are you sorry now that you never had that operation?" I could have told her then that I was soon going to have it, but I had learned my lesson ten years ago. I satisfied myself by saying only, "Yes, I *am* sorry I never had it."

I continued seeing Andy every day. He seemed to pay little attention to the changes in my body; as far as he was concerned I was the same person with whom he felt so very secure. In spite of the softening effect of the hormones, I remained fiercely protective. One evening Andy and I were riding in Central Park near Spanish Harlem; it was silly to be there in the early evening, what with night falling, but I had miscalculated the time. Suddenly three young toughs blocked the bikeway. By that time, I was hardly a ferocious-looking stud, and they probably anticipated an uncontested mugging. It infuriated me that they could stoop so low as to molest a biker with a child in tow. I accelerated, pedaling as fast as I could and aiming directly at the largest of them. I can remember baring my teeth as I leaned forward to get more leverage. Andy was laughing merrily as we flew toward them; it was like a game of chicken. At first, I don't think they believed that I'd actually ride right into them; however, when they got a good look at my snarling countenance and the ever-increasing speed of the bike, they leaped aside, and we sailed through untouched. Andy found it a delightful game, never once considering that there might have been danger. After all, Daddy was with him.

In the spring of 1975, I again consulted Dr. Laidlaw, the psychiatrist who years before had encouraged me to have faith in my own judgment. His advice had been instrumental in my decision to go to Europe. I knew that I would need a psychiatrist on my side when the time came to find a surgeon. I didn't want to go through another battery of psychological tests if I could help it; I told him what had happened to me since we last spoke. He was amazed and said, "Renée, you've been through more than you've deserved. I agree with Dr. Allenfield. Your medical colleagues have let you down. You've been frustrated and used as a guinea pig for too long. I promise that I'll do everything I can to help you find the right surgeon." He pulled out a copy of the interview I had had with him years before and said, "The answers you gave me today are the same as the ones you gave me in 1969. You've paid your dues."

Dr. Allenfield and Dr. Laidlaw began making inquiries in the ranks of those doctors who performed transsexual operations. Their highest priority was that the surgeon be competent and willing to do the operation based on my past testing. My nerves had been strained to the breaking point. I couldn't talk to any more psychiatrists, psychologists, or sociologists—the well was dry. My doctors understood this and humanely refused to accept any compromises. For awhile it looked like the spot would be Stanford. I was acquainted with some of the physicians there, and it seemed possible to cut through the red tape. I was adjusting to the idea of traipsing across the country when I received a surprising phone call from Dr. Laidlaw. "Renée," he asked, "if I could schedule your surgery in New York with no red tape and under the medical standards that you require, how would you like it?" Of course, this was simply a rhetorical question. He knew that I'd like it fine. "Do it!" I said.

The surgeon that my team had located was Dr. Roberto Granato. Ironically, his office was only one mile from my birthplace. He had already performed one hundred and fifty-seven transsexual operations; obviously, his expertise was the result of plenty of experience. I looked him up in the Blue Book and saw that his credentials were good. He had been trained initially in South America at an excellent school and had completed his training in the United States. Furthermore, I talked to physicians who had examined his postoperative patients; their comments were complimentary. The fact that he was on the faculty of the Columbia Presbyterian Medical School was also a high recommendation.

In spite of my investigations I arrived for my interview with a lot of suspicions. I was prepared to meet the same old routine: a promising beginning followed by a flaccid retreat. Dr. Granato's secretary showed me into his office, a bookish room one wall of which was covered with his various degrees. There I was greeted by the man himself. He was of medium height, Latin American in

274

appearance, and wore a thin moustache. His presentation was energetic and forthright. He spoke with an accent but was perfectly fluent in English. After the initial introductions, he sat down behind his desk and leaned forward.

"How long have you had this problem?" He didn't go in for small talk nor did he want to discuss the obvious. After all, I was sitting there in a dress.

"All my life," I answered.

"Silicone?" He pointed to my breasts.

"No, estrogens."

"How long have you wanted to be a woman?"

"All my life."

"Do you shave?"

"No, electrolysis."

"Did you want to be a woman when you were a child?"

"All my life." I realized that he was asking this same question over and over each time in slightly altered form.

"Do you live as a woman?"

"In my personal life, of course."

"And you've wanted to be a woman all your life?"

"All my life."

He stared at me intensely for about three minutes. His gaze swept over every part of my body. He held his eyes for short periods on my breasts, my face, my loop earrings, my lap, my legs, my feet, my hands. Finally, he reared back in his chair and locked his hands behind his head. "Look," he said, staring over my head, "I'm a surgeon. You come from a reputable psychiatrist who says you should have this operation. I agree with him, so I'll do it." I nearly fell off the chair. Was this man actually offering to do the deed? "You will?" I said lamely. He didn't bother to answer.

"Step into the examining room," he said brusquely, indicating a door at the rear of the office. I preceded him and was heading toward the examining table when he said, "Lift up that skirt." I stopped and turned around. Were there to be no formalities? He stood expectantly. I stepped out of my panties and, like a child playing doctor, raised the dress to display my privates. Dr. Granato grabbed my penis and pulled until I said, "Ouch!" "It is very small," he mused, "You are a tall girl and need a good-sized vagina. I will have to do a skin graft." He dropped it and grabbed my testicles. "Humph! These are shrunken. They are good for

275

nothing." I agreed. Dr. Granato straightened up and motioned me back into the office. We talked for a few minutes more.

"I want it done in the next few days," I said. He looked amused.

"I have a waiting list that goes six months into the future."

"I've been waiting ten years," I said. "Besides, I've taken the month of August off to work on a medical text. It will be a perfect cover."

"I'll tell you what, Dr. Raskind, you call me tomorrow, Thursday, and meanwhile I'll see if I can arrange for hospital admission on Sunday and surgery on Monday." Without waiting for my thanks, he hopped up and escorted me to the door. "Yes, yes, yes, Renée. I know, I'm happy to do it. Call me tomorrow."

When I called, he had done as he said he would. The operation was on. I went to his office that afternoon for a more thorough checkup. He gave me antibiotics to start taking and instructions that included daily scrubbings in my genital area with a germicidal soap. He tried to convince me to use my Blue Cross-Blue Shield coverage to pay for the operation; I refused, insisting that I be as anonymous as possible. Actually, I wished that I could use the insurance because the divorce, alimony, and child support payments had pretty much cleaned me out. I had to borrow thirty-five hundred dollars from friends to pay for the operation.

I signed only one document with my real name. This was the paper giving Dr. Granato consent to change my sex through surgery. Others I had seen used euphemisms like "sex reassignment." The one I signed said at the top: "Permission for sex change." I did like his style, no bullshit. I asked him if he considered it a big operation.

"Do you want me to describe the technique?"

"No, I just want a general idea."

"Generally, it's a hell of an operation. You'll be on the table four hours. Some patients cruise right through. Others have a rough time. You're a physician. You know that anything can happen. I'll get you a journal article reprint." He rummaged in a file cabinet and handed me a folder that I put in my purse. "I'll see you on Monday. By the way, you look terrific!" With this little stroke he dismissed me. Later that evening I took out the reprint and leafed through it. Strangely, I had never delved into the medical minutiae of the operation, though I was thoroughly familiar with the general procedure. When I came to the color-photograph plates showing the surgical steps, I couldn't retain my professional objectivity. The lurid pinks and reds jumped out of the page at me; it was all so wet and raw and bloody. I recoiled, put the article away, and have not looked at it since. I gave thanks that I was an ophthalmologist and worked in the clarity of the eye where there was no such carnage.

I spent the couple of days before Sunday at a beach house I had rented. I couldn't believe that the monumental change would take place in seventy-two hours. This speed was a professional courtesy—doctor to doctor. Ironically, the feature of my life that had scared my colleagues off for so many years was now responsible for the incredible speed of the climax. During these two days I had a houseguest at the beach, my cousin Patrice. I had originally intended to go into the hospital without a word to any of my friends or relatives; however, as I passed time with Patrice and secretly anticipated the occasion to come, I felt drawn to her. In part, I suppose it was simply that she was there, and I clung to her for companionship. On the other hand, she had been close to me in the past and had a reputation in the family for sensitivity. I'd known her since childhood and had confided in her at times in the past, though I had never told her about my transsexualism. Finally, just before I left to spend Saturday night at my Manhattan apartment, I told her what I was about to do. She listened calmly and gave me no arguments; I swore her to secrecy and told her that, if she hadn't heard from me in three days, she should start calling the hospitals. I didn't tell her where I would be or the name of my surgeon. I didn't want to be vulnerable if she couldn't keep the news to herself. As it turned out, she was as good as her word, and I was unmolested.

On Sunday, I checked into the Physicians' Hospital in Queens. I used the name Renée Frick in tribute to Josh and listed my occupation as "writer." This step was doubly necessary since my father, who had practiced medicine in Queens for forty years, was a personal friend of the physicians who owned the hospital. If the unusual name "Raskind" had appeared on any admission documents, it would almost certainly have come to their attention. Ms. Frick was conveyed to a private room. In transsexual operations a private room and private-duty nurses are required for the first forty-eight hours, postoperative. Thereafter the patient may be moved to a semiprivate room under the care of the usual nursing staff. I had made arrangements for a private room all the way. After forty years of buildup I was not about to skimp on the trimmings. The routine was standard admittance-day stuff; I had blood tests, X-rays, and a physical examination. This familiar sequence was punctuated by an unnerving visit from the anesthesiologist.

I had awaited this man's appearance with great concern. Most people don't realize how important the "gas man" is to the success of an operation. Whenever parents used to ask me about the danger of an operation, I used to say, "I can do this operation one-handed. The danger from the surgery is negligible but there is always a risk when you put someone to sleep." I realize that a doctor is supposed to project a confident image, but I always tried to cover myself because a disaster with anesthetics is almost always a major disaster. People die or are made into vegetables. During my own operations I constantly asked for reports on respiration and blood pressure, not so much because I needed them but in order to keep the anesthesiologist on his toes. A chain is only as strong as its weakest link. My surgeon might be great, but if my gas man was a dud I could end up as a female corpse.

At first glance the anesthesiologist looked benign. He was average in most respects; his attitude was that of a concerned professional. As he expressed his concerns, though, I began to wonder about his intelligence. First of all, he was worried because I had had an operation about five months before for which halothane had been used as the anesthetic. The rule of thumb on this is that there should be a six-month interval before it is used again on the same individual. His concern seemed to center around the fact that he was mostly familiar with halothane and wished he didn't have to administer a gas with which he was less expert. I longed to say, "Look, we're both medical men. We both know that there is a big safety margin built into that rule. Five months is a perfectly acceptable waiting period. Surely, you'd be safer using the stuff that you know best, don't you think?"

Of course, I was not supposed to be a doctor; I was a writer, and so I kept my teeth clenched. He left, and I was calming down—after about ten minutes by myself—when he walked back into the room and said, "Why on earth are you taking estrogens?" Was this man a complete idiot? Would I have to spell the word "transsexual" and then define it? I explained as coolly as I could that I had no ovaries of my own, so my estrogens had to come from the pharmacy; that it was kind of like a woman after a pan hysterectomy or after menopause. He nodded dully and left again. I thought to myself that I should have brought the journal reprint on transsexual surgery for him to read. I was terrified that this dolt might be my anesthesiologist. That he would be was not certain because the staff members divide the day's cases among themselves. He had visited me only because he was on duty that evening. Since there were two other staff anesthesiologists, I had one chance in three of getting him. I prayed that the odds ran true.

In spite of this unpromising visit with the gas man earlier in the day, I was feeling pretty calm by evening. The nurses and aides had seen a few other transsexual operations; so I passed the time asking them how much pain was involved. The answers ranged from, "Nothing. It's a breeze," to, "Tremendous! You'll need pain killers for at least three days." One nurse claimed that she'd heard patients say they'd never have done it if they'd known about the suffering involved. This was not good news, but I figured if they could stand it, so could I. My pain threshold had always been higher than normal. There was no reason to think I wouldn't come through better than most.

In the morning I was given an injection about an hour before the surgery was scheduled to begin. I hoped that the shot would knock me out completely, but they usually don't and my anxiety level had been steadily rising since I had awakened. That little shot didn't stand a chance; my eyes were darting around like a squirrel's as I was wheeled into the operating suite. I was greeted there by a Chinese anesthesiologist. A temporary relief flooded over me, but just seconds later I heard the voice of the rube from the night before. He was asking questions about penthrane, an anesthetic that would be the natural substitute if halothane couldn't be used. It was obvious that he knew nothing about it and was being given, milligrams per kilogram, the instructions for induction and maintenance. They were talking in a spot directly opposite the top of my head, so I couldn't see them. I kept craning around, trying to catch a glimpse of the proceedings, and hoping that some administrator would walk in and say, "There's been some mistake here. Incompetents are not allowed to practice medicine at this hospital. You'll have to go to Casablanca." Nothing like that happened, though, and my fears went racing out of control. It was not too late! I could still call it off. Yes, it would be costly, but surely that was no consideration when one's life hung in the balance. I was at the point of sitting up to make my announcement when a soothing voice said, "I am Dr. Hu. I will be your anesthesiologist today." His voice resonated with the reassuring calm of the Orient.

I relaxed momentarily but began nursing new anxieties as it became obvious that Dr. Granato was going to be late. The staff was prepared, the gas man was prepared, and the patient was prepared—all we needed was the man with the knife. The nurses were shifting from one foot to another; I was like a bomb set to go off at nine-thirty and it was now nine-forty-five. I heard the nursing supervisor yell, "Where is that Dr. Granato? I'll give him ten more minutes, and then I'm canceling the case." After a thirty-year wait, I wasn't in the mood to have some testy nurse decide my fate. If she postponed the operation I was liable to wind up the next time with Mortimer Snerd as my anesthesiologist.

Finally, the great surgeon made his entrance. He held my hands briefly; all surgeons do it. It's called "the laying on of hands." I'd done it myself hundreds of times, but I'd never realized how much it could mean. Finally, Dr. Granato retreated to the scrub room, and Dr. Hu asked me to help move myself from the stretcher to the operating table. I was aware of my strength as I slid myself with one motion onto the table. It was a willing move, smoothly executed. I hesitated only a little, marking the moment, punctuating it. When I awoke, I would be Renée. When I chose it as a child, I had not known the meaning of the name Renée. In that moment I savored its significance. Renée. Reborn. I heard Dr. Hu say, "Now, we will put you to sleep." The penthrane was turned on, and Dick was turned off.

While I was asleep Dr. Granato plied his trade. First he made an incision extending from the base of the penis down to about an inch above the anus. It was extended inward toward the area that was to become the vagina. Blood vessels were clamped, muscles dissected, and specialized structures like the urethra and erogenous tissue were prepared for future use. Extraneous structures like the vas deferens and seminal vesicles were excised. The vaginal cavity was formed by moving aside the structures occupying that space. Luckily, there is plenty of room in the body cavity for such relocation. My penis was denuded of skin and the useless leftover tissue discarded. The penile skin, along with a skin graft from my right thigh, was fashioned around a plastic mold. This form was placed in the vaginal cavity and sutured in place. My testicles were removed and the skin comprising the scrotum was used to create the vaginal labia. The urethra and nerve tissue were secured in their proper locations. The most sensitive erotic matter was located in precisely the same place as a woman's clitoris, so that my sexual sensations would parallel as much as possible a normal woman's. Packing was placed around the mold in the vagina and a catheter inserted in my urethra. During the operation I was given two units of whole blood.

The whole procedure, including the skin graft from the outer thigh of my right leg, took three-and-a-half hours. I regained consciousness in the recovery room about twenty minutes after they had finished. The first thing I was aware of was that I could not stop shaking. It was as if my whole body had been seized by a wracking chill; I was clattering like a box of marbles. It might have been simple shock or a by-product of my emergence from the anesthesia. I only knew that I was out of control; the nurse was alternately wiping my body with dry towels and checking my blood pressure, which—I found out later—was very low. My awareness of the shaking was almost immediately replaced by an overwhelming awareness of pain. My torso was afflicted with several different kinds. Sharp, shooting pains of searing intensity came from my now nonexistent penis and testicles. It was if someone was repeatedly poking a firebrand into my groin. Mixed with this was a tearing sensation; it was like someone was ripping at my organs with a pair of pliers. Underneath these sharp aspects was a dull, sickish ache such as you might have if someone had beaten you with a baseball bat in the area of your lower back. Beneath the ache was a pervasive sense of pressure, as if something inside me was enlarging, pushing outward.

It was a blessing that I was in shock; that helped to buffer my reaction to the crushingly intense flood of pain. Had I been more aware, I surely would have passed out. In spite of these incredible sensations, my mind did shift to the fact I was now a woman—and not once did I wish I hadn't done it. There was no remorse in spite of the suffering. In a way the pain seemed appropriate. It cast an intense atmosphere around a momentous occasion. Even the phantom pain in my penis was a consolation because I knew that it came from a thing that was gone from me. In a way this pain was Richard Henry Raskind's death throe. Even so, I would gladly have taken some Demerol to kill the pain, but this is not possible for anyone in shock because it might further lower an already low-blood pressure. Added to this bath of suffering was my dawning realization that I might be having a transfusion reaction that could be fatal. I was afraid, and this fear fused with the pain. I wished that I didn't know so damn much medicine. It wasn't fair that I should be afflicted by this cruel understanding when I could only lie helplessly awaiting the outcome. Finally, they gave me an injection, and I passed out.

I don't mean to give myself airs about this pain. As a doctor I've attended people who were so wracked with pain that they couldn't eat, sleep, or defecate. These are life's real sufferers, not Dick Raskind on the day his penis got knocked off. Still, this is my story and that was my pain, the worst I've ever felt. It was bad, but I asked for it, embraced it. I'm glad I felt it because it constitutes a personal testament: it showed me that I was right in becoming Renée. If ever there was an opportunity for regret it came when I was quaking in the recovery room, yet that opportunity was not seized. At that moment I realized that I would rather have died in the attempt than live any longer in a nightmare of duality.

Sometime later that day I awoke again and found that the pain had diminished somewhat. I had tubes sticking out of many of the natural orifices in my body; and out of one unnatural orifice. I had an IV bottle hooked up to each arm, a catheter in my bladder, an oxygen tube in my nose, and a plastic cylinder in my vagina. At least I had no nasogastric tube; that was a small consolation. I tried to move and received a shock of pain between my legs. It felt like someone had plunged a knife in to the hilt. I coughed in reaction to that sensation and felt the same pain again. I made a mental note: no moving and no coughing. This left me with a limited repertoire of amusements. Blessedly, my nurse was good. She sat beside me, constantly wiping my forehead and massaging my body. Her attentions made my immobility bearable; from time to time I'd risk moving my head to the right so that I could smile thankfully at her. The rest of the time I stared at the ceiling or closed my eyes and tried to guess which tube they'd take out first. Dr. Granato came by for a minute to say that everything had gone fine.

The next day was better. I could rotate a little from one side of my back to the other; and I could move my knees a little without the old knife in the groin. I still couldn't cough, though. They took the oxygen tube out of my nose, and that made me feel more human, leaving only four tubes still sticking out of me. I drank some juice and some tea. One sign that I was getting better was my irritation over the placement of the IV containing an antibiotic. They had stuck it in my left arm and it burned. Didn't they know that my left arm was my tennis arm, worth its weight in gold? On the fourth day the pain had diminished to the point where I was encouraged to get up. The philosophy after major surgery is to get the patient ambulating as quickly as possible. It seems to facilitate healing and prevents too much loss of strength from extended bed rest. Needless to say, I didn't look forward to it, but I went along with the doctor's recommendation. I stood up, passed out, and was caught by a strong nurse just before I hit the floor. When I woke up, I was back in bed. Later in the day Dr. Granato breezed in. "How do you feel?" he asked, flashing a cheerful smile.

"You must be crazy," I answered uncooperatively. I had no stomach at that point for a cheerful bedside manner. Dr. Granato pulled down the covers and lifted my hospital gown.

"Let's see what we've got here or, more accurately, what we don't got here." I wondered how often he'd made that joke. I guessed about one hundred and fifty-seven times. He removed the bandage, tinkered around down there for a few long moments, then glanced up at me. "Look here!" he waved his hand to present the area between my legs.

"I can't get into a position where I can see it," I said lamely.

"Nonsense. Don't you have a mirror?" He spotted a little stand-up mirror on a shelf over the basin. "There's one." He grabbed it and proudly lined up the reflection so that I could see it. What I saw was essentially what I had seen so many times between the legs of the women with whom I'd been intimate—a normal-looking introitus but incredibly distinctive because it was mine. I had the doctor hold the mirror at all angles so that I could see it from every possible perspective. My pubic area had been shaved for the operation, so I had a clear view of all the structures, the clearest I've ever had; there were not even any sutures visible. Dr. Granato stood by like a proud father, obviously relishing my delight. Finally, I laid my head back on the pillow.

"I was afraid to look."

"I know," he said, "that's why I made you." He smiled smugly and asked a needless question. "How do you like it?"

"Fine," I said. I'm sure he knew that it was an understatement.

On the fifth day I was lifted out of bed for a sitz bath and collapsed again in the bathroom. In a way this represented progress because it took me a lot longer to faint than it did the day before. Things started to get gray and continued until everything was gray. Not so much a blackout as a grayout. Otherwise I was doing pretty well. I was drinking more fluids, having worked my way up to diet soft drinks. The pain, though much decreased was still substantial. One of the most distressing things about it was that it was no longer directly associated with any particular structure in my body. My phantom penis pain had had only a brief life on Monday following the operation. It had soon been replaced by an unlocalized burning and tearing sensation. It didn't emanate from the vaginal area; it was just down there somewhere. It was tremendously disconcerting to have big pain and not be able to pinpoint the source. After the fifth day though, it rapidly diminished. As the major pain began to slack off, I started to feel pain in the portion of my thigh used for the skin graft. I wondered how I would explain the scar: Maybe I had slid into third base? No, that wouldn't do. A burn from a barbecue grill? It was a possibility. The one I liked best was that I had scraped it on a rusty tennis court fence while chasing a wide backhand return. As it turned out none of these fabrications was necessary. The scar is hardly visible.

With the lessening of the pain, I became a bit crankier. "Why don't you get that ten-inch plastic prick out of me?" I asked Dr. Granato irritably. "It's crushing my back and intestines." He explained that the offending object would come out about ten days after the operation. Meanwhile, it was sutured in to give the new tissue a mold to form itself around. Inside me, skin segments from my penis and my thigh were working together—knitting a vagina, as it were. And this cooperative effort was not the only miracle being wrought. This skin, that had been dry and a little leathery while in contact with the air was adapting itself to internal life, taking on a mucous quality. This change would result in my vagina being moist, and would eliminate the possibility that any of the tissue might grow together. During the healing process, my body would generate connective tissue that would further strengthen this hardy, adaptable, and accommodating skin.

By Saturday I was off Demerol completely, and my head cleared noticeably. The discomfort, though still there, was easily bearable. I ate three hearty meals and walked in the hall for exercise. I read, wrote, and watched a tennis match on television. Most significantly, I put on a little eye makeup and some lip gloss. From my years in medicine, I know that this is a sure sign that a woman in the hospital is getting well. On Monday the doctor removed the packing around my vagina but left the tube in. This relieved some of the pressure and made me feel a lot better. On Tuesday I was released from the hospital. I spent a couple of days at my apartment in the city before I went to Dr. Granato's office for a checkup. He removed the tube and examined me; there were a few places where the skin had grown together. These adhesions had to be severed, so he gave me an injection of painkiller in my newly formed genitalia; it hurt like hell. Already, I was experiencing an increased sense of vulnerability in the vaginal area. I felt rather demure as I was examined and manipulated by the doctor. At length, he gave me a clean bill of health, and I drove out to the beach, where I planned to recuperate.

When I arrived there I called Andy since I hadn't talked to him for over a week; he was chatty and full of life. I felt no strain as a result of my transformation. Naturally, he called me daddy as he had before and as he continues to do to this day. At the time of my operation he was only three-and-a-half years old. My plan was to continue relating to him as a father until he was old enough to understand. The operation made no real difference in my appearance, and if he had accepted me up to then he could surely continue to do so. Even after he was told, I didn't expect that our relationship would change. I would always be his daddy; but, at the time of this first call from the beach, that particular problem was several years away. As I talked to him I felt happy in a way that I had not felt immediately following the operation. Since waking up after the operation I had been struggling with the problems of recovery and didn't have much of a chance to feel euphoric. Even when the realization had thoroughly pressed itself on me, I felt no particular elation. I just felt like Renée, the person I knew I had been all along; however, when I heard Andy's lyrical laughter I realized how complete my life now was. I had myself; I had my son. Things had finally turned out well, and I was happy. Thereafter, I called Andy every day.

The rest of the time I spent recuperating. I slept a lot and rarely left the house for more than an hour at a time. I continued to take antibiotics for a few days after being released from the hospital, but then I required no more medication. It was just a short while, three days or so, before I dispensed with the bandage between my legs. Actually, my instructions from Dr. Granato were quite simple. I had to do two things to promote healing. First, I periodically sat in a tub of hot water laced with salt. I wasn't allowed to use soap in my genital area for a couple of weeks. The second instruction resulted in an amusing activity. I had been told that the sun's rays would be beneficial, so every day I lay in my secluded backyard presenting my newly formed anatomy to the sun. Somehow this seemed right; it smacked of some ancient ritual, as if this were Renée's introduction to the cosmos.

Another of Dr. Granato's instructions did not deal with healing so much as it did maintenance. He had supplied me with what he referred to as a dilator. This looked like nothing so much as a crudely made dildo; it is a cylindrical piece of white, rubber-like material about ten inches long. The business end tapers like a sharpened pencil but has no point; it's just lopped off bluntly. The other end sports a squarish knob that looks like it has been whittled. I guess this texturized effect is supposed to give the user a good surface to grip. The doctor told me to use this thing frequently to keep the channel open and to discourage it from shrinking. By "using it," he meant that I was supposed to insert the device and slide it in and out. Before you get a picture of me ecstatically working away with this thing, let me say that I never got a second's sexual pleasure out of it. First of all, it's too hard and, even though it's only a bit over an inch in diameter, it always feels uncomfortably big. During the first couple of months that I used the dilator, it would often come out stained with pinkish blood. Nonetheless, I faithfully continued and often slept with it inside me as I was instructed. Even now if I go through a period of extended sexual inactivity, I use my dilator.

During my first few days on the beach, my cousin Patrice came and stayed with me. I had called her from the hospital once I was coherent, to let her know that I was all right. As my only confidante, she felt rather protective and played nurse through the early period of my convalescence. Actually, aside from Dr. Granato she was the first of my friends or relatives to see me dressed as a woman after I had finally made the grade—from an anatomical standpoint. She even went with me on a shopping expedition to a second-hand store where I bought a pair of tight jeans. I remember feeling elated at the unbroken curve of my pubic area; nothing remained to be tied down or jammed up. Patrice agreed that I looked good.

By the end of my month's leave I was pretty well healed. Naturally, there were residual effects; it was a long time before I was as strong as I was before the operation. I had also been forbidden to have sex for at least six weeks. Just to be on the safe side I waited three months, resigning myself to a lengthy virginity.

Meanwhile, the doctor's warning did not keep me from doing a little sexual experimenting without a partner. I could tell right away that there was one big sexual difference between Dick and Renée. Dick had been very inhibited about his body, one might even say a bit prudish. He didn't enjoy touching his sexual parts, and he didn't enjoy having them touched. I conclude that this was a symptom of his ambivalence toward them. Renée, however, had no such ambivalence. She couldn't keep her hands off herself. I don't mean to give the impression that I was embarrassing people in public or anything like that, but finding out whether I was in good erotic working order was a high-priority item. In the first couple of weeks after the operation I was too knocked out generally and too tender specifically to do much investigating. Then again, my erogenous areas had just been sewn in, and I didn't want to risk disturbing the relocation process. I tried to remain businesslike as I looked after myself, but I discovered that erectile tissue is extremely hardy stuff. It took to its new home in a most wholehearted way. My overall contentment probably helped a lot, too. A satisfied patient is a fast-healing patient.

Whatever the reason, it wasn't long before I began to get interesting tingling sensations from my clitoral area as I went about my daily routine of self-care. Once I got past the salty sitz bath stage, for example, I could gently wash myself in the pubic area. To my delight, this excited me; little stabs of sensation originated in the area. Whatever I'd gotten in the past from down there had been associated with a penis. This was different though recognizably sexual. It wasn't as pointed; it seemed generalized yet definitely was associated with my new clitoris. I thought that this confusing vagueness might simply be the result of my unfamiliarity with the new ground rules. After all, stuff had been moved around down there. On the other hand there was less tissue than before and maybe that meant a more vague sensation. In those early stages, though, I was not inclined to overanalyze, much less to quibble. It was a relief to know that I could feel something and that it was pleasurable.

Those first nudges were indirect, the result of nonsexual activities. Gradually, as the days went by, these little flares kept bursting with greater intensity and soon demanded concentrated attention. I proceeded carefully, avoiding direct contact with the point of sensation but massaging the soft areas around my clitoris. It was indirect, but compared to the random washing movements that had excited me before, was highly focused. It was slightly higher than where my penis had been located; the one big difference was that there was no sense of projection. The sexy feelings (and by now they were intense) were more associated with the main flesh of my body. The tendency to thrust was lessened. I felt more inclined than ever to receive, to be moved toward rather than to aggress. As I continued to rub myself, the intensity of sensation grew higher. The buildup was slow, and the sensation remained more general, though it definitely strengthened and took shape as if working toward a peak of some kind. I grew more vigorous and occasionally my hand or one of my fingers would slip into direct contact with my clitoris. There was no pain or discomfort when this took place, so I felt less tentative and let it happen more often. As I went higher, I began to perceive a climax. The peculiar awareness of a finish, a final push, a barrier to be broken, loomed ahead. There is no way to adequately describe that moment when I knew for certain that I would make it.

For most people it's a given, but for Renée it was a magic place; it was almost as important as the orgasm itself—that came quickly on the heels of that instant of comprehension. It was not as well-defined as a man's orgasm. The moment of ejaculation, the clear-cut pumping of semen that is so entwined with the male orgasm, was missing. This climax was more rounded, less intense but longer-lasting, and especially gratifying in the warm sensations that flooded me and that continued to do so for some time. More than anything else it reminded me of those peculiar dreams I had experienced during my trip to Europe. I would awaken at a moment of sexual climax and find my ineffectual man's genitals responding as if with a long-lasting, low-key vibration. This sensation, though not climactic, had been intensely pleasurable. My first orgasm as a woman took me beyond this rudimentary response, but there was definitely an echo of it. As I lay there regaining my composure, I noticed that my vagina was wet, and I marveled that in this regard too, I was a woman. Over the next few weeks my ability to become excited and to give myself orgasms improved. I went through a period of shameless preoccupation with autoeroticism. This was as much a testimony to my relief at having my sexuality intact as it was to lasciviousness, though there was plenty of the latter.

In those early days I felt little need of company. I was busy getting to know Renée. In spite of my self-absorption, I did make a few trips over to Joel's nearby summer house. By that time I was a familiar sight in my women's clothes, so he had no reason to suspect that I was different in any way. I had to tell him; he didn't seem too surprised. As a matter of fact he had felt that it was in the wind. His main concern was whether I had come through all right and whether I was happy with the result. When I assured him that I was doing fine and happier than I'd been in years, he was satisfied. We went quickly back to our normal relationship, though he tended for a long time to call me "Dick." This was a problem that I had with practically everyone; the habits of many years are hard to break.

I returned to my regular routine when my vacation was ended. During the day when I practiced medicine, I dressed as a man. The rest of the time I was Renée. Gradually I informed my closest friends, sometimes one at a time and sometimes in small groups. I rather enjoyed these moments of revelation; they were invariably met with a slight, even courteous, double take. They'd look me up and down, notice nothing particularly different, and then accept whatever I wanted to tell them about the process. With virtually no exceptions, everyone was extremely tactful. Nobody asked me probing questions, although I knew that they were curious. To satisfy this natural inquisitiveness, I made a short audiotape explaining my rationale, a few details of the operation, and my hopes for the future. Sometimes I'd invite people over and simply play the tape rather than having to explain yet again. I could even leave the room if I wanted to. Afterward, I'd switch off the tape player and ask, "Any questions?" Usually, there were not. I think this tape amused most people and took the pressure off them. It's a lot easier to stare out the window to hide your uneasiness when a tape recording is holding forth than it is to do so when a real transsexual is speaking.

These sessions took place in my new apartment on the western side of Central Park at Ninetieth Street. I had incurred a lot of expenses during the operation, and maintaining Andy and Meriam in one luxury apartment and myself in another was too taxing. At the same time, I wanted a fresh start for Renée. The new neighborhood was not nearly so ritzy as where I had lived before; in fact, ritzy didn't enter in at all. There was an ethnic mix that was strange to me yet seemed appropriate for my new persona. While walking Rocco in the evenings, I'd often hear Spanish, Italian, Yiddish, and other languages, as well as various English dialects. It was an exciting composite, and I felt I could melt unnoticed into it, although even in this not-so-fashionable neighborhood I occasionally ran into one of my patients.

My social life picked up quite a bit. As Dick, I had been reclusive and hard to reach. As Renée, I started to frequent parties for the first time in years. Once I had told all my good friends, they began to invite me to parties where I would invariably contact my more casual acquaintances. In this way, a ripple of cognition began to spread out through my social stratum. Joel, for example, might be throwing a party and be asked, "Who is that tall woman? I've never seen her before." Joel would say, "Oh, don't you know? That's Renée Richards. She used to be Dick Raskind." A look of recognition would come over the inquirer's face. "My God, you're right," he might whisper. "I heard about that. I met Dick several times. Do you think she'll recognize me if I go say hello?" Joel would try to be supportive: "I expect she will. After all, the surgeon didn't remove her brain."

The new initiate would eventually work himself around to me and usually spend about a minute or two hemming and hawing

290

and staring at his shoes. I remember in particular an acquaintance who was a former tennis player turned stockbroker. When I was Dick, he was constantly pushing investments at me and explaining the beauties of the stock market. He stood in front of me as Renée, shifting from one foot to another in an agony of indecision. Finally, he looked up and said aggressively, "Renée... I have a tax shelter that you can't afford not to get into!" Generally, that was the pattern: a short period of embarrassment followed by a reversion to previous form. This reversion really wasn't total because my male friends almost immediately began to treat me as if I were a woman. I don't mean they got romantic, but they did start opening doors for me and stuff like that. My idea of how a lady is treated was formed prior to women's liberation, and these little amenities were precious to me because, however superficially, they affirmed my new role in the world. Among the most startling changes in this regard was Josh's.

At no stage of my life prior to the operation had Josh given up his abusive and obstructive attitude toward my sexual confusion. He had continued to feel that he could shame me out of it. The night I went over to tell him about the operation was no exception. The minute he opened the door and saw me in women's clothes, he started his heckling.

"Nice costume," he said. This is as close as he ever came to complimenting me on a woman's outfit.

"Thanks," I replied, as usual ignoring the barb. "I came by to tell you something important."

"Oh? Well, don't be shy. Just prop those size twelves up on the coffee table there and fire away."

"Well, you know that I've supposedly been on vacation at the beach for the last month."

"Supposedly? Don't tell me that you've run off and married the milkman."

"Josh, could you cut the sarcasm. I'm trying to be serious."

"Okay, okay, but let me move to another chair. I can see right up your skirt to no-man's-land, and it's driving me wild with desire."

"What I want to tell you," I went on between clenched teeth, "is that while I was at the beach, I was recovering from an operation."

"More breast reduction surgery?" He craned his neck. "No, I can see that wasn't it."

"I had the sex change operation," I said, taking great satisfaction from the stunned expression on his face. "Just call me Renée." He was quiet for a few seconds and when he spoke, it was in a new tone of voice.

"How'd it turn out?"

"Fine. I'm very happy, and I have no regrets even though it hurt like hell. You wouldn't believe how much it hurt."

"Oh yes I would," he answered, reflexively cupping his testicles with one hand. "Well, I'll admit that I never thought you'd do it, not after Casablanca. Are you sure they can't sew it back on? I know how changeable you are."

"Nope. With this operation, you can't go home again. Anyway, I feel like I am home. I know you've been against it, but I'm asking you to take it easy on me. There's nothing that can be done other than to accept the situation. I'm a woman now."

"Don't worry. You know me, I've always liked women better than men. Listen, as long as you're here, would you mind fixing us some coffee?"

In spite of this unpromising beginning, Josh was one of the first to treat me like a girl. With Dick he had always been comradely in an undemonstrative way. Renée was always greeted with a big bear hug. His compliments on my clothes became genuine, and he never let me open a door if he could possibly sprint ahead and do the job himself. Part of this was an exaggerated courtliness done in the spirit of fun, but the impulse sprang from a genuine change of attitude: not that he lost his sense of humor. One of his favorite pastimes still was to fix me up with dates, only now the gender had changed. Once he arranged an evening between me and a man named Al Rosenshien. He was a pleasant guy who made his living in the medical equipment business. We went to dinner and afterward spent some time playing backgammon.

The next day Josh asked him how he'd liked me. Al said, "Fine." and added that I was attractive, if a bit tall. Josh laughed. Al looked at him curiously and volunteered further that I was "pretty smart for a woman." Josh laughed longer and then inquired how I was in bed. Al looked at him reproachfully and said, "Hey, don't be crude! She's a nice girl and probably likes to make sure a man isn't just interested in her body." Josh dissolved into hysteria; Al could only look on in wonderment. I don't think Josh ever told him, but I remember Al fondly as one of my first dates after the operation: and a real gentleman at that.

During this socializing, I was busy doing an enormous job, that of having all my identification changed from Richard Raskind to Renée Richards. The first step was a legal name change; this was granted once a signed letter from Dr. Granato was presented to the proper state agency. It attested to my sex change and was the only document necessary to get the process rolling. The court granted me the name change, and after that the major problem was simply making the contacts and providing the legal documentation. In all, I had at least twenty-five separate changes to make, ranging in importance from my medical degrees to my gasoline credit cards. Passport, voter registration, driver's license, United States Tennis Association membership—the list kept getting longer and longer, and I began to realize how much paper people are involved with in this society. Some things, like magazine subscriptions, I didn't even bother to change; I just canceled them and ordered new subscriptions. This tedious process was critical to my next move. As pleasant as my new life was when compared to my old, it was still schizophrenic; I was dressing as a man during the day and as a woman at night. Plainly, this could not go on forever. It was a mirror image of the same game I had been playing all my life. I knew that I would have to make a radical relocation, considerably farther away from my former haunts than my cozy apartment on the West Side. I had already engaged a medical search organization that helped physicians find jobs in the areas where they wanted to relocate. I had given them a pretty free rein saying that I was a woman ophthalmologist who wanted to go where I was needed and appreciated. One of the places they came up with was two hours north of Duluth, Minnesota. In spite of the forbidding climate, I was giving it consideration. At any rate, no such move could be successful until all my credentials were in order; over the months following the operation I worked steadily at altering them.

Throughout this period I continued to see Andy every day—as I had ever since the divorce. Our relationship was unchanged, as I had expected. I continued to dress as a man or, at least, in indeterminate attire like tennis warm-up outfits. One time, after bringing him home from a weekend with me, I told Meriam about the operation. She was not favorably impressed and immediately called my father to spill the beans. As usual, this made no visible impression on him. He never brought it up, and we never discussed it, though I continued to see him at least once a week in our old Forest Hills home. Naturally, I extended him the courtesy of dressing as a man during these visits, but each time I climbed into men's clothes, for whatever reason, it reinforced my resolve to get out of town to a place where such distasteful charades would not be necessary.

About three months after my operation I attended a medical conference in Dallas, Texas. Even though I'd have to dress as a male, I looked forward to this trip because I knew that I'd be meeting an important friend there. He was an ear, nose, and throat man whose interest in me was not professional. We'd had a little ongoing affair since before my operation. It had been difficult because he was not only married and a father, but a homosexual as well. His advances to me before the operation had been as a gay man, but I had seen him as a masculine counterpoint to my femininity. Frankly, I think he enjoyed me in spite of my female qualities rather than because of them. He had said several times, "Renée, you don't have to get this operation on my account." I had assured him that his account had nothing to do with my reasons for getting it.

I always insisted that he relate to me as if I were a woman. When we made love it was in the missionary position even though that is not the most effective arrangement for two men. I had not had a homosexual encounter since that time long before when Jimmy, the manager of the Satin Slipper, had taken me to bed. I had made the same proviso then with regard to our lovemaking position. The one big change was that this time I was able to enjoy the experience. Being entered anally was still no real fun, though I got so that I could grin and bear it. No, the enjoyable part was having a sizeable man on top of me. I liked the weight of him and the feeling of his strength when he thrust against me. Most of all, I loved his open expression of pleasure. I got a real sense of satisfaction out of being the object of his desire and knowing that my qualities were the source of his stimulation. I didn't care that it was partly my masculinity that turned him on. All I cared was that he enjoyed me, whatever the terms.

I looked forward to the time when we could make love in a way that was even more fulfilling—when I would be a woman. So, in Dallas, we climbed the stairs to my hotel room, where I made that dream come true. It was a peculiar moment; this dear friend was gay, and I had fixed it so that he had to go straight. I know his emotions were mixed. He did really like me, and it wasn't as if he couldn't make it with a woman. On the other hand, I had heretofore been a refreshing change of pace. Now I was more like what he was getting at home. Outwardly, he remained unchanged; in fact, he was very kind. If he felt ambivalent he kept it to himself out of deference to me since, in a way, he was deflowering Renée.

If I'm a little vague on his attitude, it's because this moment was something that I had looked forward to with a mixture of anticipation and dread. I knew from my experiments in self-stimulation that I could respond sexually, but putting the new equipment to work under field conditions was another matter. Suppose I found out that it didn't respond or, worse yet, that I didn't like it as much as I thought I would? Suppose I was a flop as a lover?

I was positively demure as I unveiled my new body; I even asked for the lights to be out. Daryl came over to me and helped me take off my clothes. He was taller than I and heavier too. I felt comfortable in his arms, and as he kissed me I could feel the raspy texture of his five o'clock shadow. These masculine features were strangely comforting, and I relaxed as he guided me to the bed. He was in good shape himself, an athlete, too, of course. I could feel the various muscles of his back when he covered me with his body. There wasn't too much in the way of preliminaries that first time; both of us were nervous. He came into me, and it felt right. There was no pain, no discomfort of any kind. I had a sensation of fullness, and when he began to move in and out I knew it was going to be fine. There was no weakness or sense of artificiality about my genitals—they were sound. The firm fleshiness of Daryl's penis was in wonderful contrast to the inhuman qualities of the dilator and, though the motions were similar, the sexual response lacking in my therapy came flooding through my body when that warm extension of Daryl entered me. Tremendously exciting also were his encompassing size, the smell of him, his hairiness, and his weight pressing down on me. I had experienced all these before but never in combination with a woman's sexual response. That first time he finished quickly, and I loved that as well. I was warmed by his sense of urgency and the forceful thrusts that accompanied his climax. I didn't have an orgasm myself; in fact, I didn't come near one that time or any other time for several months. Nonetheless, I loved it. I was at last fully capable of the woman's role. I could have been content for the rest of my life with that satisfaction alone.

Daryl and I saw each other several times during my remaining months in New York. He said that the change made no difference to him, but I thought I noticed a subtle shift in his attitude. Our contacts tapered off, and once I moved away from New York we were never intimate again.

In the meantime, my resettlement plans took a great leap forward. I contacted a business associate who had settled in Irvine, California. A couple of years before Donald Waxman had set straight the business end of my medical practice. I've always been a poor bookkeeper, and my financial records had been in a shambles. Donald had introduced order and rationality into my business affairs. He had performed this service for other doctors as well, including Dr. Irving Leopold, a famous ophthalmologist whom I'd known briefly when he was a professor at Mount Sinai Hospital in New York. When Dr. Leopold had accepted the directorship of the eye department at the University of California Medical Center at Irvine, he took Donald with him to help handle the department's administrative affairs.

I saw Donald on one of his trips to New York and explained my situation; he agreed to ask Dr. Leopold if I had a chance at a job on his staff. To my delight, Dr. Leopold hardly batted an eye over my transsexualism. He was more concerned about the reaction of the local medical community if he brought in a mysterious stranger with no apparent background and placed her on a top-flight medical staff. He suggested that I practice privately for a year, build a local reputation and so ease the transition. He was kind enough to say that he'd be pleased to have me on his staff if the arrangements could be made without revealing myself or otherwise stirring up a hornet's nest. Given this encouragement I immediately set Donald to researching the local opportunities.

Had it not been for Dr. Leopold's presence, Irvine would have been the last place I'd have chosen to relocate. It is in Orange County, California, widely regarded as the most conservative county in the United States. Orange County is home base for the John Birch Society. However, with a powerful friend like Dr. Leopold, I thought I could make the transition, and besides it was a lot warmer than Duluth. In addition, there was some value in moving to such a conservative place. After all, who would ever expect it? I wasn't likely to run into many of my sophisticated New York acquaintances there, either. Furthermore, it was only an hour's drive from Los Angeles, so I would be within easy striking distance of a big city. Having lived in New York most of my life, I thought that I might miss the advantages of a metropolitan atmosphere. On balance, Orange County seemed a workable location. I had pretty much decided that "workable" was about all I could hope for. There didn't seem to be any ideal places.

By the time I was to fly out for my first interview at the Placentia Linda Hospital in Placentia, California, near Irvine, my credentials were in the name of Renée Richards. To my great satisfaction, most of my old colleagues had been willing to write letters of recommendation for Renée. There were a few holdouts who were unwilling to say that they had known such a person for years, but most considered this a subtle point, and it gave them no serious qualms. When I arrived at the Orange County Airport, I was well-documented but wracked by anxiety nonetheless. Considering all that I had been through, this interview was nothing. Still, as I drove inland toward Placentia I became more and more agitated. This was the first professional appearance of Dr. Renée Richards, and I was terrified that I would be exposed immediately. I was penetrating further and further into the heart of conservativism and that meant hard-nosed interviewers who might ask embarrassing questions. I had spent the night before the interview tossing and turning in a little motel in Newport Beach. Placentia Linda! God, just the name was enough to send cold shivers up my spine. I got up in the morning and did my makeup at least three times, scrubbing it off after each application and trying again even more meticulously. Finally, I had to settle for an imperfect face: my time was running out. I wore an extremely respectable tweed suit that had cost three hundred dollars at Bergdorf Goodman's.

When I walked into the hospital director's office, I felt about ten-feet tall rather than six-foot one. I imagined that everyone was looking at me. The chief was a man in a dark business suit, the epitome of a solid medical doctor. He suggested that we have coffee and talk. My hands shook so violently that the cup and saucer clattered whenever I picked them up. We sat in the staff lounge, and to my relief his questions weren't tough at all. Perhaps he sensed my anxiety and felt sorry for me. I presented myself as a divorcée who was seeking to start a new life. I even wondered if this talk of divorce might be too racy, but he nodded in an understanding way. After the coffee he showed me the hospital, taking every opportunity to introduce me to the doctors on the staff. They were all pretty straight but very nice to me, so by the end of the interview I was more stable. Before I left, I was given assurances that my application would be acted upon favorably. Renée's first outing had been a success in spite of my opening-performance jitters.

On my way out I was still feeling shaky; so I sat down in the lobby to regain my composure. As I gathered my faculties for the trip back to Newport Beach, I thumbed through a brochure that described the hospital and its staff. I ran my eye idly down the list of directors and suddenly gulped involuntarily. There was the name "Dr. Sol Goldman," a man whom I'd become friendly with on my tennis trip to Europe with Andy two years before. I didn't realize it at the time, but this was a prelude to many more such incidents. I was to dodge people from my past on numerous occasions—even in the wilds of Orange County. Until I tried to leave most of them behind I had no real idea how many friends I'd made over the years. Sol, however, could not be dodged; he was a director at the hospital where I might go to work. I decided to face him as quickly as possible and immediately had him paged. When he walked into the lobby, he glanced about, including me in his scan and then moved on looking for someone familiar. Then he shifted his eyes back to me; a quizzical shadow crossed his face followed by a stunned look of recognition. I had seen this sequence dozens of times before in New York. I rose, smiling, and he walked toward me as if slightly tipsy. "Dick?" he asked. "I'm Renée now," I replied. He let out a low whistle which sort of summed it up.

Sol was understanding, and he became a close friend and faithful supporter during my time in California. He promised that he wouldn't blow the whistle on me at Placentia Linda Hospital—though I never went to work there. Donald had arranged for an even more important interview; it was with the dean of Orange County ophthalmologists, Dr. Joseph Tirico. He had come to that part of the state when it was populated largely by citrus groves and had practiced there for forty years. Actually, when Dr. Leopold became chief of the eye program at the university it was Dr. Tirico who stepped down. He was then in his sixties and had decided to devote all his time to his private practice, which was the largest in the county. An admitted workaholic, he had built this huge practice and maintained it by keeping a brutal schedule. Then he decided that he'd like to spend more time playing golf; that's where I came in. He was looking for an associate with whom to split the work. Donald knew that my reputation would be made if I became the partner of the revered Dr. Tirico. In person, Dr. Tirico communicated the same sense of the Old World as Marlon Brando did in *The Godfather*. He had that same aura of power as well: vigorous, macho, gruff. I expected to run into problems with him on the basis of my femaleness; he didn't exactly strike me as a liberationist. I quickly discovered, however, that beneath the intimidating exterior he was very gentle, though I didn't think he was gentle enough to hire a transsexual. I kept that information to myself. He looked over my credentials and letters of recommendation and then offered me the job. It was that quick. We liked each other immediately, and as soon as he made the proposal, I accepted.

Back in New York, I closed out my old life as quickly as possible. My friends were sad but knew that I'd be back often to see Andy. My practice would be taken over by a young associate. I made arrangements to return periodically over the next year to finish up some previously scheduled operations. I could do the necessary surgery when I made my visits to Andy. And so, about nine months after the surgery that brought her into existence, Renée Richards headed west to start a new life.

19

Just a Quiet Life

I left New York on a cold, drizzly February day and arrived six hours later in sun-kissed southern California. Donald Waxman handed me the keys to a brand-new white Corvette bearing the license plate RRMD. We drove to a beautiful apartment complex in Newport Beach. For the same four hundred dollars per month that I had been paying for my little place in the west nineties, I moved into an apartment with a view of the Pacific ocean. Farrah Fawcett and Lee Majors maintained an apartment in my complex. They apparently used it for weekend vacations. There was a clubhouse, a weight room, a sauna, a pool—all the accouterments of the California life-style. Across the way was the John Wayne Tennis Club. I looked longingly over at it but decided against joining. Before I left New York I had been examined by a gynecologist friend of mine. He had said, "Renée, if I called one of my residents in to examine you he'd probably certify you as a normal woman. But, if you want to remain anonymous, stay away from tennis. There isn't a player in the country who wouldn't recognize that crazy windup on your forehand side." With this advice, he gave me a clean bill of health. He was overstating the case, but it was a point well made. In tennis circles I was extremely well-known, and I had to be willing to give up the game in order to live my new life.

I adapted easily to the relaxed pace of California. The highest-priority item was to establish myself as a competent doctor. At first, Dr. Tirico's patients were a little skeptical; I was also greeted with some suspicion at St. Joseph's Hospital where I performed surgery. The staff had no reason to expect that I was highly skilled, and for a while even the senior nurses were higher than me in the pecking order. I acted like a lamb through all of this; as Renée, I lacked the drive for respect and acknowledgment that had possessed me as Dick. Gradually my expertise came to be recognized. I remember one instance when an anesthesiologist was visibly disturbed about being assigned to the new kid on the block. He apparently thought that I'd be fumbling around with the scheduled surgery, a cataract operation, long past the time when a more experienced surgeon would be on the golf course. He grumpily put the patient under anesthesia. After about ten minutes, the operating nurse turned to him and said, "We'll be finished up in a few minutes. You can begin to lighten her up on the anesthesia." He looked up suspiciously and said, "When did she take the cataract out? I didn't see her do it!" Actually, I had used a technique that was not current. The favored approach nowadays is to freeze the lens with a cryogenic probe and then lift it out. There is less chance of tearing the lens capsule, but it requires bulky equipment. I had used a time-honored technique employing a pair of capsule forceps. This grasping device is shaped to fit nicely over the lens capsule, thus allowing the surgeon to ease the lens out. It is simpler and more direct than freezing, but if the forceps is badly used it can be destructive. Naturally, I never mishandled it and had no qualms about bypassing all the hassle that attended the freezing method. The gas man did not hide his amazement. Later he approached me as I was writing postoperative orders for the patient. "Dr. Richards," he said companionably, "I'll give the gas for you any day." I knew that word would get around and that I would soon be an accepted part of the team; that was all I wanted. Dick had been a star—Renée only wanted to play first-string.

Things at Dr. Tirico's offices were coming around pretty fast, too. Since the reason I was there was to take the load off him, Dr. Tirico and I were only occasionally in the office at the same time. As impressive and lovable a man as he was, he still had an air that intimidated some patients; they went to him because he was the best. As his associate, some of Dr. Tirico's glory shone on me, and I soon began to attract the patients who liked to deal with a less-overpowering personality. They figured that I must be good if Dr.

Tirico had chosen me, and at the same time I was a little less gruff. All in all, I think Dr. Tirico was pleased at what he and I offered as a team. We complemented one another well, and there was talk about a possible partnership sometime in the future.

On the home front my life was also shaping up. My apartment remained largely unfurnished (I took a drastic cut in income when I came to California) but had nonetheless become a cozy place to entertain friends. We sat on the floor or around the table in the kitchen. The most frequent visitors at first were those who knew my real story. Donald Waxman and his secretary, Olivia Henderson, who had done a lot of the legwork in getting me settled, were frequent guests. Sol Goldman also stopped by a lot; occasionally, Jeff and Bev Gaines, two friends who had known me as Dick in New York and were now living in San Diego, came up for visits. I was also meeting new people who knew me only as Renée Richards. Most of them came from the John Wayne Tennis Club.

My resolve to stay away from tennis had flagged rather quickly. For one thing, Sol was a member, and he asked me over to play as his guest. At first I played only with him and only on the far courts, well away from prying eyes, but, as my professional life started to come into shape, I began to tire of this cat-and-mouse game. I was a respected woman doctor; why shouldn't I be able to belong to a nice tennis club and have friends like anyone else? Soon I had my own membership and was playing with a few select acquaintances. This came about with no effort on my part. Anyone who watched me play could see I was good, and at a tennis club that means people want to play with you. The only way to improve is to play someone better than you.

One of my first new friends was Mike Carver, a South African. He was a short man, a little heavyset but a good tennis player and a regular member of the club. We not only played tennis together but did other things as well. Often we'd go out to dinner and then play backgammon late into the night. Almost everything was a joke to him; I found this emphasis on the lighthearted side of things to be contagious, and I enjoyed his wry approach. He lacked the intensity of my professional friends from back East, and this made it easier for me to relax when I was with him. We toyed with the possibilities of a romantic involvement and even had a little physical fun, but we soon discovered that our relationship was more that of brother and sister. Mike noticed that I was trying to keep a low profile at the club and became quite protective of me, though he never really understood why I was reclusive. It became common knowledge that if you wanted to play tennis with Renée you had to clear it with Mike. This was slightly unusual, but, as you might expect, the emphasis at the John Wayne Tennis Club is on individual rights. They were willing to abide by my rules if they wanted to play with me.

During my first few weeks in Newport Beach the tennis club became the center of my social world. I was there most evenings and quite frequently on weekends. This was a tribute to how quickly I had adjusted to being Renée. I felt so comfortable with her personality that I began to lose touch with the realities of my situation. My gynecologist's warning that I should stay away from tennis ought to have been singing in my ears—but it wasn't. Even a less-fashionable club would have been a big step in the right direction. The John Wayne Tennis Club was one of the stops on the international tennis circuit. Incidentally, I never saw John Wayne though I did meet his wife, Pilar, for whom he had built the club. His personality was simply represented by a special place called The Duke's Room. Inside were mementoes of his career. Visitors spent a lot of time looking at still pictures from his movies and at awards and trophies of every description. Everything at the Duke's tennis club was first class, and it catered to a pretty exalted clientele. This was one of its big attractions for me. The people there were the kind I understood and got along with; besides, it was right across the street from my apartment. These were the reasons I gave myself for joining, even though I would occasionally have to dart into a storeroom or some other convenient hiding place when a person from my past would show up to play a few sets while he was in the Los Angeles area.

Strangely though, the first threat to my anonymity came not from the world of tennis but in connection with my medical practice. One afternoon as I was in the changing room at St. Joseph's Hospital, Dr. Tirico stepped to the door and yelled in to me. "Renée, go to the administrator's office immediately. There is some problem with your credentials." Needless to say, my heart shot up my throat. I had been on the job only two weeks, and there was already a crisis. A secretary in the administrator's office told me that the medical license number I had given them was registered under the name Dr. Richard Raskind. Evidentally, there had been some foul-up in the changes I had requested. I told her that some mistake must have been made and promised to look into it. Under the circumstances this was as truthful as I could be. I was paralyzed with fear. Once suspicions are raised in California there is usually a thorough investigation. Because the state attracts so many kooks representing themselves as medical practitioners, it has instituted an extremely stringent procedure for determining if a person's credentials are adequate. Moreover, I knew that Dr. Tirico had been briefed by the administrator's office on my license problems.

I soon discovered that the licensing bureau had received my request but, instead of changing the name on the license, had simply added the name Renée Richards; thus the license bore two names.

Dr. Tririco apparently mulled this over for a while and then went to Donald Waxman's secretary, Olivia Henderson, whom he knew to be my friend and a part of the team that had relocated me. Olivia stalled him long enough to call me for instructions; I told her to answer him honestly. His first question gives a clue to Dr. Tirico's innocent instincts: "Olivia, is this a case of a father who always wanted a son and gave his daughter a man's name?" Olivia shook her head. His second question showed that his innocent instincts did not overshadow his good sense: "Or, is this the reflection of a sex change?" Olivia gulped and said, "Your suspicions are correct. Dr. Richards had planned to tell you eventually but wanted a few months to prove herself. She's very embarrassed at not having been truthful. It's just that she wanted you to get to know her as an individual before she brought up this thing from the past."

Olivia braced herself for a stream of vituperation from this Old World medical godfather. He was thoughtful for a moment and then in an ominously quiet voice said, "I wish I had known about Dr. Richards. I could have protected her more effectively. Our job from now on is to shield her as best we can." Olivia couldn't have been more shocked if a grizzly bear had made this statement, but Dr. Tirico went further. "You have my assurance that I will never discuss this conversation with anyone, nor will I ever bring it up to Renée. Tell her, however, that I will be glad to talk to her about it at any time if she so wishes." And with that he left. From a man who was educated at a time when transsexuals were authoritatively consigned by Krafft-Ebing to the lunatic category, this response was a sign of deep humanity.

Dr. Tirico's reaction removed one threat but left a greater one looming ahead. Within the week I was to go before the hospital's credential committee and face their cross-examination. In light of the confusion with the license, they would undoubtedly be on guard. I faced a real inquisition and doubted that my past could be suppressed. Of course, I had immediately moved to have the records amended, and I checked back as far as my college diplomas to make sure all was in order. Nevertheless, these changes take time, and it was doubtful that I would have the documents in time to present them for scrutiny at the hearing. Sure enough, on the morning of the hearing I was without a full set of credentials. Dr. Tirico had insisted that I go through with the meeting in spite of this, and at 7:30 A.M. (California medical meetings are always early) he found me sipping coffee nervously in the hospital cafeteria. The rattling of the cup and saucer was reminiscent of the Placentia Linda interview a few weeks before. He calmed me as we walked toward the board room and gave my hand a friendly squeeze; as I left him standing in the hall he smiled confidently at me. Inside, I didn't like what I saw. The chairs were arranged in a circle and were occupied by twenty committee members, all in dark suits. One chair in the circle was vacant. The chairman motioned me to it, and I sat down feeling like a heretic under the questioning of the Spanish Inquisition. In my state of mind, all these figures ranged around me looked sinister or, at best, snide. What I expected was something like the following:

"Dr. *Richards*, heh, heh, heh, you must have a mighty low opinion of the intelligence of the California medical community."

"Why no, I . . ."

"Speak when you're spoken to, Dr. *Richards!* Now, I don't know what hanky-panky you're up to. Maybe you want to sew goat glands into people, or maybe you've killed some reputable doctor and taken his place. I don't know what you've got in your twisted mind, but, believe me Dr. Richards (or should I say . . . Dr. *Raskind!*), this committee is not breaking up until we have extracted the truth!"

Actually, the chairman rather mildly said that Dr. Tirico had briefed them on my credentials and explained that the diploma had been forgotten that morning but that he, Dr. Tirico, had seen it. With that, he began the questioning.

"Dr. Richards," he asked, "how have you enjoyed practicing in California so far?"

"I've enjoyed it very much." A man across the circle caught my attention.

"I've heard that you're an excellent tennis player, Dr. Richards. Do you find that you can play more what with the California weather?"

"Yes. I've enjoyed it very much."

"Well," said the chairman, "if there are no more questions for Dr. Richards, that will be the end of the interview." Then he turned to me and after a pause that seemed like an eternity, said, "Welcome to Orange County." That marked the end of my credential troubles in California. It dawned on me that Dr. Tirico must have informed the committee that they were to take it easy with his new associate. All I had had to say was, "I've enjoyed it very much." True to his word, Dr. Tirico never talked to me directly about my past. Our relationship continued in the same way it had before the incident: amiable, productive, and stimulating.

In my private life I was getting stimulation of another kind. The pool area at my apartment complex was adjacent to a clubhouse with a weight room. The weight room could be inspected from pool side through a huge glass window. On my way to and from sunbathing I often saw a shaggy young fellow using the Universal body-building equipment. He was about my height but perhaps sixty pounds heavier because of his extensive muscular development. What I noticed most was his relaxed attitude toward his training. He exerted a lot of effort when he was actually pushing against the weight, but at all other times he seemed at ease. One day I paused by the weight room to watch him do a set of exercises. Upon finishing he unexpectedly whirled around and caught me staring. He grinned a crooked grin, and I hurried away, slightly embarrassed. Later, as I lay baking on a chaise lounge, the chair next to me creaked under a sizable weight. I looked over and was mildly surprised to see the young muscleman settling in next to me. I was flattered but not awfully surprised since I looked pretty sleek in a black one-piece suit. I was darkly tanned, and my hair had been bleached by the sun. Just that morning I had been congratulating myself. After my operation a friend had said to me, "Anyone who voluntarily wants to become a forty-year-old woman, I take my hat off to." Still, I didn't look forty. My excellent skin and active life in tennis accounted for my youthful appearance. I looked like a woman in her early thirties who was in excellent shape.

"How you doin'?" said the muscleman.

"Fine. I saw you working out. Do you live here?"

"Naw, I know somebody who lives here. I just come over to work out."

"Well, it shows," I said, looking him up and down. He was wearing a tiny bikini bathing suit.

"It ought to. I do it enough. Actually, I sell that equipment."

"That equipment in the weight room?"

"Yeah."

"Well, I'd think you'd have a setup of your own."

"Oh, I do. I just come over here to meet girls." He looked at me and smiled that crooked smile again. He reminded me of the Italian man I had met on the train to Modena. Physically they were dissimilar, but they both seemed like nice guys. There was something utterly masculine yet completely unstrained about them. I was beginning to believe that I was attracted to men who were the opposite of Dick Raskind. He had been compulsive in his masculinity. His drive for success and his macho mannerisms covered a serious gap in his manliness. The men I liked didn't have to press; their masculine auras came about because they actually were thoroughly masculine. It was as simple as that. Billy, my new acquaintance in the bikini, had this uncomplicated air in the extreme. Another thing I liked about him was that he made no pretenses to intellectualism. He wasn't unintelligent; he just didn't find cerebral pursuits as satisfying as the simpler pleasures. This suited me. I was ready for fun.

Billy and I became frequent companions and spent most of our time at my apartment in bed. Occasionally, we went out to eat or to a movie, but neither of us felt called upon to do so. We were happy with our uncomplicated evenings of pleasure; when we talked it was about travel or sports. He'd been all over the world selling muscle-building equipment, and he did a lot of consulting for sports programs. His idea of a nice evening was to have a few beers and watch television while I puttered around the apartment or worked on my cases. I'd often look up at him watching TV with a beer in his right hand and a pile of potato chips in his left, and I'd anticipate in a very domestic way the moment when he'd take me in his arms. It was almost like being married. This feeling of closeness was reinforced by the fact that he was the first man to give me an orgasm.

The secret of Billy's success was not very complicated. First, he was strong, far stronger than I. This made me feel protected and secure. Those cozy feelings were the ones I'd been longing for while living a life that forced me to provide them for others. Now somebody was doing it for me, and the sensation was great. I felt relaxed. Second, Billy liked a lot of foreplay. The other men I'd been with seemed to skim over the preliminaries, but not Billy. He gently turned me every which way and tended to all my erogenous zones. His tongue was a marvel of inventiveness. He went about this without haste and with obvious enjoyment—another turn on. The last thing that made Billy exceptional as a lover was his staying power; he was in excellent condition and was able to keep going long enough to make me peak. I don't mean that he had to continue for hours at a time, but he could last for five or ten minutes and that was all I required. I don't think it's too much to ask, but it presents a stumbling block for a lot of men.

The moment of orgasm was familiar because of my experiences with autoeroticism, but I was not prepared for the increased intensity. Relieved of the responsibility for bringing it about, I was free to concentrate on the experience itself. When the build-up began I was seized with an undeniable urge to move. It was not the compulsion to thrust that had gripped me as a man but a drive toward more random movement. Furthermore, the fact that I felt compelled to move, yet was inhibited from doing so by Billy's weight, excited me even more. It was like that experience from my childhood when I used to struggle with my pal Barry Wiseman. At a certain point I would lose my strength and collapse. This pattern found a new expression with Billy. As the excitement built, I'd feel two impulses; one to push Billy away so that I could move more freely and one to pull him down more closely. Suddenly I had a new perspective on the seemingly irrational actions of some of the women I'd made love to. They hadn't seemed sure of what they wanted, and now I was responding to the same dilemma, not out of perversity but because I was so excited that I didn't know what to do. This divided action terminated at the moment of climax. When I peaked, the wriggling motion that I had been striving for with my torso expressed itself in a free movement of my legs which was almost spasmodic. Everything went out of my mind for those few moments.

After a respectable period of postsexual affection, Billy would roll off me and eventually go to sleep. I even liked that part of it; I could lie there and watch him doze. He really did have a sweet face. Relaxed and uncomplicated even when awake, in repose that face was childlike. In many ways with Billy I resembled a bride, fascinated by all the trappings of her relationship with the man she'd chosen. Of all the sexual episodes I've had, this one stands out as the most idyllic. I often fantasize that I'm alone with Billy in some remote corner of the world where I'm unknown and where we can be as we were during my first few months in Newport Beach.

My personal life was going very nicely. My professional life, after that initial scare over my credentials, was also shaping up, and I was more relaxed than ever about my tennis. At the club I was well respected. My peculiarities were overlooked; I had made it known, for example, that I was interested only in playing for fun and would not enter tournaments. This was accepted, along with my explanation of how I could be so good and still be unknown. I said that I had played competitively up to the junior level and then given it up to pursue my education. Thereafter, I had played in some local New York area tournaments but only as an amusement—never seriously. Here in California, I was interested only in my medical practice and in a little leisure-time exercise. This story seemed plausible to the members; but I thought I caught the club professional, Ken Stewart, and his wife, Betty Ann, also a tournament player, eyeing me with a certain longing. They knew that I could strengthen the JWTC team.

The apparent success of my adjustment threw me badly off guard. I innocently thought the situation could go on forever and I ignored even the most obvious indications to the contrary. For example, when I'd call Meriam to ask about Andy, she'd often say something like, "What do you mean wearing yellow lace panties under your tennis outfit last Sunday?" Obviously she was getting information from someone, but I never found out who. I figured that whoever it was would keep his or her mouth shut out of respect for my delicate position. Clearly this was wishful thinking.

One time I looked out into the waiting room at Dr. Tirico's office, and there was one of the children I had worked on in New York. His father was sitting next to him—sporting a sly grin. He'd inquired after my whereabouts around New York, refusing to take his boy to anyone but me. Finally, he had found someone who spilled the beans, and he had flown out to have his boy treated. It was a flattering gesture, but it didn't reflect too highly on my security precautions or on the reliability of my old friends. In spite of these things my optimism was undeterred. I had an unshakable faith that somehow I'd be okay.

One day I was playing a hot game at the club. Unbeknownst to me, Bobby Riggs was in the stands. Bobby knows everyone in tennis and had been well-acquainted with Dick. He didn't recognize me personally, but he recognized something about me as a player. At first, he paid little attention to me since he had no reason to expect anything out of the ordinary. I was told later that he talked animatedly with his friends for a while and then noticed me hit a screamer down the line. His interest perked up. I hit a few more winners, and he poked the man sitting next to him and asked, "Who's that woman over there?" He was informed that she was Dr. Richards, recently arrived from New York. Bobby watched for a while longer and then observed, "She looks like a tournament player to me." This notion was pooh-poohed. She was a physician who only played on weekends. The longer he watched, the more doubtful he became. Frequently, he'd say, "She must be a tournament player." Each time he'd be assured otherwise. Finally, he saw me rush to the net and drive a forehand volley at the body of my opponent. Bobby leaped up. "You see that?" he yelled. "That's the killer instinct! Nobody but a tournament player has that!" When the match was over, he came running down to see who this mystery woman was; I looked up and saw him coming, recognizing immediately his distinctive, waddling run. Our eyes met, and at a distance of twenty feet he stopped short, grinning broadly. "Well, Dick Raskind," he said, after glancing around to make sure no one was within earshot. "How the hell are you? You look terrific!"

Of course, Bobby had heard the rumors and knew that I'd

moved west under unusual circumstances, but everything fell into place for him on that afternoon. We had a drink together, and naturally Bobby's first consideration was how he could make some money from this situation. He was entranced by the idea that a whole new person had been created. That this unknown was a dangerous tennis player gave him all sorts of ideas, most of which I turned down. On one occasion, however, he convinced me to go with him to a country club near San Diego. His hustle was as follows: he'd offer to play a couple of the better players in a doubles match with me as his partner; he would appeal to their masculine pride by intimating that he could beat them even teamed with an unknown woman. He offered to bet a thousand a corner, four thousand dollars. Naturally, they were suspicious. After all, this *was* Bobby Riggs. They wanted to see me warm up. "No problem!" Bobby shouted, quickly instructing me under his breath, "Take it easy on the warm-up sweetie." I did the best I could though I've never been too good at holding back. The suckers were still dubious, but under the sting of Bobby's taunts they finally agreed. Riggs went away four thousand dollars richer, and I had the time of my life.

All of this fun with Bobby Riggs served to further lull me into a false sense of security, and when my defenses were lowest Ken Stewart, the club pro, made me an offer I should have refused. He said in a phone conversation that he knew my stand on competitive tennis but that I was in a position to do the club a big favor. Once a year the JWTC team played an unofficial match with the tennis team of the University of California-Irvine. It was strictly local and stood for nothing except team pride. The number three woman on the club team had taken ill, and, if I wouldn't agree to stand in for her, our number four woman would have to play U.C.'s number three, our number five, their number four and so on—resulting in a series of mismatches that would almost certainly cost us the victory. In this way the honor of the John Wayne Tennis Club was placed on my shoulders. Under the circumstances it was a light load, but enough to make me think twice. Everyone had been nice to me. It was only a local team match. It was unsanctioned and would very likely go completely unnoticed. I weighed all these factors and agreed.

When I arrived the next day for the match, I was surprised to see that there were about six hundred spectators. Among them were some of my patients, who cheered loudly for me. I played well, enjoying the competition and the applause. Best of all, there were absolutely no repercussions, not a ripple.

At the time, I thought it was wonderful, but in retrospect I can see that what I really needed was an incident to scare me out of my unrealistic fog. On the other hand, if the credentials hearing or the Riggs incident hadn't done it, then probably nothing short of an absolute fiasco would have fazed me. As it was, this taste of tournament play reminded me of how much I missed organized competition. Private play is fun, but it isn't as spicy as a tournament when everyone is pumped up and you work your way through an orderly series of games to determine who is the best of a large group. I felt so comfortable as Renée that I thought once again; why shouldn't I have everything I want?

I was like Eve in the Garden of Eden but with a tennis ball instead of an apple. The match with U. C. at Irvine was my first nibble and, almost before I knew it, I was taking bigger bites. In the next few weeks I played in some mixed doubles tournaments with my South African friend Mike Carver as my partner. It was exhilarating to reach the finals even though we lost. I began to step up my practice time and started accepting invitations to play with the "A" players in the club, rather than with the lower-caliber members whom I had previously favored out of my desire to remain undiscovered. I became a familiar sight on center court hitting with the hottest players that the club had to offer. This high profile was responsible for my big mistake.

Every year a big tournament is played in La Jolla, California. It is a prestigious amateur event and is the focal point for a bit of community rivalry between Newport Beach and La Jolla. For the previous two years the tournament had been won by Robin Harris, a La Jolla resident. The interested members of the JWTC began to look around for someone to restore the prestige of Newport Beach. They didn't have to look much farther than center court, where I was swatting balls on a par with most of the best male members. Moreover, it was common knowledge that I had several times broken my rule concerning tournament play. This was perceived as a chink in my resolve. The suggestions were low-key at first. "Renée, how about entering La Jolla? I know you could do well." I resisted strongly at first, but many people had rightly discerned my relish for competition as they watched me play in the local tournaments. They were not easily convinced. "Renée," one of them said half seriously, "the reputation of Newport Beach is in your hands." As the first of July tournament date drew closer, the pressure grew more intense. Of course, I wanted to play, but I knew that I was asking for trouble stepping outside the city limits. Sensing this, the lobbyists began to downplay the importance of the tournament. "It's not really that big a deal, just a regional get-together, really, strictly local in nature. Just amateur stuff."

Given my inclination to believe them, these arguments started to sound downright sensible. Why shouldn't I play in a sectional event?

I asked Donald Waxman what he thought of the idea. "Are you crazy? Absolutely not!" I accused him of overreacting. He looked at me with amazement. "Do you want to remain anonymous or what? We've been on the brink of disaster a couple of times already, and we weren't even trying. This tournament can be nothing but trouble." Unwilling to accept only Donald's opinion, I asked Mike Carver for his advice. Though we had never discussed it, I felt that he had figured out my situation. "Gee, I don't know, Renée. That seems awfully chancy to me." I called my friends in La Jolla, Jeff and Bev Gaines. They thought it would be a mistake.

Undaunted, I asked the advice of a professional player, Frank McCabe, with whom I often practiced. Sometimes, he'd look up after I'd hit a really strong serve and say, "Renée, that's a pretty good serve . . . for a woman." The sly look on his face made me believe that he knew. His answer was more to my liking. "Of course you should play! You do whatever you damn well please. Lincoln freed the slaves." Another pro at the club, Atilio Rosetti, was likewise supportive. "Sure you'll play in it, and you'll win it, too." He was a big booster of mine and another person I thought had a good idea about my background. However, neither of these last two had any inkling of my transsexuality, though I didn't know it at the time. In typical Raskind fashion, I had shied away from confronting them directly; I preferred to go on assumptions. Thus, with hindsight, it's obvious that everyone who knew about me was against my playing in La Jolla. Those who didn't know were in favor of it, and ever optimistic, I took their advice.

Once I made the decision, Donald in Newport Beach and Jeff

and Bev in La Jolla did everything in their power to make things run smoothly. I stayed at the Gaines's house, and Bev assumed the role of spokesperson when I began to draw attention by winning match after match. Mike and Donald came down to keep me company, and a busload of Newport Beach rooters were scheduled to make the hour-and-a-half drive down to La Jolla if I got to the finals. I entered the tournament under the name Renée Clark. In retrospect, this move seems more likely to have drawn attention to me than to have protected me, but innocent that I was, I thought this measure would help if suspicions arose. Of course, it didn't protect me, and suspicions did begin to arise.

The first surprise I had was that this tournament was not the small-potatoes affair that it had been made out to be. For example, there was regular television coverage on the evening news. Moreover, every tennis buff in southern California seemed to be in attendance, and as I continued to win they became more and more inquisitive about this tall unknown woman who was playing so efficiently. One of these fans ultimately proved to be my undoing; she had come from Palm Springs to see the tournament and carried some dangerous information with her. A playboy friend of hers had told her about a prominent East Coast tennis player, a doctor, who had undergone a sex-change operation and moved to California under a veil of secrecy; a tattered veil, I might add. She made the connection when she saw a six-foot one-inch woman dominating the La Jolla tournament. After a few inquiries, she had the information that I was a doctor who had been in Newport Beach for only a few months. Naturally, this juicy discovery was too good to keep quiet, and within hours the air was vibrating with rumors, innuendoes, and assorted misinformation. Bev Gaines was continually beleaguered with questions about my background; she staunchly repeated that I was a physician friend of long acquaintance and denied any knowledge of peculiarities in my makeup. Despite her protestations, the tempest continued to mount, but as usual no one said anything to me directly. I got all my information secondhand from Donald, Mike, Bev, or Jeff. Each time I'd go on the court for a match, Donald would say, "I think the tournament officials are right around the corner, Renée. Better play fast if you want to finish this set!" This was his way of trying to lighten the atmosphere, but we all realized that the situation was getting more and more unstable. By the time I reached the semifinals, the tension was incredible.

There were no catcalls or rude remarks from the stands. On the contrary, the crowds were exceptionally polite, too polite really. It was apparent that their minds were only partially on the tennis. Beyond that, they occupied themselves with an intense scrutiny of Renée Clark. As I walked onto the courts for my semifinal match, I experienced the feeling that women so often complain about—that of being undressed by men's eyes. But I felt as though *everybody* in the place was doing it to me: men, women, and children. I couldn't keep myself from tugging down the hem of my tennis skirt, but the crowd's attitude turned out to be the least of my problems. When I stepped onto the court, I looked directly into the eyes of a black woman who had been a friend of mine in New York; her name was Andrea Glazier. I watched her register the familiar shock of recognition and saw it replaced by an expression of helplessness. This woman was the umpire. She looked uncertainly around at the huge crowd in the stands and then, without a word to me, walked dazedly to the umpire's chair. Seated nearby were Bev and Jeff Gaines, also acquaintances of hers. "What should I do?" she whispered to them. "I know who that is." Bev replied, "Just call the match." She did so, and I won.

As I strode off the court, I decided that I had pushed far enough; every indication was that things were about to spin out of control. Apparently, I was on the verge of public disclosure. Rumor had it that the president of the Southern California Tennis Association, Joe Bixler, had flown down to meet with the tournament chairman and decide on a course of action. Surely then Andrea Glazier would step forward with what she knew. I was up the creek, and the only question now was how to save myself. Shortly after I got back to the Gaines's house I received a call from Newport Beach. Unaware of the rumors concerning my identity, a busload of supporters were preparing, as promised, to come down for the finals. This was the last straw; not only was I likely to be unmasked but unmasked in front of my hometown friends. I decided to withdraw. Donald, Mike, Bev, and Jeff gave their heartfelt endorsement to this decision. Everyone, especially Bev, who had borne the brunt of the questioning and who had been forced to lie for me repeatedly, breathed sighs of relief.

I placed a call to the La Jolla Recreation Center, which served

316

as the tournament headquarters. Ironically, Andrea answered. She said that the tournament director was not there and asked if she could help. "Well," I said hesitantly, "you know the story on me. It looks like everyone associated with the tournament has one version or another of my past. The tension is building, everybody's confused, and I'm ready to withdraw from the tournament." Her response was utterly unexpected. "Renée," she said intensely, "I don't want you to withdraw. I am a member of a minority myself. My father is black, my husband is black, and my mother is a Filipino. I've been in between all my life, and I think I know a little about how you feel. I've found that when people don't know what pigeonhole to put you in, your only alternative is to show them what you are and act as if you have the right to be that. You won't be doing yourself a favor if you run away from this tournament. You'll just be giving in to stupidity. Hold your head up and play." I thanked her and hung up.

This was the first time anybody had ever put the issues in a broader perspective. The question had always been, "How can Renée stay out of trouble?" The nearest I had come to matters of principle were my vague feelings that I ought to be able to play tennis if I wanted to. My life had been largely a cat-and-mouse game with society. I had sneaked around and sneaked around, and here I was, an official woman, proclaimed so by my doctors and by the government—and I was still sneaking around. The more I thought about it, the hotter I got.

The next day in front of a thousand tense spectators, I wasn't so sure of myself. I know that I imagined this, but I had the distinct impression that no one was following the ball. All eyes seemed to be following me. As I walked out on the court, I thought I heard a murmur. I checked my tennis dress again; everything seemed to be in order. Across the net I faced a very nervous opponent. As the match progressed, I managed to put the circumstances and the environment out of my mind. I had come onto the courts thinking of myself as a kind of standard-bearer, but I was soon just a tennis player again. Unfortunately, my young opponent's concentration was not up to the task, and I won the match easily, largely on the basis of her jitteriness. The aftermath of my victory was the most incredible footnote imaginable to this crazy week.

Nobody said a thing about all the rumors. I was interviewed a dozen times by both newspaper and television reporters, and they never went any further than the stock questions that I had heard all my life. "Miss Clark, when did you feel you had the match won?" The trophy was presented to me by multimillionaire William Scripps Kellogg of Scripps's newspapers and Kellogg's cereals fame. He was the most venerated tennis supporter in the community, and his participation in the presentation seemed to put the seal of legitimacy on my title.

Back in Newport Beach I felt pretty damn good. There's nothing quite like putting your principles on the line and not having to pay any price; I had done the right thing, and that knowledge warmed me. On the other hand, I was safe back in my own nest. Of one thing I was sure. There would be no more tennis tournaments; my days as a crusader were over. I was going back to being Dr. Renée Richards. In keeping with this resolve, I was back at the office the next morning at nine o'clock. The place had never seemed better. All my shiny instruments were neatly laid out. The nurse was respectful; the patients were grateful. As I worked along I had no way of knowing that a San Diego television reporter, Dick Carlson, was busy doing his work, too. Starting with the rumors about me, he eventually tracked down the woman who had started it all. She told what he found to be a plausible story, or at least one worth checking out. My pseudonym didn't give him a moment's pause; he probably called the tennis club to find out my real name and then checked my California medical license in Sacramento—the damn thing still had two names on it! Thus rewarded, he checked back through all my school records, and everywhere he checked the name Richard Raskind kept popping up. At length, he had enough data to make a direct inquiry. At eleven o'clock the phone in my office rang. When the receptionist told me who it was, I figured that it was a reporter who needed an extra quote to round out his tournament story. Instead a voice said, "Hello, Dr. Richards, this is Dick Carlson of Channel Eight in San Diego. Is it true that you have another name on your California state medical license?" I was panic-stricken, and all my principles promptly flew out the window. "I don't know what you mean," I replied. "Do you recognize the name Richard Raskind?" he continued. "No," I said. "Please don't call me again." With that I hung up. A half hour later he called again: "Is it true that your diplomas from Rochester Medical School and from Yale University were originally made out to Richard Raskind and were subsequently changed to Renée Richards?" Again I denied it. After lunch he called with the information that the United States Lawn Tennis Association had a lifetime membership under the name Renée Richards and Richard Raskind.

As frightened as I was, I couldn't restrain myself from accepting those calls. Each time I hung up the phone I promised myself that I wouldn't speak to him again, but when the time came I couldn't resist finding out what new items he had unearthed. His fourth call was a summing up: "Isn't it true Dr. Richards, that your identity was once that of Dr. Richard Raskind, a prominent ophthalmologist and an amateur tennis player from New York City?"

Obviously there was no point in further denials: I naively decided to appeal to his better instincts. Starting out with a bit of flattery, I made the following plea: "Mr. Carlson, it would be an insult to your intelligence to deny this any further. You certainly have done quite a piece of detective work. Everything you've suggested is true, but certainly you can see that this is an extremely personal matter. Please don't reveal it to the public."

"Well, Dr. Richards, I'm a reporter, and I have to do my job. This story will be on the eleven o'clock news."

"But Mr. Carlson, that will ruin my life!"

"I don't think it will ruin your life, Dr. Richards."

"What about my son? He's only a little boy. Think what this could do to him. Can't you treat this as a personal matter? I'm just a private citizen who played in an amateur tennis tournament. Why do you want to punish me for that?"

"You were a private person until you stepped onto that court in La Jolla. After that you became a public figure, and the public has a right to know about you."

"Mr. Carlson," I said evenly, "if you break this story, I will hold you responsible for the result."

He paused for a moment and then asked, "Is that a threat?"

"No. I just want you to know that you will bear the responsibility for ruining my life." This was a pathetic parting shot, and his response was curt.

"Duly recorded," he snapped and hung up.

319

I sat numbly for about twenty minutes. I can't remember exactly what I thought about. No doubt I replayed all the ugly scenes that might flow from this news broadcast. Perhaps Andy would be taunted at school; perhaps Meriam would decide that I shouldn't see him anymore. Would the courts back her up? Would I be ostracized at the club? What would Billy think? He'd been out of town on a selling trip. Would he even bother to call me when he came back? Would my patients desert me? Would my professional life be destroyed? Would I take Dr. Tirico down with me? I stumbled through the rest of my day at the office.

That evening I couldn't bring myself to watch the news; I depended on Donald and Olivia to replay the details to me. At eleven-thirty the phone rang. It was Donald. "How bad was it?" I asked.

"It was worse than we expected," he answered reluctantly. "It seemed to go on forever, at least five minutes of air time."

"Oh my god!"

"Yeah, they had before and after pictures and everything. I don't know where they came up with that stuff, but the guy really did a job on you."

"Did he make me sound like a criminal or something?"

"Worse than that." I waited for more, but Donald didn't seem to want to say it.

"What then?"

"He claimed that you were actually a man masquerading as a woman."

"He didn't say anything about the operation?"

"No. He just said you were Richard Raskind pretending to be Renée Richards. All his evidence was presented in proof of that idea. Didn't you make it clear to him?

"Was it my job to give him information? Hell, he seemed to know everything already! Damn! Do you think this is just stupid reporting or do you think he did it maliciously?"

"Who knows? You'd think the sex change would be juicy enough. Maybe he thought that it would seem more justifiable to blow the whistle if he reported that you were really a man trying to win a women's tournament."

"I can't believe it. This creep could ruin my life just by telling the truth, and he has to make it ten times worse by broadcasting this lie. Why did I ever play in that tournament?"

"Well ..."

"Don't you dare say 'I told you so.'"

"I won't."

The rest of that night was the grimmest since I was thrown into that Spanish jail. The world outside my apartment suddenly seemed uniformly hostile. I felt the urge to throw off my clothes and run around the complex inviting people to inspect me. I heard later that Mike Carver, who knew damn well that I was a woman, had leaped up and shouted, "What's happening? That man is saying lies about Renée! He can't do that!"

Mike had watched the news broadcast in La Jolla with Jeff and Bev Gaines. They had called to console me, but it didn't do much good. A terrible falsehood had been turned loose, and I was convinced that it would destroy me. The story was picked up by the wire services, and within a day this mortifying distortion was broadcast nationwide and then worldwide. Tabloids had a field day with banner headlines, and even respectable papers gave it prominent space. All that, however, was in the future on that first lonely night. I cried steadily for an hour; then, a bit encouraged by the fact that no lynch mob had formed, I tried to sleep. At about four-thirty the next morning I was already up and arranging my wardrobe. I was determined to treat this day as I would any other; I would go to work and try to keep what was left of my life intact.

Considering the wild misgivings of the previous night, the following day was mild indeed. As usual, the waiting room was full of patients, none of whom appeared spooked. Apparently not everyone had gotten the news. I was buoyed up by this seeming normalcy, and I gratefully absorbed myself in physician's work. At lunchtime I was jarred when my secretary told me that Atilio Rosetti was on the phone. He was my coach, my friend, and my most challenging practice opponent at the club. He'd always treated me with overtones of male superiority, and I had loved it, considering this treatment a compliment to my validity as a woman. Now he was on the phone, and doubtless he had heard the news. I braced myself for the recriminations of a wounded male ego.

"Hello?" I said tentatively.

"Richards?" He always referred to me by my last name. "Listen, I've got a court at the club this afternoon at five o'clock. Can you make it?" I breathed a sigh of relief.

"I can make it. See you then."

That was the end of my crisis with Atilio. I'll never forget that gesture. It was precisely what I needed: normalcy, not sympathy, not tenderness. Atilio's gesture was representative of the treatment I received from virtually everyone in Orange County. As conservative as it's made out to be, there was no nastiness of any kind from its residents. At the John Wayne Tennis Club, everyone was protective: when I arrived for my five o'clock appointment with Atilio, the phones were already ringing off their hooks. For awhile the loudspeaker was paging me nonstop, and then it became strangely quiet. By common consent the club staff insulated me, allowing only legitimate personal calls through. The same attitude was taken toward reporters who arrived in person—none was allowed past the foyer of the club.

Most members at the club were in a good position to judge the validity of the previous night's news broadcast. I dressed in the women's facilities and had been seen naked dozens of times by female club members and staff. There couldn't have been any doubt in their minds about my anatomy; in the women's shower room there's no place to hide a stray penis. Beyond that they didn't inquire, though I began to think that my real situation was more widely known in club circles than I had guessed. On the afternoon that preceded the infamous newscast, I had come across two girls who worked in the administration offices. They were swapping sad stories about untrue boy friends and unpaid bills. Generally, they felt as if the world was treating them pretty roughly. I couldn't resist saying, "Well, I sympathize with you, but how would you feel if you knew that in four hours a man was going to go on television and blow your life inside out for an audience of millions?" They looked at me and chorused in unison, "Oh, Renée, no!" I said, "Oh, yes." These girls seemed to understand without any explanation.

I was left to wonder how many others, whom I thought I had been fooling, actually knew. Under the stress of the current crisis my rose-colored glasses were beginning to slip, and I saw that there was much more awareness around me than I had thought. I had been cleverly hiding things in ways that people saw through but politely refrained from mentioning. This endeared my neighbors to me and gave me some comfort in the face of my new and crushing notoriety.

I received this comfort with thanks, but I can't say it made much of a dent in a positively horrible week. I was badgered from as far away as Europe and the Orient. Papers were paying enormous prices for pictures of me, and everywhere I went I had to be on the lookout for photographers—who were actually hiding behind cars and fences waiting for me to come along. They would pop out and begin flashing before I knew what was happening. This was not just annoying but frightening as well, because I could never be sure one of these guys wasn't some kook with a pistol.

One morning I came out of my apartment and found a swarm of reporters and photographers lying in wait. I knew from experience that it did no good to run from them; they would just take off and snap away while stringing out behind me in a line. It was an embarrassing spectacle and could last a long time. Some of those guys were in surprisingly good shape; I guess paparazzi do a lot of running in their line of work. At any rate, I was quietly allowing them to shoot pictures of me and trying to field aggressive questions from the reporters. At this moment Billy unexpectedly rounded the corner, apparently back from his sales trip. He stood for a minute sizing up the situation and then strode up to me, clearing a path for himself by grasping newsmen's shoulders and casting them roughly to one side or the other. His progress was marked by a string of "Hey's!" and "What the's?" When he reached my side, he turned around and faced the assembly: "Renée," he asked, "how would you like me to throw these guys in the ocean?" Everyone took a step back. "No thank you, Billy. That won't be necessary," I replied. "Are you sure?" he said, looking sharply at me. "Yes." He continued to look at me for a moment. "Well, all right then." He moved off down the long porch that ran in front of the apartments. Going out, he didn't have to clear his way.

This was the last time I ever saw Billy. He and I lost touch in the whirlwind that caught me up over the next weeks. When I finally went by his apartment, I found it empty.

After a few days of this circus, it became obvious that I was going to have to do something to set the record straight. Donald and I decided to hold a press conference at the John Wayne Tennis Club. It took place about six days after Dick Carlson's news report. Media people from as far away as New York flew in for the event, which was staged on a veranda near center court.

323

There were over a hundred reporters in attendance, including the inaccurate Mr. Carlson who appeared flabbergasted at Donald's pointed invitation to him. I read a statement that summed up my story and ended with the hope that the truth would allow me to resume a normal life. Considering the subject matter and the hoopla that had preceded the press conference, it was a very restrained event. The questioning was reasonable and controlled. After it was over I felt good. Dick Carlson approached me and expressed his thanks at being invited. "You're welcome, Mr. Carlson," I answered sarcastically. "We couldn't have held it without you."

During the weeks following the press conference, I was advised constantly to go back to my practice and let things die down. It was true that I had been uncovered but at least the true story was now in circulation. There was no humiliation inherent in being a transsexual. Even my father addressed me directly on this issue: "It will die down if you let it," he said. I got more such advice from my sister and from Dr. Tirico, but there was a thorn in me that was beginning to fester. In the upsurge of publicity that followed my press conference, certain statements began to appear in the press. Officials in the governing bodies of tennis had been quoted as saying that I would not be allowed to participate in major championships for women because of my past as Richard Raskind. Up to the time I read those statements, I hadn't given a moment's thought to major women's championships. All I had ever wanted as Renée was to swat a few balls for recreation and play in local tournaments—but this refusal before the fact kind of got my dander up.

More importantly, an incredible volume of mail began to flow in from all over the world. Most of it was addressed simply: Renée Richards, Newport Beach, California. Sacks of it started piling up at the tennis club, where they kindly agreed to store it. In all, probably forty thousand letters arrived, and the peculiar thing was that it was not predominantly hate mail. Oh, there were plenty of threats and obscenities, but at least nine-tenths was positive and three-quarters of the positive comments were from people who were members of minorities. Among others, I heard from blacks, convicts, Chicanos, hippies, homosexuals, people with physical handicaps and, of course, transsexuals. These people felt they had some stake in my decisions—as had Andrea

324

Glazier, the umpire at La Jolla who had urged me so strongly to compete. She had done so on the basis of her own minority experiences. Over the years following this great outpouring of support I have come to believe that these people saw me as a member of an even smaller minority than themselves. After all, there were only a few hundred transsexuals worldwide. Other individuals who were themselves oppressed saw me as even lonelier and so, more put upon.

The ironic thing about this was that I had lived high for most of my life. I'm the first to admit that I'm basically a selfish person. All I want is my Ferrari, my beautiful apartment, and my tennis club. With these I can be happy. I've never even been very political, and here I was getting supportive letters from Black Panthers. In spite of this irony, I was susceptible to this flood of sentiment. Until you have pawed through thirty thousand letters, pleading with you to stand up for your rights and, in so doing, stand up for the rights of the world's downtrodden, you don't know what pressure is. Left to my own devices, I probably would have resolved my personal pique at being summarily barred from competition—but, my god, the whole world seemed to be looking for me to be their Joan of Arc.

To complicate matters I received a letter from my old friend Gene Scott. He told me that he had been reading all the stories about me and had been incensed by them.

He reminded me that he ran a major tournament in, of all places, Orange, New Jersey. I had played there years before as a man, and he was now inviting me back as a woman. In effect, he boldly said, "Screw you!" to the tennis administrators who had been suggesting that they would not sanction any tournament in which I played. He was putting himself in the line of fire out of loyalty to me and the principle for which I had so reluctantly come to stand. What was I to say? Sustained by the incredible wave of public sentiment, I accepted Gene's invitation.

20

Tennis in a Fishbowl

Three weeks later on my birthday, August 19, I found myself on a plane circling New York City. As I stared down into that sea of lights, I was gripped by mixed emotions: New York was Dick Raskind's town; Renée had gone through her adolescence and grown to maturity in a very different spot, Newport Beach, three thousand miles away. My only trips back East had been two schizophrenic interludes when I donned a ridiculous gray, short-haired wig and returned to do some surgery in accordance with the deal that I had made with the young doctor who had taken over my practice. I had hated every aspect of these visits except seeing Andy. Even that consolation was marred by the discomfort I had felt being back in men's clothes again. After the second visit I had realized that any further excursions would be counterproductive. I decided that thereafter I would return only to see Andy and would dispense with the suits and wig in favor of unisex clothing like jeans and shirts or athletic warm-up gear. A few weeks after this decision, my secret life had fallen apart.

What faced me in New York was a week of unbroken turmoil. The magnitude of the publicity that accompanied my decision to play in Gene Scott's tournament eclipsed the previous hoopla that took place after the news broadcast in California. The number of newsmen trailing me doubled. My acquaintances on both coasts retreated into their shells because of being badgered by reporters for background information. Furious at my uncharacteristic reference to principles and higher priorities, Meriam had sent Andy

327

off to spend the summer in Ireland, where he would be insulated from the Renée Richards Circus. Although I missed seeing Andy, I was grateful for this move and grateful that, when pressed, Meriam had grumpily admitted that Andy really had not suffered. He moved in wealthy circles and attended a private day school. Taunting was not a problem, even if any of the kids knew about his father, which was unlikely. That sort of information is not the kind that parents in good homes pass along to their three-year-old kids. Had he been older there might have been repercussions, but by the time he reached the age of understanding the heat was off. He did comprehend fairly soon that I was some kind of celebrity, but he attributed that to my medical accomplishments. It was not until years had passed that he learned the truth about me.

In spite of a secret departure from Los Angeles and a midnight arrival in New York, I was met at the airport by reporters and photographers. That flight had set the tone for the next week. I was traveling in the company of Donald Waxman, Olivia Henderson, and Jane Gross of *Newsday*, a Long Island newspaper with a special interest in me since I was a homegrown celebrity. I was interviewed all the way across the country, met at my destination by photographers who were selling pictures of me for hundreds and sometimes thousands of dollars, picked up by another reporter, Jan Perley of the *New York Post*, and interviewed again until 4 A.M. For the week prior to the tournament, I was seldom without a reporter at my side. I gave almost fifty interviews in which I repeatedly detailed my past and present motivations. I talked to reporters during my breaks from practice at the club and in the car going to and from the club. I was questioned at almost every meal as well as during any free moments I had in my hotel suite. I also spent about three hours each day on the phone talking to reporters from France, Japan, Germany—all over the world. I also accommodated American reporters who couldn't make the trip to New York. I submitted to this willingly because once I had made the decision to be a standard-bearer, I felt that I had better, by god, bear it in public. My hope was that this glare of publicity would intimidate the tennis kingpins who had refused to sanction me. I felt that I was in the right and assumed that my arguments would be accurately reflected in the media. My interview with Jan Perley of the *Post* was encouraging. The story was excellent in its accuracy and evenhanded in its analysis; the optimism that this story generated in me proved to be false indeed. Most of the other stories were riddled with misinformation and, at their worst, descended into personal attack and unsavory innuendo. The insecurities of the reporters as well as the personal revulsion some of them felt for me, showed clearly in their products.

Donald and Olivia ran interferences as best they could between me and this onslaught of newspeople, but neither of them was prepared for the incredible numbers who were bidding for my time. I continued to run myself ragged, all the time thinking that the pace would slack off. Our expectation was that this first wave of interest would break and then recede; after that, I could rest and pursue a more normal schedule. By the day before the tournament in Orange it became obvious that we had calculated incorrectly; so I was whisked away by limousine to the home of Steve Levy, a friend in Long Island who had a private tennis court. The idea was that I would practice in seclusion for my first match; even so, I gave an interview in the limousine to Neil Amdur of *The New York Times.*

When I arrived at Steve's house, I was surprised to find several of my friends from the world of tennis waiting for me. Among them were Bob Barker, Peter Fishback, Ray Garrido, and George Gondelman. Also present was Oto Mehrunka, who was to become my coach for the following year. Even Alan King, the humorist and well-known tennis buff, stopped by with his wife to wish me well. During this afternoon of companionship among my friends, I regained a little of my composure. My practice went well. There were certainly plenty of top-notch players from whom to choose opponents, and I hit balls with practically everyone there. The day was not all play, however, since Donald had agreed after much badgering to allow a network television crew to set up in Steve's backyard for just one more pretournament interview.

In the early evening I returned to my hotel. The lobby was still filled with reporters. I told Donald that I couldn't see anyone else, and donning blue jeans and a warm-up jacket I hopped into a rented car and drove to Forest Hills to keep an appointment with my father. I arrived at seven o'clock and walked into the kitchen unannounced. "You're just in time," he greeted me. "Supper's ready." We sat down and had dinner as we had so many times before, at the kitchen table. Not one word was spoken about my situation. We talked sports and medicine as we had for the last twenty years. He grumbled the questions, and I grumbled the answers and that was it. In a way, I was reassured. Earlier in the day Bob Barker had given me a copy of his newly published book, *Forty Love*. In it he had written, "To Renée. Twenty-five years of friendship in tennis. Everything changes. Nothing changes." As I sat there with my father, I felt that nothing had changed. Later I got up and said that I had to leave. "I'm playing in a tournament over in Orange, New Jersey," I added. "Well, good luck," he muttered. In spite of his taciturn approach, I could tell that he was pleased that I had left the fanfare of celebrityhood for a little dinner in his kitchen. Before I left he asked me if I needed anything from my room. I said, "No." I didn't feel that I'd ever need anything more from Dick's room.

In spite of the exhaustion I felt after a week of nonstop interviews, I slept poorly that night. My dreams had been of that peculiar variety that you can't really remember except for the fact that they concerned something very important that you had to do. I tried all night but never got it done.

At eleven o'clock Steve Levy, whose court I had practiced on the day before, arrived to take me to the tournament. He was driving his Rolls Royce and had with him Larry Parsont, a young resident at Manhattan Eye and Ear Hospital, who was a good tennis player. The three of us drove to New Jersey, followed closely by Donald, Olivia, and (naturally) a couple of reporters, all in a rented Camaro. As we approached the club grounds, we saw that cars were lined up for a mile down the highway on both sides of the entrance. "My, my," said Steve, " I wonder what's going on here? So many cars! After all, it's just a tennis tournament." He said all this in a tone of mock wonderment that was calculated to put me at my ease; if only it had been that easy. As we drove through the gates we were stopped by a club parking-lot attendant. "I'm sorry," he said, "We're full. You'll have to park in the street." Steve blinked a couple of times and then said, "I have Dr. Richards with me." The attendant started slightly. "Oh! Go in then." He motioned us on up the big circular driveway that ran in front of the clubhouse, an old mansion with columns in front. From the inside of the Rolls the scene was eerily quiet though the grounds were thronging with humanity. A huge mob of people crowded around the clubhouse entrance; I knew that they were there for me. I pushed myself deeper into the cushy seat of the Rolls Royce as we drove quietly around the driveway's huge arc. I saw heads swing in our direction, and people began to point. The crowd surged toward the car. Of course, the fact that the car was a Rolls had nothing inherently to do with me, but the crowd had decided without needing further evidence that it must belong to the star of the afternoon. If anyone else had gotten out there might have been a riot. Looking through the windows of the car I could see people craning their necks, eyes wide, mouths moving; but the deep quiet inside the car was hardly disturbed. A space was cleared and Larry opened the door. Suddenly raucous sound flooded previously calm interior. I stepped out and was relieved to see that my first contacts would be some of the ball boys and ball girls; I felt at ease with these kids. One little boy said, "Hello, Dr. Richards." I replied, "Hello. Are you going to be one of the ball boys for the match this afternoon?" He seemed proud of it. "Yes!" I was going to pat him on the head but thought better of it. I contented myself with simply saying, "That's good. It'll be fun." Then the photographers closed in, and I was surrounded by a hundred flashguns exploding repeatedly. Close behind the photographers were reporters shoving microphones in my face and yelling questions. Behind them was a crush of autograph seekers. Obviously the tournament officials hadn't anticipated such a mob, and the security was practically nonexistent. I fought my way from the car to the entrance of the clubhouse—only a few steps but a real gauntlet of grasping and yelling. At the door Gene Scott grabbed my arm and ushered me inside, where they cordoned off the hallways to create some breathing space. The crowd was pushing its way into the building in spite of these precautions, and I began to recognize the fear that must beset rock stars when they confront a huge pack of fans. I had no sense that anyone wanted to hurt me, but as a group creature they might unwittingly trample me to death. Finally, surrounded by a cordon of friends and security guards I was conveyed upstairs with some difficulty.

On the upper floor of the clubhouse, I had been assigned a little room in which to change my clothes. Reporters crowded in, one on top of another. I answered all the old questions over again. I was told that Howard Cosell was on hand to do an interview with me following my first match. Naturally, he didn't deign to wedge himself into my dressing room with the common rabble, but knowing that he was in my future didn't help me retain my composure. I retreated into a protective shell that appeared on the outside to be a transcendent calm. I looked upon the scene in the same way I looked upon a tennis match; it had to be handled through focused concentration. If the surroundings rattled you, then you lost the match. Gene Scott used the same approach, and many people remarked that we appeared to be the calmest of all. I handled each question, each incident, as a thing in itself. I worked only in the present, refusing to think about the past or the future. In this way I kept my sanity, but such concentration requires tremendous energy, and by the time I stepped onto the court I was exhausted.

Gene had arranged for a little time on an out-of-the-way practice court prior to my match. Though I left the clubhouse by climbing out my dressing-room window and down a fire escape, the crowd found me and pushed against the practice court fence, stretching their hands through the wire and begging for autographs.

Ilie Nastase was practicing on the next court, and he greeted me, wishing me luck. Ilie was one of my earliest supporters; he once made a remark to the effect that I was more feminine than some of the women already on the tour.

At length, Gene came for me. We made the long walk from the practice courts to the stadium; Gene ran interference for me. As we neared center court, the crowd got thicker and thicker. I stood in the entranceway surrounded by a solid mass of media people and heard the announcer say: "Please welcome Kathy Beene from Houston, Texas, and her opponent, Dr. Renée Richards from Newport Beach, California, and New York, New York." I pushed my way through the accumulation of photographers and other newsmen, bursting into the relatively clear sidelines around the tennis court. On all sides people, thousands in number, tiered upward; the aisles were clogged with those who couldn't find seats. I walked to my chair and put down my rackets, my towels, and my warm-up jacket. I had the same sensation I had had in La Jolla, only tenfold. All eyes were on me; I restrained an impulse to tug down my tennis dress. I had gone over myself a dozen times before I left my changing room at the clubhouse. I knew that my dress was decently long, but I still felt naked.

As I looked around the court, I spotted a familiar face. One of the linespeople was an old acquaintance, Ellen Runner. As my eyes swept the crowd, occasionally a familiar face would stand out. There were ex-patients, tennis friends and, of course, my faithful boyhood buddies; Joel, Len, and Josh. Josh had greeted me loudly as I walked into the stadium. I looked over and saw that he was standing next to a beautiful woman; I waved, and both of them waved back. Aside from these few friendly faces, the crowd was just one big blur to me. For the moment, it was noisy but under control. I had no way of knowing how long that would last.

My opponent, Kathy Beene, and I began to hit some warm-up balls. I knew nothing about her from personal experience; Gene had told me that she was the serve-and-volley type, but he hadn't seen much of her himself. As we hit the warm-up balls I noticed that Kathy was missing quite a few. I turned to Ellen Runner and said, "My god, Ellen, I think that she's more nervous than I am!" Ellen, who looked nervous herself, confirmed my impression. Of course, Kathy had every reason to be nervous. She had signed on for a tennis tournament, not a Cecil B. De Mille spectacular. The atmosphere aside, she had no way of knowing, any more than most of the people in the stands, how I'd play. Some thought I'd be super, and others thought I'd be terrible. Few knew that I'd been a good player all my life. I have the feeling that most people felt that I was a transsexual woman who had recently taken up tennis in order to exploit her supposed physical advantages. The idea was ludicrous, but then these were the same people who also insisted that I was a dentist. Certainly there had been attempts to clarify; Gene Scott had been asked to compare the way Renée Richards played with the way Dick Raskind played. Gene had raised his hand, palm down, to about the level of his scalp. "This is where Dick Raskind could play," he said. Lowering his hand to waist height he continued, "And this is where Renée Richards plays. With work, she is probably capable of playing somewhere around here." He then put his hand near his neck. He was asked if he thought Renée could beat Chris Evert. "No," he said, "Renée probably thinks she can, but that's because she's a fierce competitor. In my opinion, Renée has lost too much weight and too much strength to beat Chrissy."

As I stood there waiting for the match to start, I didn't feel as if I had the strength to beat anyone, let alone Chris Evert. My legs were so tight that I felt as if I were wearing hundred-pound

333

tennis shoes. In fact, every muscle in my body was knotted with tension. The thought of moving more than a few steps in either direction filled me with apprehension. I felt utterly weak. To compound matters, the temperature was over a hundred degrees and the humidity high: August in New Jersey. It was as if the hot, wet breath of the crowd was accumulating on the court, growing denser, heavier, and less oxygen-rich as the moments passed. I recognized my condition as nervous exhaustion, and I knew that I was in trouble—wiped out before the match had even started. From a competitive standpoint, my only ray of hope was that I could detect the same signs in Kathy Beene. She was nervous too. Even though she had less riding on the outcome of the match, she was not at her best.

The beginning of the match did nothing to increase my confidence. Kathy started serving and jumped on my first two returns. She came to the net like Jimmy Connors and killed me; I thought for sure that my goose was cooked. This girl didn't seem in the least bit nervous; however, on the next point she double-faulted. That was the start of a pattern that persisted throughout the match. In all, she double-faulted eleven times. Throughout she was inconsistent; I found that if I could just keep the ball in play she'd quickly beat herself. I won the first set six–love, losing only five points. Kathy had been overwhelmed by the emotionality of the situation. If I had any advantage it was that I had lived longer than she and suffered more. It was strictly a matter of experience.

Certainly neither of us played good or even competent tennis in that first set. The second set was worse; I was utterly exhausted, like a fighter in the fifteenth round of a slugfest. I staggered through the first game and managed to win largely on unforced errors. I lost the next one and then won again. The fourth game was a long tedious struggle; Kathy showed a lot of character in pulling herself together to win it. That evened the games at two-all. I could hear my breath loud in my ears. All the crowd sound came through as if I was at the end of a long tunnel. I had to watch my feet to make sure I didn't misstep, but when I looked up, my surroundings wavered. I inhaled, but the air did not refresh me. I stumbled a little as I walked to the baseline after a point. Donald Waxman, who was sitting nearby with Steve Levy and

Larry Parsont, saw that I was shaky; they all saw it. Few other people in the crowd had an inkling of my predicament. After all, I had won the first set 6-0 and was even with Kathy in the second. Donald, backed by Steve and Larry, called for ice-cold towels and put them on my neck at the three-two changeover. Larry searched in my bag for a bottle of potassium pills; when he found them, he promptly spilled them on the ground. The towels had cleared my head, but I still felt faint. I asked for a floppy tennis hat to protect my head from the sun. A photographer overheard my request and gave me his, which I wore for the rest of the match. I was so punchy after the break that I headed toward the wrong end of the court; an official pointed me in the right direction. I threaded my way through the photographers lining the edge of the court and made it to the correct spot.

Only my friends recognized the change in me. My dignity was intact, but my effectiveness was shot. I was moving in an awkward lockstep and didn't chase after any ball that wasn't within five feet of me. Donald was watching with the eye of a prizefight manager who has to decide whether or not to throw in the towel for his groggy boxer. It was imperative that I stay up; if I collapsed on the court I would humiliate myself and all I had agreed to stand for. Such a failure would have signaled the weakness of my claim and cruelly disappointed the hopeful thousands for whom I was a symbol of courage.

In the background I could hear the raspy voice of Howard Cosell announcing the match. I could imagine his change of tone if I went down; somehow this possibility was more chilling than any other: to have my collapse announced and analyzed by Cosell. I won the next game and went up four-two. I kept repeating to myself, "Don't fall down, Renée. Don't fall down." I considered simply stepping over to the umpire's chair and informing him that I couldn't continue. I thought better of it. All I had to do was win two more games, and considering Kathy's nerves she might do most of the work. I won the next game to take a five-two lead. I tottered over to my chair and plopped down, whereupon Donald, Steve, and Larry chorused, "How do you feel?" I looked up from underneath a towel and said, "Great." According to Steve, my face was pale, though it was disguised somewhat by my tan. "Are you really all right? Can you go on?" asked Donald. I stared blankly at them and then said from the bottom of the well: "I will not lose this match on my feet. If I lose it, it will be because I had to be carried off, but, by god, as long as I can stand up I won't lose it." With that I dragged myself up and navigated delicately to my place at the baseline.

I don't remember anything about the last game, but I recall that a huge cheer went up when I won. It was the first time in an hour that I had been aware of the crowd. My mind had been so intensely focused on survival that I had no idea whether they had been for or against me, but they yelled at the end as if I'd just won Wimbledon. I shook hands with Kathy and then with the umpire, but I never felt their flesh—I was simply numb. Donald, Steve, and Larry successively put their arms around me and I let each of them bear my weight for a while. I was thrilled but physically exhausted and emotionally drained. Supported by my friends, I was led out of the stadium. The fans near the gate gave me a big round of applause and screamed their congratulations. I looked up into the stands and saw a group of black tennis players holding up a sign that said, "The Doc is back—bigger and better than ever." In the corridor leading out of the stadium I was greeted by many friends. Notable among them was my gynecologist buddy, Donny Rubell, who had given me that prophetic warning to stay away from tennis over a year before. Others approached me, but I was in such a daze that I had to be told by them days later that they had been on hand. They said that I was cordial, but I still don't remember much about the first fifteen minutes following the match.

I began to regain full consciousness under an awning in a roped-off area of the club grounds. This corner had been set aside for my postmatch press conference. After I had arranged myself in front of about a hundred or so reporters, they began to fire questions at me. I praised Gene Scott for his courage in asking me to participate in the tournament; I praised Kathy Beene for her courage in agreeing to play me. I praised the other women who were willing to do the same. These people had refused to be intimidated by the powerful governing bodies of tennis. They had accepted me as a legitimate competitor and—by inference—as a legitimate woman. I said that I'd never forget them, and in the years since I have not.

When the press conference was over, I was led to another roped-off area where Howard Cosell waited to interview me for the "Wide World of Sports." I'll admit that I was intimidated; after all, he was not known for tact. I expected him to be tough; however, unknown to me, Steve Levy, who had known Cosell for years, had gone to him and said, "Look, Howard, this is not Muhammad Ali. Renée isn't what you might imagine. She's quiet and sensitive and not a sensation seeker. Don't be your usual abrasive self." Amazingly, Howard Cosell was both sensitive and supportive. Actually, as we looked across the lawn at thousands of people straining at the barricades, he seemed a bit nervous himself. He turned to me and said in a disarmingly Cosell-ish way, "Renée, in all my years of sports broadcasting I have never been an observer at such a scene. How can you sit here so collectedly, even serenely, in the face of all this? It must be doing all kinds of things to you. It is to me." I looked at him as calmly as I could and said, "Well, Howard, don't be misled by my surface serenity. I feel that this is a momentous event, and I am affected by it. On the other hand, I'm not going to let it overcome me. I've been through a lot in my personal life and in my life as a physician, and I've had a lot of practice dealing with unusual situations. Some of those were matters of life and death, so in that regard this can't compare. Still, I'll admit that this scene is stirring."

If the unflappable Cosell was touched, you know that the atmosphere was electric. As if in testimony, Olivia passed out just before the start of the interview and had to be revived by Larry Parsont. Once this casualty had been treated, Howard started his questioning. His manner was respectful, and the information he requested was reasonable. Perhaps most important was the fact that he treated me like a lady. I felt comfortable with him, and, amazingly, the exchange was more like an intimate conversation than an interview. It was an unlikely accomplishment considering the mob scene that surrounded us. Everybody raps Howard, but he did right by me.

After the "Wide World of Sports" segment, I was hustled upstairs to my little dressing room, where I sat staring for an hour. Every muscle was sore. My mind had taken a vacation. Occasionally, one of my friends would look in and see that I hadn't moved since the last time he checked. "You okay, Renée?" Without twitching, I'd say, "Yes. I'll be taking my shower in a minute." This probably happened seven or eight times. Before I managed that shower more reporters were shown in. I responded as if hypnotized, answering questions right up to the time I stepped into the shower. It was a rather public display of a normally personal routine. I didn't mind because I thought that it might make me seem more of a human being. The normality of gathering my effects and arranging my hair would, I hoped, help me appear average. Certainly I felt they must be curious; so I didn't make a point of asking them to leave. Following this incident, a story appeared in *People* magazine revealing that I had average-sized breasts. Not exactly world-shaking news but at least accurate.

Eventually, the crowd began to thin out and Donald, Olivia, one leftover reporter, and I climbed into the rented Camaro and started back to New York. We were still en route when five o'clock rolled around. In order to catch me on TV with Howard, we stopped in Newark, New Jersey. The neighborhood was about on a par with Harlem or Watts. It wasn't our intention to live dangerously, but the show's air time had slipped up on us. That's why we had to settle for Joe's Saloon. Inside were several old men attending to their business of getting plastered; around the pool table were more active, younger men. Some were white and some were black and one was yellow. Behind the bar was a tough-looking stevedore type. He stood there like the master of a pirate ship. I sat down and looked him over. "Are you Joe?" I asked. "Yes, I am," he replied unenthusiastically. "Well, Joe," I continued, "how about turning that TV set to Channel Seven?" Without another word he turned to the set that was perched on a high shelf behind the bar and dialed seven. The interview had just started. Howard and I were sitting there surrounded by the carefully clipped grounds of the Orange Lawn Tennis Club. Joe, the bartender, looked up at the screen and then over at me. His head swung back and forth several times before he felt that he could trust his judgment. Finally, he asked, "That you?" And I said, "That's me all right." He paused a long moment. I thought maybe he was going to punch me out, but he simply said, "What are you drinking, Dr. Richards?" To which I replied, "I'll take a beer, Joe."

As my party watched the interview unfold, we were joined by

the other patrons; one by one they wandered over, and after two or three swings of the head between the TV screen and my face, settled themselves on stools or leaned against the bar. So, surrounded by inebriates of various hues, I watched myself broadcast to an audience of millions. After it was over, I'll be damned if those scoundrels didn't queue up for autographs. Some of them looked as if they hadn't been out of the back room of Joe's Saloon for the last twenty years. Joe himself was too dignified for such silliness, but after I'd taken care of the others, I picked up a big cardboard coaster and wrote, "To Joe. You have a terrific saloon. Good luck! Renée Richards." When I handed it to him a big smile broke across his face, the first time he'd shown any emotion. Somehow, this seemed like an important approval. There were those, I knew, who would turn their noses up at me, but I had the backing of the boys at Joe's Saloon in Newark.

I soon learned that they weren't the only ones. Back in Manhattan we went for dinner to one of my old haunts on Third Avenue. As the young waiter seated us, he commented, "You *are* Renée, aren't you?" Later I heard him say to the people behind the bar, "We have a celebrity sitting over at that table." This was actually my first real awareness that my life as a private person was over. This was no newspaper reporter or tennis fan. He was an ordinary waiter who recognized me not through some special interest but because I was notorious. Later, as I walked down East Sixtieth Street on my way to a newsstand, people rolled down the windows of their cars and yelled out, "Way to go, Renée!" Others came up to me on the street and pumped my hand. Again, I was flabbergasted that a transsexual could have such a broad base of support. Those who disliked me or regarded me as a freak had the good grace to keep their mouths shut. That evening was like opening night at a hit Broadway show. At the newsstand I picked up the early edition of the *Daily News*. On the front page was the headline: RENEE ROLLS IN NEW JERSEY OPENER. Underneath in smaller type, it said, "Doc's Operation Takes Forty-six Minutes."

Finally, after champagne at the Café Pierre, we returned to the Carlton House and tried to get some sleep. It was about four o'clock in the morning but, in spite of the incredible energy drain I had gone through, I still couldn't get to sleep. So much of my life had been devoted to hiding and to pretense that I couldn't get over

339

the incredible publicness of my situation. I had been celebrated before, of course, but it had always been in spite of my sexual idiosyncrasies—never because of them. I was the heir apparent to Christine Jorgensen, but I possessed an advantage that poor Christine never enjoyed. I had an identity beyond my transsexualism. I was a doctor, a parent, and a tennis player. These dimensions made me a thorny problem for those who liked to think of transsexuals only as perverts dancing in sleazy bars. For those people, I was a puzzle, one that could not be solved by resorting to a stereotype. This was my peculiar value and, no doubt, the source of my surprising popularity.

I was desperate for sleep but it wouldn't come. I remembered an incident that had occurred as I was making my way through the mob at the clubhouse. Suddenly, from the nondescript heart of the horde a blind woman had materialized. She was probably saved from being trampled to death only by the fact that people respected her Seeing Eye dog, an aggressive-looking German shepherd. This woman moved toward me like the eye of a hurricane. All around her the tumult swirled, but she and her protective dog were unmoved. With instinctive sympathy I recognized her as a transsexual, and insisted that my party stop. She and I stood opposite one another while the tumult raged about us; she took my hand and said, "Thank you, Renée. What you're doing is so courageous!" I looked incredulously at her. "Listen," I said, "you're showing more courage right now than I ever did. Believe me, seeing you here is a great inspiration to me. Please, let's talk sometime when we're not in danger of being crushed." I kissed her on the cheek and forged ahead.

In retrospect, considering the circumstances, I think I did pretty well by her, but in the gray light of the morning after, I began to worry that I had given her the old superstar treatment. This incident began to dominate my thinking; I pictured this poor blind creature off in a corner somewhere crying, her faith in me crushed. I reviled myself for the supercilious way that I had dismissed her. I compared the problems of her life with mine and the comparison was pathetic. She was the real hero, not me. What was I? A pampered transsexual tennis bum. For an hour my anxiety continued to mount until I finally began to weep. However much I tried to pull myself together, I couldn't. Several times I almost stopped, only to burst out crying again. Olivia heard me sobbing and came in to ask if she should get a doctor for me. "What the hell do I need a doctor for?" I shouted. "I am a doctor! There's nothing wrong with me." About eight o'clock in the morning I fell asleep.

The following day I had no match to play. I awoke in the afternoon and continued the endless round of interviews and phone calls. This routine was broken only by an occasional secret practice session at a mid-Manhattan tennis club. During these breaks I was able to relieve a little of the pressure through some antics that I couldn't allow myself to perform when in public view. At one point, I hit the ball so hard against the clubhouse wall that I knocked down a picture hanging inside. Some club members came to the door and looked out questioningly. "Just relaxing," I called out.

On Monday I played a match that was in high contrast to Saturday's debacle; it was a close, three-set victory over Caroline Stoll. I was pleased that the level of tennis had improved greatly and that the emphasis had shifted more in the direction of the competition. Still, after the match I was once again besieged by the crowd and again held a press conference where I answered all the old questions once more. Eventually, though, my patience broke when one reporter stood up and asked, "How does it feel to be a woman?" I quelled an urge to rush down and knock his teeth out, politely asking him to confine his questions to tennis. In fact, I was able to remain composed through all of the grilling except for one incident. I don't even remember where or when it was; a woman reporter from Sweden had asked me a question about Andy. It wasn't even asked in a nasty way, but suddenly I burst out crying. "Please," I sobbed, "this is tough enough as it is. It seems to me that there's plenty for your readers with the trans-sexualism and the tennis and all of that. You don't have to get into my personal life and bug me about my son." The other reporters waiting for their turns shuffled uncomfortably. Finally, a spokes-man said "Renée, we'll ask you our questions another time."

My third match was against a seasoned professional, Kathy Harter, who was once ranked as high as number five in the country. I beat her in a close match, and when I came to the net to shake her hand, I said, "Kathy, you're one hell of a gal." She looked at me and with a whimsical expression on her face, said, "Renée, so are you." I knew that she was bitterly disappointed at having lost the match, but she hadn't lost her class. We walked off the court together. Near the sidelines a man rushed out of the crowd and threw his arms around me; it was Dr. Granato. He looked into my eyes and said, "Renée, this is doing so much for so many people." We embraced again, and I left him to go to yet another press conference.

Later, when I was leaving the conference area and heading toward the clubhouse, a tournament official approached me and whispered, "Somebody out there says he's your father." I hadn't spoken to him since our dinner several nights before, but I had a feeling that he'd finally show up. I walked around to where he was standing. He looked up and said, "You still don't know how to hit those low balls." I stopped in front of him and replied, "Yeh, I know. If I could just hit the low ones, I'd win the U.S. Open." Abruptly, a man from ABC rushed over and stuck a camera into my father's face. "If you value that camera," my father said ominously, "then take it away." That was the only time he made any reference to the clamor of media people around us.

As we walked to the clubhouse accompanied by an orbiting mob of people, my father and I discussed the match that I had just played. "Why the hell can't you throw the ball up higher to hit your serve?" he asked irritably. "I don't know, Dad," I replied, as ever amazed at his single-mindedness. We drove into the city in his car and had dinner together: just a typical father-and-daughter outing.

For me, the tournament came to an end in the semifinals. I lost in a close three-set match to Lea Antonopolis, a strong seventeen-year-old from California. The following year, she won the Wimbledon Junior Championship. On that day, she was the better player, and though I had been defeated I knew that it was only a small skirmish in a war with much higher stakes than a tennis trophy. I cried a little afterward, not because I'd lost but out of relief. The pressure was finally off; at my last press conference I was gracious in defeat. When I finished that swan song, I could look back with satisfaction over the past week. It had been hectic, but I felt I'd carried it off well. Surely those skittery rulers of tennis had been watching and had remarked my performance. Surely they would find me worthy.

21

The Wrong Chromosomes

The high hopes to which I had treated myself after the tournament in Orange lasted for about two weeks. I was still in New York when I read the news. The U.S. Open Committee had decided that I could play if I could pass a chromosome test. They knew that in all likelihood I could never pass such a test though it is not infallible proof of sexual identity. There are men who have the so-called female chromosomal makeup and women who have the male. It would have been a juicy joke on them if I had been one of those rare exceptions, but I wasn't about to take the test. My position was that in my case such tests were irrelevant. Of all the potential competitors, my sex was the least in doubt. It was a matter of public record based on legal documentation. The chromosome test had been available to the U.S. Open Committee for ten years, and they had not invoked it a single time. Suddenly they wanted to use it on me, a clear case of discrimination. I was willing to undergo physical examinations, but I didn't feel that the chromosome makeup that I was born with in 1934 had anything to do with my sexuality in 1976.

Despite my protests, both the United States Tennis Association and the Women's Tennis Association refused to sanction me. The USTA controlled the major tournaments like the U.S. Open, and the WTA had a lock on nearly all the prize-money tournaments in which women professionals could compete. Only a few events would be open to me without their approval. Gene Scott's tournament in Orange, for example, drew major competition on the basis of his reputation, and that was the reason he could thumb his nose at the establishment. Other tournaments, however, could not afford such gestures. Without official sanction they might well wither and die. Furthermore, a player's wins in nonsanctioned events don't count in the overall computer rankings that figure strongly in whether a player is deemed qualified to participate in major events. Without the approval of these two organizations, life as a tennis professional was denied me.

Of course, I could understand the nightmares that the governing officials were going through; I heard their objections dozens of times in the year following that first big tournament in Orange. For one thing, I looked so damn fearsome. At six-feet one-inch (or as I like to say, five-feet thirteen-inches), I was an intimidating sight standing next to some five-feet four-inch lightweight. Still, Betty Stove was six feet tall and hefty besides. So were some lesser-known pros, yet their sexuality had never been questioned. Then there was the question of muscle power. It had been asserted time and again that I had more muscle than a woman of comparable stature; this flies in the face of medical fact. A man's muscle mass is sustained by his male hormone, testosterone. Once this is taken away the muscles change in character. Their size is reduced, they elongate, and they become smoother. The muscle mass on my body was entirely appropriate for a woman my size, especially a woman athlete. As a matter of fact, I was far less strong than most women in such sports as shot-putting, discus throwing, and weight lifting. I was not even stronger than all of the world's women tennis players, though many found that hard to believe. Even if I had been, it was ridiculous to argue about strength since a tennis match is not won or lost on brute strength. One more important point needs to be made with regard to my strength: the muscles in a woman's body are small partly because they are designed to move a skeletal frame that is lighter than a man's; a woman who is six-feet tall has a considerably lighter skeleton than a man of that height. In my case, I was moving the skeleton of a man my size with the muscle mass appropriate to a woman of my size. I could have claimed that I was playing with a handicap.

These arguments were often met by officials with an attitude of indulgent world-weariness. They would emphasize that they had nothing against me personally; in fact, they would be happy to see me play. It was the precedent that they were worried about. I was

344

a serious and sincere competitor, but what about the next transsexual? Mightn't she be more intimidating than Renée Richards, who after all was, ahem, forty years old and (as was shown in Orange) beatable. The next one could be six-feet eight and three hundred pounds! Or, I would counter, five-feet two and eighty-three pounds. If size was their worry, then why didn't they just make it illegal for anyone over five-feet ten or a hundred and fifty pounds to play? Well, they would answer, that would be discriminatory.

Most of the officials whom I queried subscribed to what I came to think of as the "floodgate theory." If I was allowed to play, then the floodgates would be opened and through them would come tumbling an endless stream of made-over Neanderthals who would brutalize Chris Evert and Evonne Goolagong. Of course, this was sheer nonsense. Where would these people come from? The chances that even a mediocre player would turn out to be a genuine transsexual were low; the chances that a player capable of competing even in the top fifty would be transsexual were statistically insignificant. Did they think that anybody, just because she had once been a man, could automatically beat women professionals or even competent amateurs? This attitude was the antithesis of women's liberation.

But suppose, as had been so often suggested about me, that someone did it for money? Some player who was not quite good enough in men's tennis might decide to change only in order to overpower the women players. Even if we forget about the arguments concerning loss of strength, this fear is also pretty much groundless. How hungry for tennis success must you be to have your penis chopped off in pursuit of it? How many men would do it for a million dollars? If you could find one, would such a neurotic be likely to have the concentration to play top-flight tennis, even if he didn't go completely crazy once he'd realized what he'd done?

These arguments were all so farfetched that I had a hard time keeping a straight face while I engaged in them. Still, they had a chilling side. Born in the panicky fantasies of people who were confronting something they couldn't understand, these arguments represented all the arguments of prejudice that had ever existed. They were seductive; if unexamined, they even seemed to make a little sense. I suffered these confrontations periodically over the year following my discovery in La Jolla. The officials of the United States Tennis Association and the Women's Tennis Association gave me several hearings, but the result was always the same: request denied. The more such conversations I had, the stronger became my resolve to overcome the tennis establishment.

One of the ironies of these repeated rebuffs was that most of the women they were supposedly protecting didn't want to be protected. In fact, they were on my side. The courageous women who had played against me in the Orange tournament were just the beginning: more came to my support as time passed. The most prominent of these was the queen of tennis, Billy Jean King. More than any other player, she changed the course of women's tennis, in particular pressing for prize money on a par with the men. In feminist circles she is revered as a leader whose contributions reach far beyond her status as a tennis player. She and I had two long meetings, one in New York and one in California. Our discussions were wide ranging, and in the end she was convinced of my sincerity. Her support was to take a very concrete form in the next stage of my career.

When I announced that I would not be returning to my ophthalmological practice, everyone thought that I was crazy. Their objections took two forms. The first concerned the satisfactions of medicine as opposed to those of tennis: "As a doctor you're helping people." The second was financial: "My god, you'll bankrupt yourself!"

There is truth in the argument that by becoming a professional tennis player, I was depriving the world of a fine medical servant; this consideration caused me a lot of agonizing. I had trained for years as a physician, and I took great satisfaction from the healing that I could provide to people. On the other hand, I had been training as a transsexual all my life, far longer than I had in medicine, and the acceptance of transsexuals was the issue in my battle with the USTA and the WTA. To the average person this seems like a minor point; after all, how many transsexuals will ever want to play professional tennis? Yet, the good I could accomplish as a famous person in setting a precedent for all transsexuals could not be ignored. The problems of employment for transsexuals often take ludicrous turns; I've heard a hundred laughable yet true stories like the one about the chef who had a sex-change operation and then couldn't get her old job back because women aren't supposed to make effective chefs. This tale is good for a chuckle unless you are a bewildered transsexual trying to figure out the peculiar logic that has taken your livelihood from you. In my years as a public figure I have been approached many times by transsexuals who have told me: "I got a job when I went in and said I was a transsexual like Renée Richards." I can honestly say I looked ahead to this when I made my decision. Further, I had only to stare at the enormous stacks of mail from nontranssexuals to reassure myself that my appeal went beyond that narrow audience.

Besides, I thought it would do me good. All my life I had lived a life of intellectualization; for ten years, I lay on a psychiatrist's couch and analyzed myself and my motivations. I had spent years in school analyzing the physiology of the human body with a focus so intense that I had brought myself to a point where I knew as much about the superior oblique eye muscles as anyone else in the world. I had always found my escape from this intensity in the straightforward physicality of tennis. It had offered me a chance to suspend the rational process and exercise my reflexes and my intuitions, to escape from the obsessive professionalism of Dick Raskind. But now he was gone and Renée had taken his place; she wanted to relax, to banish Dick's compulsive attention to detail. What better place to do this than on the tennis court, where by playing her favorite game she could also strike a blow for a worthwhile principle? In this way she could exercise herself in the macrocosmic world in the same way that Dick had excelled in the microcosmic. In short, I was tired of brainwork; tennis looked good to me and I could always return to medicine once I'd made my point.

But as you may recall, there was a second objection to my choosing tennis: "My god, you'll bankrupt yourself!" This forecast was accurate: I had enough money to last me a couple of months, but beyond that was a huge questionmark. You can't win money unless you're allowed to play.

Donald Waxman was willing to function as my manager on the basis of our past relationship and on the chance that I would be granted the right to play. When that happened, he would receive a manager's commission. It wasn't long before I was out of my beautiful apartment and into the spare room at Donald's house. Over the next year I went into debt so deeply that even some of my friends sued me.

Ironically, one of the recurrent charges leveled at me by the press was that I was motivated by an unvarnished desire for money. They scoffed at my talk of principles; what these people did not realize was that my earning power as a doctor was easily over a hundred thousand dollars a year. Only a tiny fraction of the players on the professional tour make that much money, and big chunks come out of that for travel and accommodations.

To be sure, my principles were tested—and tested early. Shortly before I went back to California I was approached by a production group and asked to play a challenge match against Bobby Riggs. It would be staged at Caesar's Palace in Las Vegas, and my take was to be two hundred and fifty thousand dollars. For a person whose income had just plummeted to zero, this was a tempting offer, but I turned it down. Riggs had recently been involved in challenge matches with Margaret Court and Billy Jean King. They were supposedly staged as battles of the sexes; Bobby had beaten a nervous Margaret Court but had been soundly trounced by Billie Jean. If there was ever anything to be proven by such matches, it had already been done; Bobby Riggs playing Renée Richards would be sensationalism pure and simple, and I was interested in retaining as much sense of serious purpose as I could manage in the carnival atmosphere that surrounded me. So, in spite of the fact that my mouth watered at the prospect of an easy quarter-million dollars, I passed up the proposal—though the years ahead would have been considerably more comfortable if I had accepted.

Upon my return to California, I began training in earnest. Though I was like a boxer preparing himself with no fight in the foreseeable future, I attacked the problem of getting into shape with all-out intensity. Both Dick and Renée had been weekend athletes in the worst sense of the word. Until I went into serious training, I had smoked at least a pack of cigarettes every day and downed two martinis before dinner each night. Had I been in better shape, I would undoubtedly have borne up better under the pressures of the Orange tournament. I knew that if I was ever going to play serious competitive tennis, I'd have to be able to withstand intense pressure not only from my opponents but from the inquisitive crowds as well. When I further considered the factor of my comparatively advanced age, I knew that my only hope was to be in the best physical condition possible. In doing this I inadvertently ran into another reason to play tennis rather than be a doctor. My health and sense of well-being had improved to the point that I felt years younger. My career in professional athletics has, in essence, provided Renée with a young adulthood that might have been shorter or less intense had I continued my previous habits.

Not only did I train more and cut out old vices; I looked for wise professional instruction. I found it at La Costa where I trained with Poncho Segura. Poncho, a great champion player in his own time, has gone on to become just as well-known for coaching. His most famous pupil was the young Jimmy Connors who has always been complimentary about Poncho's contribution to his success. Poncho would set up practice matches for me and then study my technique as I played. Afterward, he'd give me a rundown, pointing out my mistakes. Even when he was playing a game three courts away, he kept track of me out of the corner of his eye, and when I made a good move I'd hear his voice, "Atta way, Renée baby!" Off the court I learned a lot from him about the tactics of match play.

After a month at La Costa, I returned to Newport Beach feeling fitter than I had in years but terribly disenfranchised. My money was disappearing at an incredible rate, yet my repeated requests for official sanction were denied unless I passed the chromosome test. I continued to practice regularly at the John Wayne Tennis Club and to stick to my training routine, but I was beginning to lose heart. The future hadn't looked so grim since before the operation.

The drought was finally broken when I received a call early one morning from Gladys Heldman who had been the main force in the development of the Virginia Slims Circuit, the first important showcase for women's professional tennis. I had met her in New York just before Gene Scott's tournament. I thought she hadn't been much impressed with me, but that early morning call proved otherwise. She invited me to participate in two professional tournaments that she was promoting in Hawaii. She was inviting me in spite of the fact that the WTA had threatened not to sanction the events and had further insinuated that there might be penalties for players who elected to compete in tournaments with me. Regardless of these threats, she assured me that the events would go ahead as scheduled and that a good field of players would be participating. I was ecstatic and accepted the invitation on the spot.

I received the call from Gladys in November of 1976, and the tournaments were planned for December. Having some real competition to prepare for made a big difference to me. Gladys had shown herself to be a true friend, and the women who had agreed to compete with me had demonstrated their independent spirit. That these people would risk reprisals from the WTA constituted tangible support at a time when, with a little cooperation from the tennis world, that organization might have been able to simply snuff me out.

The two tournaments went off without a hitch. The first was staged on the garden island of Kauai. In this beautiful setting I won the singles event, and my partner, Betty Ann Stuart, and I won the doubles. This seemed like an awfully good omen; from a practical standpoint, the prize money, though not tremendous, momentarily helped staunch my rising tide of personal indebtedness.

The second tournament was held at Kona on the island of Hawaii. I did not prevail here, losing in the finals to Karen Susman, a Wimbledon champion in 1964. In the doubles event, Betty Ann and I also lost in the finals to the team of Ceci Martinez and Mary Ann Beatty. Even these losses were not entirely unwelcome. Naturally, I hated to lose, but I could always console myself that they served to inform the public that I was not an unbeatable behemoth out to prey on helpless little girls.

The reactions of the crowd at these events set a precedent that was to be followed for many years. The incredible furor of the Orange tournament was gone, but my matches were still attended by a legion of the curious. As always, I was treated respectfully, and if there were hecklers I never heard them. Still, I was strongly aware of the intense scrutiny that the crowd directed at me when I came onto the court. This interest had nothing to do with me as a tennis player. When I first walked onto the court I was nothing more than a curiosity, but the minute I hit a ball, the tone of things changed for the better. Suddenly everyone realized that I could actually play! Somewhere in the recesses of their minds this bit of information had been stored, but the visual proof always seemed to come as somewhat of a shock. By functioning as a player I became more understandable as a human being, because everyone can understand sport.

I wish I could say that the same thing happened to the members of the press, but I sometimes wonder if they bothered to watch the games. In general, I consider that I was badly used in the early days. Seldom did any reporters try to paint me in more human terms. The tendency was to go for the obvious, to trade on my peculiar history. For example, quite a lot of ink was used on the reaction of players to my presence in the locker room. To my knowledge, no player ever complained about my dressing with everyone else; yet this question was constantly asked. My habits in the dressing room were constantly under review. In some stories I was a flagrant exhibitionist strolling around the locker room stark naked and apparently reveling in my condition. In other stories I was a secretive mole who was never spotted in the company of the other women. From my point of view these observations were not only wrong but inappropriate. All of the women who play professional tennis have been in sports for years. Part of that world is the atmosphere of the locker room. Some are more casual than others, but everyone accepts the inevitability of appearing nude in front of others. I am probably slightly less concerned about it than the average player, but at any given time a reporter might look in and see me naked—or not see me at all. From such spotty information conclusions were drawn about my general behavior. This was then reported as if it were somehow important.

Back in Newport Beach after the Hawaiian tournaments, I was once again at loose ends. I kept myself busy training and coaching, but neither of these added any money to the kitty. I was falling further and further behind in such things as rent, car payments, alimony, and child support. Soon my Corvette was gone. Things stayed pretty bleak from a professional standpoint until once again Gladys Heldman came to my rescue. She was promoting a circuit of tournaments to be called the Lionel Cup. She had been denied sanctions again by both the USTA and the WTA because of her invitation to me to participate in the events. Once again, however, a group of strong-minded women players had refused to honor that decision. Though the events were not officially recognized, they attracted quality players. Among them was my friend Billie Jean King. Her endorsement of this series was invaluable and set a precedent that no doubt convinced many players whose minds were not already made up.

Billie Jean won at the first stop on the tour, San Antonio. During the tournament we socialized a little, and she invited me to play doubles with her when the tour hit New York. She knew how much this gesture would mean to me; it was a stronger statement of her support than simply playing in a tournament in which I participated. Installing me as her partner was an unmistakable gesture of acceptance. I thankfully agreed and began to point toward that tournament, thinking that my teaming with Billie Jean might carry enough public impact to sway the USTA and the WTA. Meanwhile, I reached the finals in Little Rock and the semifinals in Tallahassee, proving that I was at least competitive against the best women I had played so far.

In New York the atmosphere had some of that old electricity. Both Billie Jean and I were big news, and the combination caused quite a stir. We played to crowds that were unusually large for a doubles event. I don't know what these people expected to see when they attended our matches, but what they did see was a pretty hot team. Billie Jean and I played well together, winning all four matches in straight sets. In fact, we had hardly lost a game by the time we reached the finals. Anyone who had been watching our progress held us to be the favorites; however, in the course of the tournament I had been stricken with the flu. When I went onto the court for the finals I was dizzy, perspiring, and sporting a fever of one hundred and one degrees. As we walked to our side of the court, I thought it best to inform my partner of the situation. "Billie Jean," I said with just a hint of self-pity in my voice, "I don't feel well, I'm not sure I'll be able to play out this match." Billie Jean glanced back at me, obviously unimpressed with my sad story. "Renée," she said, "you look fine. Let's go out and do a job." We played the first game and won, but as we changed ends I was woozy and complained again. "Billie Jean, I really feel awful." She said again, "You look terrific Renée, and you're playing great. Let's go!" We got out of our chairs and played again. After two more games, we were once again seated in our chairs; I looked over at her mournfully and said, "Billie Jean, I think I need some oxygen." She didn't even bother to look back. "We don't have any oxygen, Renée. Get up, it's your service!"

352

Billie Jean knew only one mode of play: full speed ahead. I could sense her growing frustration at being saddled with such a whiny partner. I tried to stifle myself, but after two more games the landscape was wiggling and I could hear my breath in my ears. It was similar to the way I felt at Gene Scott's tournament months before, only this time the culprit was a virus, not nervous exhaustion. Finally, I strode out to Billie Jean and said matter-of-factly, "My temperature must be at least a hundred and one. How can I play?" This I thought would be the closing statement; after all, I was a doctor. Billie Jean glanced up and said, "Listen! I won Wimbledon with a temperature of a hundred and three. Now, let's go!"

We won the first set 6–0. Afterward, I complained again. "I'm dizzy. I think I need an ambulance." Billie Jean ignored this, clapped me on the back in a comradely fashion and said, "Renée, you're playing great. Keep it up!" I staggered through three more games but felt like I was playing in syrup. Whenever I got to a ball I was amazed. Three games into the second set, I made my final statement on the situation. Approaching Billie Jean on the sidelines, I raised myself to my full height, and towering over her I said with as much dignity as I could muster, "I cannot continue. I am going to collapse." Billie Jean held me disdainfully in her gaze and then turned to the gallery. She raised herself on her toes, and throwing her arms upward in a gesture of supplication, screamed, "This is the last time I'm ever playing with a Jewish American Princess!" With that she shoved me out onto the court again, where we eventually won 6–0, 6–2. This was one of the delicate flowers that the WTA had set itself the job of protecting from me. As I stood panting during the presentation ceremony, I wondered how they could think that this marvelously strong woman could not take care of herself.

The Lionel Cup series finished in the spring of 1977. Thanks to Gladys Heldman and the cooperation of the participating players, led by Billie Jean, I had played as a professional and made enough money to keep my head above water. I had a sensation of personal triumph, but official recognition was still not forthcoming. When queried, the rulers of tennis made the same old response: if I could pass a chromosome test, I could play.

I was once again a free-floating curiosity. My debts again accrued alarmingly. In desperation, I wrote to the organizers of the Italian Open Championship in Rome and asked to be entered.

The Italian tournament was played in May and was followed closely by the French Open Championship, which preceded Wimbledon. If I could participate in these grand events, the WTA and USTA would look pretty silly if they continued to withhold their sanction. I was delighted when I received a cordial letter from Marty Mulligan, the director of the Italian tournament, granting my request to be allowed to play. This was the first and most important step in gaining access to other major European tournaments.

I redoubled my training efforts, spending much time with Oto Mehrunka, the man who had become my coach on the East Coast. Renée Richards Enterprises was still strictly a shoestring organization. The Lionel Cup money had been like gruel to a starving man: enough to prevent our demise but not enough to bring us back to health. When it came time to leave for Italy, we could barely scrape together enough money to buy tickets for Oto and me. Donald Waxman and Olivia Henderson had to stay behind. Oto and I had to depend on my tournament winnings to pay for our stay in Rome and to provide the funds to get to the French Open; even the money for a first-round loss could take care of that much if we were careful.

My arrival in Europe was celebrated as if I were a creature from outer space. I was thankful to be staying in the Holiday Inn in Rome with two hundred and fifty other tennis players, including some of the most famous ones in the world—so I was not quite the center of attention that I had been in Orange, New Jersey. The sheer numbers of journalists were less in Rome though they still managed to devote lots of time to me and were sometimes ruder than their American counterparts because neither the tournament organizers nor the local police exercised any effective control over them. I took to checking my hotel room to make sure no reporter was hanging outside the window or crouching in the closet, ready to pounce when I hung up my clothes. No move I made in public was unphotographed or unreported; somehow I coped with it, thinking that this was the price necessary for the opportunity to play tennis.

Twenty-four hours after my arrival, I discovered that the price I was paying was apparently not high enough. After a conference with a representative from the WTA, Marty Mulligan suddenly reversed his position. A messenger came to my hotel and informed me that I would not be allowed to play unless I took that damned chromosome test. I tried to call Marty several times, but he was never in. I refused to take the test and sat back to wait. One good thing about all the press hoopla was that it had whipped up public interest in seeing me play. A lot of excitable spectators were going to be disappointed. I thought this pressure might force the officials to give in. As the hours passed, however, it became apparent that the officials of the tournament had given their final word.

I was in Rome without even the money to pay my hotel bill, let alone get a ticket out. Oto was also dependent upon me; so if I went to jail he'd go too. My perception of the situation narrowed down to an unrealistically few choices, beyond which I had no ability to see. I began to consider taking the test. Though I had always maintained that it was irrelevant in my case, the chances were not 100 percent that I would fail. I had done the test on myself and had achieved borderline results. The process involves scraping some cells from the mucous membranes lining the cheek; these are placed under a microscope, and certain bodies that indicate femaleness are counted. These are called Barrbodies, and the test is called the Barrbody test. Even normal women occasionally fail because the number of Barrbodies is not consistent from one day to the next; these women are simply given the test again at another time.

I had been badgered into taking the test once before in Arkansas during the Lionel Cup tour, and I had passed! When I had attempted to turn this silly development to my advantage, the tennis authorities had demanded that I take it again. I felt far more comfortable with my original argument—that the test was irrelevant—whatever the result. Now I was facing a situation in which it seemed to me that the results of such a test were the only thing that stood between me and an Italian magistrate. I began to toy with the idea that I might be able to pass the test again; after all, one small chance was preferable to no chance at all, wasn't it? Afterward, I could still denounce the test, and if I had passed it again my denunciation would carry that much more sting. Of course, this was a shameful rationalization. Obviously, I was panic-stricken and defeated; I had simply lost my courage.

I went to the laboratory designated by the tournament committee. The doctor, a large man with white hair, seemed antagonistic. He was gruff, and when he raked the glass slide along the lining of my cheek to get the cells for the test, he abraded me unnecessarily. Oto and I sat in the corridor in front of the laboratory for four hours before an assistant emerged and curtly announced that I had failed. The only blessing was that we had eluded the reporters and were alone during this depressing albeit predictable verdict. My last chance at the Italian Open disappeared down the drain along with my self-respect.

Finally whipped, I was reduced to cabling my father for money. He sent enough for Oto to fly home and for me to go on to Paris where I planned to stay with my old friend Yvette. Her voice on the telephone was the only bright spot in the whole Roman fiasco. It had been years since we had spoken, yet in spite of a bad connection on the international circuit, she had recognized my voice immediately. When I explained my predicament, she said without hesitation, "You must come to Paris and stay with me."

I arrived in Paris feeling paranoid and disappointed with myself. Yvette met me at the airport and mothered me for several weeks. I contacted the officials who ran the French Open; they raised my hopes and then under pressure from the WTA informed me that I'd have to take the chromosome test. Listlessly, I went through it a second time. "What difference could it possibly make?" I thought. "I already compromised once. Maybe some lab technician will make a mistake." Nobody did, and I was failed once more.

I didn't think I could feel much worse than I had in Rome, but this second self-betrayal further depressed me. I guess I had continued to hold out hopes for the French Open in spite of what good sense should have dictated. Once again I was victimized by my own terribly narrow focus; I had set my sights on cracking into professional tennis, and nothing seemed to exist beyond that.

Yvette consoled me by suggesting that I could always give up the quest and return to being a doctor. Her attempts to put my situation in a wider perspective did no good. It was almost as if, after forty years of struggling with an identity problem, I couldn't do without it. Would I ever be able to settle down and recapture the seeming stability of my months in Newport Beach? It began to look as if I was more trapped by the past than I had ever imagined I would be.

These thoughts sent me into a depressive tailspin. Yvette helped as best she could, supporting me financially and listening to me talk about my confusions—both past and present. I'd run on and on until finally I'd fall into an exhausted sleep. I'd wake up late in the morning. Of course, Yvette would have gotten up and gone off to work. That would depress me further. Not only did she have a job to go to; she had a sense of duty and responsibility that got her up in the morning in spite of the previous evening's late hours.

The most constructive thing I did during my period with Yvette was to walk Lester, her dog. My outings with him reminded me of the days I'd spent in Paris with Rocco so many years before. Rocco was an elder statesman now, retired in California. He was relaxing at the country home of Bev and Jeff Gaines, too old and dignified to be wasting his energies on my wild chases around the globe. After walking Lester I'd hang around Yvette's apartment or sit in a sidewalk café sipping wine and pondering my situation. As the weeks passed, the wine began to be a more prominent part of the day, and by the end of the evening I was usually pretty well sloshed. I wasn't drinking great quantities of wine, but it didn't take much to encourage a stream of melancholy reflection, to which Yvette would listen with the patience of a saint.

Of course, this pattern of behavior solved nothing and was finally broken by an unexpected phone call that came at 3:00 A.M. Paris time. It was Donald Waxman calling from the States. I was too swacked to talk on the phone, but Yvette managed, in spite of her limited English, to comprehend the rather involved message. Joe Zingale of the Cleveland Nets was offering me a contract to play World Team Tennis; he had agreed to hire me without the sanction of the WTA. Yvette tried to make this clear to me, but I was in no condition to assimilate the news even if it was good. A second call from Donald the next day resulted in a clearer understanding of the situation. I responded, "No thanks, Donald. Those bastards will just get me over there, make a big splash in the press and then screw me. I'll never set foot on a tennis court as a member of the Cleveland Nets."

Donald and I were on the phone several more times before he finally convinced me to come home; at least the Nets were willing to pay my fare to Cleveland. Yvette propped me up and conveyed me to the airport. When I arrived in Cleveland, the flash guns popped, the press conferences hummed, and the contract got signed. Naturally, it was disapproved by the World Team Tennis League. Even in a depressed stupor I had reasoned correctly about this one.

I thought I had hit rock bottom in Paris, but one further ignominious event was forthcoming before I finally gained control of my life. After the Cleveland Nets deal fell through, I was at least back in the United States, but that also meant that I was back where my creditors were. While they were three thousand miles distant I found it easy to ignore the fact that I owed a lot and that no money was coming in. I could no longer do this. Besides, I didn't even have money for my daily expenses. Under this intense financial pressure, my resistance to temptation deteriorated further and I signed a contract for an exhibition match with Bobby Riggs.

This embarrassing production took place at the Ontario Speedway in Ontario, Canada. I was to play two matches with Bobby for five thousand dollars apiece. I wondered why, whenever I violated my principles, it always seemed to be done so ineffectually. I could have gotten a quarter of a million dollars and a trip to Las Vegas if I had caved in only a year before. As it was, I found myself in a cramped dressing room under the infield bleachers of a racetrack. The walls were gray cement block with a row of hooks at about head height; these were my "closet." The only piece of furniture in the room was a wooden bench. Outside, it was drizzling rain and in spite of the fact that it was July a cold breeze stirred the rain. A horde of at least two hundred people was gathering to see the famous transsexual and the famous hustler play tennis. From my point of view the only good thing about the whole scene was that hardly anyone was there. It had not been publicized outside Canada, and what promotion there had been locally was ineffectual. Everything about the arrangements was half-baked except for the dinner party the night before. That had been nice. Otherwise, the production had the same designation as was indicated on my dressing room door, "D."

Across the hall in dressing room "A," Bobby Riggs was psyching himself up. What most people don't realize is that Bobby is an intense competitor; at every stage of his life he has been a champion. He was a boys champion, a U.S. Boys Champion, a U.S. Juniors Champion, a Wimbledon Champion, a U.S. Professional Champion, a U.S. Thirty-Five and Over Champion, a Forty-Five and Over Champion, and so on. For him there are no inconsequential matches. He may be playing in a dress while carrying an umbrella over his head, but that doesn't mean he isn't interested in winning. Aside from being a great athlete, his competitive spirit is the element that has made him a successful hustler.

As we walked onto the temporary tennis court, constructed at no great expense for our match, I caught some of Bobby's fever. In spite of the pathetic smattering of applause that quickly dissipated into the vastness of the speedway, I began to feel the same tension that I would have felt before a crowd of thousands. I looked up into the largely empty bleachers and felt a surge of kindly feeling for the people sitting there. Huddled miserably in the drizzle, they were willing to stick it out to see Bobby and me. Like all the crowds before them, they craned their necks curiously at me. I threw a ball into the air and saw it arc up against the makeshift lights on the infield side of the court. It was surrounded in its flight by little droplets of mist illuminated in the night air. My racket came around and met the ball creating a little explosion of moisture, and I could feel the mood of the crowd change as it had so many times before. She can play! Bobby jumped on the serve and sent it back with authority. Again I felt the crowd shift. He can play! In the middle of that dark speedway, in front of those bedraggled and somewhat surprised spectactors, Bobby and I played a damn good match. We put everything we had into it, and what we had was plenty good. Best of all, I won seven-five, seven-five. Afterward, our ragtag audience gave us a warm round of applause, which was a great tribute on a cold and rainy night. The next day I beat him again in the afternoon in front of a slightly larger gallery. The score was almost the same as it had been the night before: seven-five, seven-six. Again we played a fine match; Bobby, who had had me three set points in the second set, was exhausted and furious at himself afterward. Everytime I see him he mentions those three set points.

I don't mean to make this speedway affair sound too much like a triumph of the human spirit. Seedy is seedy, and Bobby and I both realized that we really were one step away from the carnival level of entertainment. The thing that made me think twice was that, even in a crummy atmosphere the game itself had meant something. The competition had lifted the event to a level that no one had expected. It began to gall me more and more that I was being deprived of a proper showcase for my competitive spirit. The more I thought about it, the more my blood boiled—when I got back to New York I looked for a good lawyer.

22

Renée Is Official

I found Roy Cohn through Alan King, who said he was controversial but the best there was. I first met him at his brownstone apartment on East Sixty-eighth Street off Madison Avenue, and he greeted me in a bathrobe. On the way over I had been rehearsing my speech. I would give him some personal background, tell him why I felt I should play professional tennis, review my career so far, and run through the arguments in my favor. When he slumped into the room in his bathrobe, I was a little taken aback; but there was no misjudging the forceful cut of his jaw or the penetrating way he fixed his gaze on me. I stuttered a little, "Mr. Cohn, I . . . I'm Renée Richards and I . . . I . . ." He held up his hand and said: "I know, I know. You want to play in the U.S. Open." I was unnerved by his directness. Didn't he want to hear my speech? "Well, yes, but . . ." He held up his hand again and said, "I'll take the case." I didn't quite know what to make of this news. Of course I was happy, so I decided to thank him. "Oh, Mr. Cohn . . ." He held up his hand again. "I'll tell you what you do," he said. "You meet me in East Hampton this weekend, and we'll talk at greater length." He handed me a card upon which he had scribbled the address. As we shook hands I started to thank him again, "Mr. Cohn, I want to thank you so much. This means a lot to me." This time he couldn't raise his hand to stop me because I was shaking it.

On the way to East Hampton, I rehearsed the speech I had planned to make at our first meeting. The home at the address

Roy Cohn had given me was palatial. He was the weekend house-guest of a man whose family fortune came from manufacturing safes. We sat down in an airy drawing room, and after the usual greetings I prepared to start my speech. I had trimmed it down to include only the arguments in favor of my being allowed to play professional tennis. I figured that I had been mulling them over for the previous year and could give Mr. Cohn a good start on preparing my case. I started to speak, but he held up his hand and proceeded to articulate in detail every one of the points I had intended to make, with a clarity and precision of logic that put to shame the speech I was about to make. From that point on I didn't bother opening my mouth. I just committed the whole process into his hands. He didn't handle my case personally but turned it over to his partner, Mike Rosen, who sat in on our East Hampton meeting. Figuring that there was little for me to add, I went home to my dad's house in Forest Hills.

There, within shouting distance of the courts upon which the U.S. Open would be played in a couple of weeks, I lounged around in my old room. The days passed pleasantly now; the months of personal struggle were over. What I could do, I had done. The rest was in the hands of the legal system. Rather than fixing my thoughts constantly on the litigation that was approaching, I felt more inclined to cast my mind back over the bizarre path that I'd followed—and the heroes and villains who had populated my life. Interestingly, there have been few that I'd care to label villains. The world as I've seen it is a confusing place. Regardless of how hard I study it, looking for causes and effects, I can never be sure that I've sized them up correctly. For example, I could fix the blame for my transsexuality on the people in my environment and next year have to eat my words when someone finds a bio-chemical cause for it. In the final analysis, all the people involved were responding to forces over which they had little control. Who knows why people are afraid or intolerant or spiteful or weak? I can hardly blame them any more than I can blame myself for what I am. Yet, I do recognize villains; I recognize them by the degree of bitterness that sweeps over me when I think of them. My mother, the stern and overpowering Dr. Bishop, is thus a villain. My sister is a villain. She brutalized me as a child; as an adult she disapproved of what I had become. The indomitable Dr. Bak was so obsessed with his own theories that he was blind to any other reality. The villains are those who loaded me with guilt and made so much of my life a lonely struggle. During those days of waiting I thought about the villains and hoped they would have no more victories over me.

But no matter how much time I spent on the villains, I spent far more on the heroes. There have been so many people in my life who have helped me, probably because I needed so much. While I waited in my father's house, they came back to me—an endless procession of benign ghosts. There were intimate friends as well as unknown citizens: people who long ago spoke kindly to a slender girl in Forest Hills or whistled at a tall woman in Milan. There were physicians by the score: those who taught me and those who treated me. And there were women: women who gave me love in the face of an unkind destiny. Many times I'd thought myself alone, abandoned and far beyond the reach of remedies; yet my mind's eye filled with a legion of those whose lives had mixed with mine. I had moved through a world filled with heroes because my life had called for them. Torn by forces that daily threatened my destruction, I had reached out a thousand times and found someone to save me. I have no idea why I've lived the life I have. Maybe it was in order to create heroes.

The telephone sounded. I ran down the hall to my room and picked it up. A voice said, "Renée, you've won."

Afterword

Since I won my case, I've been able to play anywhere in the United States or South America. I'd have to go to court to win the right to play in Europe, and I've never felt up to it. Though the WTA and the USTA grumbled about an appeal they never followed through. Judge Alfred Ascione came down pretty hard on them, as anyone who reads the decision can clearly see. Then again, none of the fears that drove them to ban me ever proved warranted. I certainly haven't dominated the world of women's tennis. In that year, 1977, with Betty Ann Stuart, I was a U.S. Open doubles finalist. After that I had some good wins and often gave the top players as much as they could handle, but my income remained low. The flood of transsexuals that they predicted would follow my lead never materialized; there hasn't been even a single one, but if someone like me ever does come along she'll find a saner world to greet her. I'm proud of that.

In 1981 I decided to go back to medicine. I felt that I had done as much as I could as a player and as a pioneer. I had to admit that I was a better doctor than I was an athlete, and I missed the wonderful feedback from grateful patients. After years as a public curiosity, the security and personal rewards of a physician's life were once again attractive.

I arranged to take a refresher course at Harvard and found it exciting. The more I exercised my old skills, the more at home I felt. For the first time since my unmasking in 1976, I could look forward to a well-regulated life. In order to break in moderately,

I took over a friend's practice while he was on vacation. I discovered that I still had a good rapport with patients and that their problems and the solutions to them were pretty much the same as they were in 1976. The way seemed clear for my return to medicine.

I had only one thing left to do and that was to play in the 1981 U.S. Open. This was to be my last big tournament, and I had trained hard. Even that late in my tennis career, I continued to believe that I could win it, though the closest I had come was when I was 1979 U.S. Open 35-and-over singles champion.

In 1981, however, I was eliminated in the first round by a good young player, Andrea Leand. It left me with an empty feeling; I had been as fit as at any time in my career and, optimistic as always, had confidently set aside the whole two weeks of the tournament. Like a bride left standing at the altar, I felt that I should be doing something, but what? Of course, I could sit in the stands and watch others play, but I felt that the physical edge I had trained so hard to achieve would simply go to waste if I did that. Since I could no longer compete myself, I turned my attention to how I might help someone else—my first thought was of Martina Navratilova.

I had known Martina since I had played against her in that U.S. Open doubles final. She and I had hit it off immediately. Maybe it was that we were both estranged, she from her homeland and me from the world at large. Whatever the reason, we formed a lasting friendship. When we were playing in the same tournaments, we often warmed each other up. Once, shortly after we had first met, Martina eliminated me in the second round of a tournament in Sao Paulo, Brazil. It was a brutal match—7-6, 7-6—and I was exhausted and depressed afterward. Home was a long way away, and outside the locker room an aggressive band of paparazzi lay in wait. Martina walked over to me and said, "Renée, stay with it. You'll make it." She was already the second-ranked player in the world and didn't owe me the time of day. She just said it because she's nice, and it meant a lot to me in those lonely circumstances.

I had noticed two important things about Martina's style. First, she could not hit a backhand drive. Second, she won most of her games through the force of her athletic ability. Her tactical game was not nearly as strong. Since tactics are one of my strong points,

I felt that Martina could profit from the strategies that I would not be able to use. And I felt that I could correct her backhand, as well.

Through August of 1981, Chris Evert Lloyd had been Martina's nemesis. The last time they'd played, Martina had lost: 6-0, 6-0; but I knew that Martina could win if she'd just stick to a sensible game plan.

I went to her and said, "This is my last tournament, and now I'm out of it. If you like, I can devote myself to helping you win." She said, "Good, let's get started." The ease with which we assumed our roles made it seem as if we were fulfilling an unspoken agreement though we had never before discussed my coaching her.

Because it seemed inevitable that Martina would meet Chris in one of the later rounds, we spent almost the entire two weeks of the U.S. Open preparing for her. I worked out some techniques that I thought would be effective, and started correcting her backhand, a move that, in the long run, was probably my greatest contribution to her game.

When their confrontation came, it was one of the finest semifinal matches in U.S. Open history. During the match a friend turned to me and said, "I'm having an incredible sense of déjà vu because this is so much like your practice sessions with Martina." This gratified me since I've always felt that I have a special talent for coaching, and one important element in coaching is to be able to anticipate what form a match is likely to take. Once that has been done, techniques can be created that will alter that form to your player's benefit.

Martina won the match; we were both incredibly high until she lost to Tracy Austin the next day. In our fever to prepare for Chris, we had neglected to do likewise for Tracy, whose game, though similar to Chrissie's, requires a little different approach.

In spite of the loss to Tracy, it was obvious that Martina and I made a good team; so I agreed to coach her for the fall on a trial basis. In October we went to the U.S. Indoor Championships in Minneapolis where I helped her prepare for Tracy, whom she beat 6-0, 6-2. After the match Martina said, "Well, Coach, did I execute okay?" My answer, "Pretty good," was certainly an understatement.

Though this success was gratifying, I was torn by an ironic

dilemma. For years I had tried to make a major success in professional tennis; then, when I had decided to give it up and return to medicine, a success had sort of fallen into my lap. I should have been ecstatic, but I kept thinking about medicine. I don't mean that I didn't enjoy the routine of preparation with Martina; it just seemed that I was postponing my inevitable return to ophthalmology. Furthermore, I found myself dreading the plane rides and the hotels in strange places. What a baffling turn of events! I was rapidly becoming one of the most famous coaches in tennis, and I couldn't relax and enjoy it. I kept thinking, "This is what I've wanted. I should be happy."

It was this feeling that I *should* be happy (along with my personal commitment to Martina) that spurred me to accompany her on a tour that included Germany, Japan, and Australia. Everywhere we went Martina won, climaxed by the Australian Open championship. Once again I was pleased but uneasy. After the Australian Open win, Martina took the microphone and said, "I'd just like to thank one person. I'd like to thank my coach, Renée Richards. Without her, I would never have won."

This is the kind of recognition that should have provided me a deep satisfaction. Instead, I found myself writing a letter of resignation to Martina. In it I explained that I was being drawn back to medicine, and as much as I had enjoyed our winning streak I wanted to get on with what seemed to be the major current in my life.

Shortly after Martina received the letter she called me and said, "Renée, I've read your letter five times. I know it by heart, but I don't want you to quit." I expected this reaction, and that was a large part of why I had put my resignation in a letter form rather than announcing it in person. "Renée," she went on, "You know that winning the Australian was as big a high for you as for me."

"Yes," I said, "I'll admit that."

"Well . . ." she said, expectantly.

"All right. All right. I *would* like to see you win the French and Wimbledon. But after that I'm going back to medicine."

It was as simple as that; all she had to do was insist. Our winning streak together is a matter of record; it was climaxed with a dramatic three-set victory over Chris Evert Lloyd in the 1982 Wimbledon final.

At the victory dinner I was approached repeatedly with congratulations. Many people said something like "Well, now you've coached a Wimbledon champion. Most coaches would give their eye teeth for that credit. What are you going to do with it?"

"I'm going back to New York to be an ophthalmologist," I replied.

To tell the truth I'm still a little surprised myself by this decision. My success with Martina probably would have enabled me to pick pretty much whomever I wanted to coach or to have any sort of tennis camp that I might desire. Only a couple of years before, this would have seemed like heaven; yet I've never regretted going back to medicine—I feel it's where I belong.

I wish I could say that my personal life had finally come into focus as nicely as my professional life, but that would be a little too much to hope for. Still, things have turned out fairly well considering the strange transit that has dominated my life. Some relationships were lost, some stayed the same, and some continue to grow.

My sister and I are permanently estranged. For her, my notoriety was the ultimate example of "acting out." I visited her once after I had become a public figure. I arrived at her house wearing a sweater and skirt. She invited me to change into something more comfortable. I replied casually that I was perfectly comfortable as I was. She insisted. It was then I realized that what she really meant was something more comfortable for her. This was a strange turnaround for a person who, forty years before, had lovingly helped me into a silk slip. I don't think that I'll ever see her again.

My father and I have yet to discuss my transsexuality. Often when people phone his house and ask for Dr. Richards, he answers, "He's not here." Still, he accepts me. I'll never forget the sight of him in his car, racing after me as I drove out of Forest Hills one day. He was blowing the horn and waving something. When he pulled abreast of me he leaned across the front seat and thrust the object through the window on the passenger's side. "You forgot this!" he shouted. It was my purse.

Near the beginning of this book I showed some bitterness toward my dad, but make no mistake, I love him. He's never been the hugging and kissing type, but if I come into Kennedy Airport at three in the morning, he's there to pick me up. And if the weather's bad, he's got my raincoat.

Andy continues to be, as he puts it, the most important thing in my life. The fame that has come to me has had little direct effect on him. We've protected him well; I feel good that I was an attentive and masculine father through the first five years of his life. I'm a Freudian and believe that those years are the most important in the formation of a healthy personality. I've seen no signs of sexual confusion on his part; he is secure in his masculinity. I feel far more regretful about my divorce than I do about my transsexuality. If anything has affected Andy negatively it has been my estrangement from Meriam, but for that I am no more blameworthy than any of the world's other divorced parents. When I see Andy I follow a ritual that is practiced on weekends by what seems like half the fathers in New York City. I drive up to the apartment house where my son lives with his mother and stepfather; out the front door comes my son and away we go for the day.

Very soon after I went public Andy got onto the fact that I was some sort of celebrity. He noticed that I drew attention, but in all that time there has never been an ugly incident. Andy attributes most of my notoriety to the fact that I am a noted physician; as a matter of fact, he is capable of being a bit smug about it. Once, when we were rowing in Central Park he turned to some people in a nearby boat and shouted, "This is Dr. Richard Raskind, the famous eye doctor!" Beyond these infrequent outbursts Andy shows little more than the usual childish pride in his father.

On occasion, he has noted that I have characteristics different from the average dad. Once he said, "Daddy, I'm glad that you got rid of your beard and don't have to shave it off anymore." When I asked why, he answered, "Because a beard is okay for Grandpa, he's an old guy, but you're young. I don't think that you should have a beard." Another time he asked, "Daddy, why is your hair so long?" I told him that I just preferred a longer style; he nodded and said, "Yes, I know. It suits your face better." In spite of these comments, he has never shown any doubt about my ability to fulfill the masculine role. When we are reunited after a separation of more than a few days, he always runs directly at me and leaps into my arms, completely secure in the knowledge that I'll protect him from falling. (As he has gotten older and bigger, this has become more and more and more taxing.) He is currently fascinated with guns and armaments of all kinds. I am regularly grilled on my naval career; he wants to know if I ever killed anybody. When I explain that I was more in the lifesaving end of it, he seems vaguely disappointed: a typical eight-year-old.

After my operation, Meriam and I engaged an eminent child psychiatrist to advise us in the tricky matter of helping Andy adjust. He suggested that we put off telling him as long as possible. We judged that unless he accidentally found out he should be left untroubled until he was at least eight or nine years old. For years he was protected from a direct discussion of the situation and was cooperative in his own behalf. I told him that he might hear somebody on radio or television criticizing me. He said, "Daddy, I won't listen to them. I'll turn it off."

Inevitably though the time came when he had to be told. Meriam did it when I was not present so as to allow him to react without worrying about my feelings. She reported that he took it pretty calmly. One of his comments was, "Well, I can see why you and Daddy had to get a divorce. Two women can't be married." A day or so later she took him to see the psychiatrist in case there was any aspect of it that he didn't feel comfortable discussing with those directly involved. The doctor reported that he was as calm as any eight-year-old who would rather be out playing soccer. "How's your daddy?" asked the psychiatrist. Andy looked over at him and said, "Mommy told me that my daddy changed into a lady." The doctor nodded encouragingly. "But," Andy offered in summation, "that's crazy." I'll have to admit the kid's got a point.

During our regular phone calls, he had little to say on the subject. We discussed the usual stuff like whether or not I was going to buy him an air rifle. Occasionally, for no discernible reason, an identity-related question would pop irrelevantly into the conversation. "Daddy, do you have breasts?" I tried to treat these as matter-of-factly as possible. "Yes, I do." I'd wait expectantly, but the next comment would be back on the subject of air rifles. So far, our most prolonged interaction on the subject occurred the first time I saw him after he'd been told. I was in New York for the U.S. Open, and we spent a day fishing off Long Island. The trip got off to a suggestive start. While the attendant at the boat-rental place was getting our gear together, I went back to the car for our bait. Meanwhile, the attendant finished and turned to Andy. "When your mother gets back," he said, "have her come over to the office." Upon my return, Andy laughingly repeated what the man had said. I chuckled along with him, but I could see that the incident had started him thinking.

As always, Andy insisted on piloting the boat. He's a bit reckless, sometimes driving right into the wakes of larger boats rather than crossing them properly at an oblique angle. I always sit next to him in order to keep us from being swamped. As we sped along, a lively argument developed over where the fish would most likely be. The boat-rental man had given us some hints, but his directions were open to interpretation. Finally, we anchored and made our preparations. As usual, Andy wanted things done without delay. "Bait the hook, Daddy! Bait the hook, Daddy!"

We dropped in our lines and soon found out that the crabs were more interested in our worms than were the flounder. Consequently, our lines were in and out of the bay a dozen times per hour on false alarms. Invariably, it seemed that our hooks came up empty or with crabs dangling pugnaciously from them. After each of these episodes Andy would urge me on again, "Bait the hook, Daddy!" I would always hurry to do as he asked, but after awhile our supply of worms was sadly depleted. Occasionally, we'd change locations in an attempt to foil the crabs, but they were everywhere. Eventually, I had to cannibalize one of the two flounders that we did catch in order to have enough bait to last for the rest of the day. Throughout our fishing adventure Andy and I kept up our good-natured bantering over whose fishing technique was most likely to produce results. Considering the dismal catch of crabs and trash fish, neither of us could really claim much of an edge, but the argument was entertaining.

Every once in awhile, Andy would suddenly ask a question about my femaleness. "Did you use a pillow to hide your breasts from me when I was little?" he asked. "No," I answered. "I just wore baggy shirts. You never seemed to notice." He didn't confirm or deny my comment but simply turned his attention back to his fishing. Once as I was trying to make a piece of flounder stay on Andy's hook he hit me with a more direct question. "Do you have all of a woman's private parts?" I answered but didn't look up because I was at a critical point with the flounder. "Yes." I handed him his hook and he tossed it into the bay, feeding out the line until he felt it hit bottom. "I wonder if the crabs like the flounder as much as they do the worms?" he asked with another abrupt change of subject. "I don't think they can afford to be very choosy," I said, pulling up my own empty hook. "There's your answer. It didn't take them any longer to get the flounder off my hook than it did the worms. I think they like my bait better than yours though!" He stared disdainfully at me. "They can't tell the difference. Crabs don't have any brains." Naturally, I couldn't let this go unchallenged. "Who told you they don't have brains?" He pulled up his hook. "They don't have brains like humans do. Bait the hook, Daddy!" I grabbed it and stuck on a piece of flounder. "But they have a brain of sorts. Not much of a brain, it's true, but a brain nonetheless." Andy was settling his hook again. "Can you have babies, Daddy?" This question sounded strange even to me. "No, I can't. I have a vagina, but I don't have a uterus. You see, a baby needs . . ." Andy cut off this lecture on reproduction. "Let's go over there. I think that man said there were a lot of fish over by that big dock." I looked where he was pointing. "All right, but I hate to leave this spot, what with the crabs biting so well."

And that's the way we spent our day. The most mundane father-and-son chatter was occasionally interrupted by comments of the most bizarre kind. Actually, Andy asked very few questions, considering the richness of the subject matter. I think that this is his defense mechanism. He ventures to find out what he can handle and calls a halt when he has had enough. I imagine that this process will continue for years to come. The questions will grow more complicated until finally he will ask the ones that I cannot answer—then he will face his own moment of truth.

But, looking at him on that August afternoon as he steered heedlessly homeward, I couldn't dread that day. The sun was setting behind us, splashing everything with red. Andy's face was thrust aggressively into the breeze. He was so brave and so unruffled by his responsibility as a skipper. He took us into a wake at the wrong angle and the boat slipped dangerously. I put my hand over his on the throttle and righted us. He looked up at me with a petulant expression. "You trying to kill us both?" I asked with exaggerated gruffness. He broke into a smile. "You wouldn't let anything happen to me!" he laughed. "What makes you think that?" He twisted the throttle for more speed. "Because I'm the most important thing in your life!"